Global Lessons from the AIDS Pandemic

Bradly J. Condon . Tapen Sinha

Global Lessons from the AIDS Pandemic

Economic, Financial, Legal and Political Implications

 Springer

Dr. Bradly J. Condon
Departamento Académico de
Administración
Instituto Tecnológico Autónomo de
México (ITAM)
Rio Hondo No. 1
Col. Tizapán San Ángel
Mexico, D.F., 01000
bcondon@itam.mx

Dr. Tapen Sinha
Departamento de Actuaría
Instituto Tecnológico Autónomo de
México (ITAM)
Rio Hondo No. 1
Col. Tizapán San Ángel
Mexico, D.F., 01000
tapen@itam.mx

ISBN 978-3-540-78391-6   e-ISBN 978-3-540-78392-3
DOI 10.1007/978-3-540-78392-3

Library of Congress Control Number: 2008927607

© 2008 Springer-Verlag Berlin Heidelberg

Cover design: WMXDesign GmbH, Heidelberg, Germany

Printed on acid-free paper

9 8 7 6 5 4 3 2 1

springer.com

We dedicate this book to the HIV-positive people of the world, past, present and future. Faith, hope, love, compassion and courage. The authors' royalties will be donated to AIDS-related charities.

Preface

We began to research for this book in 2000, with the idea that we might contribute to the search for solutions to the global HIV/AIDS pandemic by combining perspectives from different disciplines. Much has happened in the intervening years.

First, the severity of the HIV/AIDS pandemic in sub-Saharan Africa – and the threat it posed for many others regions of the world – led to a movement among several countries to correct the imbalance between producers and users of pharmaceutical products. This effort produced a clarification of the right of governments to produce generic medicine under compulsory licenses and an amendment of the World Trade Organization's TRIPS Agreement to allow exports of generic medicines from one WTO Member to another. In 2007, the amended rules were put into practice, with Canada authorizing the export of generic antiretroviral drugs to Rwanda. However, at the same time, global patent laws have been undermined due to regulatory capture, most notably in free trade agreements and through political pressure on countries like Thailand to not to exercise their right to issue compulsory licenses for pharmaceutical products.

Second, the amount of money available for the treatment and prevention of HIV/AIDS has increased dramatically, with the establishment of the World Bank Multi-Country HIV/AIDS Program for Africa (MAP), the Global Fund to Fight AIDS, Tuberculosis and Malaria and the US President's Emergency Plan for AIDS Relief (PEPFAR), among other funding initiatives. The increase in funding has meant that many millions of people now have access to treatment compared to the time when we began to work on this book. Yet, millions more still need treatment and cannot afford it. In this regard, the US President's effort in 2007 to double the funding available under PEPFAR is a very encouraging sign. At the same time, the proliferation of donors and programs for HIV/AIDS has created new challenges – the need to coordinate donor policies to minimize the administrative burden for recipients and the need to ensure that donor policies are based on science, not ideological or political interests.

Third, in 2007, UNAIDS began to use new methodologies to estimate the number of individuals living with HIV/AIDS, the number of new infections and the number of people who die each year. The new statistics are at once encouraging and discouraging. It now appears that the percentage of infected adults in some countries is lower than it was initially thought and that the epidemic has peaked in some of the worst affected countries. Nevertheless, there are still over 30 million people living with HIV/AIDS worldwide and new infections are on the rise in several other countries. Therefore, hope must not give way to complacency, and prevention efforts need to be scaled up globally if we are to bring the HIV/AIDS pandemic under control. Achieving this goal will require new and different ways of thinking about where our economic and political interests lie.

Fourth, in the new millennium, some fast-moving infectious diseases with high mortality rates appeared on the scene – severe acute respiratory syndrome (SARS) and the H5N1 influenza virus. These new viruses led us to consider what lessons we need to learn from our experience with the HIV/AIDS pandemic and have led us to the conclusion that the significance of the world's successes and failures with respect to HIV/AIDS go far beyond addressing the human immunodeficiency virus.

Fifth, path-breaking research has appeared in the past couple of years with respect to the economics of HIV/AIDS and the economics of patents. An economic boom can have the unintended consequence of increasing HIV/AIDS infection in a given population. The new economics of patents show that the long-held belief that granting patent protection is the only way to boost research and development for new drugs may not be true after all.

Sixth, the concept of mortality bonds has evolved into a financially viable product in the past three years. Without the epidemiological developments of HIV, SARS and H5N1 influenza, these products would simply not exist today. There are signs that they will become important financial instruments in the coming decades.

Seventh, the failure of "3 by 5" (the goal of expanding treatment to three million AIDS patients in developing countries by 2005) has provided an impetus for scaling up treatment around the world. In 2000, such a goal seemed a distant dream. Today, the possibility of achieving universal access to treatment within a few years seems very real. It will not avert the tragedy that HIV/AIDS has already caused for millions of people, but it will stop the biggest killer of our times from prematurely taking the lives of tens of millions of others.

Mexico City
May 2008

Bradly Condon
Tapen Sinha

Acknowledgements

The authors acknowledge the help, support, and encouragement of the following people: Enrique de Alba, Carlos Alcérreca, Rebecca Benedict, Michele Boldrin, Ashok Chaudhuri, Cathy Condon, Kip Condon, Peter Doherty, Ali DuBose, Sean Fay, Alberto Febronio, Arturo Fernández, Lorna Guinness, Stephen Heeney, Diego Hernández, Bernard Hirschel, Georgina Jarquin, Jenny Lanjouw, David Levine, Douglas Keir, Julio Montaner, Mark Nordman, Emily Oster, Mit Philips, Suzanne Scotchmer, Dipendra Sinha, Kent Smetters, María de la Luz S. de Uriarte and Duncan Wood.

We thank the Instituto Tecnológico Autónomo de México and the Asociación Mexicana de Cultura AC for their generous support of our research. We are grateful to our publisher, Springer-Verlag, for seeing the value in this topic. We deeply appreciate the diligent work of the editors at Springer-Verlag, in particular Sundardevadoss Dharmendra, Katharina Wetzel-Vandai and Christiane Beisel.

Contents

List of Abbreviations

ABC	Abstinence, Be Faithful, Condom
ACSI	Absolute Component Summed Index
ADB	African Development Bank
AIDS	Acquired Immunodeficiency Syndrome
ANC	Antenatal Clinic
ART	Antiretroviral Therapy
ARV	Antiretroviral Drugs
BPAS	Best Practice AIDS Standard
CAFTA-DR	Central America-Dominican Republic-United States Free Trade Agreement
CAP	Corporate AIDS Prevention Program
CCM	Global Fund Country Coordinating Mechanism
CDC	US Centers for Disease Control and Prevention
CHAI	Clinton Foundation HIV/AIDS Initiative
CMS	Commercial Market Strategies
CNJR	Rwanda National Youth Council
CSI	Component Summed Index
CSW	Commercial Sex Workers
DAC	Development Assistance Committee of the OECD
EC	European Communities
ELISA	Enzyme-Linked Immunosorbent Assay Test
EU	European Union
FDA	US Food and Drug Administration
FSW	Female Sex Workers
G7	Group of Seven Industrialized Countries
GAMET	Global AIDS Monitoring and Evaluation Support Team
GBC	Global Business Coalition on HIV/AIDS
GDP	Gross Domestic Product
GIST	Global Joint Problem-Solving and Implementation Support Team
GNP	Gross National Product
GTT	Global Task Team on Improving AIDS Coordination among Multilateral Institutions and International Donors
HAART	Highly Active Antiretroviral Therapy
HIV	Human Immunodeficiency Virus
IADB	Inter-American Development Bank
IBRD	International Bank for Reconstruction and Development
IDA	International Development Association
IDU	Injection Drug User
IHR	International Health Regulations

IMF	International Monetary Fund
ILO	International Labor Organization
IOM	International Organization for Migration
ISO	International Standards Organization
MAP	World Bank Multi-Country HIV/AIDS Program for Africa
MSF	Médicins sans Frontières (Doctors without Borders)
MSM	Men who have Sex with Men
NGO	Non-Governmental Organization
OECD	Organization for Economic Cooperation and Development
OED	World Bank Operations Evaluation Department
PEPFAR	US President's Emergency Program for AIDS Relief
PhRMA	Pharmaceutical Research and Manufacturers of America
PLWH/A	People Living with HIV/AIDS
PPP	Purchasing Power Parity
PSI	Population Services International
RCSI	Relative Component Summed Index
R&D	Research and Development
SARS	Severe Acute Respiratory Syndrome
SIV	Simian Immunodeficiency Virus
STD	Sexually Transmitted Disease
STI	Sexually Transmitted Infection
TB	Tuberculosis
TRIPS	Agreement on Trade-Related Aspects of Intellectual Property Rights
UNAIDS	Joint United Nations Program on HIV/AIDS
UNDP	United Nations Development Program
UNFPA	United Nations Population Fund
UNGASS	United Nations General Assembly Special Session
UNHCR	United Nations High Commissioner for Refugees
UNICEF	United Nations Children Fund
USAID	United States Agency for International Development
USTR	United States Trade Representative
WHO	World Health Organization
WIPO	World Intellectual Property Organization
WTO	World Trade Organization

List of Boxes

List of Figures

List of Tables

1 Introduction to the Economic, Financial, Political and Legal Implications of Global Pandemics

"We shall require a substantially new way of thinking if mankind is to survive."

Albert Einstein

In this chapter, we begin with an assessment of the risks posed by *fast-moving* global pandemics. We then examine the origin and nature of the *slow-moving* global HIV/AIDS pandemic. The remainder of this chapter summarizes the topics that will be covered in the subsequent chapters of this book.

1.1 The Threat of Global Pandemics

In the summer of 2007, researchers from the University of Washington confirmed for the first time that the H5N1 influenza virus had been transmitted from human to human. A woman on the Indonesian island of Sumatra caught the virus from poultry in May of 2006 and transmitted the virus to her 10-year-old nephew, which was then transmitted to other relatives. Seven of eight family members who caught the disease died. This incident showed that there is a serious threat of an H5N1 influenza pandemic that could spread quickly and have a high and rapid mortality rate (Waters 2007). Human-to-human transmission of the H5N1 influenza virus was also suspected in Pakistan in November 2007 (McPherson 2007). The World Health Organization (WHO) uses six phases of pandemic alert to estimate the level of a threat. In December 2007, H5N1 was in phase 3, because it is a new influenza virus subtype that is causing disease in humans, but is not yet spreading efficiently and sustainably among humans. However, there is no way of knowing when such a pandemic might occur (Nebehay 2007). Figure 1.1 shows how often recorded influenza epidemics occurred during the second millennium, and how they have increased in frequency over time. This pattern is not surprising because fast-moving pandemics require close contact between groups of people. Over time, people began living together in bigger groups in cities. They also increased interactions due to faster modes of transportation.

The number of deaths of the next influenza pandemic could surpass the estimated 50–100 million deaths caused by the 1918–1919 global flu pandemic, commonly referred to as the Spanish Flu (Taubenberger and Morens 2006). The 1918–1919 influenza virus had a mortality rate of 2.5%, significantly higher than previous influenza epidemics, which were less than 0.1% (Taubenberger and Morens 2006; Billings 1997). Moreover, unlike other flu pandemics, almost half of the influenza-related deaths were in young adults, 20–40 years of age (Taubenberger and Morens 2006). In this regard, the 1918–1919 virus was like HIV/AIDS,

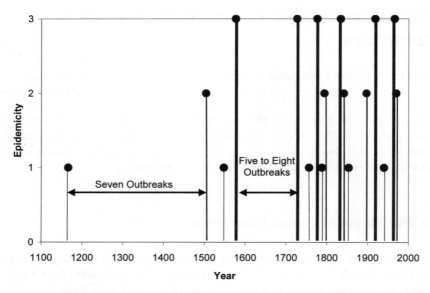

Fig. 1.1 Frequency and severity of influenza 1100–1980 AD. Notes: 1, epidemic; 2, probable pandemic; 3, pandemic. Source: Potter, C.W: Textbook of Influenza, Nicholson, Webster, Hay, Blackwell Science 1998

which also affects young adults in the most productive years of their lives and has a correspondingly greater economic impact.

The experience with HIV/AIDS mortality in South Africa (see Chap. 3) is a stark reminder of what happened during the Spanish Flu epidemic in the United States. Figure 1.2 reproduces the mortality experience in the United States during 1918 and compares it with the experience of the previous 7 years (1911–1917). Both the HIV/AIDS epidemic and the Spanish Flu epidemic have one important common element – they both affected adults. They did not affect the young and the old with weak immune systems, as had happened in the case of other epidemics like the plague in the fourteenth century. If the excess deaths occur mainly among the very young and the very old, the economic implications are different, since the young have not accumulated much human capital and society has not spent many resources on them yet. Similarly, if the very old die, they do not affect production in a society. However, when adults die in the prime of their productive years, it reduces economic growth significantly.

The reason that HIV/AIDS affects mostly adults is reasonably clear – it is largely a sexually transmitted disease. While mother-to-child transmission, transmission by contaminated needles and transmission through blood transfusion make it possible to see the impact on other age groups, the bulk of HIV transmission is still due to sexual contact.

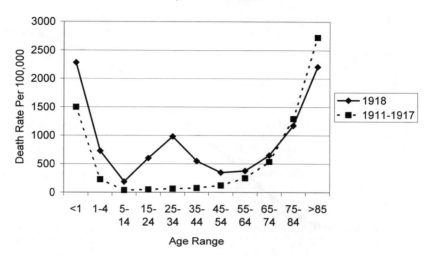

Fig. 1.2 Rising mortality due to Spanish Flu. *Source*: CDC Data

It is still unclear why the Spanish Flu affected the most able-bodied persons at a higher rate. One plausible hypothesis is that the flu itself was not the cause of their deaths. Rather, the virus produced a reaction that caused the patients' own organs to attack the body. Since able-bodied persons have the most vigorous organs, they were affected the most. It is also important to remember that the Spanish Flu was not identified as flu until more than a decade later. Thus, most of what we know today about the Spanish Flu is the result of postmortem analysis of the disease.

The one striking difference between the increases in mortality in these two pandemics was time. In the case of the Spanish Flu, the impact was swift. Everything happened within a span of 3 years. In the case of HIV/AIDS, the impact has unfolded over decades (see Fig. 1.3).

Like the 1918–1919 virus, H5N1 is an avian virus (Taubenberger and Morens 2006). The 1918–1919 influenza virus spread along trade routes and shipping lines, along with the frontlines of World War I (Billings 1997). A century later, what might the impact of such a fast-moving virus be? Trade routes have increased dramatically, as have the means for transporting humans around the globe. Figure 1.4 shows the dramatic increase in global airline traffic in the second half of the twentieth century. These factors suggest that an H5N1 influenza pandemic could unfold much more rapidly and cause many more deaths than the 1918–1919 pandemic.

The evolution of science and international institutions over the past century are mitigating factors that could help to contain the effects of a fast-moving global

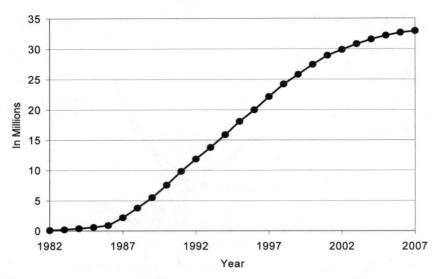

Fig. 1.3 Increasing worldwide prevalence of HIV/AIDS. *Source*: UNAIDS, Avert.org, and own calculations

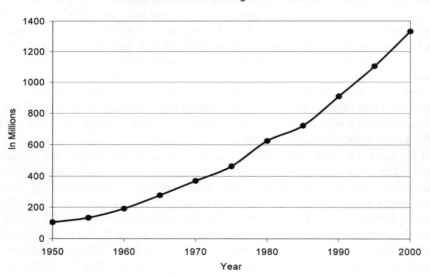

Fig. 1.4 Global airline traffic 1950–2000. *Source*: World Health Organization and World Tourism Organization

pandemic in the twenty-first century. However, as the experience with severe acute respiratory syndrome (SARS) showed, modern air travel means that contagious diseases can spread rapidly around the globe (see Fig. 1.5). Even with modern antiviral and antibacterial drugs, vaccines, and prevention knowledge, the return of a pandemic virus equivalent to the virus of 1918–1919 would probably kill more than 100 million people worldwide, and a pandemic virus with the pathogenic potential of the H5N1 virus could cause substantially more deaths (Taubenberger and Morens 2006).

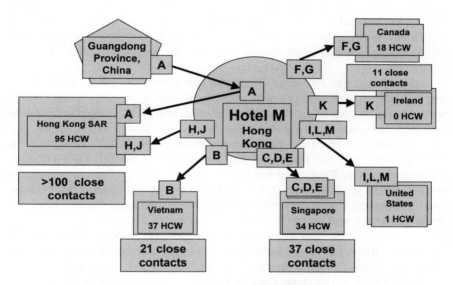

Source: WHO/CDC, HCW stands for healthcare workers

Fig. 1.5 International amplification and transmission of SARS by guests at Hotel M, Hong Kong, 21 February–26 March. *Source*: WHO and CDC

Globalization, together with global climate change, also means that diseases that were formerly confined to tropical developing countries are now spreading to temperate developed countries. This is occurring through a combination of vector migration – the movement of mosquitoes from the tropics to temperate regions – and human travel. West Nile virus, which is transmitted by mosquitoes, is now found throughout the continental United States and Canadian provinces. Chikungunya, a tropical disease that is related to dengue fever, is normally found in the Indian Ocean region. However, in the summer of 2007, a chikungunya epidemic occurred in northern Italy, where tiger mosquitoes now can thrive in the warming climate of southern Europe. An Italian, who had traveled to Kerala, India, returned to Italy with chikungunya in his blood, where it was spread by the tiger mosquitoes. This was the first epidemic of a tropical disease in a developed, European country in modern times (Rosenthal 2007). The movement of developing country diseases to developed countries provides another reason to view developing country diseases, which have been largely neglected, as a global problem that requires a global response.

Infectious diseases can also originate in developed countries. In November 2007, a new and virulent strain of adenovirus was reported in parts of the United States. The US Centers for Disease Control and Prevention (CDC) reported that two of the ten people who died from the new strain were infants and 50 of the 140 affected people were hospitalized, including 24 admitted to intensive care units. The new strain of adenovirus first appeared in May 2006 in New York, and spread to Oregon, Washington state and Texas. This particular adenovirus can make healthy young adults severely ill, which is unusual for an adenovirus (Dunham 2007).

Understanding past outbreaks of diseases can lead to new public health measures and other interventions to more effectively address existing diseases and to better prepare the world for future diseases. Sherman (2007) has examined how several diseases have influenced society, politics and culture and spawned new ways to address diseases and their consequences: (1) porphyria and hemophilia, which affected the royal families of Europe, influenced the political fortunes of England, Germany, Russia and the United States; (2) late blight, which caused the Irish potato famine in the 1850s, led to a wave of immigration that changed the politics of the United States; (3) cholera, which prompted sanitary measures, promoted nursing and led to the discovery of oral rehydration therapy; (4) smallpox led to a vaccine that eradicated the disease; (5) bubonic plague, which caused the "Black Death" in the fourteenth century, promoted quarantine measures; (6) syphilis led to a cure through chemotherapy; (7) tuberculosis led to attenuated vaccines; (8) malaria and yellow fever provided the basis for vector control; and (9) influenza and HIV/AIDS, two pandemics that continue to challenge humanity.

The main focus of this book is the AIDS pandemic – a slow-moving global pandemic with a high mortality rate. This slow-moving pandemic has revealed some of the flaws in our international economic, financial, legal and political institutions and provides many lessons on how to improve the ways that the world addresses global diseases. Unlike other diseases that disproportionately affect developing countries, HIV/AIDS has not been neglected because it also affects developed countries. This chapter begins with a brief description of the origins and nature of the HIV virus, then provides an overview of the issues that will be analyzed in this book.

1.2 The Origins of the HIV Virus

There are two major groups of HIV viruses: HIV-1 and HIV-2. HIV is a *lentivirus* that attacks the immune system. "*Lentivirus*" literally means a slow virus, thus named because of the time it takes to produce any adverse effect on the body. *Lentiviruses* are in turn part of a larger group of viruses known as retroviruses. Retroviruses have been found in a number of different animals, including cats, sheep, horses, monkeys and cattle.

There is evidence that the origin of HIV is the Simian Immunodeficiency Virus (SIV), which affects monkeys. Scientists believe that HIV is a descendant of SIV because certain strains of SIV bear a very close resemblance to HIV-1 and HIV-2. The more virulent strain of HIV, HIV-1, is the closest to SIVcpz, the SIV strain found in chimpanzees. Nevertheless, this virus is still significantly different from HIV. HIV-2 corresponds to SIVsm, a strain of SIV found in the sooty mangabey (also known as the green monkey). This monkey is indigenous to western Africa (Gao et al., 1999).

There are several theories about how *zoonosis* (the process by which a virus is transferred between animals and humans) caused SIV to mutate into HIV. The most commonly accepted theory is the "hunter" theory. According to this theory, SIVcpz was transferred to humans when hunters killed and ate chimpanzees or when the chimpanzee's blood infected the hunters' cuts or wounds. Most of the time, the hunter's body would have fought off SIV. However, in a few instances, SIV would adapt to its new human host to become HIV-1. This "hunter" theory finds support in the existence of several different early strains of HIV, each with a slightly different genetic make-up (with the most common strain being HIV-1 group M). Every time the virus passed successfully from a chimpanzee to a human, it would develop in a slightly different way and thus produce a slightly different strain (Wolfe et al., 2004).

Although clear cases of AIDS were identified in the early 1980s in the United States, a plasma sample taken in 1959 from an adult male living in what is now the Democratic Republic of Congo showed the presence of HIV-1 (Zhou et al., 1998). Similarly, HIV-2 seems to have come from Guinea-Bissau. By analyzing samples of two different subtypes of HIV-2 (A and B) taken from infected humans and SIV samples taken from sooty mangabeys, Vandamme et al. (2003) concluded that both subtypes A and B had passed into humans in the 1950s (with a margin of error of 15 years). It is entirely possible that transmission from monkeys to humans had occurred decades, or even centuries, earlier. However, if groups of infected humans did not come into close contact with other groups, they might have died out.

1.3 The Nature of HIV/AIDS

HIV destroys the human immune system, leaves millions of adults vulnerable to a wide range of lethal illnesses in the prime of their life and kills millions of children whose lives have barely begun. HIV enters the human body via fluids such as blood or semen, attaches itself to the infection-fighting CD4 cells of the immune system, injects its RNA into the DNA of the host CD4 cells and then uses the CD4 cell's division mechanism to replicate. These copies of HIV then enter the blood stream, attach themselves to other CD4 cells and continue replicating. Over time, the quantity of HIV in the blood increases and the number of CD4 cells decreases. Some people begin to have symptoms within months, while others can be without symptoms for more than 10 years. However, the virus continues to multiply, infecting and killing the cells of the immune system, and can be transmitted to other people through unprotected sex, blood transfusions or organ transplants and the sharing of needles, even though the infected person has no symptoms.

When the immune system is sufficiently weakened, it is no longer able to fight off infections caused by common bacteria, virus, fungi and parasites, such as: *mycobacterium avium* complex (which causes night sweats, weight loss, abdominal pain, fatigue, diarrhea and anemia); tuberculosis (which causes night sweats, weight loss, loss of energy, poor appetite, fever and a cough), *salmonellosis* (which causes diarrhea, fever and abdominal pain and cramps); *bacillary angiomatosis* (which causes skin lesions and can affect internal organs, including the brain, bone marrow, heart, lungs, larynx, tongue, esophagus, stomach, colon, diaphragm, kidneys, adrenal glands, pancreas, uterine cervix and vulva); *cyto-megalovirus* (which can cause fever, fatigue, rash, chills, fatigue, headache and blindness); viral hepatitis (which can cause loss of appetite, nausea, vomiting, fever, weakness, fatigue and aching in the abdomen); herpes (which can cause painful blisters, headache, muscle ache and fever); human *papillomavirus* (which can cause genital warts and pre-cancerous changes in the cervix, vulva, anus or penis); progressive *multifocal leukoencephalopathy* (which can cause mental deterioration, vision loss, speech disturbances, a loss of coordination, paralysis and coma); *candidiasis* (which can cause burning pain in the mouth or throat, pain and difficulty when swallowing and vaginal yeast infections); *cryptococcal meningitis* (which can cause severe headache, nausea, vomiting, blurred vision, sensitivity to bright light, stiff neck, seizures, confusion, behavioral changes and coma); *pneumocystis carinii pneumonia* (which can cause fever, chest tightness, shortness of breath, lack of energy, dry cough and weight loss); *toxoplasmosis* (which can cause damage to the brain, eyes or other organs); and *cryptosporidiosis* (which can cause diarrhea, dehydration, weight loss, stomach cramps or pain, fever, nausea and vomiting). HIV-positive people can also get cancers, such as Kaposi's sarcoma (which can cause lesions on the skin, mouth, throat, lungs and the intestinal tract) and lymphoma (which can cause fever, chills, weight loss, night sweats and lack of energy).

HIV treatment involves the use of antiretroviral drugs that prevent the virus from replicating, thereby reducing the amount of virus in the body. However, these drugs do not eliminate the virus from the body and become ineffective if the virus mutates and develops resistance to the drugs. Drug resistance is delayed by using two or more classes of anti-HIV drugs in combination, each of which attacks the virus in a different way. Other medical interventions focus on preventing or treating the opportunistic infections listed above. We examine HIV/AIDS treatment issues in greater detail in Chaps. 3 and 9.

1.4 HIV/AIDS Strategies in Developed and Developing Countries

In Chap. 2, we provide an overview of the global AIDS pandemic and the three central issues that form part of a comprehensive AIDS strategy – prevention, treatment and human rights protection. Each of these issues is inter-related and must be considered in the context of specific countries or regions, in order to take into account variations in cultural values, affected groups, infection rates, legal systems, economic resources and human resources. Chapter 2 therefore analyzes these key issues in country-specific and region-specific contexts. Prevention, treatment and human rights protection also raise other issues, such as the cost of patented medicine, the right of governments to suspend patent rights and the use of litigation and international political pressure to increase the cost of life-saving medicines.

In 2007, there were an estimated 30.6–36.1 million people living with HIV/AIDS worldwide, 1.8–4.1 million new infections and 1.9–2.4 million people dying from AIDS-related illnesses. HIV/AIDS disproportionately affects the most marginalized groups in each society – the poor, commercial sex workers, men who have sex with men, injection drug users and women. However, the degree to which these groups are marginalized varies from one society to the next and within each society. As a sexually transmitted disease, the stigma associated with AIDS further isolates the people who live with this condition and makes HIV difficult to discuss openly. Widespread societal taboos regarding sex, negative attitudes regarding the groups of people most affected by the virus and the fear that is kindled by infectious disease have proved to be powerful allies for a virus whose transmission would be otherwise more easily prevented. The stigma associated with HIV/AIDS and a lack of legal protection against discrimination may deter people from seeking testing and treatment. The lack of access to treatment and information also can discourage people from seeking testing, which in turn can contribute to the spread of the disease. Moreover, antiretroviral treatment reduces the amount of HIV in the body, thereby reducing the risk of transmission.

The course of the HIV/AIDS pandemic in different settings underlines the importance of early intervention with appropriate policies to prevent and contain the spread of global diseases. The source of HIV/AIDS in animals and its transmission to humans through *zoonosis* shows that the world community needs to be vigilant regarding other such events. For example, H5N1 influenza, which is a more infectious disease, would spread much more rapidly than HIV/AIDS. In order to prepare for such a pandemic, the lessons of the HIV/AIDS pandemic would have to be applied *before* the pandemic occurs. The HIV/AIDS epidemic in Africa has demonstrated how health issues can become security issues. It has also demonstrated the importance of political leadership and accurate information in containing the spread of disease.

The experience in Brazil and Thailand indicate that a well-designed HIV/AIDS program that is tailored to the specific epidemic and to the specific context of the country in question can be successful, at least in middle-income countries with relatively low prevalence rates. The lesson from Brazil and Thailand is not that other countries should duplicate these two countries' programs. Rather, the lessons from Brazil and Thailand are that: (1) responses to HIV/AIDS need to be tailor-made; (2) governmental and NGO leaders have a crucial role to play; (3) early intervention is necessary in order to contain the spread of the virus; and (4) health infrastructure and human resources need to be adequate.

The incorporation of a human rights program appears to be an important element that has contributed to Brazil's success. The stigma associated with HIV/AIDS in South Africa has hampered that country's efforts, whereas the relative absence of stigma surrounding the commercial sex trade in Thailand has meant the absence of such a barrier to action in that country. Similarly, the stigma associated with injection drug users in Russia hampered the implementation of an effective HIV/AIDS strategy in a country where injection drug users make up 50% of the epidemic. Thus, social conditions may be highly relevant to the design of an effective HIV/AIDS program. Finally, the nature of the epidemic must be taken into account in each context. In both Brazil and Thailand, efforts have focused on high-risk groups, which differed in the two settings – with commercial sex workers being the main focus in Thailand and Brazil's efforts focused on men who have sex with men, injection drug users and commercial sex workers.

Providing universal access to antiretroviral therapy requires adequate financial resources in the face of a particular prevalence rate. The manner in which governments deal with negotiations with other governments and patent owners has a direct impact on the cost of treatment, as demonstrated by South Africa, Thailand and Brazil. However, financial resources do not necessarily correlate with the design of an effective program, as the case of Japan demonstrates. Moreover, even middle-income countries can face disaster where political leadership is replaced by inaction and denial, as the case of South Africa shows. Both the Japanese and the South African experiences demonstrate that cultural or psychological predispositions can hobble the capacity of a country to respond effectively to the threats posed by epidemics. These factors therefore need to be taken into account in the design of international responses to the threat posed by global diseases.

The difficulties faced by developing countries in confronting the HIV/AIDS epidemic have direct effects on the developed world. The HIV/AIDS pandemic has influenced World Trade Organization (WTO) policy regarding patent protection for pharmaceutical companies that are primarily located in the developed countries. In this regard, the epidemic has begun to change an important element of international economic policy. The migration of natural persons across the borders of an increasingly integrated global economy means developed country interests are also at stake in addressing the HIV/AIDS pandemic in developing countries. Borders do not prevent the spread of the virus and closing borders is not an option in a globalized world. Perhaps most significantly, national and global experiences with the HIV/AIDS pandemic provide lessons for addressing not just HIV/AIDS, but other global diseases and pandemics as well. A complete picture of the HIV/AIDS pandemic requires an analysis of its effects on human health, security, international relations, business, international economic policy, national economic growth and social dynamics. However, this multi-faceted analysis serves not only to ensure effective strategies for confronting this disease and this pandemic, but to underline the importance of a multidisciplinary approach to other global health issues.

1.5 Insurance, Mortality, Treatment Costs and the Business Impact of HIV/AIDS

In Chap. 3 we analyze financial aspects of HIV/AIDS. HIV/AIDS was first identified in developed countries, where the insurance industry was the first business to be deeply affected by HIV/AIDS. Later, HIV/AIDS became a financial issue for all industries offering health care for their employees, as well as governments concerned with public health expenditures. In developing countries, with a few exceptions like Thailand and Brazil, the reaction to HIV/AIDS was slower.

Chapter 3 focuses on the data and financial tools used by insurance companies to address the financial risks associated with the HIV/AIDS pandemic. We first examine these issues in the context of developed countries, focusing on the United States. We then examine these issues in the context of developing countries, focusing on high-prevalence countries in sub-Saharan Africa and, in particular, South Africa. We then consider public and private sector strategies that might be adapted to South Africa's situation. Finally, we demonstrate that the potential financial benefits to companies in high-prevalence countries from funding prevention and treatment programs for their employees are likely to exceed the costs of such programs.

In the early 1980s, the insurance industry in the developed world was concerned about the impact of HIV/AIDS, due to long-term, individual life insurance policies for which they could not deny renewal and due to their inability to identify and exclude persons with HIV from group insurance coverage. In the late 1980s, it appeared that AIDS would cause death within 2 years and that the number of cases would exceed 1.2 million by 1998 in the United States alone. This new risk not been priced into insurance premiums and might have threatened the solvency of many life insurance companies.

However, once the nature of HIV transmission was understood, prevention reduced the actual numbers. In addition, in 1996, the advent of triple combination antiretroviral treatments for HIV/AIDS reduced mortality significantly and dramatically increased the number of years people could live with HIV/AIDS. With a correct assessment of survival probabilities for HIV-positive individuals, insurance companies could accurately calculate the financial reserves they needed to set aside. These developments lowered the financial risks of having long-term life insurance policies on HIV-positive individuals. Moreover, the cost of the new treatments did not pose a threat to private health insurers, since most health insurance policies were renewable annually and could be factored into their premiums.

In addition, by the late 1990s, it became possible to estimate the cost of treatment for HIV/AIDS. The result is that the insurance risks associated with HIV/AIDS are now similar to those for diabetes and can be priced accordingly.

In many developing countries the situation is very different, for the following reasons: (1) prevalence rates are much higher in many developing countries and vary widely; (2) HIV/AIDS has expanded beyond high-risk groups to the general population; (3) healthcare infrastructure is inadequate in many developing countries; and (4) mechanisms for estimating prevalence and tracking the spread of HIV/AIDS are less developed. For example, in 2007 a major revision of HIV/AIDS prevalence in India reduced the estimated number of cases from 5.7 million in 2004 to 2.47 million in 2006. The accuracy of HIV/AIDS estimates is important, both for governments involved in assessing the scale of prevention and treatment needs and for the private sector, particularly the insurance industry. The correct pricing of insurance products requires an accurate assessment of the frequency and severity of risks.

South Africa has the most HIV/AIDS cases in the world and one of the highest prevalence rates. Moreover, mortality rates are high and survival probabilities are low, due to a lack of access to treatment. However, the highly developed South African insurance industry was not severely affected by the dramatic rise in HIV/AIDS prevalence in South Africa, because most life insurance policies in South Africa were short-term policies and South African insurance companies used income and education levels to categorize risk. However, while the insurance industry in South Africa has been able to survive HIV/AIDS, this has come at the cost of reduced access to life insurance and limited access to health insurance that might cover part of the cost of treatment for HIV/AIDS. Thus, while South Africa is a middle-income country, it has not achieved universal access to treatment for people living with HIV/AIDS. Achieving this goal in South Africa is further complicated by its high prevalence rate.

Mexico has expanded access to HIV/AIDS treatment primarily through the purchase of higher cost patented drugs. While both South Africa and Mexico are middle-income countries, there is a big difference in their HIV prevalence rates. This means that the Mexican approach would not be affordable in South Africa. While the Mexican public health insurance model could work in South Africa, the purchase of antiretroviral medication for South Africa would have to be funded by external sources. In addition, South Africa would have to pursue the same strategy as Thailand and Brazil, by substituting generic equivalents for more expensive patented drugs. However, for middle-income countries with prevalence rates like South Africa, expanding access to treatment for HIV/AIDS is likely to require a mixture of public and private sector strategies.

In the United States and other developed countries, a financial mechanism was developed to convert terminally ill patients' savings through life insurance into viatical settlements. Viatical settlement companies give cash to terminally ill patients in exchange for their life insurance policies. When the patient dies, the company collects the death benefits. This process enabled terminally ill patients to pay for medical treatment. In Chap. 3, we demonstrate that a properly regulated viatical market, combined with insurance regulation that provides access to life insurance for HIV-positive individuals, provides a mechanism to enhance private sector coverage of the cost of HIV treatment. A viatical market serves as a complement to coverage under a public health care system. However, unlike South Africa, the United States has a prevalence rate of below one percent and is a high-income country. Moreover, in South Africa there is no viatical market. Nevertheless, while South Africa is a middle-income country, it has the most developed insurance market in the world as a percentage of gross domestic product (GDP). In this regard, South Africa is different from most developing countries. Given the level of development in the South African insurance market, the development of a viatical market is a viable option for South Africa.

Viatical markets represent one example of a broader category of financial instruments, known as securitization. Securitization of mortality is a new financial mechanism that can be used to hedge against the risk of a fast-moving epidemic, such as influenza. The loss of life and health care costs of such a pandemic could be catastrophic for life and health insurance companies. Securitization can be used to insure otherwise unmarketable risks and thereby reduce the financial risks of insurance companies. It is also a way to expand life and health insurance coverage to the risk of a serious, fast-moving pandemic. However, securitization only works where there is a low probability of such a high-loss event occurring. For this reason, it is unlikely to work in the case of HIV/AIDS in countries with high prevalence, since this is no longer a low probability event in those countries.

1.6 The Economics of HIV/AIDS

In Chap. 4, we use macroeconomic and microeconomic analysis to examine how economic conditions affect HIV/AIDS and how HIV/AIDS affects economic development. We examine the relationships between HIV/AIDS and poverty, inequality and social capital, and consider whether economic differences between countries explain differences in HIV prevalence. Since HIV/AIDS disproportionately affects people of working age, we use a macroeconomic model to examine the potential economic impact of HIV/AIDS. We show how microeconomic and epidemiological models about behavioral responses to HIV/AIDS can help to determine the effectiveness of specific HIV/AIDS prevention strategies. Economics plays a significant role in the propagation of HIV/AIDS in high incidence countries. The economics of HIV/AIDS also shows us the likely economic returns on actions that prevent HIV infections.

There is evidence that the substantial difference in the transmission rates between the United States and sub-Saharan Africa are due to untreated bacterial sexually transmitted infections. One implication of this evidence is that expanding treatment of other sexually transmitted infections may prove to be a cost effective way to reduce the incidence of HIV/AIDS. Another implication is that lower levels of economic development are not necessarily the root cause of higher rates of HIV/AIDS prevalence or vice versa. Another variable, such as war, inadequate health or poor education, may explain the relationship between poverty and HIV/AIDS. While there is a significant negative correlation between social capital and income inequality, on the one hand, and HIV/AIDS, on the other hand, it is not clear what policy prescription should flow from these findings. Reducing income inequality by taxation and redistribution of wealth can negatively affect individual incentives and the policies that might increase social capital are not obvious. Poverty reduction is too broad a goal to constitute what might be termed an HIV/AIDS prevention strategy. Moreover, there is no clear evidence that reducing poverty and income inequality will necessarily reduce HIV/AIDS prevalence.

It is difficult to predict the impact of HIV/AIDS on economic development. In theory, rising HIV/AIDS prevalence could cause the labor participation rate to rise, to fall or to remain the same. Rising rates of HIV/AIDS would reduce the supply of labor, but would also reduce the population. If HIV/AIDS were to reduce the supply of labor and the population to the same degree, then labor per capita would remain the same. Since HIV/AIDS strikes the population at a productive age, it may reduce the labor force more than the entire population, and the labor participation rate would fall. However, a decline in the supply of labor would lead to a rise in capital per labor unit in the short run. Nevertheless, in the long run, the supply of capital may fall if rising HIV/AIDS leads to less saving and investment.

Falling life expectancy and rising mortality due to HIV/AIDS may lead to lower future economic growth due to the importance of human capital for long-term accumulation of wealth. On the societal level, an HIV/AIDS epidemic can affect the size, growth rate and age and skill composition of the future labor force. In addition, the slow-moving nature of HIV/AIDS produces higher costs of treatment and palliative care than epidemics that kill quickly. These additional costs can decrease GDP growth by reducing savings and investment. On the individual level, HIV/AIDS can reduce income and increase costs. The diminished working capacity of individuals with HIV/AIDS reduces income and lower life expectancy reduces lifetime income. Higher costs, such as medical expenses and caring for orphans, lead to less education for children and lower savings. HIV/AIDS destroys human capital in a number ways and reduces the transmission of human capital between generations, leading to declining levels of education. However, it is difficult to determine the impact of HIV/AIDS on all macroeconomic variables. For example, rising incidence of HIV/AIDS can lead to rising or falling total fertility rates, which also affect human capital and economic growth. As a result, the impact of HIV/AIDS on overall economic welfare, in the form of changes to GDP, remains unclear.

Microeconomic and epidemiological models in Uganda show that promoting sexual abstinence before marriage and monogamy are less effective HIV/AIDS prevention strategies than condom promotion. Moreover, behavioral responses to HIV/AIDS risk depend on life expectancy. Individuals with higher incomes and longer life expectancy are more likely to respond to HIV risk. In regions in Africa with high rates of malaria, people already face a high risk of death from malaria and have little incentive to change their sexual behavior. Reducing the risk of death from malaria would increase incentives to change sexual behavior to reduce HIV risk. The reduction of malaria risk is relatively inexpensive, making malaria prevention a cost effective way to reduce HIV risk.

Evidence from Uganda regarding the connection between exports and HIV suggests that targeting prevention at vulnerable groups would be an effective strategy in generalized HIV epidemics. Increased exports lead to increased transportation of goods and more people movement. Truckers and other migrants are important drivers of the overall epidemic, which means that targeting prevention activities at that group would decrease HIV transmission. In addition, if increases in economic activity make the HIV epidemic worse, economic growth strategies need to incorporate HIV prevention strategies.

Another economic issue raised by HIV/AIDS is the side-effect of large increases in foreign aid to combat HIV/AIDS in high-prevalence, low-income countries. Where foreign aid increases the money supply, inflation may rise and the balance of payments may deteriorate. Large inflows of resources could significantly raise the real value of the local currency, thereby producing low economic growth, increased international debt, higher imports and lower exports. Additional expenditures would raise the wages of skilled professionals, making the private sector less competitive in the long run. The economy would become significantly more dependent on aid and remain that way for the indefinite future. Thus, foreign aid is not an unmitigated blessing.

Another question is whether we can justify singling out HIV/AIDS for increased funding when lives could be saved in other, less expensive programs. For example, prevention programs targeted at sexual transmission and transmission among injection drug users could avert 28 million new infections at a cost of USD 3,900 for each life saved. Extending maternal and newborn health coverage to 95% of the poorest countries could save over 100 million lives at a cost of USD 390 for each life saved. Nevertheless, we argue that there are a number of justifications for spending money on HIV/AIDS (and other infectious diseases). First, since HIV/AIDS is infectious, HIV prevention saves more than the life of the person who avoids HIV infection. Second, prevention targeted at vulnerable groups is a cost effective means to reduce disease propagation among the general population. Third, where HIV/AIDS funding is spent to strengthen general healthcare systems, the benefits are not limited to HIV/AIDS alone.

1.7 The Political Economy of Patents and Global Health Threats

In Chap. 5 we examine the problem of regulatory capture through the lens of national and international regulation of pharmaceutical patents. National regulatory capture can lead to de facto international regulatory capture when the national government in question has disproportionate influence in international organizations, such as the World Bank, or disproportionate bargaining power in international negotiations, such as trade negotiations at the WTO or in regional trade agreements. The source of the influence or bargaining power can include the percentage of world trade of a country, the size of its market, its spending power with respect to foreign aid, the size and percentage of its monetary contributions to international organizations and its ability to facilitate membership in a desirable economic group (such as the European Union or WTO). The degree of bargaining power or influence for the same national government can vary with the context. For example, the bargaining power of the United States is greater in free trade negotiations with small developing countries than it is in the WTO context, where the bargaining power of the United States is offset by the bargaining power of the European Union or other coalitions of influential countries. Where an industry succeeds in capturing the regulatory process of one or more national governments, that regulatory capture can lead to the indirect capture of international regulatory processes, leading to international rules that favor the industry at the expense of global welfare.

In Chap. 5, we show how the threat of compulsory licenses in the United States and Canada, to address real and imagined threats of anthrax, respectively, undermined their initial bargaining position in WTO negotiations on compulsory licensing of pharmaceuticals in developing countries. The severity of the HIV/AIDS crisis in many parts of the developing world, combined with the duplicitous policy of Canada and the United States regarding patent rights, prompted several developing countries to adopt a common position calling for clarifications to the rights of governments to issue compulsory licenses to protect public health and, in particular, to promote access to medicines for all. The resulting Declaration on the TRIPS Agreement and Public Health also identified a gap in the Agreement on Trade-Related Aspects of Intellectual Property Rights (TRIPS), under which only countries with adequate pharmaceutical manufacturing capacity could in practice exercise the right to issue compulsory licenses on pharmaceutical products. Two years of multilateral negotiations on this issue ultimately led to a decision to amend the TRIPS Agreement (known as the Paragraph 6 Decision), but it took two more years to adopt the amendment formally and it has yet to be adopted by the two-thirds of the WTO Members required for it to enter into force. However, the most interesting aspect of these negotiations was the extent to which the Pharmaceutical Research and Manufacturers of America (PhRMA), which lobbies the US government on behalf of its member companies, succeeded in dictating the US government's position in the negotiations.

This instance of international regulatory capture was later followed by two other examples, in several free trade negotiations between the United States and developing countries and in the exercise of the US Trade Representative's authority to identify and apply political pressure to countries that are considered to be undermining US commercial interests. For example, the Central America-Dominican

Republic-United States Free Trade Agreement (CAFTA-DR) not only created new obstacles to compulsory licensing of pharmaceutical products in several small developing countries, but also overrode the clarifications to the rights of governments that were achieved in the WTO negotiations. When Thailand – a country that did not negotiate this type of free trade agreement with the United States – exercised its rights under WTO law to issue compulsory licenses on some pharmaceutical products (including antiretroviral drugs for its HIV/AIDS treatment program), the US Trade Representative placed Thailand on its priority watch list of countries and characterized the Thai government's decision as "further indications of a weakening of respect for patents". This kind of political pressure from the governments of the major pharmaceutical companies discourages the use of compulsory licensing to increase affordable access to medicine in developing countries and undermines the international rule of law.

In Chap. 5 we show why strong patent rights for pharmaceutical products in developing countries are not necessary to provide research incentives to invent new medicines. We also argue show why parallel imports of cheaper drugs from developing countries are unlikely to undermine research incentives in developed country markets. We then analyze whether patents are necessary for innovation to occur and argue that patent rights in fact have the effect of stifling innovation by providing an incentive to patent holders to invest in legal action to extend the life of their patents and to prevent others from developing new innovations. In economic terms, this is an inefficient way of allocating economic resources. Striking the right balance between incentives to invent new medicines and affordable access to those medicines is a key issue in addressing global diseases.

1.8 Global Diseases, Global Patents and Developing Countries in WTO Law

Chapter 6 analyzes the key patent provisions of the WTO TRIPS Agreement, in light of the relevant WTO jurisprudence that has interpreted these provisions and other WTO provisions that relate to the special and differential treatment of developing countries in the WTO system.

Governments grant patents to inventors on the national level, which means that they only have legal effect in the jurisdictions where the application for a patent has been granted. One of the conditions for granting a patent is that the inventor disclose the data used in the producing the invention. TRIPS established minimum standards for the protection of intellectual property rights in the national laws of WTO Members. TRIPS requires that patents be granted for a minimum of 20 years and that they provide patent owners with the exclusive right to prevent third parties from making, using, selling or importing a patented product without the owner's consent. However, TRIPS allows exceptions to these patent rights, including the right of governments to issue compulsory licenses under certain conditions. A compulsory license authorizes a third party to produce and sell the invention without the patent owner's consent. This exception plays a key role in balancing the rights of patent owners against the needs of consumers of patented products. The right to issue a compulsory license on a patented drug provides countries with bargaining power to extract price concessions for patented drugs or to issue compulsory licenses if price negotiations fail. However, this bargaining power applies only to countries that have the manufacturing capacity to produce generic drugs, since the generic drugs must be used to predominately supply the national market of the country that issues the compulsory license. Countries that lack domestic manufacturing capacity would need to be able to import generics manufactured under compulsory licenses in other countries in order to enjoy a comparable level of bargaining power. The Paragraph 6 Decision established rules to allow this to happen.

The Paragraph 6 Decision waives an exporter's obligation to supply predominantly its domestic market, enabling any country with manufacturing capacity to issue a compulsory license to produce generic drugs for export to countries that have insufficient or no manufacturing capacity, subject to several conditions. No formal restriction on the countries that are eligible to import exists under the Paragraph 6 system. All WTO members, other than least-developed countries, are required to notify the WTO of their intention to use the Paragraph 6 system. Some countries have made a commitment not to use the Paragraph 6 system as importers, while several others have committed to using the system as importers only in situations of national emergency or extreme urgency. The latter have agreed, in effect, not to use the system simply to lower the general cost of purchasing medicine for public health care systems. No restrictions exist regarding the countries that are eligible to export.

The Paragraph 6 system does not apply to countries that have sufficient manufacturing capacity to issue compulsory licenses to meet the needs of their own populations. The question in a given case is whether the importing country has manufacturing capacity for the pharmaceutical product in question. For example, countries like China, India and Brazil, if they lack capacity for a particular medicine, could use the Paragraph 6 system to import drugs from generic manufacturers in other countries. However, where developing countries do have manufacturing capacity, they will have to determine whether and how to use compulsory licensing to reduce the cost of providing treatment by issuing licenses to their own generic manufacturers. When a country issues a compulsory license to its own generic drug manufacturers to serve its own market, the Paragraph 6 Decision will not apply.

Among the policy objectives of the TRIPS Agreement is to balance intellectual property rights against development needs. In WTO law more generally, there are numerous provisions that provide for differential treatment based on the level of development of WTO members. We make a distinction between global diseases (diseases that are prevalent in both developed and developing countries, such as HIV/AIDS) and neglected diseases (developing country diseases that are not prevalent in developed countries, such as malaria). The economic issues are different for these two categories, because the markets for drugs that treat the diseases are different. We argue that global patents not necessary to provide research incentives for neglected diseases, nor are global patents necessary to provide research incentives for global diseases. Moreover, drug patents have neither a positive economic impact on developing countries nor meet their development needs.

We propose to eliminate the obligation of eligible developing countries to provide patent rights for pharmaceutical products, through waivers for developing countries and extended transition periods for least-developed countries. In this regard, Chap. 6 proposes a categorization of the WTO membership in the form of an index that can be used to achieve a more equitable balance between the rights of producers and users on a market-by-market basis. This proposal is grounded on economic considerations and takes into account the need to apply a systematic international standard to determine the particular needs of developing countries. The proposed index addresses the needs of a country not just based on its level of poverty, but also based on a threshold level of infection rate for a particular disease. The index serves to promote affordable access to medicine using criteria that are tailored to address the specific circumstances surrounding global or neglected diseases.

The applicability of the index to diseases and pandemics other than HIV/AIDS depends on the speed at which the disease spreads. In the case of other slowing-moving global diseases, such as tuberculosis and diabetes, the index is applicable because the disease rate can be determined. In the case of a fast-moving global disease, such as SARS or influenza, or the use of biological agents in war or terrorism, such as anthrax, governments may wish to stockpile medical treatment before the disease occurs. In these circumstances, the disease rate cannot be determined before the government needs to acquire the necessary medical treatment. However, WTO members can exercise their right to issue compulsory licenses to address a national emergency or other circumstances of extreme urgency under TRIPS Article 31 or the Paragraph 6 System or use the threat of a compulsory license to expand production or to lower the cost of the drugs that they need to stockpile.

1.9 Bilateral and Multilateral Financing of HIV/AIDS Programs

Chapter 7 examines the activities of the World Bank, the International Monetary Fund (IMF), the Global Fund, bilateral donors and the private sector. We examine the relationships among bilateral donors and international organizations, what distinguishes their roles in the global HIV/AIDS pandemic and the extent to which their activities overlap. We show how funding strategies and parameters affect the effectiveness of AIDS funding in preventing transmission and providing treatment.

Multilateral institutions, such as the World Bank, the IMF and the Global Fund, and bilateral donors, including non-governmental organizations (NGOs) and national governments, need to coordinate and harmonize their policies and financing conditions in order to reduce the administrative burden on recipients and in order to avoid imposing conflicting conditions on recipients. Donors also need to be careful with respect to the role assigned to the private sector in delivering aid, in order to avoid the unnecessary diversion of funds away from the core goal of healthcare.

The global response to the HIV/AIDS pandemic has highlighted the need to strengthen healthcare infrastructure in developing countries. It is important to address the HIV/AIDS pandemic in a way that strengthens the ability of national governments and multilateral organizations to address health concerns more generally. Particularly in the case of fast-moving infectious diseases, equitable and effective distribution should be paramount, since such diseases are unlikely to respect socio-economic boundaries.

The global business community has an important role to play in addressing global diseases. It is important to integrate health issues into the overall business strategy of firms. In addition, there is a need to standardize best practices on a more systematic basis and to create incentives for those best practices to be adopted by suppliers and business partners of global companies.

1.10 The Successes and Failures of Global Health Organizations

Chapter 8 examines the activities of the WHO, UNAIDS, Médicins sans Frontières (MSF), the US President's Emergency Program for AIDS Relief (PEPFAR) and the CDC. The ineffectiveness of the WHO in addressing the HIV/AIDS pandemic and the advent of SARS and H5N1 influenza highlighted the need for reforms to make the WHO a more effective multilateral health institution. In 2005, reforms to the WHO International Health Regulations (IHR) enhanced the ability of the WHO to coordinate and implement a global response to global diseases and future pandemics. The effectiveness of the IHR, which entered into force in 2007, has also been enhanced by the advent of modern communications technologies, which facilitate the dissemination of news on outbreaks of contagious diseases. The IHR focus on fast-moving contagious diseases and reflect the core competencies of the WHO. While the IHR have norms that discourage the use of disproportionate trade and travel restrictions in response to disease outbreaks, health-related trade restrictions are regulated by the WTO. However, the risk assessments conducted by the WHO under the IHR are likely to influence the application of WTO rules to such cases.

UNAIDS has filled the gaps left by the WHO with respect to the HIV/AIDS pandemic, but the creation of such disease-specific agencies is not the best approach to addressing fast-moving global diseases. Moreover, even the creation of

UNAIDS has been insufficient to provide adequate multilateral leadership on HIV/AIDS within the UN system.

MSF has moved in to fill the gaps left by the UN system. However, while MSF has filled an important need, its withdrawal from collective efforts sets an unfortunate precedent in an environment where a multiplicity of players and approaches requires greater harmonization and coordination of efforts in order to ensure the efficient use of resources. Nevertheless, the creation of UNAIDS and the approach of MSF both serve to highlight the need for ongoing reforms to improve the effectiveness of global health institutions and have led to innovative approaches that may serve as models for such reforms.

PEPFAR has injected much-needed funding for HIV/AIDS. However, the policies that have been imposed on funding for treatment have favored the commercial interests of the US pharmaceutical industry, thereby undermining the goal of increasing access to treatment. The policies imposed on funding for prevention have favored the ideological interests of conservative Christian organizations in the United States, thereby undermining the goal of effective, science-based prevention efforts. While the use of funding should be monitored to ensure its effective use, substituting science-based strategies with strategies that cater to the domestic political interests of donor governments can hamper efforts to address pandemics effectively.

The CDC is part of the US Department of Health and Human Services. In addition to its work in the United States, the CDC is involved in global health activities. The CDC is a recognized source of expertise, particularly in responding to outbreaks of infectious diseases around the world. The CDC responds to outbreaks of infectious diseases by deploying staff, monitoring the spread of disease and training public health staff from other countries. The CDC is also a valuable source of research and publications on public health issues. Its work outside the United States, with national partners and the WHO, represents a valuable contribution to global health and a recognition of the interconnectedness of global health issues.

1.11 Prevention, Treatment and Human Rights

In Chap. 9, we emphasize the importance of integrating prevention, treatment and human rights to manage HIV/AIDS effectively. The primary reason that human rights need to be addressed in conjunction with prevention and treatment is because discrimination keeps people away from both prevention and treatment programs. Moreover, stigma and discrimination have reduced the effectiveness of prevention programs by excluding vulnerable groups. The less effective prevention programs are, the more treatment is required and the less affordable the goal of universal access to treatment will be.

Global access to antiretroviral therapy for people living with HIV/AIDS has been scaled up significantly in recent years. Many developing countries now have universal access to treatment, including low-income countries, such as Rwanda, and middle-income countries, such as Thailand and Brazil. However, prevention needs to be scaled up considerably in order to make universal access to treatment an affordable goal on a global scale. Without adequate prevention, new infections will rise and millions more people will need treatment. The increase in new HIV infections in several high-income countries highlights the need for effective prevention programs in all countries. This requires an evidence-based focus on high-risk groups and locations to achieve the best possible results, including programs for commercial sex workers and needle exchange programs. The need to focus prevention efforts on the most vulnerable groups remains an issue in both developed and developing countries. Proven HIV prevention strategies for sexual transmission, blood-borne transmission, mother-to-child transmission, as well as social strategies to reduce vulnerability to HIV/AIDS, need to be focused according to the specific nature of the epidemic in different settings. Strategies that increase stigma and discrimination against vulnerable groups ignore the fact that people at high risk of contracting HIV/AIDS do not live in isolation from the general population.

With the advent of triple combination therapy, the focus has shifted from the effectiveness of treatments for HIV/AIDS to the cost of making effective treatments accessible. This is why the issue of drug patents has become so important. However, increasing the number of people receiving treatment will require addressing the capacity constraints of treatment providers, which include limited health infrastructure and human resources, management capacity and the ability to identify new patients through testing and counseling. While high-income countries and middle-income countries with low prevalence rates are in a position to pay for HIV/AIDS treatment, middle-income countries with high prevalence rates and most low-income countries are not. Low-income countries with high prevalence rates in particular will have to depend on external funding sources, such as PEPFAR and the Global Fund, to expand access to treatment and then to maintain treatment.

Scientists have been trying to develop an HIV vaccine for more than 20 years, but without success. Moreover, HIV/AIDS vaccine trials to date reveal a pattern of development of potential vaccines not in the subtypes where the needs are the greatest, but where the biggest monetary rewards are expected. The economics of HIV/AIDS vaccines suggest that funding for vaccines for the worst-effected countries are unlikely to come from the private sector.

HIV/AIDS-related human rights are the area where the least progress has been made and need to become a central focus in the global fight against HIV/AIDS. This requires the reform and repeal of laws that discriminate against vulnerable groups and HIV-positive people, and the introduction or strengthening of laws that prohibit discrimination against vulnerable groups and HIV-positive people. For example, laws that prohibit sexual acts between consenting adults in private, laws prohibiting sex work that involves no victimization and laws prohibiting measures such as needle exchange create obstacles to treatment and prevention. Laws and cultural traditions in some countries increase women's vulnerability to HIV/AIDS, either within marriage or by forcing them to support themselves and their children as sex workers. Laws that criminalize HIV transmission and travel restrictions based on HIV status discriminate directly against people with HIV/AIDS and often ignore scientific evidence. On the plus side, courts in a variety of countries have applied constitutional law, international law and other legislation to uphold the rights of people living with HIV/AIDS with respect to employment and access to HIV-related medical care and treatment.

The United Nations International Guidelines on HIV/AIDS and Human Rights acknowledge the inherent limitations in using law reform to enhance human rights. The effectiveness human rights laws depend on the strength of the legal system in a given society and on the access of its citizens to the system, both of which vary considerably from one country to the next. Moreover, the law cannot serve as the only means of educating, changing attitudes, achieving behavioral change or protecting people's rights. Nevertheless, since laws regulate conduct between the State and the individual and between individuals, they can either support or undermine the observance of human rights, including HIV-related human rights.

1.12 Increasing the Effectiveness of Global Disease Management

Understanding past outbreaks of diseases can lead to new public health measures and other interventions to more effectively address existing diseases and to better prepare the world for future pandemics. While medicine and science have a crucial role to play in addressing pandemics, whether slow-moving (like HIV/AIDS) or fast-moving (like influenza), the social, legal, political, financial and economic ramifications of pandemics can not be ignored. Well-considered social, legal, political and financial strategies are essential in order to address any pandemic effectively, but they are particularly important when it comes to addressing fast-moving pandemics.

International human rights law and international health law are far less developed and much less effective than international trade law. However, as we show in Chap. 4, global pandemics are also of great importance to economic growth. The key difference between international trade and pandemics is that the former is a positive force for economic growth, while the latter has a negative impact. International trade raises standards of living, whereas pandemics lower standards of living and the length and quality of life. If economic importance is the key reason for having effective global policies, laws and institutions, then the further development an effective global framework to address the negative consequences of pandemics should be given much greater priority.

References

Billings M (1997) The Influenza Pandemic of 1918. http://virus.stanford.edu/uda/. Accessed 6 September 2007

Dunham W (2007) Virulent form of cold virus spreads in U.S. Reuters, 15 November 2007

Gao F, Bailes E, Robertson DL, Chen Y et al. (1999) Origin of HIV-1 in the chimpanzee Pan troglodytes troglodytes. Nature 397:436–444

McPherson S (2007) All eyes on Pakistan as H5N1 H2H transmission grows more probable. http://www.scottmcpherson.net/journal/2007/12/14/all-eyes-on-pakistan-as-h5n1-h2h-transmission-grows-more-pro.html. Accessed 14 December 2007

Nebehay S (2007) Mixed scenario seen behind Pakistan birdflu spread. http://www.reuters.com/article/latestCrisis/idUSL18866730. Accessed 19 December 2007

Rosenthal E (2007) As Earth Warms Up, Tropical Virus Moves to Italy. http://www.nytimes.com/2007/12/23/world/europe/23virus.html?hp. Accessed 23 December 2007

Sherman IW (2007) Twelve Diseases That Changed Our World. American Society for Microbiology Press, Washington, DC

Taubenberger JK, Morens DM (2006) 1918 Influenza: The Mother of all Pandemics. Emerging Infectious Diseases. http://www.cdc.gov/ncidod/EID/vol12no01/05-0979.htm. Accessed 23 October 2007

Vandamme AM et al. (2003) Tracing the origin and history of the HIV-2 epidemic. Proceedings of the National Academy of Sciences of the United States of America 100(11): 6588–6592

Waters J (2007) Bird flu could have become worldwide pandemic: study. http://www.abc.net.au/news/stories/2007/08/31/2021231.htm. Accessed 31 August 2007

Wolfe ND, Switzer WM, Carr JK et al. (2004) Naturally acquired simian retrovirus infections in Central African Hunters. The Lancet 363:932

Zhou T, Korber B, Nahinias AJ (1998) An African HIV-1 sequence from 1959 and implications for the origin of the epidemic. Nature 391:594–597

2 HIV/AIDS Prevention and Treatment Strategies in Developed and Developing Countries

"The world must do more, much more on every front in the fight against AIDS. Of course, it means dramatically expanding our prevention efforts, but the most striking inequity is our failure to provide the lifesaving treatment to the millions of people who need it most. The single most important step we must now take is to provide access to treatment throughout the developing world. There is no excuse for delay. We must start now. If we discard the people who are dying from AIDS, then we can no longer call ourselves decent people."
Nelson Mandela, 15 July 2003, International AIDS Society Conference in Paris

AIDS is a truly global disease. As such, it raises issues that local or regional diseases do not (although some issues may be the same). For example, because AIDS affects both rich and poor countries, AIDS has become a treatable disease far more quickly than regional, poor-country diseases such as malaria. However, patented treatments for AIDS, while affordable for patients in rich countries, have not been widely available to many patients in poor countries. AIDS is also an infectious disease that is largely preventable. This means that public education and prevention measures (such as free condom distribution and needle exchange programs) are capable of slowing the spread of the disease. AIDS is also a sexually transmitted disease (although it can also be transmitted through blood transfusions, needle-sharing, and mother-to-child). Many cultures have taboos about sex in general and homosexual intercourse in particular. This aspect of the disease complicates both treatment and prevention due to the stigma associated with sexually transmitted diseases. Combine such taboos with the fear associated with infectious, life-threatening diseases, and the discriminatory treatment of marginalized members of society, and you have a potent and complex global problem that defies easy solutions.

Due to the nature of the disease itself, prevention, treatment and human rights protection must all form part of any comprehensive AIDS strategy. These are the three central issues that must be addressed simultaneously in order to deal effectively with the AIDS pandemic. Each of these issues involves a host of subsidiary issues. For example, treatment raises issues such as the cost of patented medicine, the rights of governments to suspend patent rights, the availability of health workers and infrastructure and the availability of international aid to finance national AIDS strategies. Moreover, prevention, treatment and human rights protection are inter-related issues. For example, the rights of women affect their ability to use prevention strategies. Moreover, the stigma associated with HIV/AIDS, together with a lack of legal protection against discrimination, may deter people from seeking testing and treatment. Finally, a lack of access to treatment can create a sense of

25

futility with respect to seeking testing, which in turn can contribute to the spread of the disease.

This chapter will examine these issues in different parts of the globe. While AIDS is a global disease, its impact varies from one country to the next and from one region to the next. Variations in cultural values, affected groups, infection rates, legal systems, economic resources and human resources mean that HIV/AIDS must be considered in specific contexts. This chapter therefore seeks to paint a global picture of the AIDS pandemic one issue, one country and one region at a time, by analyzing the key issues in country-specific and region-specific contexts. The chapter ends with a consideration of how experiences with HIV/AIDS might inform the strategies adopted to address the global pandemics of the future, such as H5N1 influenza.

2.1 The Global Statistics

HIV/AIDS ranks among history's worst epidemics. With the 2007 revisions to the United Nations' global estimates of the number of people infected with HIV/AIDS, it now appears that this pandemic has peaked (UNAIDS 2007). (In Chap. 3, we analyze the methodology used for HIV/AIDS estimates.) In 2007, there were an estimated 1.8–4.1 million new infections (see Table 2.1), down from 2.1 to to 4.4 million new infections in 2001. However, an estimated 1.9–2.4 million people died from AIDS-related illnesses in 2007 (see Table 2.2) and the number of people living with HIV/AIDS has continued to increase, rising to 30.6–36.1 million (see Table 2.3), compared to 26.9–32.4 million in 2001 (UNAIDS 2007). While the estimated number of new infections declined in sub-Saharan Africa and South and Southeast Asia between 2001 and 2007, they increased during this period in Eastern Europe, Vietnam and Indonesia (see Table 2.6). Moreover, a mutated HIV virus could emerge that might be more easily transmitted or more drug resistant. The battle against HIV/AIDS is far from over.

Low- and middle-income countries are disproportionately affected by HIV/AIDS, accounting for over 96% of new infections in 2007 (UNAIDS 2007). Table 2.4 shows the regional distribution of HIV/AIDS in 2007 and 2001 and the adult prevalence rate in 2007. Sub-Saharan Africa remains the region most affected by

Table 2.1 People newly infected with HIV in 2007

	Range of estimate
Adults	1.4–3.6 million
Children under 15 years	350,000–540,000
Total	1.8–4.1 million

Source: AIDS Epidemic Update, December 2007, UNAIDS, Geneva

HIV/AIDS, with 20.9–24.3 million individuals infected (68% of all cases world-wide) and 1.5–2.0 million deaths (76% of global deaths) in 2007. Almost 90% of children with HIV live in sub-Saharan Africa. Women are the most affected group in this region, making up 61% of the total number of people living with HIV, compared to 43% in the Caribbean, and 29% in Asia (UNAIDS 2007). HIV prevalence exceeded 15% of the adult population in eight southern African countries in 2007. According to population-based surveys, the highest adult (15–49 years of

Table 2.2 AIDS deaths in 2007

	Range of estimate
Adults	1.6–2.1 million
Children under 15 years	310,000–380,000
Total	1.9–2.4 million

Source: AIDS Epidemic Update, December 2007, UNAIDS, Geneva

Table 2.3 Number of people living with HIV in 2007

Group	Range of estimate
Adults	28.2–33.6 million
Women	13.9–16.6 million
Children under 15 years	2.2–2.6 million
Total	30.6–36.1 million

Source: AIDS Epidemic Update, December 2007, UNAIDS, Geneva

Table 2.4 Regional distribution of HIV/AIDS in 2007 and 2001

Region	2007	2001	Adult prevalence 2007 (%)
Sub-Saharan Africa	20.9–24.3 million	19.7–23.6 million	4.6–5.5
North Africa and Middle East	270,000–500,000	220,000–400,000	0.2–0.4
South and South-East Asia	3.3–5.1 million	2.9–4.5 million	0.2–0.4
East Asia	620,000–960,000	350,000–910,000	<0.2
Oceania	53,000–120,000	19,000–39,000	0.3–0.7
Latin America	1.4–1.9 million	1.2–1.6 million	0.4–0.6
Caribbean	210,000–270,000	180,000–250,000	0.9–1.2
Eastern Europe and Central Asia	1.2–2.1 million	490,000–1.1 million	0.7–1.2
Western and Central Europe	600,000–1.1 million	500,000–170,000	0.2–0.4
North America	480,000–1.9 million	390,000–1.6 million	0.5–0.9
Total	30.6–36.1 million	26.9–32.4 million	0.7–0.9

Source: AIDS Epidemic Update, December 2007, UNAIDS, Geneva

Table 2.5 Estimated adult HIV/AIDS prevalence rates, population-based surveys

Rank	Country	Population-based survey of adult prevalence (year)
1	Swaziland	25.9 (2006–2007)
2	Botswana	25.2 (2004)
3	Lesotho	23.5 (2004)
4	Zimbabwe	18.1 (2005–2006)
5	South Africa	16.2 (2005)
6	Zambia	15.6 (2001–2002)
7	Malawi	12.7 (2004)
8	Uganda	7.1 (2004–2005)
9	Tanzania	7.0 (2004)
10	Kenya	6.7 (2003)
11	Central African Republic	6.2 (2006)
12	Cameroon	5.5 (2004)
13	Cote d'Ivoire	4.7 (2005)
14	Burundi	3.6 (2002)
15	Chad	3.3 (2005)
16	Equatorial Guinea	3.2 (2004)
17	Rwanda	3.0 (2005)
18	Haiti	2.2 (2005–2006)
19	Ghana	2.2 (2003)
20	Burkina Faso	1.8 (2003)
21	Sierra Leone	1.5 (2005)
22	Guinea	1.5 (2005)
23	Ethiopia	1.4 (2005)
24	Mali	1.3 (2006)
25	Dominican Republic	1.0 (2002)

Source: AIDS Epidemic Update, December 2007, UNAIDS, Geneva. Note: Population-based surveys are not available for all countries

age) prevalence rates were as follows in the years in which surveys took place: Swaziland: 25.9 (2006–2007); Botswana: 25.2 (2004); Lesotho: 23.5 (2004); Zimbabwe: 18.1 (2005–2006); South Africa: 16.2 (2005); and Zambia: 15.6 (2001–2002) (see Table 2.5).

South and South-east Asia is the second most affected region, with 3.3–5.1 million people living with HIV, 180,000–740,000 new infections and 230,000–380,000 deaths in 2007. Latin America and Eastern Europe/Central Asia follow, with 1.4–1.9 and 1.2–2.1 million people living with HIV in each region, respectively. However, HIV is spreading more rapidly in Eastern Europe/Central Asia than in Latin America, with 70,000–290,000 new infections in the former in 2007, compared to 47,000–220,000 in the latter (see Table 2.6). A decrease in new infections in Eastern Europe/Central Asia was mainly due to a decrease in the Russian Federation. However, the number of persons with HIV increased 150% in Eastern Europe between 2001 and 2007. The estimated number of deaths due to AIDS in Latin America in 2007, at 49,000–91,000, was greater than in Eastern Europe/Central Asia, at 42,000–88,000 (UNAIDS 2007).

Table 2.6 Newly infected adults and children by region in 2007 and 2001

Region	2007	2001	Change
Sub-Saharan Africa	1.4–2.4 million	1.7–2.7 million	Decrease
North Africa and Middle East	16,000–65,000	17,000–58,000	Stable
South and South-East Asia	180,000–740,000	150,000–800,000	Stable
East Asia	21,000–220,000	49,000–130,000	Increase
Oceania	11,000–26,000	3,000–5,600	Increase
Latin America	47,000–220,000	56,000–220,000	Stable
Caribbean	15,000–23,000	17,000–25,000	Decrease
Eastern Europe and Central Asia	70,000–290,000	98,000–340,000	Decrease
Western and Central Europe	19,000–86,000	19,000–76,000	Increase
North America	38,000–68,000	40,000–63,000	Stable
Total	1.8–4.1 million	2.1–4.4 million	Decrease

Source: AIDS Epidemic Update, December 2007, UNAIDS, Geneva

North America and Western/Central Europe also have large numbers of people living with HIV (480,000–1.9 million and 600,000–1.1 million, respectively), but had relatively fewer deaths from AIDS in 2007 (18,000–31,000 and less than 15,000, respectively), due to greater access to medical treatment. North America and Western/Central Europe also had fewer new infections than other regions, relative to the number of people living with HIV, at 38,000–68,000 and 19,000–86,000, respectively. While the Caribbean has fewer people living with AIDS than the foregoing regions, at 210,000–270,000, it has the second highest adult prevalence rate in the world, at 0.9–1.2%, behind sub-Saharan Africa, where the adult prevalence rate was 4.5–5.5% in 2007 (UNAIDS 2007).

UNAIDS developed a special program called "3 by 5". The aim of the program was to deliver antiretroviral therapy (ART) to three million individuals with AIDS in developing countries by 2005. However, the goal was not met. The program managed to reach around one million individuals by December 2005 (http://www.eurosurveillance.org/ew/2005/051124.asp). A 2007 report found that scaling up access to treatment was being impeded by high prices, patent barriers, registration barriers and misinformation, with the result that many countries were using AIDS treatments that are not preferred by World Health Organization (WHO) guidelines (International Treatment Preparedness Coalition 2007).

2.2 The African Epidemic: HIV/AIDS Becomes a Security Issue

The African HIV/AIDS epidemic represents the worst-case scenario. The severity of HIV infection rates in Africa prompted the United Nations Security Council to treat the AIDS crisis as a security issue. UN Security Council Resolution 1308, passed in July 2000, states that "the HIV/AIDS pandemic, if unchecked, may pose a risk to stability and security." This was the first time the United Nations had ever considered a health issue to be a security issue.

The epidemic threatens security in many different ways. HIV threatens individual security. Most of HIV sufferers live in developing countries. Most people in developing countries depend on agriculture. Agricultural production will be threatened by the lack of young people working the fields. Lack of food supply puts strains on families and communities. Tension between ethnic and social groups mounts. Economic migration gets worse and more refugees are created (Garrett 2005).

AIDS is an economic security problem. If economic progress is threatened, violent conflicts become more common. Daly (2000) suggests that even an adult prevalence rate of 10% would reduce the *growth* of GDP by 30%. At infection levels above 20%, a report by the WHO shows that the GDP would *decline* between 1 and 2% per year (WHO 2000).

AIDS is a communal security issue. It directly affects police forces, civil servants, teachers, and healthcare professionals. In South Africa, one in seven civil servants was HIV positive in 1998 (McNeil 1998).

AIDS is also a national security problem. The effect on military personnel can be devastating. In many African countries, peacekeeping forces transmit the disease from one area to the other. The military is vulnerable to HIV/AIDS for four main reasons. (1) The majority are men under 25 years of age who spend long periods deployed away from family and partners. (2) The military tend to have access to cash, enabling soldiers to "buy" sex partners, to drink heavily, and to use drugs off duty. When they are drunk or drugged, people are more likely to have unprotected sex. (3) Military work increases opportunities for men to use coercion to obtain sex. (4) The vast majority of (voluntary) military come from poorer and less educated families. Lower education and unprotected sex go hand in glove (UNAIDS 2005). For example, South Africa, with the best-equipped and best-trained military force on the African continent, does much of the region's policing. Seven out of ten military deaths in South Africa are AIDS-related. A quarter of its uniformed soldiers are infected with HIV/AIDS. Since the United Nations bars countries from sending HIV-positive soldiers on international missions a quarter of South African troops are unable to engage in UN peacekeeping missions.

US Vice President Al Gore, in an address to the UN Security Council, in January 2000 put it all very succinctly. He declared that HIV/AIDS is a security issue because "it threatens not just individual citizens, but the very institutions that define and defend the character of a society. This disease weakens workforces and saps economic strength. AIDS strikes at teachers, and denies education to their students. It strikes at the military, and subverts the forces of order and peacekeeping." (http://www.aegis.com/news/usis/2000/US000102.html)

The severity of sub-Saharan Africa's AIDS crisis is the result of a number of factors. First, since the AIDS epidemic originated in Africa, most probably through the transmission of a mutated virus from primates, it has had more time to spread there than in other parts of the world. Indeed, there is a high probability that people were dying from AIDS-related causes in Africa long before the appearance of AIDS in North America led to its diagnosis. One doctor reports having treated patients in Africa in the 1970s with symptoms that were consistent with an AIDS diagnosis. Second, a lack of public education programs aimed at prevention, combined with a cultural resistance to the use of condoms, allowed the virus to spread. Third, many in the affected societies responded to the crisis with denial, resulting in silence rather than a search for solutions. In South Africa, for example, President Thabo Mbeki (Nelson Mandela's successor) continued to question whether AIDS was caused by HIV even as the World Conference on AIDS was convening in his country in 1999. In 2000, he condemned the view that HIV/AIDS was sexually transmitted as a racist Western view (Cullinan 2004). Fourth, neither African governments nor the vast majority of infected individuals have the financial resources to pay for treatment. Pharmaceutical manufacturers resisted providing AIDS drugs to African countries at prices they can afford. Greater access to drug treatments could have reduced infection rates in Africa. By lowering the amount of virus in the blood, the drugs may significantly reduce the risk of sexual or intravenous transmission. Short-term treatments can substantially reduce mother-to-child transmission for a relatively low cost. Similarly, short-term treatments can be used as a prophylactic measure immediately after exposure to the virus in cases of rape or accidental exposure of healthcare workers.

To deal effectively with the crisis, African nations need to reduce both infection rates and mortality rates. They must use public education to change cultural attitudes to reduce infection rates. They also need access to the relatively inexpensive drug treatments to prevent mother-to-child transmission and accidental transmission to health-care workers. Both of these strategies are affordable enough to be viable options. With respect to mortality rates, these societies require affordable access to drug treatments.

2.3 South Africa: International Politics and Lack of Political Leadership

South Africa is the most populous country in the sub-Saharan African region. It has approximately 45 million people (estimate of December 2005). The adult prevalence rate of HIV/AIDS for South Africa is 16.2% (see Table 2.5). Few countries in the world have a higher prevalence rate. South Africa has the most people with HIV/AIDS of any country in the world.

In spite of the severity of the AIDS epidemic in South Africa, the South African government has been remarkably slow to develop an effective AIDS strategy. AIDS is the object of strong social stigma in South Africa and hinders prevention and treatment efforts, but has not been addressed. It took until 2004 for South Africa to launch a public anti-retroviral drug program and the program's implementation has remained slow, with tens of thousands of prospective patients still unable to access treatment. The private sector in South Africa began to provide ART treatment to employees at least 2 years before the South African government, in mining companies such as Anglo American and De Beers, and in manufacturing companies like DaimlerChrysler. Right into the twenty-first century, South African president Thabo Mbeki raised doubts about whether HIV causes AIDS and questioned the basic strategies to address the epidemic, even suggesting that the drugs commonly used to treat HIV would be ineffective. In 2005, South African Health Minister Manto Tshabalala-Msimang continued to espouse garlic and olive oil instead of antiretroviral drugs for people with HIV. President Mbeki's predecessor, Nelson Mandela, was also slow to address the AIDS issue during his presidency, although he has dedicated time to lobbying for greater action during his retirement.

On 12 December 1997, South African President Nelson Mandela signed into law amendments to the South African Medicines Act (www.polity.org.za/html/ govdocs/legislation/1997/act90.pdf). This amendment prompted a group of multinational pharmaceutical companies to sue the South African government (www. cptech.org/ip/health/sa/sa-timeline.txt). In May 1997, a representative of the Pharmaceutical Research and Manufacturers of America (PhRMA), Mr. Harvey Bale, sounded the alarm over how the proposed changes could affect the rights of the owners of patented medicine. Different representatives of the federal government of the United States, along with PhRMA representatives, pressured the government of South Africa to abandon the amendment. The US government implicitly threatened trade sanctions and the revocation of reciprocal tax treaties. The response of South African Health Minister Nkosazana Zuma was to declare that "It is unacceptable for South Africa to pay higher prices than Australia" for medicine.

The eye of the storm was centered on the following passage:
Section 15C
The minister may prescribe conditions for the supply of more affordable medicines in certain circumstances so as to protect the health of the public, and in particular may

> (a) Notwithstanding anything to the contrary contained in the Patents Act, 1978 (Act No. 57 of 1978), determine that the rights with regard to any medicine under a patent granted in the Republic shall not extend to acts in respect of such medicine which has been put onto the market by the owner of the medicine, or with his or her consent;

> (b) Prescribe the conditions on which any medicine which is identical in composition, meets the same quality standard and is intended to have

the same proprietary name as that of another medicine already registered in the Republic, but which is imported by a person other than the person who is the holder of the registration certificate of the medicine already registered and which originates from any site of manufacture of the original manufacturer as approved by the council in the prescribed manner, may be imported:

(c) Prescribe the registration procedure for, as well as the use of, the medicine referred to in paragraph (b).

In essence, paragraph (a) establishes a system of international exhaustion of patent rights and paragraph (b) authorizes parallel imports. Under a system of *international exhaustion*, as soon as the product is put on the market of any country by the patent holder, he can no longer block the importation of that product into any other country. Such importations are known as parallel imports. Exhaustion of patent rights cannot be raised in a dispute before the World Trade Organization (WTO), meaning that the member countries are free to establish a system of international exhaustion of patent rights and to authorize parallel imports, just as South Africa did with its Section 15C amendment.

While the WTO Agreement on Trade-Related Aspects of Intellectual Property Rights (TRIPS) requires that patent holders be granted the exclusive right to prevent third parties from making, using, selling or *importing* their product without consent, Section 15C could not form the basis of a WTO complaint under TRIPS. Members of the WTO must seek permission through the WTO dispute settlement system in order to impose trade sanctions for violations of WTO agreements. Thus, while the South African amendment might violate one provision of TRIPS, a different provision of TRIPS prevents the use of the dispute settlement system to resolve the matter. As a result, any trade sanctions imposed unilaterally against South Africa for this alleged violation of TRIPS would be illegal under WTO law. This meant that the international dispute settlement system of the WTO could not be used against South Africa in this case. Nevertheless, the potential threat of WTO action was used, together with other threats, to pressure the South African government.

It was not just the US government that raised concerns about Section 15 (c). The Vice President of the European Commission, Leon Brittan wrote (on 23 March 1998) to the then Deputy-President, Thabo Mbeki, arguing that the Act "would appear to be at variance with South Africa's obligations under the WTO TRIPS agreement … and its implementation would negatively affect the interest of the European pharmaceutical industry." (www.oxfam.org.uk/policy/papers/safrica/safrica3.htm). In July 1998, the President of France voiced his concern over the issue as did the heads of state of Switzerland and Germany. Thus, governments of most developed countries with high concentrations of pharmaceutical patents sided with the Pharmaceutical Manufacturers' Association of South Africa in pressuring the South African government to withdraw Section 15(c) of the Act.

The next step the American government took to pressure South Africa was the introduction of the omnibus appropriations law, which contained a provision inserted by Rep. Rodney Frelinghuysen (R-NJ) that cut off aid to the government of South Africa. This provision established that "..None of the funds appropriated under this heading may be available for assistance for the central Government of the Republic of South Africa, until the Secretary of State reports in writing to the appropriate committees of the Congress on the steps being taken by the United States Government to work with the Government of the Republic of South Africa to negotiate the repeal, suspension, or termination of Section 15 (c) of South Africa's Medicines and Related Substances Control Amendment Act No. 90 of 1997" (See Omnibus Consolidated and Emergency Supplemental Appropriations Act, Public Law No 105–277, 112 Stat 2681 1999). This bill was originally part of the House of Representative Bill HR 4328 (available at www.bts.gov/lawlib/docs/hr4328.pdf).

The position of the American government kept hardening. In April 1999, the United States Trade Representative put South Africa on the so-called 301 Watch List – a list of countries that could face trade sanctions over laws that affected American business interests. Vice President Al Gore continued to express his displeasure at the passage of the South African Medicines Act. Thus, both the executive and legislative branches of the American government got involved in the campaign against South Africa's quest for more affordable medicine to treat the world's largest population of people with HIV/AIDS.

In the case of Mr. Gore, the dramatic turn around came when he wrote on, 25 June 1999, the following letter to James E. Clyburn, the Chair of the Congressional Black Caucus, "I want you to know from the start that I support South Africa's efforts to enhance health care for its people including efforts to engage in compulsory licensing and parallel importing of pharmaceuticals – so long as they are done in a way consistent with international agreements" (Love 1999). Why did the dramatic turn-around take place? There are two possible reasons. First, on June 16, 1999, Mr. Gore declared that he would run for the presidency of the United States in 2000. Immediately, he was attacked by AIDS activists on the ground that he was fighting against South Africa's position on parallel imports. Given that Mr. Gore was trying to get the support of the gay community, this might have influenced his view. Second, perhaps more importantly, on June 24, 1999, the US Supreme Court ruled that state governments cannot be sued for patent infringement (Florida Prepaid Postsecondary Education Expense Board v. College Savings Bank et al.). Thus, it became amply clear that if the states within the United States could not be sued for patent infringement, it would be all but impossible to make the political case for taking action against another sovereign nation like South Africa. (As noted above, there was no basis for filing an international legal complaint against South Africa at the WTO).

While the international legal route was doubtful, and the international political campaign was in progress, pharmaceutical companies launched a third prong in their attack on the South African law. On 18 February 1998, the Pharmaceutical Manufacturers' Association of South Africa, along with 39 pharmaceutical companies, sued South African President Nelson Mandela over this issue (Pharmaceutical Manufacturers' Association of South Africa v. President of the Republic of South Africa, Case No 4183/98).

Despite the three-pronged campaign, the South African government still refused to budge. For example, in December 1999, South African Health Minister Nkosazana Zuma declared:

> We have a right in South Africa to put public health before profit – public health should be supreme and commercial interest second. The most important asset of South Africa is its people. That does not mean that pharmaceutical companies should not make a profit. But their profit margins should still allow people to afford medicine. We need to fight for this position in multilateral organisations. Even the World Trade Organisation (WTO) intellectual property rights regime recognises that you cannot leave essential medicines to unfettered market forces. There has to be intervention to make sure that medicines are affordable. This is not a uniquely South African problem. It is an issue that developing countries should take on together. But, poor people in developed countries also cannot afford these medicines. (www.igd.org.za/pub/g-dialogue/interviews/zuma.html)

On 10 May 2000, President Clinton signed an Executive Order which prohibited sanctions against sub-Saharan African countries that violated American patent law in obtaining AIDS medications and/or treatments (for the full text of the Executive Order, see Appendix). There are two notable features of the Executive Order. First, it refers *only to* HIV/AIDS. In other words, the Executive Order cannot be applied to other kinds of diseases. Thus, for example, in the case of malaria, the Executive Order would have no effect. Second, it only exempted sub-Saharan Africa. Any other country anywhere else cannot benefit from this Executive Order. For example, Haiti has an HIV/AIDS infection rate comparable to some sub-Saharan African countries. But, by definition, it would be excluded.

Remarkably, the pharmaceutical companies did not change their position on the South African law even after this Executive Order. They continued to hold the line. Only after the inauguration of George W. Bush and his clear message that he would not reverse the Executive Order did the pharmaceutical companies back down. They dropped the case unconditionally in April 2001. This also coincided with a turn of events in the South African court hearing the case that would have required the patent owners to disclose confidential information regarding the cost of producing the medicines at issue. Others believe that "international outrage" played a pivotal role. For example, 't Hoen (2002) wrote, "Eventually, the strong international public outrage over the companies' legal challenge of a developing country's medicines law and the companies' weak legal position caused the companies to unconditionally drop the case in April 2001."

Why did the pharmaceutical companies invest so much in opposing that particular clause in the South African law? Given that South Africa only represents a very tiny part of their global profits, it seems unlikely that this effort resulted from a desire to maintain economic incentives to engage in research and development for South African diseases (see Lanjouw 2001). A more logical reason would be a concern that price reductions in developing countries might increase pressure from governments in developed countries to lower prices there as well. In the case of South Africa, the battle between patent owners and the government centered upon the issue of parallel imports. In the next section, we examine the case of Brazil, where the main issue in this regard was the compulsory licensing of patented medicine (see Harris 2001).

The case of South Africa is instructive in many ways. The legal dispute over parallel imports in South Africa set an important precedent that influenced the perception of developed country governments, such as the United States and European governments, on the correct balance between the rights of patent owners and the rights of patients, particularly in developing countries that face serious AIDS epidemics. A more unfortunate lesson from South Africa is that failure to address the AIDS epidemic early and effectively can have disastrous consequences for a country and, indeed, a region – as it has in many parts of sub-Saharan Africa. In retrospect, the lack of political leadership in South Africa – which prevails even as we write this book in the form of bizarre and dangerous statements on the part of the minister of health – has been a significant factor in the spread of AIDS in a middle-income country that might have faced a brighter future had its leadership responded differently. South Africa stands as a cautionary tale regarding the danger of inaction and denial.

2.4 AIDS Strategy in Brazil: Integrating Prevention, Treatment and Human Rights

In terms of *absolute numbers*, Latin America and the Caribbean have the third highest number of cases of any region, after Africa and South/Southeast Asia (see Table 2.4). In terms of infection rates, the Caribbean has the highest infection rate outside of Africa (see Table 2.5). In 2007, there were an estimated 1,610,000–2,170,000 people living with HIV/AIDS in Latin America and the Caribbean (see Table 2.4). This compares to 480,000–1,900,000 in North America (the United States and Canada), 3,300,000–5,100,000 in South and Southeast Asia, and 20,900,000–24,300,000 in sub-Saharan Africa. In Latin America and the Caribbean, the highest infection rate is 2.2 in Haiti (2005–2006), while Brazil has the highest number of cases, with an estimated 620,000 (370,000–1,000,000) (figures for 2005) people living with HIV (UNAIDS 2007). Between 1980 and June 2007, 474,273 cases of AIDS were reported in Brazil: 289,074 in the Southeast; 89,250 in the South; 53,089 in the Northeast; 26,757 in the Central/West; and 16,103 in the North (Brazil Ministry of Health 2007).

In 1992, the World Bank predicted that 1.2 million Brazilians would be infected by 2002. The actual number is half of that figure and demonstrates Brazil's success in tackling the epidemic. Moreover, the epidemic shows signs of stabilization in Brazil, with the incidence (of new cases) now decreasing. In 2006, 32,628 new infections were reported, compared to 38,816 in 2002 (Brazil Ministry of Health 2007). However, the trends in Brazil vary by region, with new infections on the rise in the North and Northeast and declining in the rest of the country (see Table 2.7).

Between 2002 and 2006, the number of AIDS-related deaths increased in the North (42.4%), Northeast (15.7%) and Central/West (14.9%) regions of Brazil, but decreased in the South (46.5%) and Southeast (11.76%) (Brazil Ministry of Health 2007) (see Table 2.8).

Table 2.7 Incidence of new infections in Brazil in 2002 and 2006 per 100,000 by region

Region	2002	2006
North	10.8	13.6
Northeast	9.4	10.1
Southeast	29.2	20.5
South	33.3	25.6
Central/West	20.1	15.8

Source: Brazil Ministry of Health, Boletim Epidemiológico, 2007

Table 2.8 AIDS-related deaths in Brazil in 2002 and 2006 by region

Region	2002	2006
North	415	591
Northeast	1,341	1,552
Southeast	6,496	5,732
South	2,246	1,046
Central/West	557	640

Source: Brazil Ministry of Health, Boletim Epidemiológico, 2007

Brazil's AIDS program dates from 1982, when the first AIDS cases were diagnosed there. Brazil adopted a three-pronged strategy based on (1) early and sustained prevention (since 1983, starting in Sao Paulo with gay NGOs), (2) the promotion and protection of human rights (since 1988), and (3) universal access to treatment and care (starting in 1991 with AZT and with ART in 1996, the year effective triple-combination therapy became available). Most critically, Brazil's state-of-the-art prevention program has focused on high-risk groups (men who have sex with men (MSM), injection drug users (IDUs), and commercial sex workers (CSW)), but has also expanded to at-risk populations (female sex partners of MSM and IDUs and persons with multiple sex partners) and, more generally, women, youth, rural populations and the poor. This has increased awareness and healthier sexual behavior among the general population, especially younger populations and high-risk groups. Brazil has kept higher prevalence rates largely limited to high-risk groups: IDUs (36.3%), MSM (10.8%), and CSW (6.5%) (World Bank 2004).

Brazil has contained the epidemic, with adult prevalence in the general population at 0.6% (Brazil Ministry of Health 2007). Since the beginning of the epidemic in Brazil, there have been 314,294 cases of AIDS reported in men and 159,793 in women. However, the nature of the epidemic in Brazil has changed over time. In 1985, the ratio of men to women with HIV/AIDS was 15 to 1, whereas this ratio was 1.5–1 in 2007 (Brazil Ministry of Health 2007). In 1996, of the men, 29.4% were homosexual or bisexual; 25.6% were heterosexual; and 23.6% were intravenous drug users. In 2006, 42.6% were heterosexual; 27.6% were homosexual or bisexual; and 9.3% were intravenous drug users. Among women over 13 years of age, in 1996, 86.1% were heterosexual and 12.6% were intravenous drug users. In 2006, 95.7% were heterosexual and 3.5% were intravenous drug users (Brazil Ministry of Health 2007).

In 1988, the new Brazilian Constitution made health a universal right and a duty of the state. That same year, Congress passed a law that expanded the human rights of workers with incapacitating or terminal illness to include people living with AIDS. Since the 1980s, all levels of government and civil society have been involved in human rights activities related to HIV/AIDS. In 2003, there were about 140,000 patients receiving ART and a further 196,000 HIV-positive asymptomatic cases being monitored. Between 1997 and 2001, Brazil saved approximately USD 2.2 billion by reducing hospitalizations by 70% and by reducing the cost of ART through local manufacturing of generic drugs and aggressive negotiation of price reductions for patented drugs. Mortality and opportunistic infection rates have declined sharply since 1997 and incidence rates have also dropped considerably (World Bank 2004).

Figure 2.1 shows the dramatic decline in the new infection rate in Brazil since 1995. This decline can be attributed to the vigorous campaign that Brazil has pursued among different risk groups. It also shows the drop in the rate of new infections in the United States. However, the new infection rates (or incidence rates) in the United States are still far ahead of the other three countries in the figure. It is important to keep the terminology consistent. In epidemiology, the term *prevalence rate* is used to mean the proportion of population infected with HIV/AIDS whereas *incidence rate* refers to the number of new cases in a given year. They can represent quite different things. For example, the prevalence rate might fall simply because of death of a large number of HIV/AIDS patients.

In contrast to the lack of leadership in South Africa, strong leadership in Brazil's government and civil society created effective partnerships among governmental, non-governmental and private sectors. These partnerships created synergies of

New Infection Rate per 1000

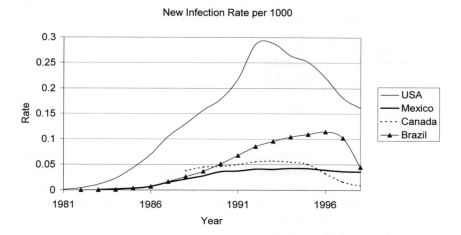

Fig. 2.1 New infection rate per 1,000 people in Brazil, Canada, Mexico and USA. *Source*: Data from UNAIDS Country Fact Sheets, 2002. Population figures from the CIA Factbook, 2002

expertise and resources that expanded the range and coverage of HIV/AIDS programs. In this regard, key elements contributing to Brazil's success have been democratic institutions (public accountability, channels for public opinion, and a free press) and the participation of NGOs in policy formulation and evaluation and program delivery, particularly among vulnerable groups. Human rights protection has proved to be an essential component, encouraging high-risk individuals and communities to address the disease openly and to get diagnosed and treated. Brazil benefited from better health infrastructure (hospitals, clinics, counseling centers and laboratories) and human resources (other than the number of nurses) than most middle-income developing countries. Brazil's prevalence rate (0.6%) is relatively low compared to sub-Saharan African countries, and its per capita expenditure on health (USD 308) is relatively high compared to other developing countries, making Brazil's HIV/AIDS program affordable at 0.07% of GDP (Oliveira-Cruz et al., 2004). However, the average cost of treatment has risen quickly, from USD 1,350 per patient in 2003, to USD 2,500 in 2005 (Camacho 2006).

Making universal access affordable has been a key element of Brazil's HIV/AIDS strategy, through manufacturing generic drugs and rigorous price negotiations with patent owners. In 2001, Brazil extracted price concessions from Merck and Roche by threatening to issue compulsory licenses on their patents in order to manufacture generic versions of their HIV/AIDS drugs. The TRIPS Agreement permits WTO members to issue compulsory licenses on patents without negotiating compensation in cases of non-commercial public use, national emergency or extreme urgency. The term "non-commercial public use" would cover the manufacture of generic AIDS drugs for free distribution through the government's

AIDS program. Brazilian law incorporates these TRIPS provisions and provides that a national emergency might arise from a threat to the public's health or nutrition, the environment, or the country's social, economic or technological development (Chartrand 2001). Thus, in addition to the "non-commercial public use" basis, compulsory licenses could also be issued for AIDS drugs on the grounds of "national emergency". The effect of TRIPS rules on compulsory licensing on the bargaining power of Brazil in its negotiations with patent owners has had a direct impact on the cost of providing access to HIV/AIDS treatment for Brazilian patients.

In 2001, the United States filed a complaint at the WTO over Brazil's requirement that patent owners manufacture their products in Brazil in order to maintain full patent rights (Brazil – Measures affecting patent protection, Complaint by the United States, WTO Document WT/DS199). Brazil's Industrial Property Law (which came into effect in 1997) also makes patents subject to compulsory licensing if the product is not manufactured in Brazil. Had the dispute proceeded, the outcome would have been uncertain, since a lack of consensus on the issue of local working requirements resulted in ambiguous WTO provisions on this issue (Champ and Attaran 2002). The United States argued that the Brazilian law violated TRIPS obligations to make patents available without discrimination as to whether the products are imported or produced locally. However, the United States dropped the case after world leaders and health organizations said the case could hurt Brazil's HIV/AIDS program. The United States and Brazil notified the WTO of their mutually agreed solution on 5 July 2001.

Brazil has been manufacturing HIV/AIDS drugs in its government laboratory, which make generics for the free drug program. Brazil did not need to issue any compulsory licenses to manufacture these AIDS drugs in Brazil. These HIV/AIDS drugs produced by the government laboratory (called "Farmanguinhos") were not protected by patents in Brazil, as patent protection for pharmaceuticals only began after 1997 with the Industrial Property Law, and those drugs were already on the market before that. Consequently, anyone was free to produce them without a (compulsory or voluntary) license from the patent holders, as they were off-patent. However, on 5 September 2003, Brazil implemented legislation to authorize imports of generic versions of *efavirenz*, *lopinavir* and *nelfinavir* from India and China after it failed to reach a satisfactory agreement in price negotiations with the patent owners.

Brazil's HIV/AIDS program has driven down both drug prices and deaths from HIV/AIDS. The program has reduced the nation's death rate from HIV/AIDS by half. The health ministry spent $444 million on HIV/AIDS drugs in 2000, 4% of its health budget. The decline in hospitalizations from opportunistic infections from 1997 to 1999 saved the health ministry $422 million (Rosenberg 2001). The money that the government saved on treatment for patients who would otherwise have been hospitalized exceeds the cost of the drugs by 60%.

Since Brazil began making the generic copies of HIV/AIDS drugs, it has reduced the price of the patented equivalents. The Brazilian state laboratory makes eight of the 15 HIV/AIDS drugs used in the country. The price of HIV/AIDS drugs with no generic competition fell 9% between 1996 and 2000 (Baldwin 2002). The price of those that faced generic competition fell 79%. This has enabled Brazil to produce some triple therapy for USD 3,000 per year and to expect the price to drop to $700 per year in the future. This compares to a cost of USD 10,000 to USD 15,000 per year in the United States (Rosenberg 2001).

In August 2001, the Brazilian health minister announced that his government would issue a compulsory license on Roche's HIV/AIDS drug *nelfinavir* and begin manufacturing a generic copy in government laboratories in 2002. The announcement came after negotiations between the Swiss drug company and Brazil failed to produce an agreement on price reductions. The health minister said that over a quarter of his HIV/AIDS program budget was being spent on *nelfinavir* alone. Even if the company agreed to reduce its price by an additional 40%, the health minister said that would be insufficient to stop the government from proceeding with its plan (Petersen 2001). The reason for the government's refusal of the offer was that it would still be less expensive for the government laboratory to carry out the local manufacturing of *nelfinavir* than to accept Roche's proposal. The government reasoned that in order to avoid the compulsory license, the price reduction by Roche would have to be as advantageous as the cost of manufacturing in the government laboratory.

The company responded by pointing out it had already reduced the price in Brazil to 50% of the cost in the United States and had donated thousands of doses of the pediatric syrup version to Brazil. The company stated its intention to begin manufacturing Viracept (the brand name of *nelfinavir*) in Brazil in 2002 and to continue to provide the medicine free to Brazilian children with HIV/AIDS. It sought further negotiations, which the health minister described as an attempt to delay preparations to manufacture the drug in the government's laboratory. Financial analysts said the dispute would affect public relations more than finances, with Roche's overall sales of Viracept rising 5% to USD 132.6 million in the first half of 2001 (Shields 2001).

On August 31, 2001 the Brazilian health minister announced an agreement with Roche to reduce the price by a further 40%, making the Brazilian price 30% of the US price. In March 2001, a similar threat to the patent on two HIV/AIDS drugs produced by Merck led to an agreement to reduce the price of *indinavir* and *efavirenz* by about 60% in Brazil (Rich 2001). In both cases, the decision of the Brazilian government to purchase the patented drugs, rather than issue compulsory licenses to government laboratories, indicates that the negotiations succeeded in reaching the optimal price for the drugs. Assuming that Brazil's decision was based on cost alone, the difference between the cost of manufacturing in the Brazilian laboratory and purchasing the patented drugs at a discount must have been too small for Brazil to issue a compulsory license.

Brazil, as a developing country that did not provide patent protection when TRIPS came into force, was not required to fully implement its TRIPS obligations until 2005. However, Brazil chose not to use the full transition period that was available.

TRIPS requires patents to provide patent owners with the exclusive right to prevent third parties from making, using, selling or importing a patented product without the owner's consent. Articles 30 and 31 authorize exceptions to these rights. Article 30 permits "limited exceptions". Article 31 permits WTO members to allow "other use of the subject matter of the patent", and covers compulsory licensing of patents. The term "other use" means "use other than that allowed under Article 30". Under Article 31, a government may issue a compulsory license authorizing the government or a third party to produce generic drugs without the authorization of the patent holder where negotiations fail to obtain authorization on reasonable commercial terms. However, the use of the patent must be to supply "predominantly" the domestic market and the patent holder must be paid adequate remuneration, based on the economic value of the license. As noted above, the negotiation requirement may be waived in cases of national emergency, extreme urgency, or non-commercial public use. Members are not obliged to comply with the negotiation requirement or to serve predominantly the domestic market where the use is permitted to remedy anti-competitive practices.

The TRIPS provisions relating to compulsory licensing strengthened Brazil's position in its price negotiations with Roche and Merck. Brazil met the necessary conditions to halt negotiations because the generic versions would have served a non-commercial public use and predominantly supplied the domestic market. Since the term "adequate remuneration" is not defined, the pharmaceutical companies could not predict with certainty what compensation they would have received in the Brazilian courts had Brazil walked away from the negotiations (see Box 2.1). This gave the companies an added incentive to determine the price through negotiation.

At Doha in 2001, the WTO Ministerial Conference agreed in the Declaration on TRIPS and Public Health that TRIPS "does not and should not prevent Members from taking measures to protect public health…and, in particular, to promote access to medicines for all". This Declaration also confirms that WTO members have "the right to grant compulsory licenses and the freedom to determine the grounds upon which such licenses are granted". It also clarifies that members have "the right to determine what constitutes a national emergency or other circumstances of extreme urgency, it being understood that public health crises, *including* those relating to HIV/AIDS, tuberculosis, malaria and other epidemics, can represent a national emergency or other circumstances of extreme urgency" (emphasis added). Thus, the scope of this Declaration is not limited to a specific number of diseases (such as HIV/AIDS, tuberculosis or malaria), nor to specific types of health crises, such as epidemics. The definition of "national emergency" or "extreme urgency" is not limited to public health problems and could cover other matters as well.

In the context of HIV/AIDS, the Declaration clarifies that "national emergency" and "extreme urgency" can be interpreted according to the *nature* of the disease rather than just the *number* of infections in a particular country. There is research that suggests that once a population reaches an adult infection rate of 1%, it becomes much more difficult to prevent HIV/AIDS from spreading much more

Box 2.1 Determining compensation for compulsory licenses in the courts

Calculating compensation for compulsory licenses is likely to be an uncertain process in any legal system. Since TRIPS permits the process for calculating remuneration to differ from one WTO member to the next, uncertainty increases in the international context. TRIPS Article 31(h) requires that "the right holder shall be paid adequate remuneration in the circumstances of each case, taking into account the economic value of the [compulsory license]." Article 31(k) allows "the need to correct anti-competitive practices" to be taken into account in determining the amount of remuneration. Article 31(j) requires that "any decision relating to remuneration...shall be subject to judicial review or other independent review . . . in that Member." Article 1 provides that "Members shall be free to determine the appropriate method of implementing [TRIPS] within their own legal system and practice." The general nature of these compensation obligations, together with the flexibility permitted under Article 1, means that the specific manner in which compensation is determined may vary from one WTO member to the next, as may the principles that apply to judicial review or its equivalent in each legal system.

For example, in the United States, courts apply a 15 factor test to assess damages as a reasonable royalty (Georgia-Pacific Corp. v. United States Plywood Corp. 1971; Gargoyles Inc. and Pro-Tec Inc. v. The United States 1997). Moreover, in the words of the United States Court of Appeals for the Federal Circuit, "the facts of each case (and royalty determination) differ", making it difficult to predict the outcome (Gargoyles Inc. and Pro-Tec Inc. v. The United States 1997, p. 9).

In addition, the patent owner may fail to prove a claim for lost profits. In Gargoyles Inc. and Pro-Tec Inc. v. The United States (1997), the US Federal court upheld the finding of the Claims Court that: (1) due to insufficient manufacturing capacity, the plaintiff could not have met the demand for its product had no compulsory license been issued; (2) there was an acceptable substitute product that could have been used in place of the plaintiff's product; and (3) the plaintiff did not properly quantify its lost profits. Under US jurisprudence, the correct measure of compensation is what the owner has lost, not what the taker has gained (Leesona Corp. v. United States 1979; Hughes Aircraft Co. v. United States 1996; Gargoyles Inc. and Pro-Tec Inc. v. The United States 1997).

A final factor that currently contributes to the uncertainty surrounding the level of compensation that may be forthcoming under US law is the standard of proof required. The standard is clear with respect to lost profits in private cases for damages, where the patent owner must show only a "reasonable probability" that, but for the infringement, it would have made the sales made by the infringer (Rite-Hite Corp. v. Kelley Co. 1995). However, it is not clear whether the same standard applies in cases that involve the government, where lost profits are awarded only after the strictest proof that the patentee would actually have earned and retained those sums in its sales to the Government (Gargoyles Inc. and Pro-Tec Inc. v. The United States 1997; Tektronix Inc. v. United States 1977). Moreover, a royalty could not be awarded in addition, since that would constitute double counting (Leesona Corp. v. United States 1979). Since TRIPS permits the process for calculating remuneration to differ from one WTO member to the next, uncertainty increases in the international context.

On 7 September 2007, the U.S House of Representatives passed the Patent Reform Act of 2007 (H.R. 1908, http://www.govtrack.us/congress/billtext.xpd?bill=h110-1908). The bill still had to pass in the Senate in 2008. The proposed law would allow a court to replace the existing 15-factor test with a single concept of "apportionment." Under Section 5, damage calculations could be limited to the economic value properly attributable to the patent's specific contribution over prior inventions. However, where the patent's specific contribution over prior inventions is the predominant basis for market demand for an infringing product or process, damages may be based upon the entire market value of the products or processes involved that satisfy that demand. The bill could significantly limit damage awards. The US pharmaceutical industry opposed to the Patent Reform Act of 2007.

rapidly and widely in the population (see Box 2.2). Indeed, the nature of HIV/AIDS is such that the United Nations views HIV/AIDS as not only a global health crisis, but a threat to peace and security. Thus, countries with relatively low prevalence rates for HIV/AIDS, like Brazil's rate of 0.6%, could consider HIV/AIDS a national emergency or a situation of extreme urgency, although the threshold at which a situation would qualify still remains somewhat ambiguous. Greater clarity would be useful so that WTO members can take action in borderline cases with greater confidence that it would not result in a complaint being filed at the WTO or the withdrawal of international aid or other benefits from developed countries whose pharmaceutical lobbies exert pressure on their governments.

The case of Brazil demonstrates that developing countries with manufacturing capacity have the power they need to reach the optimal price in negotiations with patent owners. If the cost of manufacturing generic versions under compulsory license (or of importing from generic producers in other countries) is lower than the cost of buying from the patent owner, the country will do the former. This price competition ensures that the drug in question is supplied at the lowest possible cost. Thus, the level of bargaining power a country enjoys ultimately affects the price it pays for medicine and the affordability of treatment for HIV/AIDS. This has a direct impact on the number of patients that get access to treatment.

Brazil's AIDS program has been remarkably successful on many measures. It's three-pronged strategy – prevention, human rights protection, and universal access to treatment – serves as a model for other countries to follow, whether developed or developing. Universal access to ART is a hallmark of the success of Brazil's program, but having brought the epidemic under control is Brazil's most important achievement (Oliveira-Cruz et al., 2004). However, high drug prices could still threaten the sustainability of universal access to ART (Galvao 2002).

Box 2.2 The one percent debate

The exact 1% figure is subject to assumptions in a mathematical model. However, the general thrust of the result is as follows. If the infection rate is below some threshold level, the disease eventually dies out. If it is above certain threshold, then the disease grows according to a Gompertz curve, first rising rapidly to some level of the population and then stabilizing. The early model where this was demonstrated was known as the SIR model with three stages of an organism: susceptible (S), infective (I) and removed (R). In biomedical literature, the first such demonstration was provided by Barbour (1975). However, the theorem was derived under the condition that there is equal likelihood of disease transmission in the entire population. In the case of HIV/AIDS, this is not true. The transmission mechanism in the developing countries tends to follow poverty, not ignorance and sexual "promiscuity" as is popularly believed. In reviewing the evidence, Galvao (2002) write "Many of those at greatest risk already know that HIV is a sexually transmitted pathogen and that condoms could prevent transmission. Their risk stems less from ignorance and more from the precarious situations in which hundreds of millions live; gender inequality adds a special burden, and is the main reason that, globally, HIV incidence is now higher among women than among men." (p. 404). Given that poverty occurs in clusters or networks (that is, if I am poor, my relatives and my children are likely to be poor as well), we need a different model for explaining the propagation of HIV/AIDS. A model with correlated agents can produce "synthetic communities." A recent example of such a model has been powerfully illustrated by Boguna et al. (2003). Such models have been used in studying patterns of clustering of collaborative research, connectivity of pages on the Internet, growth of cities and many other phenomena. They all point to the same general conclusion. Beyond a certain threshold, there is takeoff point. Dezso and Barabasi (2002) show that in the presence of a threshold value of an epidemic, a policy of containing the disease by spending resources in a random fashion (without attacking the nodes of the network) can never eradicate the disease.

In 2006, Brazil continued to play a leading role in tackling the AIDS pandemic, hosting 18 other Latin American countries to discuss ways to achieve universal access to anti-retroviral drugs by 2010 in the region, through collective purchasing and production of medicine. Pedro Chequer, coordinator of Brazil's National STD/AIDS Program, urged other countries to reject non-scientific approaches to prevention, such as the refusal to use condoms for religious, philosophical or cultural reasons. Brazil itself planned to distribute 1.5 billion condoms in 2006.

In May 2007, Brazil issued a compulsory license to import generic versions HIV/AIDS drug *efavirenz* from laboratories certified by the World Health Organization. Merck's patent for *efavirenz* is in force until 2012. *Efavirenz* costs Brazil USD 580 per patient per year for the 75,000 patients taking this medication in Brazil, whereas the generic version costs about USD 166 per year.

2.5 Thailand: Successful Prevention in the Sex Trade

In 2007, there were about 500,000 people living with HIV/AIDS in Thailand, of whom approximately 100,000 were receiving first-line retroviral treatment and 50,000 will require second-line treatment in the near future, due to the virus developing resistance to first-line treatment (Thai Ministry of Public Health 2007). In 2007, Thailand issued compulsory licenses for *efarivenz* (the preferred first-line treatment) and Kaletra (the preferred second-line treatment), in order to achieve universal coverage for HIV/AIDS treatment using the best available medicines (Thai Ministry of Public Health 2007). We discuss these compulsory licenses at the end of this section.

In the case of Thailand, our focus is on prevention strategies in the sex trade. Thailand adopted early a strategy of 100% condom use in 100% of sexual contacts in risk groups. This strategy was pursued vigorously over a decade. In this way, Thailand has essentially avoided an explosion in the number of infections that would have almost surely happened had it not taken this strategy. It shows us how a middle-income country can devise a behavior-modifying strategy to cope with the disease if adopted early enough.

The explosion of HIV infection in Thailand came in the late 1980s. In 1988, a repeat survey among drug users found that, in one single year, the prevalence rate of HIV increased from 1 to 44% (Uneklabh et al., 1989). A study by Weniger et al. (1991) found that, in the northern province of Chiang Mai, 44% of commercial sex workers were HIV positive. In addition, in a survey among 16–49 year old males, 28% admitted having premarital or extramarital sex during the past year. Of these, 75% said they had sex with commercial sex workers (Sittitrai et al., 1992).

Thailand has had a long history of controlled commercial sex. Commercial sex was tolerated in certain zones (the most famous being the Patpong district of Bangkok). As a result, sex workers were centralized and highly structured.

After HIV infection hit, the Thai government undertook a program to ensure 100% condom use in brothels. The program launched a mass advertising campaign to promote condom use in commercial sex. The federal government sponsored explicit television commercials as part of a massive education campaign. It started a workplace education program targeting the potential brothel visitors. The government undertook a direct education campaign targeting male and female sex workers and their clients. It started distributing free condoms where high-risk commercial sex was taking place. Government doctors tested and treated individual sex workers with routine examinations and distributed condoms. The government set up a system of prevention, testing and treatment for health workers. The government instituted a reporting system for male patients with sexually transmitted diseases, a system which triggered outreach programs. Finally, the program introduced a series of mobile clinics.

In Thailand, there was strong political and financial commitment at local and national levels, including: local STI/AIDS units, provincial health officers, provincial governors, district officers, the police and regional disease control offices. The police held formal meetings with brothel owners to ensure compliance with the program. Thai Prime Minister Anand Panyarachun appointed Mechai Voravaidya, an individual with strong NGO roots, to be in charge of HIV issues and to report directly to the Prime Minister.

To ensure compliance in the sex trade, the government introduced "secret shoppers" – inspectors who visited brothels at random. Violators faced the threat of sanctions, such as brothel closures. The government monitored data on sexually transmitted infections. There was testing and treatment of sex workers through routine examinations. The inspectors also monitored the number of condoms used in each brothel (Weniger 2006).

The results of the Thai measures can clearly be seen in Fig. 2.2. Between 1989 and 1994, condom non-use fell dramatically as well as sexually transmitted diseases reported in males. Since HIV is a slow-moving *lentivirus*, often researchers see early results of behavior change in other sexually transmitted diseases. By 1995, it became very clear that the program implemented by Thai government had worked.

The effect can also be seen by how HIV/AIDS has unfolded in Thailand over time. Figures 2.3 and 2.4 show how the spread of HIV/AIDS would have taken place had there been no change in behavior. Assuming no behavioral modification, a model generated the projection figure to 2020. It shows that by 2004, there would have been more than 8 million people with HIV/AIDS in Thailand. That would have meant a prevalence rate of 13% by the end of 2003. Instead, in 2003, Thailand only had a prevalence rate of 1.5%.

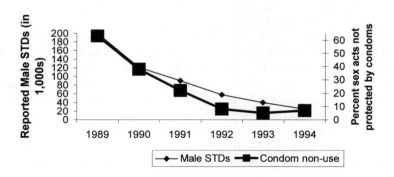

Fig. 2.2 Reported male STDs and percent of sex acts without condoms. *Source*: Ministry of Health, Thailand, 2000

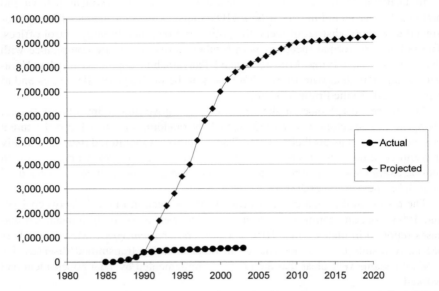

Fig. 2.3 Actual and projected HIV patients in Thailand. *Source*: Ministry of Health, Thailand, 2002

Thailand provides a number of lessons for other middle-income countries. However, it does not mean that we could expect the same degree of success in all countries. Timing is crucial, and Thailand was able to time its interventions very well. Thailand already had an infrastructure for detecting sexually transmitted diseases among sex workers. In other countries, where the sex industry is more diffuse and less organized, this kind of success might be hard to achieve. There are other factors that could complicate the implementation of such programs in other countries. Lack of political commitment could be an important obstacle to the successful implementation of a program like Thailand's. Limited financial resources could be another problem for less developed countries (Smith-Fawzi et al., 2001). In Thailand, the police chose to cooperate with the brothel owners. In other countries, this kind of coorperation may be harder to achieve. Finally, Thailand's focus on the sex trade was well suited to Thailand's situation, since that was the main source of the threat. The difference in the number of actual and projected cases of HIV/AIDS shows that this was the right strategy for Thailand to pursue.

In November 2006 and January 2007, the Thai government announced that it would issue compulsory licenses to produce lower-cost generic versions of Merck's antiretroviral *efavirenz* and Abbott Laboratories' Kaletra, respectively (Kaiser Daily HIV/AIDS Report 2007). Thailand also announced that it planned to issue a compulsory license for Sanofi-Aventis' anti-blood clotting pill Plavix, which is used to treat heart disease, not HIV/AIDS. In issuing the licenses, Thailand would set an important precedent for other developing countries by extending the use of compulsory licensing beyond health emergencies such as HIV to treatments for heart disease (Kazmin and Jack 2007). In the case of Plavix, the justification for the compulsory license under TRIPS Article 31 would be non-commercial public use, rather than national emergency, which the 2001 TRIPS Declaration indicates as the basis for HIV/AIDS medications. The US threat to issue a compulsory license on Cipro, in order to reduce the cost of stockpiling that drug in case of a terrorist attack using anthrax, preceded the similar actions of the Thai government by over 6 years (see Chap. 5).

A controversy erupted, even though Thailand, like other members of the WTO, has a right to issue compulsory licenses for domestic manufacture of patented products by virtue of TRIPS Article 31 or for importation under the Paragraph 6 Decision. The United States placed Thailand on a priority watch list of countries. The European Union's Trade Commissioner Peter Mandelson sent a letter lamenting Thailand's disregard for Abbott's intellectual property. However, the US government routinely grants compulsory licenses for purely commercial reasons, largely to streamline production of consumer electronics and military hardware. Five such licenses were issued in the last year alone, one of them specifically to Abbott. More than half of all antiretroviral drugs were researched entirely on US government grants. Both *lopinavir* and *ritonavir*, the two antiretroviral agents in Kaletra, were researched with public money. The reason for the protest over Thailand's action is the pharmaceutical industry's fear that Thailand's compulsory license could inspire other developing countries to issue licenses for a series of drugs (Santoro 2007).

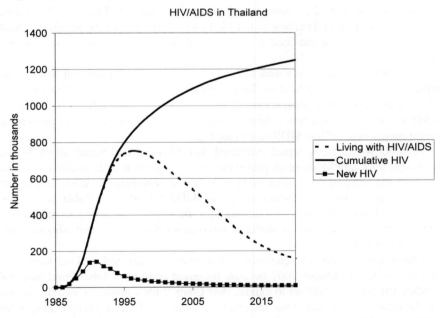

Fig. 2.4 HIV/AIDS in Thailand 1985–2020. *Source*: Ministry of Health, Thailand, 2007

Population

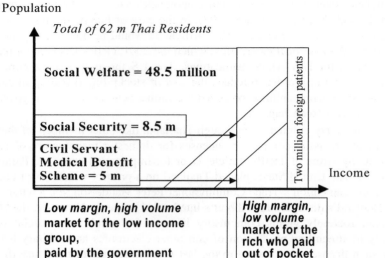

Fig. 2.5 Private and public drug markets in Thailand. *Source*: Facts and evidences on the ten burning issues related to the Government use of patents on three patented essential drugs in Thailand, Ministry of Health, Thailand, 2007 http:// www.moph.go.th/hot/White% 20Paper%20CL-EN.pdf

However, as Fig. 2.5 shows, compulsory licensing of drugs for the public health care system in Thailand is not likely to affect sales in the relatively small private market for the patented drugs, although it will affect sales to the government.

The Thai government planned to use the nearly USD 15 million it would save from issuing compulsory licenses for prevention activities. From 1991 to 1994, the Thai budget for AIDS prevention activities increased from USD 2.6 million to USD 462 million. As a result, new infections fell by more than 80%, preventing an estimated two million AIDS cases (see Fig. 2.4).

A 2006 World Bank report estimated that Thailand had saved about $43 in treatment for every $1 spent on prevention. However, from 2001 to 2006, the Thai government reduced prevention budgets by about two-thirds in favor of offering universal access to anti-retroviral drugs for AIDS patients (see Table 2.9). However, prevalence rates increased among specific groups, including teenagers, the spouses of men who visit sex workers, intravenous drug users, men who have sex with men and migrants.

One series of safe sex television advertisements, targeted at Thai teenagers, stopped airing in October 2007 because the grant from the Global Fund that was funding the program was set to expire. (See Chap. 7 for a more detailed discussion of the Global Fund and other international donors). With a limited budget for

Table 2.9 Budget for universal access to ARV (million Bahts) and universal care (Bahts per capita)

Year	Napha (million Bahts)	Global fund (million Bahts)	Total (million Bahts)	Per capita in Bahts
2002	278	–	278	1,202
2003	282	–	282	1,202
2004	715	96	811	1,308
2005	1,118	199	1,317	1,393
2006	2,542	307	2,849	1,659
2007	3,473	226	3,699	1,899

Source: Presentation of Suwit Wibulpolprasert, M.D., Senior Advisor on Disease Control Ministry of Public Health, Thailand May 10th, 2007, Berlin, Germany. www.medico-international.de/kampagne/gesundheit/downloads/ppp_ panel1_suwit.pps

HIV/AIDS, Thailand has had to make choices in the allocation of funds between prevention and treatment. This highlights the need for sustained funding from donors, such as the Global Fund, and the importance of compulsory licensing as a means to reduce the cost of treatment, even in middle-income countries (Ten Kate 2007).

One day after Abbott Laboratories and Thailand failed to reach an agreement on the price of Abbott's antiretroviral drugs Aluvia and Kaletra, the Thai Health Minister offered to not issue compulsory licenses if the pharmaceutical companies offered prices lower than those charged by generic drug makers. Aluvia is a heat-stable version of Kaletra that eliminates the need for refrigeration and doesn't need to be taken with food, both advantages in a tropical developing country such as Thailand. (In other markets, such as Mexico, the heat-stable version of Kaletra is also called Kaletra and has replaced the older version of the drug.) Abbott offered to sell Aluvia in Thailand for USD 1,000 per person annually on the condition that the country agree not to allow generic versions of the drug into the market, that Thailand not to seek compulsory licensing for Aluvia and that the price of Aluvia could not be reduced any further. Indian generic drug maker Matrix Laboratories offered to sell a generic version of Aluvia to Thailand for USD 695, per person annually (Kaiser Daily HIV/AIDS Report 2007). Abbott had reduced its price for Kaletra in Thailand to USD 2,200 per patient per year in 2006 (Kazmin and Jack 2007).

Abbott threatened to not register the patent for Aluvia in Thailand and to not sell it in Thailand, in order to block the option of compulsory licensing (Health News 2007). By not registering the patent, Abbott would not have to disclose to the Thai government its patented process for making Aluvia and there would be no Thai patent for which to issue a compulsory license. Thus, Abbott's strategy would undermine the credibility of Thailand's threat to issue the compulsory license on Aluvia (though not on Kaletra) and strengthen Abbott's negotiating power with respect to the price for Aluvia in Thailand. Abbott also withdrew applications to sell six other new medications in Thailand (Stone 2007).

The Thai government applies the following criteria to determine whether to issue a compulsory license on patented drugs and medical supplies: (1) they are listed in the National Essential Drugs list; or (2) they are necessary to solve important public health problems; or (3) they are necessary in emergency or extreme urgency; or (4) they are necessary for the prevention and control of outbreaks/epidemics/pandemics; or (5) they are necessary for saving life. Moreover, the price of the patented product must be too high to be affordable by the government to supply the beneficiaries of the national insurance health schemes in order to achieve universal coverage. In the case of Kaletra, the cost of achieving universal coverage was equal to the government's entire budget for anti-retroviral drugs (Thai Ministry of Public Health 2007).

According to the Thai government, only 15% of all patented medicines are eligible for compulsory licensing under the foregoing criteria. Moreover, most of the new patented drugs do not have any significant benefit compared to existing non-patented drugs, obviating the need for compulsory licensing. Finally, compulsory licensing of drugs in Thailand for the public healthcare system does not remove the patented versions from the market, which still exists for two million foreigners and wealthy Thais that buy their medication privately, which is the principal market for patented drugs in Thailand. The Thai government implemented TRIPS in 1992, 8 years before it was required to do so, but this did not have a positive impact on investment in the pharmaceutical industry, with the number of drug factories in Thailand declining from 188 in 1992 to 166 in 2006 (Thai Ministry of Public Health 2007).

Following its decision to issue compulsory licenses on these drugs, the Thai government received letters of support from the Executive Director of UNAIDS, the Director General of the World Health Organization, Médecins san Frontières and the Clinton Foundation, among others (these organizations are discussed in Chaps. 7 and 8) (Thai Ministry of Public Health 2007).

2.6 Japan: The Xenophobic Denial Strategy

HIV/AIDS was first reported in Japan in 1983. Since then, the incidence of HIV and AIDS (the number of new cases) has gone up almost continuously (see Fig. 2.6). The absolute number of cases is still very small compared with other developed countries. There have been just over 5,000 cases of HIV since 1983.

During the first decade of the spread of HIV and AIDS in Japan, Japanese politicians, commentators and other Japanese experts argued repeatedly that HIV/AIDS was not a Japanese problem – it was the "foreigners" who were infected. Indeed, although the foreigners represent less than 2% of the population living in Japan, they represent over 30% of the HIV cases in Japan (Nemoto 2004).

In Fig. 2.7, we plot HIV incidence every year by nationality and sex. There are several notable features. (1) The number of Japanese females with new infection has stayed very low over the past two decades. (2) The number of foreign male workers with HIV is fairly low. However, as a proportion of population in Japan, the number is high. (3) Among the female foreign workers, the incidence grew quickly between 1990 and 1994 but fell later in the decade. (4) The incidence of HIV among Japanese males has outstripped all other groups over the past two decades.

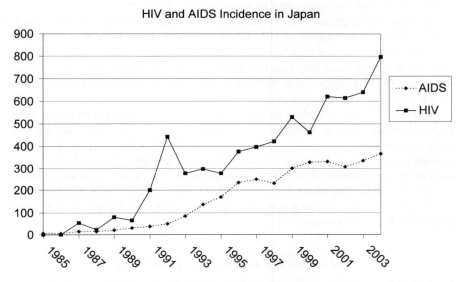

Fig. 2.6 Incidence of HIV and AIDS in Japan 1985–2004. *Source*: Database of the National Institute of Infectious Diseases, Japan

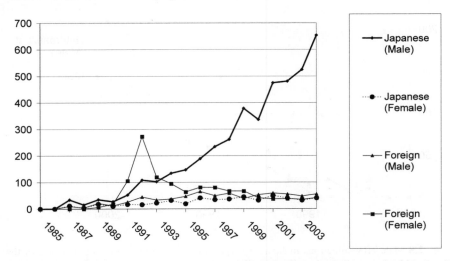

Fig. 2.7 HIV Incidence by sex and nationality 1985–2004. *Source*: Database of the National Institute of Infectious Diseases, Japan

Due to labor shortages during the Japanese boom in the 1980s, many foreign male workers were brought into Japan for construction and other manual work. Most female workers were brought in to work in brothels, massage parlors and other high-risk activities. Not surprisingly, many of these female sex workers were infected. It is not clear whether they were infected before they came to Japan or they were infected after they came to Japan (Kihara et al., 2003).

In Japan, most of new cases of HIV have occurred through Japanese men. There are two main sources of HIV infection among men: through heterosexual activities or through men who have sex with men (MSM). Figure 2.8 shows that, until 1996, heterosexual infection and MSM infection numbers were very similar. After that, MSM numbers have doubled over the next years whereas heterosexual infection numbers have stayed relatively stable.

Where are Japanese males contracting HIV? Are they coming from Japanese tourists abroad (such as Bangkok or Hawaii)? Nemoto et al. (2003) argued that such tourists could potentially be a factor. Anecdotal evidence from the 1980s suggested that many Japanese tourists went on "sex tours" of high-risk areas around the world, contracted HIV and brought it back to Japan. However, systematically collected data about the origin shows (see Fig. 2.9) that at least since 1990, more than 80% of infections among men occurred in Japan. By 2003, this proportion had risen to over 95%.

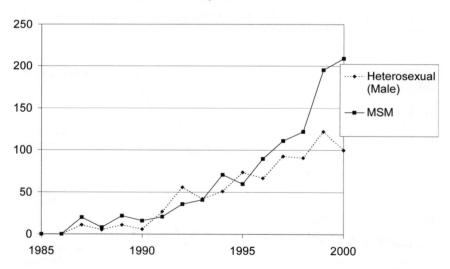

Fig. 2.8 Male HIV infections in Japan by type of sexual activity. *Source*: Database of the National Institute of Infectious Diseases, Japan

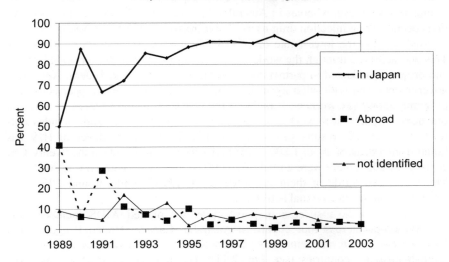

Fig. 2.9 Place where Japanese men contracted HIV. *Source*: Database of the National Institute of Infectious Diseases, Japan

Japan has been fortunate in that the absolute number of HIV/AIDS cases is very low. However, this appears to be based on luck more than a well-designed HIV/AIDS strategy. Xenophobia has colored Japan's response to HIV/AIDS, resulting in a strategy that might be described as xenophobic denial – that is, denying that HIV/AIDS is a problem for Japanese people based on incorrect assumptions that it is a problem for foreigners and Japanese who interact with foreigners.

2.7 Australia: Nondiscriminatory Education and Prevention

The incidence of HIV rose rapidly in the early 1980s in Australia. The government took prompt and rational actions. It instituted several programs immediately. There was remarkable consensus about the policies across the political parties.

It became clear that the single biggest risky group was men who have sex with men. Government at the federal, state and local levels started various campaigns among gay and other homosexually active men between the mid 1980s and the late 1990s. The mobilization and action of the gay community has been central to the effectiveness of these campaigns. Education and prevention were linked with nondiscriminatory HIV/AIDS testing, treatment and care.

Australia instituted a needle and syringe program to keep HIV/AIDS rates low among injection drug users. The program made fresh needles accessible to all the injection drug users. They were not only available in the hospitals and clinics but also community centers and even in churches. The results are dramatic. In the United States and Canada, about 25% of newly acquired HIV infections are attributed to injection drug use, whereas in Australia, less than 5% of newly acquired infections occur among injection drug users (Department of Health and Ageing 2002).

Australia has the lowest rate of HIV/AIDS among sex workers in the world. This was achieved through the work of community-based sex worker organizations and projects conducted in partnership with State, Territory and Federal Australian governments, and with other agencies. The foundation has been a peer education program among sex workers. It includes the provision of information on safe sex practices, requires new workers to implement these practices and includes outreach services. The results can be seen in Fig. 2.10. The incidence of HIV has fallen from a peak of about 1,800 in the mid 1980s to under 700 in the twenty-first century. In 2003, there were a total of 14,000 people living with HIV in Australia. More than two thirds of them got infected via MSM, while around 20% were infected through heterosexual activities.

To put Australia's success in perspective, we plotted AIDS incidence per 100,000 people across four countries: Australia, Canada, United Kingdom and United States. There are remarkable differences in AIDS incidence among these English-speaking countries (see Fig. 2.11). The rate in the United States has stayed ten times as high as Australia. Australia has followed in the footsteps of the

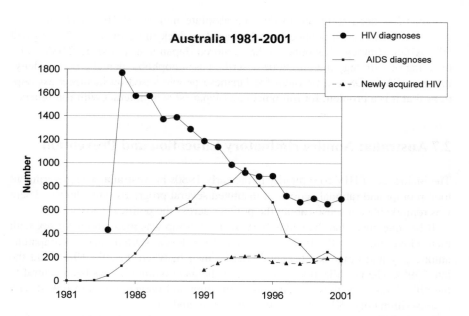

Fig. 2.10 HIV and AIDS diagnosis in Australia. *Source*: National Notifiable Diseases Surveillance System, Australia

United Kingdom. In fact, many of the safe sex practices in Australia were imported from the UK. Weaver et al. (2005) have shown that sex education has also produced a better set of results in Australia compared with the United States (but not as good as in the Netherlands).

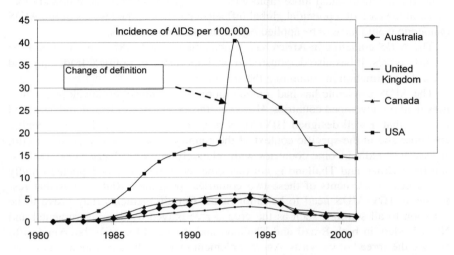

Fig. 2.11 AIDS incidence in Australia, Canada, UK and USA. *Source*: National Notifiable Diseases Surveillance System, Australia

Australia, in contrast to Japan, represents a case of a developed country that has been successful in keeping the number of HIV/AIDS cases low through a well-thought-out strategy, rather than relying on luck. Unfortunately, Australia is now having problems sustaining this success. The National Notifiable Diseases Surveillance System showed that from 1999 to 2004 the notification rate of chlamydial infection increased from 76.1 to 179.7 per 100,000 persons. There has been a corresponding rise in hepatitis C infection among the population. A clear but smaller increase in gonorrhea has also been noted during the same period (Mindel and Kippax 2005). Whether these increases in other sexually transmitted diseases will be followed by an increase in HIV/AIDS we do not know. However, Australia's success with respect to HIV/AIDS stands in sharp contrast to its current experience with other sexually transmitted diseases.

2.8 Implications for Other Global Diseases

This brief survey of the course of the AIDS pandemic in different settings underlines the importance of early intervention with appropriate policies to prevent and contain the spread of global diseases. The source of AIDS in animals and its transmission to humans through *zoonosis* shows that the world community needs to be vigilant regarding other such events. The most obvious contemporary parallel is avian influenza. As a more infectious disease and one that is transmitted more easily (that is, in the environment and through casual contact), avian influenza would spread much more rapidly than HIV/AIDS and kill more quickly too. Thus, in the case of a potential global influenza pandemic, the lessons of the AIDS pandemic would have to be applied *before* the pandemic occurs.

The AIDS epidemic in Africa has demonstrated how health issues can become security issues. It has also demonstrated the importance of political leadership and accurate information in containing the spread of disease.

The AIDS pandemic has had a much more severe impact on developing countries than on developed countries. However, the experience in Brazil and Thailand indicate that a well-designed HIV/AIDS program that is tailored to the specific epidemic and in the specific context of the country in question can be successful, at least in middle-income countries with relatively low prevalence rates. The lesson from Brazil and Thailand is not that other countries should duplicate blindly the successful elements of these two countries' programs. Rather, it is that responses to HIV/AIDS need to be tailor-made. Certain elements may prove to be common to all settings, such as the crucial role played by the governmental and NGO leaders in both Brazil and Thailand and the need for early intervention to contain the spread of the virus. Another element that may be a common denominator is the need for adequate health infrastructure and human resources. However, the absence of this element does not necessarily mean that taking action would be futile. In Haiti – a very poor country with a relatively high prevalence rate where social institutions have broken down – NGOs have managed to deliver treatment and testing to people living with HIV/AIDS in remote areas of the country. Similarly, the role played by democratic institutions in Brazil does not appear to have been an essential element in Thailand. However, the incorporation of the human rights element appears to be an important element that has contributed to Brazil's success. The stigma associated with HIV/AIDS in South Africa has hampered that country's efforts, whereas the relative absence of stigma surrounding the commercial sex trade in Thailand has meant the absence of such a barrier to action in that country. Similarly, the stigma associated with injection drug users in Russia has hampered the implementation of an effective HIV/AIDS strategy in a country where injection drug users make up 50% of the epidemic (Rhodes et al., 1999). Thus, social conditions can be highly relevant to the design of an effective HIV/AIDS program. Finally, the nature of the epidemic must be taken into account in each context. In both Brazil and Thailand, efforts have focused on high-risk groups, which differed in the two settings – with commercial sex workers being the main focus in Thailand and Brazil's efforts focused on MSM, injection drug users and commercial sex workers.

Providing universal access to ART requires adequate financial resources in the face of a particular prevalence rate. The manner in which governments deal with negotiations with other governments and patent owners has a direct impact on the cost of treatment, as demonstrated by South Africa, Thailand and Brazil.

Financial resources do not necessarily correlate with the design of an effective program, as the case of Japan demonstrates. Moreover, even middle-income countries can face disaster where political leadership is replaced by inaction and denial, as the case of South Africa shows. Both the Japanese and the South African experiences demonstrate that cultural or psychological predispositions can hobble the capacity of a country to respond effectively to the threats posed by epidemics. These factors therefore need to be taken into account in the design of international responses to the threat posed by global diseases.

The difficulties faced by developing countries in confronting the HIV/AIDS epidemic have direct effects on the developed world. The epidemic has influenced WTO policy regarding patent protection for pharmaceutical companies that are primarily located in the developed countries. In this regard, the epidemic has begun to change an important element of international economic policy. The migration of natural persons across the borders of an increasingly integrated global economy means developed country interests are also at stake in addressing the epidemic in developing country neighbors. Borders do not prevent the spread of the virus and closing borders is not an option. Perhaps most significantly, national and global experiences with the AIDS pandemic provide lessons for addressing not just HIV/AIDS, but other global diseases and pandemics as well. A complete picture of the AIDS pandemic requires an analysis of its effects on human health, security, international relations, business, international economic policy, national economic growth and social dynamics. However, this multi-faceted analysis serves not only to ensure effective strategies for confronting this disease and this pandemic, but to underline the importance of a multidisciplinary approach to other global health issues.

References

Baldwin K (2002) Latin American AIDS Activists Turn on Brazil. Reuters, 25 May 2002

Barbour AD (1975) The Duration of the Closed Stochastic Epidemic. Biometrika 62:478, Theorem 2:478–479

Boguna M, Pastor-Satorras R, Diaz-Guilera A, Arenas A (2003) Emergence of Clustering, Correlations, And Communities In A Social Network Model. Unpublished manuscript

Brazil Ministry of Health (2007) Boletim Epidemiológico 2007. http://www.aids.gov.br/data/Pages/LUMISE77B47C8ITEMID2814D2BBCB3A4044A05D457001332BCFPTBRIE.htm. Accessed 27 November 2007

Camacho K (2006) Latin America seeks consensual approach to AIDS/STD. Agencia Brasil

Champ P, Attaran A (2002) Patent Rights and Local Working Under the WTO TRIPS Agreement: An Analysis of the US-Brazil Patent Dispute. Yale Journal of International Law 27:365

Chartrand S (2001) Patents: In Health Emergencies, Brazil Allows the Copying of Drugs. New York Times, 19 February 2001

Cooper H, Zimmerman R, McGinley L (2001) Drug Makers' Fight For Patent Rights Puts Them in a Vise – AIDS Suit in South Africa May Be a No-Win for Them – Industry Loses US Government's Backing. Wall Street Journal, 5 March 2001

Cullinan K (2004) Aids Infected by toxic ideas. Financial Mail, 7 May 2004

Daly K (2000) The Business Response to HIV/AIDS: Impact and Lessons Learned. Joint United Nations Program on HIV/AIDS

Department of Health and Ageing (2002) Return on Investment in Needle and Syringe Programs in Australia, report prepared by Health Outcomes International in association with the National Centre in HIV Epidemiology and Clinical Research and Professor Michael Drummond, Canberra

Dezso Z, Barabasi AL (2002) Halting viruses in scale-free networks. Physical Review E 2002 May;65(5 Pt 2):055103. Epub 2002 May 21

Galvao J (2002) Access to Antiretroviral Drugs in Brazil. The Lancet 360:1862–1865

Gargoyles Inc. and Pro-Tec Inc. v. The United States (1997), 113 F 3d 1572. http://www.law.emory.edu/fedcircuit/may97/96-5089.html. Accessed 20 May 2004

Garrett L (2005) HIV and National Security: Where are the Links? Council on Foreign Relations, New York

Georgia-Pacific Corp. v. United States Plywood Corp. (1971) 318 F Supp 1116, 1120, 166 USPQ 235, 238 (SDNY), Modified and Affirmed, 446 F 2d 295, 302, 170 USPQ 369, 374 (2d Cir 1971)

Harris G (2001) Adverse Reaction: AIDS Gaffes in Africa Come Back to Haunt Drug Industry at Home – Price Cuts Abroad Deepen Domestic Trouble as Firms Reveal 'True' Cost of Pills – John le Carre's New Villain. Wall Str J 23 April 2001

Health News (2007) Thai HIV Activists Scale up Protests Against AIDS Drug Blockade. http://news.monstersandcritics.com/health/news/article_1333921. php. Accessed 24 July 2007

Hughes Aircraft Co. v. United States (1996) 86 F 3d 1566, 1571–72, 39 USPQ 2d 1065, 1069 (Fed Cir 1996)

International Treatment Preparedness Coalition (2007) Missing the Target #5: Improving AIDS Drug Access and Advancing Health Care for All. http:// www. aidstreatmentaccess. org/itpc5th.pdf. Accessed 15 December 2007

Kaiser Daily HIV/AIDS Report (2007) Thailand Will Not Issue Compulsory Licenses for Patented Drugs if Pharmaceutical Companies Match Generic Prices, Health Minister Says. http://www.kaisernetwork.org/daily_reports/rep_index.cfm? DR_ID=44931. Accessed 18 May 2007

Kazmin A, Jack A (2007) Thailand Confirms Switch to Generic Drugs. Financial Times, 29 January 2007

Kihara M et al. (2003) HIV Surveillance in Japan 1984–2000. Journal of the Acquired Immune Deficiency Syndrome 35:S55–S63

Lanjouw J (2001) A Patent Policy Proposal for Global Diseases. The Brookings Institution. http://www.brook.edu/views/papers/lanjouw/20010611.htm. Accessed 24 July 2004

Leesona Corp. v. United States (1979) 599 F.2d 958, 966, 202 USPQ 424, 432-33 (Ct. Cl. 1979)

Love J (1999) Congressional Testimony. www.house.gov/reform/cj/hearings/99.7.22/Love.htm. Accessed 24 May 2004

McNeil DG Jr (1998) AIDS Stalking Africa's Struggling Economies. New York Times, 15 November 1998

Mindel A, Kippax S (2005) A National Sexually Transmissible Infections Strategy: The Need for an All-Embracing Approach. Medical Journal of Australia 183:10

Nemoto T (2004) HIV Surveillance and Prevention Studies in Japan. AIDS Education and Prevention, Special Supplement, June 2004, 27–42

Nemoto T et al. (2003) Potential Vector Toward High HIV Prevalence in Japan. Unpublished manuscript. University of California – San Francisco

Oliveira-Cruz V, Kowalski J, McPake B (2004) The Brazilian HIV/AIDS 'success story' – can others do it? Tropical Medicine and International Health 9:292–297

Petersen M (2001) Roche Asks for Meeting With Brazil Health Minister. New York Times, 24 August 2001

Rhodes T, Ball A, Stimson G et al. (1999) HIV Infection Associated with Drug Injecting in the Newly Independent States, Eastern Europe: The Social and Economic Context of Epidemics. Addiction 94:1323–1336

Rich JL (2001) Roche Reaches Accord on Drug with Brazil. New York Times, 31 August 2001

Rite-Hite Corp. v. Kelley Co (1995) 56 F 3d 1538, 1545, 35 USPQ 2d 1065, 1069 (Fed Cir) (in banc), cert denied, 116 S Ct 184

Rosenberg T (2001) Look at Brazil. New York Times, 28 January 2001

Santoro L (2007) Cheap HIV Drugs are More Important than Patents. LA Times. http://www.latimes.com/news/opinion/sunday/commentary/la-oe-santoro9 oct 09,0,7919978.story?coll=la-sunday-commentary. Accessed 9 October 2007

Shields M (2001) Drug Maker, Brazil Near Accord on AIDS Drug Price. Reuters, 23 August 2001

Sittitrai, W et al. (1992) Thai Sexual Behavior and the Risk of HIV Infection. Chulalongkorn University

Smith-Fawzi MC, Koenig SP, Castro A, Becerra MC, Sachs J, Attaran A, Kim JY (2001) Community-Based Approaches to HIV Treatment in Resource-Poor Settings. Lancet 358: 404–409

Stone R (2007) Thai Health Minister Defends Controversial Drug-Patent Policy. Science 316:5830/1408

Tektronix Inc. v. United States (1977) 552 F 2d 343, 349, 193 USPQ 385, 391 (Ct Cl), modified, 557 F 2d 265 (Ct Cl 1977)

Ten Kate D (2007) Calling Mr. Condom: Thailand Renews Prevention Efforts to Stem an Uptick in HIV Infections. Asia Sentinel. http://www.asiasentinel.com/index.php?option=com_content&task=view&id=761&Itemid=31. Accessed 12 October 2007

Thai Ministry of Public Health (2007) Facts and Evidences on the 10 Burning Issues Related to the Government Use of Patents on Three Patented Essential Drugs in Thailand. http://www.moph.go.th/hot/White%20Paper%20CL-EN.pdf. Accessed 25 November 2007

't Hoen E (2002) TRIPS, Pharmaceutical Patents, and Access to Essential Medicines: A Long Way From Seattle to Doha. Chicago Journal of International Law 3:27

UNAIDS (2005) On the Frontline. http://data.unaids.org/UNA-docs/Report_SHR_OnFrontLine_18 july05_en.pdf?p. Accessed 27 June 2006

UNAIDS (2007) 2007 AIDS epidemic update. http://data.unaids.org/pub/EPISlides/2007/2007_ epiupdate_en.pdf. Accessed 30 November 2007

Uneklabh C et al. (1989) Prevalence of HIV Among Drug Users in Thailand. Paper Presented at the Fourth International Conference on AIDS, Stockholm, Sweden

Weaver H, Smith G, Kippax S (2005) School-Based Sex Education Policies and Indicators of Sexual Health among young people: a Comparison of the Netherlands, France, Australia and the United States. Sex Education: Sexuality, Society and Learning 5:171–188

World Bank (2004) Project Performance Assessment Report Brazil. Report No. 28819, April 2004

Weniger BG (2006) Epidemiology of HIV Infection in Thailand, AIDS 5: S65–S71

WHO (2000) HIV, TB and Malaria – Three Major Infectious Disease Threats. Backgrounder No. 1 July 2000

Appendix

Text of the Executive Order No. 13155

ACCESS TO HIV/AIDS PHARMACEUTICALS AND MEDICAL TECHNO-
LOGIES By the authority vested in me as President by the Constitution and the
laws of the United States of America, including Sections 141 and Chap. 1 of
title III of the Trade Act of 1974, as amended (19 USC. 2171, 2411–2420), Section 307 of the Public Health Service Act (42 USC. 2421), and Section 104 of the
Foreign Assistance Act of 1961, as amended (22 USC. 2151b), and in accordance
with executive branch policy on health-related intellectual property matters to
promote access to essential medicines, it is hereby ordered as follows: Section
1. Policy. (a) In administering Sections 301–310 of the Trade Act of 1974, the
United States shall not seek, through negotiation or otherwise, the revocation or
revision of any intellectual property law or policy of a beneficiary sub-Saharan
African country, as determined by the President, that regulates HIV/AIDS pharmaceuticals or medical technologies if the law or policy of the country: (1) promotes access to HIV/AIDS pharmaceuticals or medical technologies for affected
populations in that country; and (2) provides adequate and effective intellectual
property protection consistent with the Agreement on Trade-Related Aspects of
Intellectual Property Rights (TRIPS Agreement) referred to in Section 101(d)(15)
of the Uruguay Round Agreements Act (19 USC. 3511(d)(15)). (b) The United
States shall encourage all beneficiary sub-Saharan African countries to implement
policies designed to address the underlying causes of the HIV/AIDS crisis by,
among other things, making efforts to encourage practices that will prevent further
transmission and infection and to stimulate development of the infrastructure necessary to deliver adequate health services, and by encouraging policies that provide an incentive for public and private research on, and development of, vaccines
and other medical innovations that will combat the HIV/AIDS epidemic in Africa.
Section 2. Rationale: (a) This order finds that: (1) since the onset of the worldwide
HIV/AIDS epidemic, approximately 34 million people living in sub-Saharan
Africa have been infected with the disease; (2) of those infected, approximately
11.5 million have died; (3) the deaths represent 83% of the total HIV/AIDS-
related deaths worldwide; and (4) access to effective therapeutics for HIV/AIDS is
determined by issues of price, health system infrastructure for delivery, and sustainable financing. (b) In light of these findings, this order recognizes that: (1) it is
in the interest of the United States to take all reasonable steps to prevent further
spread of infectious disease, particularly HIV/AIDS; (2) there is critical need for
effective incentives to develop new pharmaceuticals, vaccines, and therapies to
combat the HIV/AIDS crisis, including effective global intellectual property standards designed to foster pharmaceutical and medical innovation; (3) the overriding
priority for responding to the crisis of HIV/AIDS in sub-Saharan Africa should be
to improve public education and to encourage practices that will prevent further

transmission and infection, and to stimulate development of the infrastructure necessary to deliver adequate health care services; (4) the United States should work with individual countries in sub-Saharan Africa to assist them in development of effective public education campaigns aimed at the prevention of HIV/AIDS transmission and infection, and to improve their health care infrastructure to promote improved access to quality health care for their citizens in general, and particularly with respect to the HIV/AIDS epidemic; (5) an effective United States response to the crisis in sub-Saharan Africa must focus in the short term on preventive programs designed to reduce the frequency of new infections and remove the stigma of the disease, and should place a priority on basic health services that can be used to treat opportunistic infections, sexually transmitted infections, and complications associated with HIV/AIDS so as to prolong the duration and improve the quality of life of those with the disease; (6) an effective United States response to the crisis must also focus on the development of HIV/AIDS vaccines to prevent the spread of the disease; (7) the innovative capacity of the United States in the commercial and public pharmaceutical research sectors is unmatched in the world, and the participation of both these sectors will be a critical element in any successful program to respond to the HIV/AIDS crisis in sub-Saharan Africa; (8) the TRIPS Agreement recognizes the importance of promoting effective and adequate protection of intellectual property rights and the right of countries to adopt measures necessary to protect public health; (9) individual countries should have the ability to take measures to address the HIV/AIDS epidemic, provided that such measures are consistent with their international obligations; and (10) successful initiatives will require effective partnerships and cooperation among governments, international organizations, nongovernmental organizations, and the private sector, and greater consideration should be given to financial, legal, and other incentives that will promote improved prevention and treatment actions. Section 3. Scope. (a) This order prohibits the United States Government from taking action pursuant to Section 301(b) of the Trade Act of 1974 with respect to any law or policy in beneficiary sub-Saharan African countries that promotes access to HIV/AIDS pharmaceuticals or medical technologies and that provides adequate and effective intellectual property protection consistent with the TRIPS Agreement. However, this order does not prohibit United States Government officials from evaluating, determining, or expressing concern about whether such a law or policy promotes access to HIV/AIDS pharmaceuticals or medical technologies or provides adequate and effective intellectual property protection consistent with the TRIPS Agreement. In addition, this order does not prohibit United States Government officials from consulting with or otherwise discussing with sub-Saharan African governments whether such law or policy meets the conditions set forth in Section 1(a) of this order. Moreover, this order does not prohibit the United States Government from invoking the dispute settlement procedures of the World Trade Organization to examine whether any such law or policy is consistent with the Uruguay Round Agreements, referred to in Section 101(d) of the Uruguay Round Agreements Act. (b) This order is intended only to improve the internal management of the executive branch and is not intended to, and does not create, any right or benefit, substantive or procedural, enforceable at law or equity by a party against the United States, its agencies or instrumentalities, its officers or employees, or any other person. WILLIAM J. CLINTON, THE WHITE HOUSE, May 10, 2000.

3 Insurance, Mortality, Treatment Costs and the Business Impact of HIV/AIDS in Developed and Developing Countries

"AIDS is also a business opportunity, with the potential for private sector providers to deliver products, healthcare services, insurance and management."
Business and AIDS. Financial Times Editorial, 1 December 2006

In this chapter, we analyze financial aspects of HIV/AIDS. HIV/AIDS was first identified in a number of developed countries. Later, it was recognized in a very large number of countries in sub-Saharan Africa. In the developed countries, the first industry to be gravely concerned with HIV/AIDS was the insurance industry. Later, it became a general concern for all industries offering health care for their employees. In both cases, the preoccupation was financial – they were concerned about rising costs of indemnization. In addition, the governments in developed countries began to realize that HIV/AIDS could have a big impact on public health expenditures. In developing countries, with a few exceptions like Thailand and Brazil, the reaction to HIV/AIDS has been slow. In the case of sub-Saharan African countries, with a few exceptions like Uganda, many countries refused to acknowledge the very existence of the problem.

This chapter will focus on the development of the analysis of HIV/AIDS data and financial tools used by insurance companies to address the financial risks associated with the HIV/AIDS pandemic. We first examine these issues in the context of developed countries, focusing on the United States. We then examine these issues in the context of developing countries, focusing on high-prevalence countries in sub-Saharan Africa and, in particular, South Africa. We then consider public and private sector strategies that might be adapted to South Africa's situation. Finally, we examine the economic incentives for companies to fund prevention and treatment programs for their employees in high-prevalence countries.

3.1 HIV/AIDS in Developed Countries

In this section, we show how advances in understanding the nature of HIV/AIDS and the effect of medical advances on mortality from HIV/AIDS have affected the insurance business in developed countries, focusing on the example of the United States. Uncertainty regarding the nature of the disease and the extent of its potential financial impact on insurance companies led to the development of better methodologies for projecting the course of the epidemic in developed countries. Once the nature of HIV transmission became clear, prevention programs changed the course of the epidemic. The HIV/AIDS epidemic also led to the development of new financial instruments and markets. The development of effective medical treatments changed the nature of the financial risks that HIV/AIDS posed for insurance companies, as well as public perceptions regarding the importance of HIV/AIDS as a public health issue.

3.1.1 The Insurance Industry and HIV/AIDS in Developed Countries

AIDS was first identified in 1981. The first sign of a new disease was the appearance of a rare form of cancer (Kaposi's sarcoma) among the "wrong" patients. It was accompanied by an increase in pneumonia caused by a normally harmless protozoan (*Pneumocystis carinii pneumonia*). It became evident that an infectious form of immune deficiency had appeared. Since the syndrome of immunodeficiency was acquired, the name Acquired Immunodeficiency Syndrome (AIDS) was coined. The identification of a specific virus (HIV-1) occurred in 1983. At that time, it became clear that certain groups were more vulnerable than others. These groups were identified as men who had sex with men, hemophiliacs, intravenous drug users and Haitian refugees in the United States. At that point, it was not clear how to combat HIV-1. Later, a blood screening antibody test was developed that could indicate the presence or absence of this virus.

Axidothymidine (AZT) was formulated in the 1960s as an anti-cancer drug. It was a failure. In 1984, companies began testing AZT's effectiveness against AIDS. In 1985, after successful trials, the US Food and Drug Administration approved AZT for treating AIDS, with a newer generic name, *zidovudine*. It quickly became clear that AZT therapy was not a long term solution, as *zidovudine* had only a short-term effect in prolonging life among AIDS patients (more on the drug AZT appears below). It appeared that it prolonged life between two and three extra years. From the perspective of life insurers, the gain from the introduction of AZT was very small.

The insurance industry in the developed world viewed HIV/AIDS with great alarm. The problem with individual life policies was that a number of them were long term policies where it was all but impossible to deny renewal. The problem with group policies was that it was yet not clear how to identify persons with HIV-1, in order to exclude them.

3.1.2 Problems of Mortality Projections and Insurance

In the late 1980s, it seemed that there was no relief in sight as far as the insurance industry was concerned. Moreover, the Task Force of the Society of Actuaries brought out a report in 1988 showing a very grim future of HIV infection and death from AIDS in the United States. At that time, it appeared certain that full-blown AIDS would cause death within 2 years. The forecast for the United States

Actual and Forecast Cumulative AIDS cases circa 1986

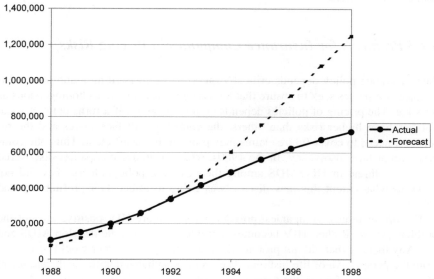

Fig. 3.1 Wrong forecast of AIDS cases. *Source*: Society of Actuaries Task Force Report, 1988

in Fig. 3.1 (made in 1987) assumed that there would be no new infections starting in 1998. Reality turned out to be completely different. The actual numbers were slightly over half of what was forecast. Moreover, new infections did not dramatically fall to anywhere near zero.

In 1986, HIV/AIDS looked like a money losing proposition for many insurance companies, through their exposure to existing life insurance and health insurance policies. It was seen as a big problem. The conservative forecast for 1998 was a cumulative number of persons with full-blown AIDS of more than 1,200,000. The dire projection did not materialize. The cumulative number of AIDS cases rose to about 700,000 by 1998.

The problem of wild over-projection appeared not just in the United States. The Report of the Task Force of the Society of Actuaries also reported that the number of HIV-positive persons in Australia would rise to 50,000 (we examined HIV/AIDS in Australia in Chap. 2). In fact, the number of HIV-positive people in Australia never rose to more than 16,000.

Once it became clear that the disease was sexually transmitted, people in developed countries started using condoms more than before – especially people in high-risk groups – thereby reducing the incidence of HIV. It turned out that the insurance industry's forecast was inaccurate. The inaccurate forecasts meant that insurance companies in developed countries did not have a good estimate of the future cost of HIV/AIDS. In the following subsection, we discuss the problems of different types of insurance policies as a result of this uncertainty about the future course of HIV/AIDS.

3.1.3 Problems for Insurance Companies in Pricing Risks

Any insurance policy depends critically on correct underwriting assumptions. Insurance companies seek to ensure that the policies they sell are as homogeneous as possible. The pricing of policies depends on homogeneity. If it turns out that some policies have higher risks than others, the company will face losses and the reserves it needs to cover future claims may prove to be insufficient. Thus, the company might face insolvency. In the 1980s, when insurance companies discovered the "new" threat of HIV/AIDS among their existing policyholders, they did not know to what extent this new disease was going to affect their profitability and solvency.

For *life* insurance companies, policyholders who are HIV-positive are not the problem *per se*. Rather, HIV becomes a problem when people develop AIDS and die. Any therapy that did not prolong the life of the policyholder would be useless from the perspective of life insurers. The prognosis changed with the development of new therapies, first in the form of a single drug and then in the forms of dual and triple therapies. Insurance companies in developed countries began to accept group life insurance policies, in which some members of the group would be HIV-positive, without adjusting the premiums once it became clear that the number of persons in a group would not be significant. They also started accepting individual policies, but with higher premiums and additional conditions.

For *health* insurance companies, it was a different matter. They are concerned not just with the eventual death of the policy holder, but with the cost of treatment until death. Thus, if the appearance of a new disease suddenly raises the average cost of treatment, it spells trouble for health insurance companies. However, health insurance companies had one big advantage over life insurance companies. Almost all health insurance policies are *annually* renewable. Health insurance policies are rarely long-term contracts. Unless there are some guarantees explicitly spelled out in the contract regarding future premiums, the company can raise the premiums. Life insurance policies are often long-term contracts. Thus, it is usually not possible to change the premiums midstream.

3.1.4 Comparing HIV/AIDS with Diabetes

There have been similar episodes in the history of insurance with respect to other diseases. For over 2000 years, diabetes was recognized, but it had no known treatment. As a result, diabetes patients were not insurable. Beginning in the 1920s, the discovery of insulin led to new treatments, but the outcome remained uncertain.

Thus, insurance became possible, but at a very high cost. In the 1970s, treatment improved. Over the following decades, the methods of administering insulin became standardized. Patients themselves could administer insulin without the need for doctors or nurses. As a result, diabetes patients can now get standard treatment for insurance policies. However, they do not pay the same premiums; they pay an extra charge (a loading), as with other kinds of additional risks.

The case of diabetes is not exactly the same as the case of HIV/AIDS. First, diabetes is can not be transmitted between people. Second, it is known that HIV/AIDS is associated with certain risky activities. Thus, an injection drug user is much more likely to become HIV-positive than a person who is not. By the same token, a person with diabetic parents is much more likely to become diabetic. It is a legal question whether insurance companies should be using these types of information for underwriting risk classification and charging additional premiums.

There is an inherent tension between human rights law and insurance practices. The very nature of the insurance business requires companies to discriminate against particular groups, based on their risk profile, in determining insurability and premiums. For this reason, in many human rights laws the practices of insurance companies in determining insurability and premiums constitute an exception to the prohibition against discrimination based on disabilities. However, this does not give insurance companies an unlimited right to discriminate. For example, Australian courts have found it lawful for insurance companies to take into account physical impairment or disability to classify risks and set premiums, where it is based on the advice of actuaries, statistical data and the practice of prudent insurers. However, in Zurich Insurance Co v. Ontario Human Rights Commission (1992), the Supreme Court of Canada ruled that business convenience alone cannot override human rights. Thus, where individualized testing is an alternative to statistically-based discrimination according to membership in a group, it must be used. Moreover, the mere absence of statistical evidence is not enough to prove that there is no alternative to the discriminatory practice. The British Columbia Human Rights Tribunal applied this Supreme Court decision to rule that an insurance company could not refuse coverage to an HIV-negative man whose wife was HIV-positive, in the absence of actuarial and statistical evidence establishing the risk of insuring the man (Ramaroson 2003).

3.1.5 The Advent of Effective Treatment

Figure 3.2 shows the number of years drugs for treating HIV/AIDS had been available in 2000. By 2000, AZT had been available for 14 years. *Nevirapine* had only been available for 4 years. Initially these drugs were used only for patients who already had full-blown AIDS. Now it has become clear that the same drugs are useful in keeping the onset of full-blown AIDS at bay. It has also become clear that some combinations of drugs are better than treatment with single drugs. Drugs like *nevirapine* also have been proven effective to reduce mother-to-child transmission of HIV.

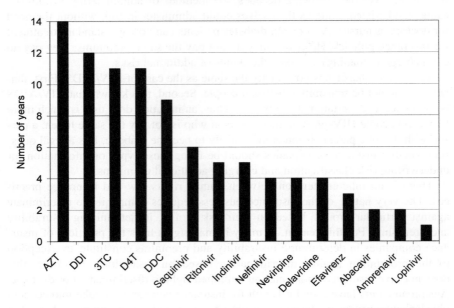

Fig. 3.2 Years various drugs have been available (calculated for the year 2000) *Source*:
Various

As we noted earlier, *zidovudine* (AZT) was the first drug approved for the treatment of AIDS and HIV infection. Jerome Horwitz first synthesized AZT in 1964,
under a US National Institutes of Health grant. It was intended to treat cancer, but
failed to show efficacy. In February 1985, Samuel Broder, Hiroaki Mitsuya, and
Robert Yarchoan from the National Cancer Institute, collaborating with Janet Ride-
out and several others, started working on AZT as a treatment for AIDS patients.
After showing that this drug was an effective agent against HIV in a petri dish, the
team conducted the initial clinical trial that showed that it could increase CD4 cell
counts in AIDS patients. The definition of the onset of AIDS is measured in terms
of CD4 cell counts. Drugs for HIV/AIDS increase CD4 cell counts. AZT became
the very first drug that showed some effectiveness against full-blown AIDS.

A placebo-controlled randomized trial of AZT showed that it could prolong the
life of patients with AIDS. The pharmaceutical company Burroughs Wellcome
filed for a patent on AZT in 1985. On 20 March 1987, the US Food and Drug
Administration (FDA) approved the drug through the recently instituted fast-track
system for use against HIV, AIDS, and AIDS Related Complex (a now-defunct
medical term for pre-AIDS illness). AZT was approved as a preventive treatment
in 1990.

Two years later, the FDA approved the next important drug, DDI. Some researchers postulated that a combination of AZT and DDI might be more useful than each drug by itself. However, it was quickly shown that the combination actually reduced the efficacy of both the drugs.

When new classes of drugs were developed, it turned out that combination therapy worked far better using each drug individually. However, getting the drug companies to cooperate in trying out various combinations turned out to be difficult, as various drugs were developed by different companies and they had different regimens (for example, one might have to be taken once a day and another three times a day). It turned out that therapy with three drugs produced better results (for a meta-analysis of existing studies, see Yazdanpanah et al., 2004). However, governments in developed countries did not aggressively move to get patent owners to form a patent pool so that the drug regimes could be harmonized. A patent pool is an agreement to share patents. It is generally formed by a number of businesses in the same industry. There are many examples of privately agreed patent pools, such as MPEG-2 standards for selling digital movies. In matters of national importance, patent pools have been used to bind an industry for many decades. For example, an aircraft patent pool was founded in the United States in 1917. It was brought in by Franklin D. Roosevelt, then Secretary of the Navy. It encompassed practically all airplane manufacturers in the US, resolved all pending infringement claims and bound its members to give each other non-exclusive licenses of all airplane patents.

3.1.6 The Impact of Drugs on Survivability

In Fig. 3.3, we examine the percentage of patients dying under various regimes for people who have full-blown AIDS. We report the results of Montaner et al. (1998) from the INCAS trial. The data came from trials in Italy, the Netherlands, Canada and Australia, collectively called the INCAS. The curve to the left shows the probability of dying without any drugs. Within 8 months, 25% had died. The dotted curve next to it is the estimated death profile of those who were taking a single drug. Although the initial response to the single drug regime was better than no drug at all, the quick mutation of the virus quickly made the drug ineffective. Thus, after eight months, the mortality experience of the patients on the single drug regime became virtually identical to the ones without any drugs. The fatter dotted line shows the mortality rates for the patients on a dual drug regimen. They fared better. However, their mortality rate also reached 25% after 15 months. The solid line to the right shows the strikingly different response of patients on triple drug cocktails. After 15 months, only 4% had died.

A more recent study of Swiss cohorts confirmed the earlier results by carefully following a group of 10,977 Swiss patients over a period of 12 years (Keisera et al., 2004). The objective of the Swiss cohort study was to compare three groups: (1) individuals who were HIV-negative; (2) HIV-positive patients who were not

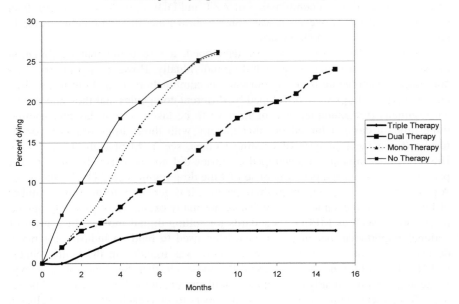

Fig. 3.3 Survival probabilities on mono/double/triple therapies. *Source*: Montaner et al. (1998)

on Highly Active Anti-Retroviral Therapy (HAART, a combination of three or more antiretroviral drugs); and (3) HIV-positive patients who were on HAART. The survival probabilities of these three groups are shown in Fig. 3.4. It shows that for a 20 year old, without HAART treatment, the chance of surviving 10 years was about 50%. The patients with HAART would have a 50% chance of living another 35 years. It also shows the limitations of HAART. Compared with the HIV-negative group, the survival probability is still low. The HIV-negative group would live at least another 40 years with more than 90% probability.

Insurance companies set their premiums based on two primary indicators: age and sex. They modify the rates based on medical conditions. Thus, diabetics get a loading factor because of their medical condition. Given that the survival probabilities are so different for HIV/AIDS patients, it is important for the insurance companies to know the changing portfolios of risks. For individual policies, it may be possible (depending on the regulatory structure) to outright refuse coverage for HIV/AIDS patients. Alternatively, it might be possible to offer policies with higher premiums for the same coverage. For group policies, the cost of testing everyone would be high. Moreover, in most developed countries, by law, it would not be possible to refuse coverage for HIV-positive employees. Thus, for setting reserves, it became indispensable for insurance companies to have a correct assessment of survival probabilities for HIV-positive individuals.

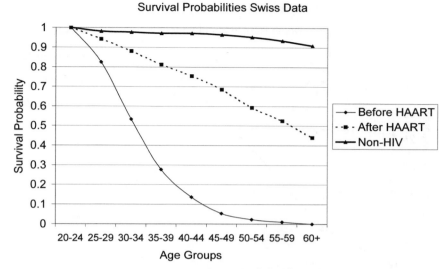

Fig. 3.4 Swiss cohort data on survival. *Source*: Keisera et al. (2004)

By the mid 1990s, the prevalence of HIV and the corresponding death rates of insurance buyers began to drop significantly in developed countries. For example, Doll (1997) reported that, during 1996, many insurance companies in the United States saw a 50% reduction in death rates from AIDS in some of their life insurance portfolios. It appeared that the death rates had peaked in the United States from HIV/AIDS. The dramatic effects can be seen in Fig. 3.5. In the early 1980s, the biggest killers of 25–44 old year men were accidents (about 36 per 100,000), cancer (about 25 per 100,000 and homicide (about 15 per 100,000). By 1994, deaths from HIV/AIDS had overtaken deaths from all the other causes. But, by the turn of the century, deaths from AIDS had taken a very sharp downturn.

The outcome that Fig. 3.5 depicts in the change of mortality is not surprising in light of the new drug therapies that have become available over the past two decades, especially since the discovery of the efficacy of triple drug cocktails. A recent study by the US Centers for Disease Control (CDC) shows how much survival rates have improved over time once a patient is diagnosed with full-blown AIDS in the United States. As Fig. 3.6 shows, the 5-year survival rate for the 1981–1992 cohort was less than 20%. The same 5-year survival rate for the 2001–2003 cohort has been estimated at 85%, up from 50% a decade earlier.

Along with the general decline in HIV prevalence in the population, public concern over HIV/AIDS has fallen. When a random sample of over 1,000 Americans were asked an open-ended question, "What would you say is the most urgent health problem facing this country at the present time?" 68% said HIV/AIDS, in 1987. By 2006, the concern over HIV/AIDS was virtually gone (see Table 3.1). It was a remarkable decline in public perception. No other public health issue has shown such a dramatic decline in public concern in a span of 20 years.

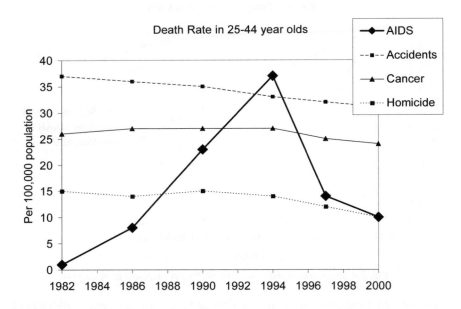

Fig. 3.5 US death rates from various causes. *Source*: Statistical abstracts of the United States, various years

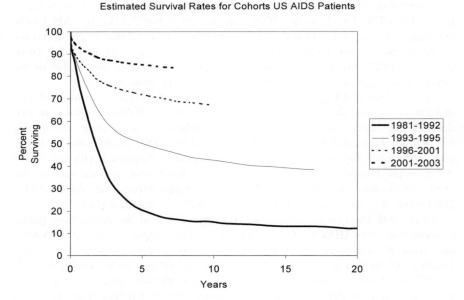

Fig. 3.6 Effectiveness of drugs: US cohort data. *Source*: www.cdc.gov

Table 3.1 Gallup poll of health care concerns 1987–2006 "What would you say is the most urgent health problem facing this country at the present time?" [Open-ended]

Date	Health care insurance costs (%)	Access to health care (%)	Cancer (%)	Obesity (%)	HIV/AIDS (%)
1987	1	0	14	3	68
1991	20	0	6	0	55
1992	30	0	5	0	41
1997	9	13	15	0	29
1999	13	1	23	1	33
2000	25	13	20	3	18
2001	14	8	19	4	7
2002	25	14	21	7	8
2003	27	25	13	7	8
2004	29	29	9	7	5
2005	25	17	15	9	6
2006	29	22	14	8	6

Source: http://www.data360.org/dsg.aspx?Data_Set_Group_Id=1505

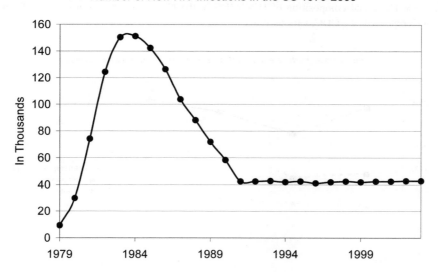

Number of New HIV Infections in the US 1979-2003

Fig. 3.7 US centers for disease control estimates of new infections *Source*: Data from the Centers for Disease Control, Atlanta, 2006

Since 1991, the number of new cases of HIV/AIDS has stabilized in the United States (see Fig. 3.7). It peaked in 1983–1984 and then started to decline until it reached slightly over 40,000 new infections a year in 1992. After that, it stayed at that level for the next decade. However, using a better methodology, estimates of new cases of HIV/AIDS in the United States are higher (see Chap. 8).

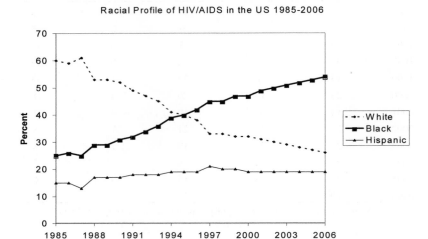

Fig. 3.8 The racial composition of HIV/AIDS in the US 1985–2006. *Source*: Data from various reports of the CDC, various years

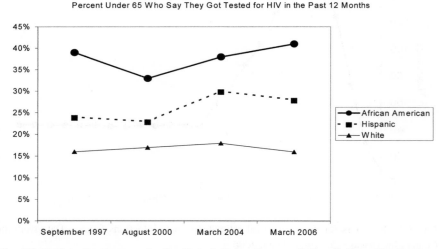

Fig. 3.9 HIV testing by race in the United States *Source*: Gallup Poll on Health Care, 1987–2006

As Fig. 3.9 shows, HIV testing statistics do not reflect the racial profile of HIV/AIDS in the United States. Even though Hispanics have the lowest rate among the three big groups, they are more apt to get tested than the whites. African-Americans are three times more likely than their white counterparts to have HIV/AIDS and they are three times as likely to get tested. However, over time, the testing done by African-Americans should have increased in proportion to the rise in the rate of infection in the community. This has not happened.

Box 3.1 The changing color of HIV/AIDS in the USA

Two clear trends have become evident in the spread of HIV/AIDS in the United States. First, as we noted in the previous subsection, the incidence (new infections) per year has stabilized at 40,000 per year. However, as Fig. 3.8 shows, the racial profile of HIV/AIDS has undergone a remarkable transformation. In 1985, whites bore 60% of the HIV/AIDS burden. African-Americans accounted for 25% of HIV/AIDS cases. Hispanics accounted for another 15%. Thus, African-Americans, who accounted for 15% of the population in 1985, represented a proportionally larger number of HIV/AIDS patients. Over time, this trend has become worse. By 1994, the proportion of HIV/AIDS patients among whites and African-Americans had become equal, at 40% each, and Hispanics accounted for 19% of the disease burden. The statistics for 2006 showed that the proportion of HIV/AIDS patients among Hispanics had remained stable, at 19%. However, the proportion of HIV/AIDS patients among African-Americans had shot up to 54% and the proportion for whites had dropped to 26% (Asians and Pacific Islanders accounted for the remaining 1%). Thus, the African-Americans, who account for less than 15% of the population, are almost four times as likely as their white counterparts to be infected with HIV. In 2005, African-Americans accounted for 18,121 (49%) of the estimated 37,331 new HIV/AIDS diagnoses in the United States.

In Washington, DC the HIV prevalence rate was 5% in 2007 (about the same as Rwanda). More than 80% of the HIV cases diagnosed in DC between 2001 and 2006 were among black men, women and adolescents. Ninety percent of women who tested positive for HIV were black. About 37% of HIV cases were transmitted through heterosexual contact, compared with 25% that were transmitted among men who have sex with men (Medical News Today 2007).

3.1.7 Estimating the Cost of HIV/AIDS Treatment in the Developed World

In developed countries, most people with HIV/AIDS depend on public sources to pay for medical services. In developing countries, this is not necessarily so. For planning public expenditures, credible estimates of the cost of treating HIV/AIDS patients are essential for policy makers at all levels.

However, estimating the cost of treating HIV/AIDS is not straightforward even in a developed country like the United States, for the following reasons. First, only some states report information to the CDC about individuals who have been diagnosed with HIV, but all states report information about individuals diagnosed with AIDS. Second, information with personal identifiers is not released, to protect the identity of people with HIV/AIDS. Third, federal laws prohibit state Medicaid programs from disclosing the names of people living with HIV. Thus, no readily accessible list of people is available to researchers.

The most common national estimate of the cost of treating people with HIV/AIDS was calculated using data from the HIV Cost and Services Utilization Study. The payer-based approach uses data about the flow of funds from payers to the providers of care, and the provider-based approach uses data about funds received by providers of care. A third method uses patient-based estimates.

In theory, estimates derived from these three approaches should be the same. In reality, this is not so because each approach is based on a different set of assumptions. The accuracy of patient-based estimates depends on how well the sample represents the universe of patients with HIV/AIDS who receive care. The accuracy of estimates based on the amount of money spent by payers depends on the precision of the methodology used by each payer to calculate the proportion of their payments attributable to people with HIV/AIDS, as well as the completeness of the list of payers. Similarly, the accuracy of estimates based on the funds received by providers depends on the precision of the methodology used to derive estimates of the money received by these providers for treating people with HIV/AIDS, as well as on the completeness of the list of providers.

Hellinger and Fleishman (2000) estimated the national cost of treating people with HIV/AIDS, using two approaches (payer-based and provider-based), by synthesizing disparate data sources and comparing these estimates to existing estimates derived using a patient-based approach. They used data from the following sources: (1) surveys of people with HIV/AIDS from studies of federal and state expenditures for HIV/AIDS; (2) consulting firms that collect data on drug costs; (3) the federal agency that maintains a data base composed of hospital discharge abstracts from many states across the country; and (4) a survey of private insurers supported by the Health Insurance Association of American and the American Council of Life Insurance. They found that the cost of treating all people with HIV in 1996 was between 6.7 and 7.8 billion dollars. This produces an average annual cost of treating a person of between USD 20,000 and USD 24,700, using the payer/provider based approaches.

3.2 HIV/AIDS in Developing Countries

In developing countries, problems regarding HIV/AIDS are different from developed countries. First, no developed country has a prevalence rate that exceeds 1% of the population. Among developing countries, the rates vary enormously. In sub-Saharan Africa, the prevalence rate exceeds 15% in several countries (see Chap.2).

In the Middle East and in North Africa, the prevalence rate is usually less than 0.4%. Second, in developed countries, the problem is far more severe among men who have sex with men (MSM) than any other identifiable group. Since MSM do not represent a very large proportion of the entire population, the problem has not expanded to the rest of the population. In many developing countries, especially in sub-Saharan Africa, the epidemic has expanded into the general population. A very large proportion of heterosexuals, both men and women, are infected. Third, due to available public healthcare infrastructure in the developed world, there are mechanisms to deal with the management of the disease. In most developing countries, such help simply does not exist. Fourth, in the developed world, relatively good mechanisms exist for tracking the spread of HIV/AIDS. In most developing countries, such mechanisms are absent. Fifth, not every person in a given developing country is poor. There is a wider variation in wealth and income in developing countries than in developed countries. Thus, certain aspects of HIV/AIDS are exactly the same for the rich in the developing world as for most people in the developed world.

In this section, we begin by examining different methods for estimating HIV/AIDS prevalence in developing countries, using the examples of India and South Africa. Next, we focus on the impact of the HIV/AIDS epidemic in South Africa. We then examine the insurance industry in South Africa and how it has addressed the HIV/AIDS epidemic in that country.

3.2.1 Errors in Measuring the Prevalence of HIV/AIDS in India

As we noted above, tracking the disease is a big problem in the developing world. We highlight the problem with the example of India. The 2006 Report on the Global AIDS Epidemic by the UNAIDS reported that India had overtaken South Africa as the country with the highest number of people with HIV/AIDS. It was officially estimated at 5.5 million people (http://www.unaids.org/en/HIV_data/2006GlobalReport/default.asp). Figure 3.10 shows the rise in estimated HIV/AIDS prevalence in India between 1980 and 2004.

Actuarial projections of HIV/AIDS prevalence in India, based on the South African Antenatal Clinic model, are depicted in Fig. 3.11. Based on the available data up to 1999, by 2005 the prevalence rate in India would have exceeded 5% of the population and, by 2015, would have exceeded 10% of the population. These alarming projections made headlines.

In July 2007, news reports noted a major revision of HIV/AIDS prevalence in India (Zaheer 2007). The revision reduced the median estimate from 5.7 million in 2004 to 2.47 million in 2006. HIV/AIDS prevalence was now estimated to be around 0.36%, down significantly from the earlier estimate of 0.9%. This big drop was due to a statistical error.

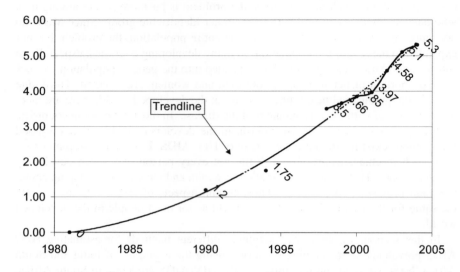

Fig. 3.10 Estimated HIV/AIDS prevalence in India 1980–2004 using antenatal clinic method. *Source*: Derived from NACO database

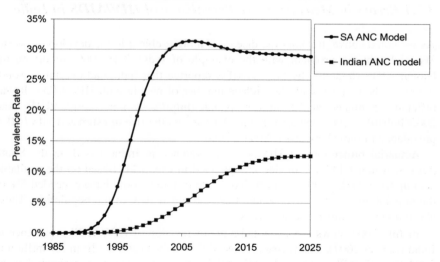

Fig. 3.11 Projection of prevalence rates of HIV/AIDS in South Africa and India. *Source*: Stuart Land, RGA Reinsurance Company of South Africa, modelling the HIV/AIDS epidemic in India, Presented at the 4th Global Conference of Actuaries, 14–15 February 2002

3.2.2 Problems with Estimating Prevalence Using Antenatal Clinic Data

To determine the source of the statistical error in estimating HIV/AIDS prevalence in India, we need to understand the methods of estimating the number of people with HIV/AIDS in a region or a country. No country in the world tests everyone for HIV/AIDS, even though the cost of testing using saliva has come down tremendously. The most common method for estimating the number of people with HIV/AIDS is to use data from visits to Antenatal Clinics.

However, there are a number of caveats when using Antenatal Clinic data to estimate the prevalence of the general population. First, only pregnant women are eligible for testing for HIV/AIDS. This introduces a structural bias in the process of generalizing from the universe of pregnant women to all women and then to the entire population. Second, women who become pregnant and attend Antenatal Clinic facilities are, by definition, sexually active women who are not using contraceptives. This introduces a self-selection bias when we try to generalize from this universe to the entire population. Third, various factors associated with HIV influence attendance at an Antenatal Clinic. For example, HIV-positive women might be less likely to attend a clinic. Moreover, HIV-positive women might be less likely to become pregnant. Fourth, women in urban areas are generally more likely to visit an Antenatal Clinic before childbirth than their rural counterparts. If urban women are more likely to be HIV-positive, this would introduce another bias. Fifth, attending public Antenatal Clinics in developing countries is associated with poverty. Poorer women are not only more likely to attend public clinics; they are also more likely to be less educated. Education is strongly negatively correlated with HIV/AIDS in developing countries, as women with higher education are more likely to use methods of contraception such as condoms. The use of condoms substantially reduces the likelihood of contracting HIV/AIDS.

Recently, a number of studies have shown that the upward bias generated by Antenatal Clinic data can be quite significant when compared to population-wide surveys. In Fig. 3.12, we cite one such example from Rice et al. (2007).

Figure 3.12 shows that for every age group of women, estimates of HIV/AIDS prevalence are substantially (and statistically significantly) higher with the Antenatal Clinic Method than with the population survey method. This difference has now been documented not just in high prevalence countries, like South Africa, but in several other countries with varying degrees of prevalence. We illustrate this difference Fig. 3.13 (using data from Wilson 2007).

The accuracy of HIV/AIDS estimates is important, both for governments involved in assessing the scale of prevention and treatment needs and for the private sector, particularly the insurance industry. Prior to the revision of Indian HIV/AIDS estimates, it appeared that India would surpass South Africa as the country with the highest number of cases in the world. While it now appears that this will not be the case, India, like South Africa, still has a large-scale problem, even if the number of HIV/AIDS cases is much smaller as a percentage of the population.

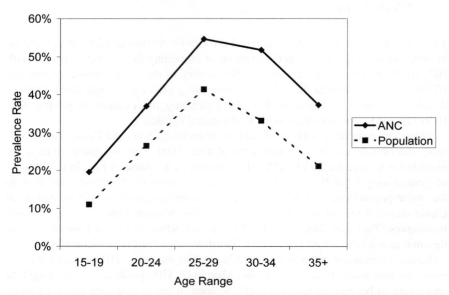

Fig. 3.12 Antenatal clinic data versus population survey data, South Africa. *Source*: UNAIDS database

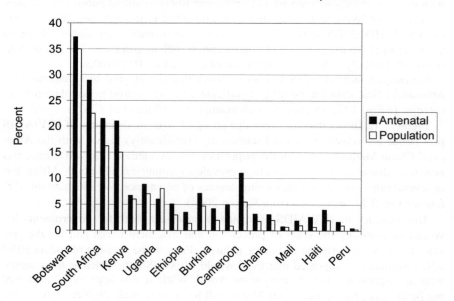

Fig. 3.13 Antenatal clinic method produces higher prevalence rate. *Source*: UNAIDS database

3.2.3 Insurance Companies' Problem with HIV/AIDS

In an insurance company, the main task of an actuary is to create a group with homogenous risks and price each group according to their risks. The outbreak of HIV/AIDS in the 1980s created a problem for life insurance companies. The risks that they thought were homogenous became heterogeneous due to the presence of HIV/AIDS among policy holders. HIV/AIDS raises mortality risks substantially. At the time, mortality among HIV/AIDS patients was extremely high because effective treatments for HIV/AIDS were still unavailable. The groups that were deemed homogeneous suddenly appeared extremely heterogeneous. Heterogeneity of a group means rising risks of insolvency for a line of business.

In the 1980s, insurance companies were concerned about two problems. First, HIV/AIDS meant they could lose a lot of money from their existing policies. Second, in the future, more people with HIV/AIDS could buy policies. If the companies had a costly method of determining the HIV status of a person, it would mean either losing business or underwriting policies with faulty assumptions about the policy holders. Either way, it would be a problem for the life insurance business.

After 1985, the enzyme-linked immunosorbent assay test (ELISA) became the most frequently used test. ELISA was quick and inexpensive, but it produced a large number of false positive results. Over 10% of HIV-negative people tested HIV-positive using ELISA. A technically more difficult and more costly test, called the Western Blot, used electrophoretic separation of virus proteins and glycoproteins to give a profile of bands characteristic of HIV when antibodies to HIV were present.

As we noted earlier, insurance policies have one important characteristic that other long-term contracts do not have. An insurance contract is unilaterally binding on the insurance company. If a policy holder simply stops making the payments on a 20-year policy after 1 year, the policy holder can still benefit from the residual value of the policy. However, 1 year after an insurance company has agreed to a set premium payment on a 20-year policy, if the insurance company finds out that the policy holder is HIV-positive, it can neither cancel the policy nor raise the premiums after the fact. It has to stick to the original premium rates to which it agreed.

In order to price an insurance product correctly, an actuary in an insurance company has to assess accurately two elements of risk: frequency and severity. With the rise of HIV/AIDS in the 1980s, insurance companies could not determine either with accuracy. They did not know what proportion of their portfolio was at higher risk of contracting HIV/AIDS. That is, they did not know what percentage of their existing or prospective clients had HIV/AIDS.

Figure 3.14 plots the survival probabilities for three different classes of 30-year-old males, using data for 1987 from Daykin et al. (1988): men with full-blown AIDS, HIV-positive males and HIV-negative males.

Survival Distribution 30 Year Old Male

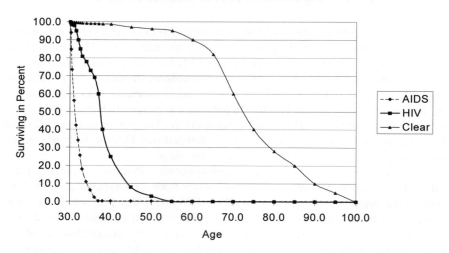

Fig. 3.14 Survival probabilities for three classes of 30-year-old males. *Source*: Daykin et al. (1988)

The most striking feature is how different the survival rates are. In 1.5 years, more than half the people with AIDS would have died. For HIV-positive men, it would be 7.5 years. Half of HIV-negative men would live another 42.5 years. The additional life expectancy for a 30-year-old, HIV-negative male was 46.6 years. This corresponded to a life expectancy of 77 years for an HIV-negative male. For a 30-year-old, HIV-positive male, the additional life expectancy was 8.2 years. The additional life expectancy of a 30-year-old with AIDS was only 1.5 years.

If the HIV prevalence rate is even 5%, the losses from life insurance policies on HIV/AIDS patients alone could cause the insolvency of an insurance company. If we add the financial implications of health care insurance, it would be even worse.

3.2.4 The South African Life Insurance Business and HIV/AIDS

South Africa has had a highly developed life insurance market for decades. As a proportion of GDP, it had the highest penetration of life insurance in the world in 1990. South Africa still had the highest penetration of life insurance in the world in 2006. Life insurance penetration is calculated as the total life insurance premium paid as a percentage of GDP in a given year. In Table 3.2, we compare rates of life insurance penetration in 2001. Japan, a developed country, had a life insurance penetration rate of 9%. Similarly, for the United Kingdom, life insurance penetration was 10%. In South Africa, a middle-income country, life insurance penetration exceeded 14%. There were 60 registered life insurance offices in

Table 3.2 South Africa leads the World in life insurance penetration

Country	Life insurance penetration (%)
USA	4
Japan	9
UK	10
France	6
Germany	3
India	1
Brazil	0.4
Chile	3
South Africa	14

Source: Data from Swiss Re database for the year 2001. Life insurance penetration means life insurance premium paid as a percentage of GDP

South Africa. However, the market was highly concentrated. The two largest insurance companies had a market share of 47% and the four largest had 74% of the market.

A rise in HIV/AIDS prevalence to over 30% of the adult population would have spelled disaster for the life insurance market in any developed country. Yet, the insurance industry was not severely affected by the rise of HIV/AIDS in South Africa. The reason is that most of life insurance policies in South Africa were short-term policies; most expired within 5 years of issue. However, most life insurance policies in *developed* countries are long-term policies that last for 10–20 years. Given that an insurance policy is a unilateral agreement on the part of the company, South African insurance companies did not have to commit themselves for long.

South Africa was one country where the problem of estimating countrywide HIV/AIDS prevalence using Antenatal Clinic data was known at least since 2000. For example, Keir (2001) estimated HIV/AIDS prevalence using two different methods. First, he used Antenatal Clinic data and second, he used indirect methods using population weighting. In the second method, special attention is paid to the fact that urban areas tend to produce more cases than rural areas. The results are shown in Fig. 3.15. There are two notable features in this figure. First, the prevalence rate is much higher using the Antenatal Clinic method. Second, the projection based on the weighted method showed that the prevalence rate would peak in 2006–2007. Updated data from UNAIDS in 2007 appears to confirm that this peak has been reached.

Keir (2001) also presented mortality rates for 2000 and projected the mortality for 2006. Normally, mortality rates show a J shape. Childhood mortality is typically higher than adult mortality. Mortality falls in adolescence and then rises slowly until 70. Then it rises relatively rapidly. With HIV/AIDS, a largely sexually transmitted disease, mortality rises during the peak of fertility for women and

Prevalence in South Africa: 1985-2010

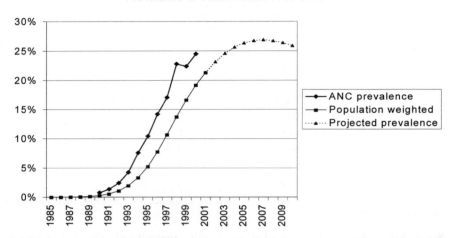

Fig. 3.15 HIV prevalence in South Africa, using ANC and population weighting. *Source*: Keir (2001)

Death Per 1000 of 45 Year Olds Over 15 Years

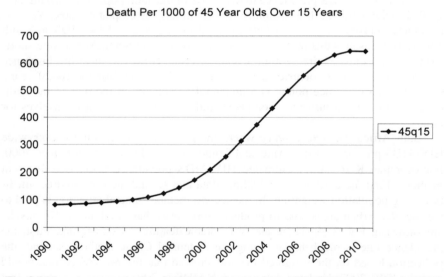

Fig. 3.16 Long term survival probabilities in South Africa 1990–2010. *Source*: Keir (2001)

the sexually active period for men. It shows a classic W shape – an expanding mortality bulge for the age group 25–55.

Keir also showed how this rise in mortality would continue until at least 2010, by plotting the mortality of 15 year olds for the next 45 years (denoted by 45q15). As Fig. 3.16 shows, this rate changes from 83 per thousand in 1990 to 645 per

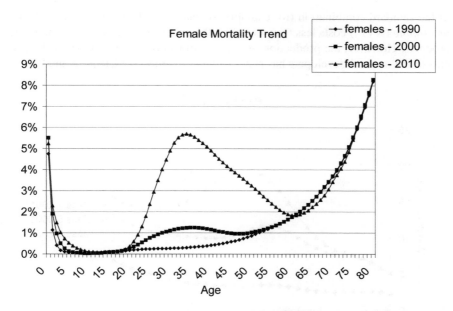

Fig. 3.17 Female mortality trends in South Africa 1990–2010. *Source*: ASSA database

1,000 in 2010. Two decades would produce a dramatic eightfold rise in the mortality of people aged 15–60 – the prime working age. This change has a dramatic impact on human capital and has grave consequences for economic growth (see Chap. 4).

Most of this change in mortality is taking place in the 20–55 age range, as the Fig. 3.17 illustrates. The change from a J shape to a W shape is most pronounced for women in South Africa. The most dramatic change takes place in the 33–34 age range. Between 1990 and 2010, women's mortality rises by 20-fold in this range.

South Africa has used a classification system for insuring lives. The system uses income and education as proxies for calculating the mortality differential in the population (in addition to age and as a marker for mortality that is commonly used elsewhere). Individuals are classified by five different levels of income and education. At one extreme, high income/high education people get a rating of 1 and low income/low education people get a rating of 5. According to Keir (2001), the mortality of Class 1 individuals was one-third of the mortality of Class 5 individuals in 2001. As Fig. 3.18 shows, the effect of income and education on mortality is amplified in the projected number for 2006. Most of this difference is due to the effect of HIV/AIDS.

The cost of getting triple therapy for patients in developing countries can very expensive. To overcome the problem, countries like Thailand and Brazil have started producing generic versions of the drugs domestically. The generic version of the standard combination (for example, *stavudine* (d4T) + *lamivudine* (3TC) + *nevirapine* (NVP)) costs less than a tenth of the prices charged for the brand name products. However, the production of generic drugs prior to the expiry of the patents of the original developers has generated controversy (see Chaps. 5 and 6).

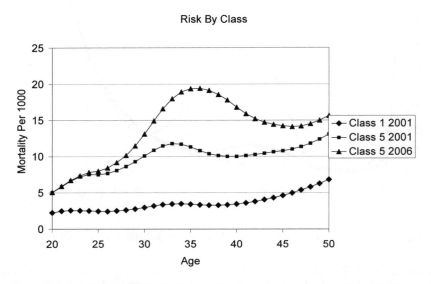

Fig. 3.18 Survival probabilities in South Africa by risk class. *Source*: Keir (2001)

Table 3.3 Five-year survival probabilities for patients without HAART with CD4 cell counts of 200–350 cells per mm^3

Type of country	Probability (range)
Industrialized countries	72.6% (48.6–86.7%)
Resource-limited countries	52.7% (15.7–80.2%)

Source: Zwahlen and Egger (2006)

3.3 Public and Private Sector Health Care Strategies in Developing Countries

In the this section, we consider public and private sector strategies that have been used with respect to health insurance, the first in another middle-income country (Mexico), and the second in a developed country (the United States). In the case of Mexico, we examine the expansion of access to HIV/AIDS treatment through the public health insurance system. In the case of the United States, we examine the use of insurance regulation on access to private sector insurance. In this regard, the US provides an example for insurance companies in the private sector. We also consider the incentives for private sector employers to expand access to treatment in the workplace. For middle-income countries with prevalence rates like South Africa, expanding access to treatment for HIV/AIDS is likely to require a mixture of public and private sector strategies.

3.3.1 The Cost of Treatment in a Middle Income Country: Mexico

In the first part of this chapter, we discussed the cost of treatment in a high-income country. In this section, we will discuss the changing cost of treatment in a middle-income country – Mexico. A study by Bautista et al. (2003) highlights the many issues that developing countries have to address in order to expand and maintain access to treatment for existing HIV/AIDS patients. There are three important features of the Mexican treatment program. First, Mexico switched to triple therapy very quickly after the appearance of this new treatment. Second, it did so by buying the drugs from the patent holders. Third, it made drugs available to all Mexican residents regardless of their affiliations to the patchwork of medical coverage. All of these features have a big impact on financing of the treatment of HIV/AIDS.

There are three subsystems in Mexico through which the government provides treatment for HIV/AIDS: (1) the Ministry of Health; (2) the Mexican Social Security Institutes – one for the private sector (IMSS), one for the public sector (ISSSTE) and one for the Armed Forces (ISSFAM); and (3) the National Institutes of Health. Mexico spends nearly 6% of GDP on healthcare, with an equal split between the private and the public sector. Compared with other countries with a similar level of development, the share of the private spending on healthcare is surprisingly large. The estimated prevalence of HIV/AIDS in Mexico is well below 1%.

Mexico started providing antiretroviral drugs (ARVs) through the public health care system in 1997. By 1999, 55% of people living with HIV/AIDS had regular access to ARVs. In theory, every part of the health care system should have access to ARVs. Official norms state that all patients have the right to prescribed treatment at any facility and in any subsystem. In practice, access to ARV treatment and care varies considerably across socioeconomic groups. In the beginning, the Ministry of Health services did not cover the cost of ARVs (although federal, state and local governments provided some coverage).

The change in the cost of providing different types of drugs in Mexico has been dramatic, as Table 3.4 shows. In 1997, almost 70% of all ARV costs were for double therapy. By 2001, over 88% were for triple therapy. Bautista et al. (2003) followed 1,062 randomly selected patients with sample stratification by system of coverage and rural/urban strata. The study selected only people over 18 whose HIV diagnosis was confirmed by Western, Elisa or laboratory culture or who had symptomatic AIDS during 2000–2001.

Table 3.4 Recurrent costs of ARVs in Mexico 1997–2001

	1997 (%)	1998 (%)	1999 (%)	2000 (%)	2001 (%)
Triple	26.50	51.40	69.30	88.70	88.10
Double	69.40	46.40	27.90	10.20	10.10
Mono	4.10	2.20	2.80	1.10	1.80

Source: Bautista et al. (2003)

Switching to triple ARV therapy (also known as highly active antiretroviral treatment or HAART) led to a dramatic rise in cost of treatment per patient, as Fig. 3.19 shows. Before the introduction of triple ARV therapy, the average cost of treatment was just under USD 1,000 per year. After the introduction of this treatment, the cost per patient shot up threefold. The most notable feature of Fig. 3.19 is that by far the largest component of treatment costs is for triple ARV therapy. As we saw in Chap. 2, the struggle by Brazil and Thailand to switch to generic drugs was precisely to avoid this kind of cost escalation. Of course, it is also important to keep in mind that the prevalence of HIV/AIDS in Mexico is not in the same league as Brazil or Thailand. Brazil's prevalence rate is twice that of Mexico and Thailand's rate is twice that of Brazil (https://www.cia.gov/library/ publications/the-world-factbook/fields/2155.html).

Average Annual per Patient Cost of Treatment

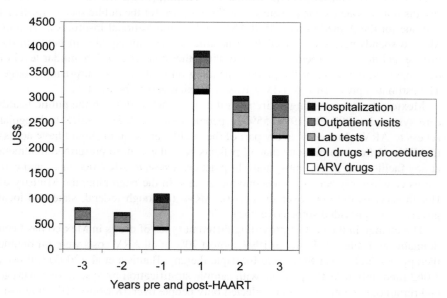

Fig. 3.19 Pre- and post- HAART cost of treatment in Mexico. *Source*: Bautista et al. (2003)

While both South Africa and Mexico are middle-income countries, there is a big difference in their HIV prevalence rates. This means that the Mexican approach would not be affordable in South Africa. While the Mexican public health insurance system could work in South Africa, the purchase of antiretroviral medication for South Africa would have to be funded by external sources (see Chaps. 7 and 8). In addition, South Africa would have to pursue the same strategy as Thailand and Brazil, by substituting generic equivalents for more expensive patented drugs (see Chap. 2). However, for middle-income countries with prevalence rates like South Africa, expanding access to treatment for HIV/AIDS is likely to require a mixture of public and private sector strategies. In the next section, we examine the example of insurance regulations in the United States, which affect the provision of insurance in the private sector.

3.3.2 Viatical Settlements: A Financial Byproduct of HIV/AIDS

If there is a sufficient proportion of people in the portfolio of an insurance company and if they can be tested cheaply, it is possible to set up a separate mortality table for that group. In the beginning, the tests were too expensive to be performed on every new potential policy holder even in developed countries. It has become cheaper to test for HIV over time. In the past decade, the cheapest method has been oral fluid testing. Oral fluid testing for HIV has been one of the major screening tools of life insurance underwriting since 1997 in the United States. The prevalence of HIV-positive individuals appears to have stabilized since 1995 in the United States. Nevertheless, testing continues to provide insurers with a low-cost, non-invasive and relatively accurate means of identifying HIV prevalence for correct risk classification. Most life and health insurance companies use the oral fluid method, which cost USD 18 in 2005.

In spite of the advent of a low-cost HIV testing method, the creation of a separate mortality table for HIV-positive individuals did not happen. In fact, regulatory bodies in many countries did not allow a separate table be used for individuals with HIV for selling life and other insurance policies. Instead, another method was developed to convert terminally ill patients' savings through life insurance into viatical settlements.

Viatical settlements give cash to terminally ill patients in exchange for their life insurance policies. Viatical settlement companies buy these life insurance policies from the patients. They then become the sole beneficiaries of the policies and pay the premiums until the patient dies. When the patient dies, the company collects the death benefits. The first such transactions arose in the context of HIV, allowing terminally ill patients, with previously illiquid assets in life insurance policies, to convert them into cash through immediate settlement. This process reduced the problem of payments of medical bills and prescription drugs for terminally ill patients.

Box 3.2 Oral fluid testing

Oral fluid testing (OFT) for HIV has been one of the major screening tools of life insurance underwriting since 1997 in the United States. Even though the prevalence of HIV-positive individuals has stabilized since 1995, testing continues to provide insurers with a low-cost, noninvasive and highly accurate means of identifying HIV prevalence for correct risk classification. Over 150 life and health insurers employ OFT in their underwriting schemes (Bergstrom 2005). An interesting question arises. At what face value of a life insurance policy should a company test for HIV? In 2005, each test cost USD 18. Suppose the prevalence rate is one in ten thousand. If everyone who buys a life insurance policy is tested for HIV, the company will incur a cost of USD 180,000 (18 × 10,000) to detect one HIV-positive person. Thus, unless the savings from testing that person (who might be denied coverage or charged a higher premium) is USD 180,000, the cost of testing is higher than the benefits generated. Of course, in reality, there are a number of factors have to be taken into account. First, the prevalence rate varies with age. Generally, HIV prevalence is relatively high for persons in their twenties. It gradually falls with age. Thus, we have to take into account this factor to find the proportion of people who will be HIV-positive. Second, some people who buy ten- or 20–year life coverage will not continue with their policies. Thus, we have to take into account the lapse rate of policies. Third, the announcement of testing for HIV will deter some people who know (or think) they are HIV-positive and they will drop out of the potential buyer pool, thus making the proportion of HIV-positive individuals smaller than the general population (the so-called sentinel effect). Fourth, to calculate the present value of benefits of testing we need a discount rate. For insurance companies, for long-term life insurance, it is common to use a discount rate of 7%. Bergstrom (2005) performs a series of calculations taking into account all the effects described above. Testing becomes surprisingly cost effective at a very low face value of life insurance policies. For example, if 1,000 policies are issued at age 42 for a face value of USD 25,000, it would generate savings in terms of present value of excess mortality of USD 81,250. Thus, deducting the testing costs of USD 18,000 for these 1,000 tests yields a net savings of USD 63,250 to the company. Thus, even for life insurance policies with a face value of USD 25,000 each, it is cost effective to test for HIV. He also shows that for life insurance policies with face a value of more than USD 100,000, the rate of return on testing is over 40% for individuals above age 40.

Recognizing the rights of terminally ill patients, in 1996 the US Congress passed the Health Insurance Portability and Accountability Act, which exempted the proceeds from viatical settlement transactions from federal income taxes. The viatical settlement industry grew from USD 500 million in the United States in 1995 to over a billion dollars in 1998. By 2005, the viatical market had transformed itself into a market for life settlements, which applies to all life insurance policies, not just those of terminally ill patients. The viatical market grew to USD 12 billion in the United States alone. Bernstein Research (2006) has forecast a viatical market of USD 150 billion by 2015.

There was one peculiar element of viatical settlements – they were not considered insurance products. Thus, viatical settlement companies are not bound by insurance regulations. Most viatical companies doing business in the United States do not fall within the regulatory jurisdiction of the United States, because they are not domiciled in the United States and they write the contracts outside of the United States. Usually, they operate through brokers, who act as intermediaries to make the deals possible. Most policies are in excess of one million dollars.

The National Association of Insurance Commissioners in the United States issued model legislation in 1994, to serve as a guideline for state regulators. The model legislation recommended that viatical settlement companies should be licensed by the Department of Insurance in each state. There should be provisions for a "cooling off " period of at least two weeks during which the seller can cancel a viatical settlement contract without penalty. The model legislation also stipulated that consumers must receive a minimum percentage of the face value of the life insurance policy. These minimum payments are based on the life expectancy of the consumer and the credit rating of the life insurance company that originally issued the policy. Table 3.5 below gives the minimum payment levels stipulated by the model regulation.

Table 3.5 Mandated minimum prices as a percentage of face value

Life expectancy	Minimum percentage of face value (%)
Less than 6 months	80
At least 6 but less than 12 months	70
At least 12 but less than 18 months	65
At least 18 but less than 24 months	60
Greater than 24 months	50

Source: National Association of Insurance Commissioners, 1997, Model Regulation for Viatical Settlements, Kansas City, Missouri. *Note*: The percentage maybe reduced by 5% for policies from insurers rated less than the top four categories of A.M. Best credit rating

California became the first state to implement viatical regulation. It was followed by Florida, Illinois, Indiana, Kansas, Louisiana, Minnesota, New York, North Carolina, North Dakota, Oregon, Texas, Vermont, Virginia, Washington and Wisconsin in quick succession. The rest of the states did not follow suit.

Sood (2003) provides data on demographics of the sellers of viatical settlements from Texas for the period 1995–1997 (see Table 3.6).

Table 3.6 Demographics at baseline and participation in the viatical market

Variables	Entire sample	Sold life insurance	Did not sell
Age	35 years	37 years	35 years
Male (%)	81	88	80
Have college degree (%)	26	33	26
Race			
White (%)	60	78	56
African-American (%)	24	16	26
Hispanic (%)	11	5	12
Other Races (%)	5	1	6
Monthly Income			
<$500 (%)	15	13	16
$501–$2,000 (%)	41	41	40
>$2,000 (%)	44	46	44
Liquid assets			
<$5,000 (%)	72	65	74
$5,001–$25,000 (%)	13	16	13
>$25,000 (%)	15	19	13
House ownership (%)	32	35	31
Non-liquid assets			
<$10,000 (%)	69	61	71
$10,001–$50,000 (%)	14	19	12
$50,001–$200,000 (%)	11	12	11
>$200,000 (%)	6	8	6
Disease Stage			
Asymptomatic (%)	9	9	9
Symptomatic (%)	51	38	54
AIDS (%)	40	53	37
CD4 T-cell levels			
<50 cells per ml (%)	12	15	11
50–200 cells per ml (%)	25	41	22
201–500 cells per ml (%)	42	32	44
>500 cells per ml (%)	21	13	23
Sample size	$N = 1,009$	$N = 165$	$N = 844$

Source: Sood (2003)

Analyzing the data, Sood (2003) concluded the following: "The existing price regulation in the viatical settlements market is binding for the relatively healthy consumers but has no effect on market outcomes for the relatively unhealthy consumers." Thus the regulatory scheme imposed by most states discriminates against the relatively healthy HIV population and rules out certain viatical settlements for this population trades that are otherwise appropriate.

This imposes a daunting prospect for HIV/AIDS patients with life insurance but limited liquidity. They would like to finance treatment by selling their life insurance in the early stages of infection – thereby forestalling progression to AIDS and eventual mortality – but regulatory restrictions require them to let their health deteriorate before they can find a buyer of their policy."

The case of insurance regulation in the United States provides an example for insurance companies in the private sector. However, unlike South Africa, the United States has a prevalence rate of below 1% and is a high-income country. Moreover, in South Africa there is no viatical market. Nevertheless, while South Africa is a middle-income country, it has the most developed insurance market in the world as a percentage of GDP. In this regard, South Africa is different from most developing countries. The foregoing discussion of the US viatical market demonstrates that a properly regulated viatical market, combined with insurance regulation that provides access to life insurance for HIV-positive individuals, is a mechanism to enhance private sector coverage of the cost of HIV treatment. In this regard, a viatical market serves as a complement to coverage under a public health care system. Given the level of development in the South African insurance market, the development of a viatical market is a viable option. Viatical markets represent one example of the broader category of financial instruments, known as securitization (see Box 3.3).

Box 3.3 Securitization

Securitization is a form of insurance applied to assets and liabilities. It is a way to make illiquid assets, such as a bank's mortgage and credit card portfolios, more liquid. Securitization can also work on the liability side, by allowing insurers to sell their liabilities in the market. For example, it is a mechanism that reinsurers can use to prevent themselves from losing money from catastrophic events (such as hurricanes, earthquakes and pandemics) by convincing other people (the investors) to risk their money instead.

In the early 1990s, catastrophic property risks were securitized in the capital market. This mechanism entails the creation of a special-purpose company. That company floats special bonds that are sold in the capital market. The characteristics of such bonds are as follows. If a certain trigger event happens, the bond does not pay interest. If some other specified trigger event happens, the bond does not pay the principal. For example, if it is a bond that covers earthquake risks in a specific area, the first trigger event may be an earthquake of a certain magnitude. The second trigger may be an earthquake of a bigger magnitude. If the frequency and severity of earthquakes are known from past data, risk pricing is done just as it is with other insurance products. However, the advantage of securitization is that we need not know the actual extent of the damage caused by the earthquakes. The payments are made simply on the basis of the magnitude of the earthquake, without having to verify the extent of the damage caused.

Mortality securitization has the same basic structure that is used in catastrophic risk securitization. A reinsurer (or in some cases an insurer) forms a special-purpose company. Initially, the reinsurer pays the insurance premiums. The investors buy bonds of two kinds: collateral bonds and default-free bonds. Later, the income from the bonds, either in coupons or in redemptions, is used to fund obligations to the reinsurer and investors. In some years there will be benefits paid to the reinsurer, and in some years there will be benefits paid to the investors, in the form of bond coupons or maturity values. The program is set up so that the cash flows from the bond portfolio always match the benefits to the reinsurer and the benefits to the investors. In a somewhat different context, the structure is very similar to a currency swap.

The first such mortality securitization was executed by Swiss Re in December 2003. It was a 4-year mortality bond that matured in January 2007. Swiss Re guaranteed the payment of the coupons. The interest rate on the bond was priced at 1.35% over the London InterBank Offered Rate (LIBOR).

The mortality rate was based on the weighted average mortality from all causes of the United States (70%), the United Kingdom (15%), France (7.5%), Italy (5%) and Switzerland (2.5%). The weights were chosen according to the exposure that Swiss Re had in each of these countries. There was an option to reduce repayment on the bond if mortality exceeded 130% of the 2002 weighted average mortality rate. The payment of the principal was to be reduced 5% for every 0.01 increase in mortality over the threshold until it reached a peak of 150%. Vita Capital (called Vita I) was the special-purpose company. Had something gone wrong and the index had moved in such a way that the mortality rates were higher than those stipulated, the bond investors were at risk, since they would have lost a portion of their maturity value.

Why did Swiss Re enter into such a deal? Discussions with some of the negotiators revealed several reasons. First, Swiss Re wanted to get investors comfortable with the idea of this type of investment vehicle. Second, the securitization could be a private transaction that did not have to go through any regulatory body in order to be executed. Third, this was a hedge against an epidemic over the next 4 years. The securitization was structured so that, had there been an epidemic, like the 1918 influenza epidemic, Swiss Re would not have had to pay the bond holders the principal, just the interest. The securitization worked as follows. The investors paid Swiss Re for the bonds. The UK government, in order to hedge against the risk of an influenza pandemic, then received that money via Swiss Re. The UK government paid the interest on the bonds to the investors, which was guaranteed. Since such an event did not take place, Swiss Re had to pay back the capital to the investors and the UK government had to pay back the capital to Swiss Re. Thus, the securitization provided a way to insure against the risk of a pandemic, a risk that would not have been marketable otherwise.

A simulation by Swiss Re showed that the only event since 1906 that would have triggered the bond and excused the UK government from repaying the capital would have been the 1918 influenza epidemic. It would not have been triggered by the deaths during the two World Wars, by deaths during the worst years of AIDS mortality in these countries or by deaths caused by the influenza epidemic of 1956.

Clearly, such instruments have relevance for any future unexpected events that affect mortality. After the success of the launch of Vita I, Swiss Re launched a more ambitious and more complex mortality bond in 2005 called Vita II and another in 2006 called Vita III. This success has attracted other companies to the field. Since Swiss Re is making money on this new type of financial instrument, other companies are issuing mortality securitization bonds too. In 2006, Scottish Re launched Tartan and AXA launched Osiris.

Mortality securitization can also be used by insurance companies, not just governments, in order to insure against the risk of the losses that would be caused by an influenza pandemic. The loss of life and the health care costs from such a pandemic could be catastrophic for life and health insurance companies. In this way, securitization can be used to insure otherwise unmarketable risks and thereby reduce the financial risks of insurance companies. It is also a way to expand life and health insurance coverage to the risk of a serious, fast-moving pandemic. However, securitization only works where there is a low probability of such a high-loss event occurring. For this reason, it is unlikely to work in the case of HIV/AIDS, since this is no longer a low probability event.

In the case of the South African epidemic, tackling HIV/AIDS will require a variety of policy responses. Therefore, in the next section we also consider the incentives for private sector employers to expand access to treatment and prevention programs in the workplace.

3.3.3 Economic Incentives for Companies to Pay for Prevention and Treatment

As we saw in Chap. 2, sub-Saharan Africa has the highest rates of HIV infection in the world. In several countries in the region, the prevalence rate exceeds 15%. We have also seen that the disease disproportionately affects sexually active people in the most productive years of their working life. That means that their employers are affected too. When employees have HIV/AIDS, productivity falls, absenteeism rises and health care costs increase. The economic impact of HIV/AIDS has the same effect as a tax on the business.

There are several components of HIV/AIDS-related expenditures where a significant proportion of workers suffer from HIV/AIDS. Table 3.7 provides an example of expenditures for two companies in Côte d'Ivoire, broken down by various categories. The first important feature of the table is that the costs are not the same across all companies. For example, for company 1, the medical care component accounts for 25.2% of HIV/AIDS-related expenditures. For company 2, this component is 13.0%. The cost of sick leave is 9.3% for company 1 whereas it is 18.2%

for company 2. Similarly, the cost of lost productivity and reorganization is 13.3% for company 1 and 20.5% of total for company 2. Therefore, it is all but impossible to generalize the size of each component for all companies. It depends on the type of company (for example, whether the company is in an agribusiness, a mining business or a service industry).

Table 3.7 Breakdown of costs of HIV/AIDS for two companies in Côte d'Ivoire

Cost item	Company 1 (%)	Company 2 (%)
Medical care	25.2	13.0
Prevention	1.0	1.2
HIV screening	0.6	–
Wage bill for medical personnel	5.2	12.5
Increased health insurance costs	5.0	–
Disability pensions	23.7	–
Sick leave	9.3	18.2
Attendance at funerals	3.1	3.3
Dismissals and severance pay	–	1.1
Recruitment and training	–	5.2
Lost productivity and reorganization	13.3	25.0
Funeral costs	13.5	20.5
Total HIV/AIDS-related costs	100.0	100.0
Total as percentage of wage bill	1.3	0.8
HIV incidence among company employees	1.9	1.1

Source: Aventin and Huard (2000)

A study by Simon (2005) illustrates how productivity is affected by the presence of HIV/AIDS among workers in a study of tea estates owned by a large agribusiness in the Kericho District in the highlands of western Kenya. The company has around 10,000 tea pluckers (79% male), who are paid by the number of kilograms of tealeaf plucked. Thus, the company has detailed records for each worker and their productivity. There is free on-site medical care for all workers and their dependents. Workers get paid sick leave. For a number of years, the company's medical facilities had been treating opportunistic infections and providing palliative care for employees with AIDS. At the time, they did not have antiretroviral drugs. Thus, the situation provided ideal conditions for estimating the productivity differential for workers who were and who were not infected with HIV/AIDS.

Two groups were separated. The first group (called HIV Cases), are tea pluckers who died at company health facilities of AIDS-related causes. Data were collected for this group using their past record of tea plucking. The second group (called Controls), are pluckers who were working in the same fields over the same time period as the first group and did not present any symptoms. There were approximately four times as many workers in the Controls group as in the HIV Cases

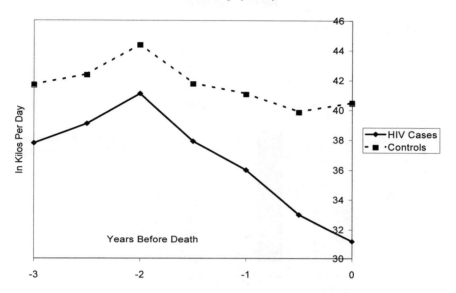

Fig. 3.20 Productivity decline due to the onset of AIDS. *Source*: Simon (2005)

group. In Fig. 3.20, we show the amount of leaves plucked by each group before their death. The differential becomes clear at least 3 years before the death of the workers. The differential widens until productivity differs by more than 20%. Thus, HIV/AIDS substantially reduces the productivity of the workers.

The foregoing example clearly demonstrates that having HIV/AIDS-infected employees affects the productivity of workers substantially. This raises an important issue. Is it cost effective for companies to provide treatment for the workers from a purely financial point of view? An analysis by Sabin (2003) demonstrates that the answer is affirmative under certain reasonable assumptions. The study examines a particular company and divides all the employees into three categories: unskilled worker; skilled worker; and manager. Then it assumes that treatment is provided 8 years after HIV infection. It assumes that drug therapy increases the working life of the workers by 5 years. It assumes that there are no associated morbidity effects. All of these are extremely conservative assumptions. The study then calculates the net benefits over time from treatment, assuming two sets of prices for the treatment. One is a low-cost scenario, in which the drugs for treatment cost USD 500 a year, and the other is a high-cost scenario, in which the drugs for treatment cost USD 1,000 a year. In Chap. 5, we show that under certain circumstances, it is entirely feasible to have treatment regimes whose costs are in the range considered here (see Fig. 5.1, showing how drug costs have come down

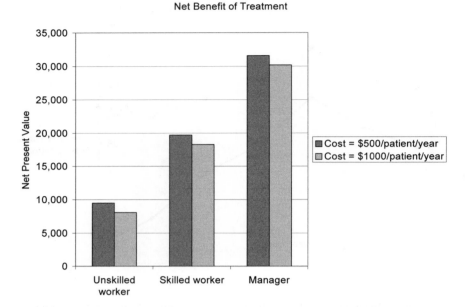

Fig. 3.21 Net present value of treatment under two scenarios. *Source*: Sabin (2003)

over time). The study shows that, with an annual discount rate of 10%, the net present value for each scenario for each class of employee is positive and large. As one would expect, the gains are larger for employees with more skills. These results are demonstrated in Fig. 3.21.

Do prevention programs work for companies from a purely financial point of view? Once again, the Sabin (2003) study demonstrates that the answer is affirmative. To estimate the net benefit of a prevention program, the study compared the cost of providing a prevention program to the entire workforce with the net benefits of such a program. It is difficult to estimate the cost of a prevention program. Thus the study assumed two scenarios – a low-cost program of USD 5 per employee per year and a high-cost program of USD 10 per employee per year. On the benefit side, the study assumed that infections in the year of the prevention program would be cut by 50%. This number was based on discussions with industry leaders in South Africa. The results are shown in Fig. 3.22. It clearly shows that prevention programs also benefit the company. The net benefit is positive and large under both scenarios.

How do companies deal with HIV/AIDS in the workplace in Africa? Very few large-scale studies have been conducted to find out the general practice of businesses in Africa (Bloom et al., 2002). One study by Ramachandran et al. (2006) examines manager and worker perceptions of HIV/AIDS, and how firms in the private sector respond to HIV/AIDS through various measures. Using a survey

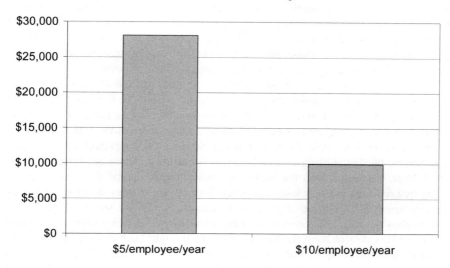

Fig. 3.22 Benefits for a company of prevention program under two scenarios. *Source*: Sabin (2003)

sample of 860 firms and 4,955 workers from Uganda, Kenya and Tanzania, the study shows that 32% of firms engage in HIV/AIDS prevention activity. The percentage of firms conducting pre-employment health checks in their samples ranges from 20% in Uganda to over 50% in Tanzania. This is somewhat surprising, given that HIV/AIDS prevalence is lower in Tanzania.

The analysis shows that larger firms and firms with higher skilled or better-trained workforces tend to do more to prevent HIV/AIDS. These firms are also more likely to conduct pre-employment health checks to screen out sicker applicants. Firms where a majority of workers are unionized are also more likely to carry out AIDS prevention activities and pre-employment health checks. Managers with concerns about absenteeism are more likely to carry out AIDS prevention activities. The study found that, if it is costly to replace workers, firms attempt to mitigate this cost by engaging in prevention activities or by screening new applicants. The study also found that 75% of workers are willing to pay to be tested for HIV. The study also showed that increasing the incentives for large firms not yet engaged in prevention would significantly increase the coverage of workers with respect to AIDS prevention activities.

3.3.4 Business Strategies in High Prevalence Countries

There are three possible HIV/AIDS strategies for a business operating in high prevalence countries.

The first option is for business leaders to stick to the status quo, and do nothing. This may seem like a costless option, but it is not. First, without any action, HIV/AIDS prevalence will continue to rise. Thus, it will become a bigger problem in the future. Second, it is always costly to replace a valuable worker. Therefore, doing nothing is costly. Third, investing in prevention and treatment now can actually translate into a positive financial outcome for the company.

The second option is for business leaders to attempt to shift the burden from their own companies to governments or individuals. They can fire individuals with HIV/AIDS. However, this option may not be possible, due to human rights legislation (see Chap. 9). Even if they can legally dismiss individuals with HIV/AIDS, it may be expensive, again due to legislation. Simon (2005) reported that, in Southern Africa, burden shifting is a widespread occurrence. There are three methods used. First, companies shift the burden by greater use of capital to invest in equipment that replaces workers with machines. Second, companies shift the burden by simply firing HIV-positive employees. However, as we will see in Chap. 9, discrimination against HIV-positive employees is illegal in many countries. While most workers do not have the financial means to fight such discrimination, their cause is often taken up by human rights or AIDS organizations. Third, companies replace full-time workers by contract workers. This circumvents the problem of carrying the burden of HIV-positive workers.

The third option is for business leaders to invest in fighting the epidemic. This would entail taking proactive measures within the workplace to help prevent the epidemic from spreading and to mitigate its negative impact on workers. In Chap. 7, we discuss how this option is being pursued worldwide by the Global Business Coalition on HIV/AIDS, which has 220 member companies, headquartered in 30 countries, employing over 11 million people in more than 200 countries.

A comprehensive study by Rosen et al. (2007) of a range of companies from South Africa, Uganda, Kenya, Zambia, Ethiopia and Rwanda produced the following results. (1) HIV prevalence ranged from 5 to 37% of the workforce. (2) The average cost per employee lost to AIDS varied from 0.5 to 5.6 times the average annual compensation of the employee affected. (3) Labor cost increases were estimated at 0.6–10.8%. Antiretroviral treatment at a cost of USD 360/patient per year was found to have positive financial returns for most companies. (4) Managers of small and medium-sized enterprises (SME) reported low AIDS-related employee attrition, little concern about the impact of AIDS and relatively little interest in taking action. (5) AIDS was estimated to increase the average operating costs of SMEs by less than 1%.

The impact of HIV/AIDS affects a company through various channels (see Fig. 3.23). Internally, there are direct and indirect costs for the company. Direct costs include medical costs, which in turn include health care insurance, disability insurance and life insurance. In addition, when workers leave permanently due to illness or death, there is an additional cost of recruiting and training new workers. There are a series of hard-to-measure indirect costs that come from productivity loss, increased absenteeism and additional time spent on managing the disease inside the company. In addition to internal costs to the company, there are external costs – the disease can affect the product demand through various channels as well as the supply chain to the company.

Some industries, by the very nature of their work, are vulnerable to employee infection with HIV/AIDS. Such is the case for hospitals. Cases of health care staff refusing to attend patients with HIV/AIDS still happen (as we will see in the example from Philadelphia in Chap. 9). In developing countries, it is far worse. Most hospitals (at least in theory) have risk management procedures in place to manage the risk of contamination through patients coming in with wounds or patients who undergo surgery. This applies not just to HIV/AIDS; it applies to all other diseases that can be transmitted by coming in contact with the blood of a patient. In addition, there is a reverse problem too. HIV-positive doctors and nurses can infect patients. There was a famous case of a Florida dentist who had infected at least five patients during invasive surgery (Morbidity and Mortality Weekly Report 1991).

The porn industry is another example where, by the very nature of the work of the actors and actresses, there is high risk of spreading HIV/AIDS. Thus, protection is essential in the industry to save lives. Here, the American industry has

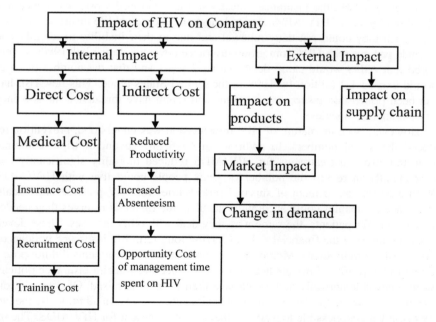

Fig. 3.23 Impact of HIV/AIDS on a company. *Source*: Elaborated from Vijayasekar Kalava-konda, Managing HIV/AIDS Risks, World Bank, Capital and Risk Management Unit, Financial Operations and Policy Department, June 2005

taken a completely different route compared with other countries that produce a substantial number of porn movies. Following a series of high-profile infections and deaths of porn stars (most notably the death of John Holmes), the American porn industry adopted frequent testing of all actors and actresses. Over 90% of American porn actors and actresses perform without condoms. At present, there is a centralized depository of all the test results so that they can be viewed at one location. Over the period of 1995–2005, only a handful of porn actors and actresses contracted HIV/AIDS. For an industry with 1,500 regulars, it is a remarkable result. In Europe and elsewhere (most notably in Brazil), more than 90% of on-screen sex acts are performed with condoms. Because of the lack of centralized data, HIV/AIDS infection rate among porn actors and actresses is not known. The difference can also create an entry point for the disease in the industry. There was a well-publicized case of Darren James, an American porn actor, who performed sex acts in several movies in Brazil and then infected a number of American actresses upon return, after he performed without condoms in Brazil.

3.4 Implications for Other Global Diseases

In the early 1980s, the insurance industry in the developed world was concerned about the impact of HIV/AIDS, due to long-term, individual life insurance policies for which they could not deny renewal and due to their inability to identify and exclude persons with HIV from group insurance coverage. In the late 1980s, it appeared that AIDS would cause death within 2 years and that the number of cases would exceed 1.2 million by 1998 in the United States alone. This new risk had not been priced into insurance premiums and might have threatened the solvency of insurance companies.

However, once the nature of HIV transmission was understood, prevention reduced the actual numbers. In addition, in 1996, the advent of triple combination antiretroviral treatments for HIV/AIDS reduced mortality significantly and dramatically increased the number of years people could live with HIV/AIDS. With a correct assessment of survival probabilities for HIV-positive individuals, insurance companies could accurately calculate the financial reserves they needed to set aside for patients, the same way they deal with other diseases. These developments lowered the financial risks of having long-term life insurance policies on HIV-positive individuals. Moreover, the cost of the new treatments did not pose a threat to the profits of private health insurers, since most health insurance policies were renewable annually and could have their premiums raised. Of course, it did mean an additional burden for national health care systems. In addition, by the late 1990s, it became possible to estimate the cost of treatment for HIV/AIDS. The result is that the insurance risks associated with HIV/AIDS are now similar to those for diabetes and can be priced accordingly.

The situation is very different in developing countries with high prevalence rates and in which HIV/AIDS has expanded to the general population, health care infrastructure is inadequate and mechanisms for estimating prevalence are less developed. The accuracy of HIV/AIDS estimates is important, both for governments involved in assessing the scale of prevention and treatment needs and for the private sector, particularly the insurance industry. The correct pricing of insurance products requires an accurate assessment of the frequency and severity of risks. While the Mexican public health insurance system could work in South Africa, the purchase of antiretroviral medication for South Africa would have to be funded by external sources. In addition, South Africa would have to pursue the same strategy as Thailand and Brazil, by substituting generic equivalents for more expensive patented drugs. However, for middle-income countries with prevalence rates like South Africa, expanding access to treatment for HIV/AIDS is likely to require a mixture of public and private sector strategies.

A properly regulated viatical market, combined with insurance regulation that provides access to life insurance for HIV-positive individuals, provides a mechanism to enhance private sector coverage of the cost of HIV treatment. While South Africa is a middle-income country, it has the most developed insurance market in the world as a percentage of gross domestic product. In this regard, South Africa is different from most developing countries. Given the level of development in the South African insurance market, the development of a viatical market is a viable option for South Africa.

Viatical markets represent one example of the broader category of financial instruments, known as securitization. Securitization of mortality is a new financial mechanism that can be used to hedge against the risk of a fast-moving epidemic, such as influenza. The loss of life and health care costs of such a pandemic could be catastrophic for life and health insurance companies. Securitization can be used to insure otherwise unmarketable risks and thereby reduce the financial risks of insurance companies. It is also a way to expand life and health insurance coverage to the risk of a serious, fast-moving pandemic.

References

Auvert B, Taljaard D, Lagarde E, Sobngwi-Tambekou J, Sitta R, Puren A (2005) Randomized, controlled intervention trial of male circumcision for reduction of HIV infection risk: the ANRS 1265 trial. PLoS Medicine 2:298

Aventin L, Huard P (2000) The cost of AIDS to three manufacturing firms in Côte d'Ivoire. Journal of African Economics 9:161–188

Bailey RC (2007) Male Circumcision: The Road from Evidence to Practice. Division of Epidemiology, School of Public Health, University of Illinois at Chicago

Bautista S, Dmytraczenko T, Kombe G, Bertozzi S (2003) Antiretroviral Treat-ment Costs in Mexico. WHO/UNAIDS Workshop on Strategic Information for Anti-Retroviral Therapy Programmes, 2 July 2003

Bernstein Research (2005) Life settlements need not be unsettling, July 20, New York

Bergstrom R (2005) The protection value of oral fluid testing. On the Risk 21:63–64

Bloom DE, Mahal A, and River Path Associates (2002) HIV/AIDS and the Private Sector – A Literature Review. American Foundation for AIDS: Washington, DC

Daykin C, Eves M, Clark P, Haberman S et al. (1988) The Impact of HIV Infection and AIDS on Insurance in the United Kingdom. Journal of the Institute of Actuaries 115: 727–837

Doll DC (1997) AIDS Death Claims on Ordinary Life Insurance. Product Development News, Society of Actuaries, May 1997, pp. 4

Hellinger FJ, Fleishman JA (2000) Estimating the national cost of treating people with HIV disease: patient, payer, and provider data. Journal of Acquired Immune Deficiency Syndromes 24:182–188

Keir D (2001) HIV/AIDS in South Africa. Life Convention, 18–20 November 2001, Birmingham Hilton Metropole, UK

Keisera O, Taffe P, Zwahlen M, Battegay M, Bernasconi E, Weber R, Rickenbach M (2004) All cause mortality in the Swiss HIV cohort study from 1990 to 2001 in comparison with the Swiss population. AIDS 18:1835–1843

Medical News Today (2007) Washington, D.C., Releases New Data On HIV/AIDS. http://www.medicalnewstoday.com/articles/89856.php. Accessed 27 November 2007

Montaner JS, Reiss P, Cooper D, Vella S, Harris M, Conway B, Wainberg MA, Smith D, Robinson P, Hall D, Myers M, Lange JM (1998) A randomized, double-blind trial comparing combinations of nevirapine, didanosine, and zidovudine for HIV-infected patients: the INCAS Trial. Italy, The Netherlands, Canada and Australia Study. JAMA 279:930–937

Morbidity and Mortality Weekly Report (1991) Update: transmission of HIV infection during an invasive dental procedure – Florida. 18 January 1991

Ramachandran V, Shah MK, Turner G (2006) Does the Private Sector Care About AIDS? Evidence from Investment Climate Surveys in East Africa. Working Paper, Georgetown University, Washington

Ramaroson M (2003) The Human Right of HIV Positive Persons to Non-discrimination in Getting Life Insurance in South Africa. LL.M. Thesis, University of Pretoria

Rice BD, Bätzing-Feigenbaum J, Hosegood V, Tanser F, Hill C, Barnighausen T, Herbst K, Welz T, Newell ML (2007) Population and antenatal-based HIV prevalence estimates in a high contracepting female population in rural South Africa. BMC Public Health 7:160–176

Rosen S, Feeley F, Connelly P, Simon J (2007) The private sector and HIV/AIDS in Africa: taking stock of 6 years of applied research. AIDS 21:S41–S51

Sabin L (2003) Corporate Responsibility in a World of AIDS: The Economic Case for Investing Now. Center for International Health and Development, Boston University School of Public Health, Boston

Simon J (2005) HIV/AIDS and its Impacts on African Labor Markets. Center for International Health and Development, Boston University School of Public Health, Boston

Sood, N (2003) Cashing Out Life Insurance: An Analysis of the Viatical Settlements Market, the RAND Graduate School Dissertation, Santa Monica, California

Wilson D (2007) The Evolving HIV Epidemic: What Have We Learned Since the MAP Began? World Bank, Washington

Yazdanpanah Y, Sissoko D, Egger M, Mouton Y, Zwahlen M, Chêne G (2004) Clinical efficacy of antiretroviral combination therapy based on protease inhibitors or non-nucleoside analogue reverse transcriptase inhibitors: indirect comparison of controlled trials. British Medical Journal 328:249

Zaheer K (2007) HIV cases highly overestimated, survey shows. Reuters, 6 July 2007

Zwahlen M, Egger M (2006) Progression and mortality of untreated HIV-positive individuals living in resource-limited settings: Update of literature review and evidence synthesis. UNAIDS, Obligation HQ/05/422204

4 The Economics of HIV/AIDS

"A reliable AIDS vaccine would be a public good and so would be subsidizing the use of condoms, through sex education and through making condoms readily available at zero price."

Tomas J. Philipson and Richard A. Posner (1992) In: The Optimal Regulation of AIDS

Economics is inextricably linked with HIV/AIDS. Economic conditions affect HIV/AIDS and, in turn, HIV/AIDS affects an economy at both the macro and micro levels. Thus, the link works in both directions. In this chapter, we examine the relationships between HIV/AIDS and poverty, inequality and social capital, and consider whether economic differences between countries explain differences in HIV prevalence. As we have noted in Chap. 3, HIV/AIDS disproportionately affects people of working age. In this chapter, we examine the potential economic impact of HIV/AIDS, using a macroeconomic model. This is followed by a review of microeconomic and epidemiological models that try to answer questions about the behavioral response of people who are either at risk of or actually living with HIV/AIDS. Such studies provide a useful mechanism for determining the effectiveness of HIV/AIDS prevention strategies (a topic we explore further in Chap. 9). Economics plays a significant role in the propagation of HIV/AIDS in high incidence countries. The economics of HIV/AIDS also shows us the likely economic returns on different strategies to prevent HIV infections.

4.1 Sexually Transmitted Infections and HIV/AIDS

The link between economic conditions (as measured by per capita income) and HIV/AIDS is very different from common sexually transmitted diseases (although HIV/AIDS is not exclusively a sexually transmitted disease, it is largely so). In Table 4.1, we show the correlation between per capita income in each state in the United States (excluding Washington DC) and HIV/AIDS, Chlamydia, Gonorrhea and Syphilis. It turns out that HIV/AIDS is strongly linked to gonorrhea and syphilis but not with chlamydia (Bleakley 2003). Income per capita, however, is not directly correlated with any of these diseases (Bleakley and Lange, 2005).

To see the importance of the correlations between HIV/AIDS and other sexually transmitted infections, we discuss a pioneering study by Oster (2005). She concentrated on two facts. (1) There is little difference between the sexual behavior of Americans and sub-Saharan Africans. (2) The transmission rate of HIV from men to women is three times as high in sub-Saharan Africa as it is in the United States. She builds a model that uses sexual behavior as an input, along with transmission of HIV as another input, which produces HIV prevalence as an output. Her model produces results that match the actual outcomes in terms of HIV prevalence in the United States and sub-Saharan Africa.

Table 4.1 Correlation between per capita income and HIV/AIDS, chlamydia, gonorrhea and syphilis by state, United States, 2003

	Chlamydia	Gonorrhea	HIV/AIDS	Syphilis	Income
Chlamydia	1.00	0.67[a]	0.29	0.41[a]	−0.16
Gonorrhea		1.00	0.53[a]	0.58[a]	−0.16
HIV/AIDS			1.00	0.70[a]	0.36[a]
Syphilis				1.00	0.04
Income					1.00

Source: Own calculations. Significant at 1% level of significance

What is the cause of the substantial difference in the transmission rates between the United States and sub-Saharan Africa? Oster argues that it comes from other untreated sexually transmitted infections. Untreated, open sores from chlamydia, syphilis and gonorrhea are the main reasons for the vast difference in HIV transmission. Her results indicate that treating bacterial sexually transmitted infections could prevent as many as 24% of new infections over a decade, at a cost of less than USD 80 per infection. This has clear policy implications for HIV/AIDS. The most cost effective way to deal with HIV/AIDS may not lie in tackling HIV/AIDS directly. It may lie in the treatment of other sexually transmitted infections.

4.2 Social Capital and HIV/AIDS

There are three different types of capital: (1) human; (2) physical; and (3) social. We would expect human and physical capital to have strong relationships with HIV/AIDS (Cohen, 1998 and 2002). Human capital gets eroded due to HIV/AIDS because HIV/AIDS affects disproportionately people at a productive age. However, we never directly observe human capital. We use different proxies to measure it. Per capita income (or the level of schooling) is sometimes used as a proxy (Papageorgiou and Stoyetcheva, 2004). Table 4.1 shows that, at least with state level data in the United States, per capita income is not related to any of the sexually transmitted diseases.

Given that per capita income is not related to HIV/AIDS, researchers have investigated whether other types of capital are related to HIV/AIDS. Holtgrave and Crosby (2003) found that social capital is indeed strongly related to the prevalence of HIV/AIDS across the states in the United States (see Table 4.2).

The idea of social capital has been around for quite some time. Robert D. Putnam has pioneered quantitative measures to capture social capital. Putnam (2000) produced a composite index to measure it over time. He explained that " ....the core idea of social capital theory is that social networks have value". The central factors include trust, reciprocity and cooperation among members of a social network that aims to achieve common goals. Muntaner and Lynch (2002) discuss Putnam's use of the term social capital. Since sexually transmitted diseases result from social interactions, any relation between social capital and such diseases are of interest. It is important to note that social capital is different from human capital as well as physical capital.

Table 4.2 shows that, for a developed country, poverty is not correlated with HIV, gonorrhea or syphilis. Income inequality, on the other hand, is correlated with HIV. However, social capital is strongly correlated with all four diseases.

Table 4.2 Correlation between poverty, social capital, income inequality and HIV/AIDS, Chlamydia, Gonorrhea and Syphilis

	Gonorrhea	Syphilis	Chlamydia	HIV/AIDS
Poverty	0.204	0.232	0.358[a]	0.099
Social capital	−0.671[a]	−0.591[a]	−0.532[a]	−0.498[a]
Income inequality	0.203	0.133	0.395[a]	0.469[a]

Source: Holtgrave and Crosby (2003). Significant at 1% level of significance

4.3 Relationships Between HIV/AIDS and Poverty, Inequality and Social Capital Using Global Data

David (2007) undertook a more ambitious study of the relationship between HIV/AIDS and social capital, at the international level. Using data from 80 countries around the world, and using the World Value Survey at the national level for each country as a proxy for social capital, he finds that, under most specifications, HIV/AIDS is related to social capital. His interpretation of the data was to claim that HIV/AIDS causes a decline in social capital at the national level. However, given that his data is cross-sectional, there is no way of proving the causality he claims. We can just as easily envision a decline of social capital leading to an increase in HIV/AIDS.

There is a significant negative correlation between social capital and income inequality, on the one hand, and HIV/AIDS, on the other hand. However, it is not clear what policy prescription should flow from these findings. Changing income inequality in a country is not a simple matter. It involves social engineering on a large scale. A policy of reducing income inequality by taxation and redistribution of wealth can backfire because it can negatively affect individual incentives. Policies to increase social capital are even less obvious.

Using data from over 110 countries, we can also see the relationship between poverty and HIV prevalence. Figure 4.1 shows a strongly positive relationship between HIV prevalence and poverty, as measured by the proportion of the population living under USD 2 per day. This association does not mean that HIV/AIDS is the root cause of poverty, nor vice versa. For example, poverty and education go hand

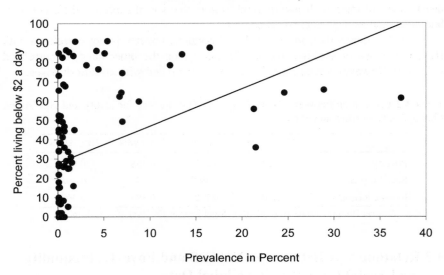

Fig. 4.1 HIV prevalence and absolute poverty. *Source*: Own calculations

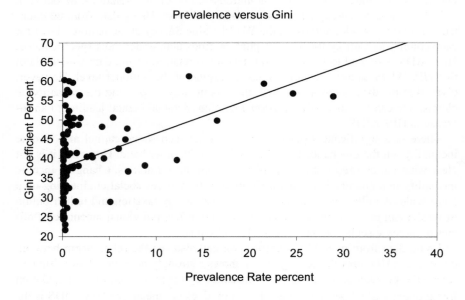

Fig. 4.2 Prevalence of HIV/AIDS and relative income inequality. *Source*: Own calculations

in hand. Thus, a high incidence of absolute poverty might cause a high incidence of HIV/AIDS. To put it differently, it is impossible to tell whether absolute poverty causes HIV/AIDS or vice versa – or whether another variable, such as war, inadequate health or poor education, explains the relationship.

We can also see the relationship between (relative) income inequality, as measured by the Gini coefficient, and the prevalence of HIV/AIDS, using data from over 110 countries. Figure 4.2 shows that higher inequality is associated with higher prevalence of HIV/AIDS. Once again, such an association cannot be interpreted as evidence of causality.

Bloom and Mahal (2001) have also noted relationships between poverty and income inequality and the prevalence of HIV/AIDS. However, in terms of policy implications, such studies do not offer much in the way of concrete proposals. Poverty reduction is too broad a goal to constitute what might be termed an HIV/AIDS prevention strategy. Moreover, there is no clear evidence that reducing poverty and income inequality will necessarily reduce HIV/AIDS prevalence. In Chap. 9 we examine HIV/AIDS prevention strategies in greater detail.

4.4 The Economic Impact of HIV/AIDS in a Macroeconomic Growth Model

The economic impact of HIV/AIDS takes place over many years and many generations. Therefore, the long-term economic impact of HIV/AIDS is very different from the short-term impact. Moreover, in any given economy, there are many evolving variables affecting the economy at the same time. Therefore, we use economic modeling to isolate the economic effect of one variable (HIV/AIDS).

We first use a standard one-sector macroeconomic model as a framework for exploring the macroeconomic impact of HIV/AIDS. The total output (Y) is a function of capital (K) and labor (L): $Y = F(K, L)$. Y is assumed to be an increasing function in both K and L. In addition, we make a distinction between labor (or workforce) (L) and the population (N). Thus, we can express the production function in per capita terms as $Y/N = F(K, L)/N$. Under the assumption that F is a homogeneous function of degree one, we can write the equation as $Y/N = F(K/N, L/N)$. Growth theory tells us that output per capita (Y/N) will rise or fall depending on capital per capita (K/L) and labor per capita or the labor participation rate (L/N). Economic growth comes from three different sources in this model: (1) a higher labor participation rate (rising L/N); (2) a higher capital labor ratio (K/N); and (3) technology (that causes the function F to shift upwards).

In theory, rising HIV/AIDS prevalence could cause the labor participation rate (L/N) to rise, to fall or to remain the same. Rising rates of HIV/AIDS would reduce the supply of labor (L). It would also reduce the population (N). If HIV/AIDS were to reduce the supply of labor and the population to the same degree, then labor per capita would remain the same. However, HIV/AIDS strikes the population at a productive age. If HIV/AIDS reduces the labor force (L) more than the entire population (N), then the labor participation rate (L/N) would fall. However, a decline in the supply of labor would lead to a rise in capital per labor unit (K/L) in the short run. Thus, in the short run, the total impact of HIV/AIDS is ambiguous in this model. However, in the long run, the supply of capital (K) may fall if rising HIV/AIDS leads to less saving and investment.

Empirical evidence on the loss of labor force due to HIV/AIDS is very clear in sub-Saharan African countries, as Table 4.3 shows. Over the next several decades, there could be a massive decline in the labor force in these countries. Such spectacular falls in the labor force have not been seen anywhere in the world since the Black Death in Europe during 1348–1350, when some 30–50% of the population died due to bubonic and pneumonic plague.

Table 4.3 Percentage of labor force lost due to HIV/AIDS

Year	Botswana	Lesotho	Malawi	Moz	SA	Namibia	Tanz	Zimb
2005	−17.2	−4.8	−10.6	−9.0	−12.8	−10.8	−9.1	−19.7
2020	−30.6	−10.6	−16.0	−24.9	−35.1	−24.9	−14.6	−29.4

Source: Husain and Badcock-Walters (2002). Notes: Moz Mozambique; SA South Africa; Tanz Tanzania; Zimb Zimbabwe

In conclusion, a classical model of economic growth does not give us any definite conclusion about the macroeconomic impact of HIV/AIDS. The impact depends critically on the specification of the model based on facts. Unfortunately, most facts are not unambiguous. They also vary between countries.

4.5 Macroeconomic Models: HIV/AIDS and Economic Growth

The literature on HIV/AIDS and economic growth provides a mixed picture. A large number of studies show a negative effect of HIV/AIDS on long run economic growth: Over (1992); Bonnel (2000); Bell et al. (2004); and Corrigan, Glomm, and Mendez (2005). However, in one of the first direct macroeconomic studies, Bloom and Mahal (1997) found that there is no relationship between HIV and economic growth in the long run. Werker et al. (2006) reaffirmed this result with the additional use of the variable of circumcision across countries (Poulin and Muula, 2007). In addition, two studies by Young (2005, 2006) show that HIV/AIDS actually will have a positive impact on the welfare of the surviving population over the next 100 years. We will discuss some of these studies in detail.

4.5.1 The Impact of HIV/AIDS on Per Capita Income

Bloom and Mahal (1997) published one of the earliest empirical studies of the impact of HIV/AIDS on the per capita income growth. They gathered data on 51 developing countries for the years 1980–1992. Their conclusion was startling: "HIV/AIDS has no statistical impact on per capita income growth". Their reasoning was fortified by a number of reasonable arguments. (1) In many developing countries, there is surplus labor. This surplus could be absorbed without much visible impact on GDP per capita. (2) Since the poor use less medical services, the drain on resources would be relatively minor in developing countries. (3) Community-based and family-based networks will deal with medical requirements. (4) Projections of the number of people with HIV/AIDS tend to be overstated. However, their paper relied heavily on the model of evolution of HIV/AIDS called EPIMODEL, developed by Chin (1994). The model was very sensitive to the specifications of initial conditions. It turned out that the expansion of HIV/AIDS was far more severe in many countries than were addressed in the model. The scale of the rise in mortality had not reached the proportions that were to be reached over the next decade. Hence, the macroeconomic impact that did not appear in their study was to show up in later studies (see below).

Bloom and Mahal also compared the current and forthcoming impact of HIV/AIDS with that of the Black Death in the 1300s. They argued that evidence shows that the Black Death actually caused an increase in the standard of living among the survivors. However, the same argument would not apply to HIV/AIDS today. In the 1300s, the main source income was agriculture that had very little input of human capital. Education hardly played any role in the (mostly agricultural) production process. Even the actual sowing season was not known with precision. Today, the agricultural production process is vastly different. Almost everywhere in the world, the use of artificial fertilizer and pesticides is commonplace. Thus, even in agriculture, human capital has become a factor in the production process. This was not relevant in the 14th century. Therefore, it is critical to take into account in the model the impact of HIV/AIDS on human capital.

4.5.2 The Role of Human Capital

Bloom and Mahal downplayed two critical elements of HIV/AIDS. First, HIV/AIDS affects people who are sexually and economically active. This is in stark contrast with other important diseases like malaria. Therefore, the HIV/AIDS epidemic affects the size, growth rate, age and skill composition of the future labor force that feeds into the growth rates of potential output and of productivity. Second, unlike other killer diseases, like the bubonic plague or influenza, HIV/AIDS is slow-moving, both within society and within the human body. As a result, society must bear higher costs of treatment and palliative care relative to other comparable killer diseases (Moore and Viscusi, 1988). This affects the level and composition of future consumption demand of households (as they have to incur additional private costs) and of governments (that provide public health services). These additional costs dampen savings and investment, thereby reducing the future GDP growth rate. The economics of HIV/AIDS is therefore quite distinct from other diseases with similar epidemiological and demographic characteristics.

A key factor for long-term accumulation of wealth in a given country is its human capital. Therefore, we modify the model to take into account human capital. We show that in the long run, HIV/AIDS can trap a country in poverty for many generations. To explain the human capital argument, we first document the fall in life expectancy due to HIV/AIDS in selected African countries (Acemaoglu and Johnson, 2005).

The impact of HIV/AIDS on life expectancy is large in many countries – especially in sub-Saharan Africa. As Table 4.4 demonstrates, the effect of HIV/AIDS on life expectancy at birth for males is staggering. In Mozambique, the life expectancy falls from 44.32 years in 1990 to 39.74 years in 2012, a drop of more than 10%. In Tanzania, the impact is somewhat smaller and it recovers over the 20-year period (Biswalo and Lie, 1995). The effects in South Africa and Namibia are far larger. In South Africa, life expectancy at birth for males falls by more than 25%. In Namibia, it falls by more than 30%. Botswana is the country hardest hit by this. Life expectancy males at birth falls by 36% in just 10 years (Botswana Sentinal Survey, 2001). Such a reduction in life expectancy over such a short period of time is without historical precedent (Ainsworth and Over, 2001).

What impact would a reduction of 5–20 years of life expectancy have on human capital? To answer that question, we turn to the evidence produced by Bils and Klenow (2000). Although their study was focused on the impact of schooling on economic growth, they also shed some light on the channels through which economic growth is caused by (and in turn, causes) schooling. They show that a 1-year rise in life expectancy at birth leads to 0.25- to 1-year rise in schooling on the average. Thus, a 5-year drop in life expectancy could lead to up to a 5-year drop in average schooling.

What are the microeconomic channels through which falling life expectancy can lead to lower future economic growth? Bonnel (2000) provides a list of microeconomic effects through two main channels: reduced income and increased costs. Reduced income results from the reduced working capacity of workers with HIV/AIDS and lower lifetime income due to lower life expectancy.

Higher costs come from a variety of sources: (1) higher medical expenses due to HIV/AIDS; (2) the dissolution of households that leads to increased social costs; and (3) the cost of caring for orphans that falls either directly on the family or on the society. Higher costs also lead to less education for the children and less saving at the macro level. They all contribute to falling future levels of income through falling productivity (which is linked to education) of future generations.

In summary, HIV/AIDS destroys human capital through a number of mechanisms. (1) It weakens mechanisms for human capital formation. (2) When parents die, it weakens knowledge transmission between generations. (3) Children stay out

Table 4.4 Male life expectancy at birth: 1995–2015

Year	Botswana	Mozambique	Namibia	South Africa	Tanzania
1990	NA	44.32	62.05	59.67	48.34
1991	NA	44.35	62.58	59.81	48.20
1992	NA	44.34	62.95	59.83	47.94
1993	NA	44.43	63.13	59.66	47.59
1994	NA	44.50	63.03	59.13	47.20
1995	54.62	44.48	62.51	58.30	46.50
1996	50.75	44.37	61.28	57.15	45.79
1997	46.96	44.15	59.57	55.70	45.16
1998	43.65	43.87	57.52	54.04	44.66
1999	40.95	43.52	55.31	52.30	44.27
2000	38.85	43.12	53.19	50.58	44.00
2001	37.31	42.70	51.27	48.98	44.09
2002	36.22	42.27	49.53	47.58	44.26
2003	35.48	41.83	48.13	46.44	44.52
2004	35.04	41.41	47.10	45.57	44.83
2005	34.81	41.01	46.38	44.96	45.17
2006	34.73	40.65	45.94	44.59	45.55
2007	34.77	40.35	45.73	44.42	45.95
2008	34.88	40.09	45.72	44.42	46.35
2009	35.05	39.91	45.86	44.64	46.73
2010	35.22	39.78	46.1	44.96	47.11
2011	35.39	39.74	46.4	45.34	47.48
2012	35.54	39.74	46.72	45.75	47.83
2013	35.67	39.81	47.03	46.16	48.17
2014	35.77	39.93	47.31	46.55	48.49
2015	35.86	40.09	47.56	46.93	48.8

Source: US Census Bureau, International Programs Center, unpublished tables

of school due to lost labor and income. (4) Lower life expectancy reduces the pay-off from education. (5) Teachers become sick and die due to HIV/AIDS. They are costly to replace.

The impact of HIV/AIDS on mortality during productive years is striking. This can be seen in the two following figures. Figures 4.3 and 4.4 show the precise nature of where AIDS strikes in terms of excess mortality. The figures are calculated from the mortality tables produced by the Actuarial Society of South Africa (ASSA). First, we normalize the mortality in South Africa to the year 1985. Thus, the mortality for every age group 15–19, 20–24, etc. are set to 1. The logic of choosing 1985 was that it would be last year in which the effect of deaths due to AIDS had not yet shown up in the mortality of the population. We then calculate

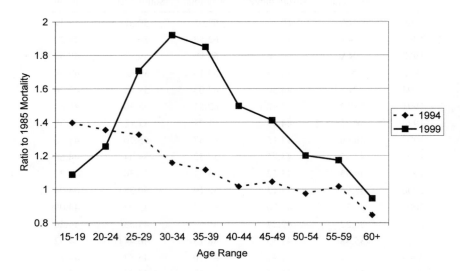

Fig. 4.3 Male mortality in 1994, 1999 as a proportion of male mortality in 1985. *Source*: South African Actuarial Society database

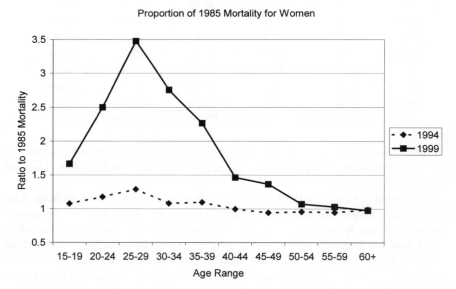

Fig. 4.4 Female mortality in 1994, 1999 as a proportion of female mortality in 1985. Source: South African Actuarial Society database

the mortality of males and females for every age group for the years 1994 and 1999 in relation to their corresponding rates for 1985. Thus, Fig. 3.5 for females of age group 25–29 for the year 1999 implies that the mortality for that age group was 3.5 times higher than their figure for the year 1985. These kinds of staggering reversals of longevity of prime-age people in such a short time have never been seen in any society in the past century.

4.5.3 The Transmission of Human Capital

Bell et al. (2004) took a different tack. They proposed an overlapping generations model with a central role for human capital instead of a classical Solow growth model. They explicitly modeled the transmission of human capital between generations through costly education. They list all the channels through which a disease like HIV/AIDS strikes.

> We begin by listing what are arguably the primary effects of morbidity and mortality in the age groups that AIDS typically strikes, namely, young and prime-aged adults. It is useful to order such effects, whether due to AIDS or to other causes, in the following way: (a) Morbidity reduces productivity on the job or results in outright absenteeism. If the worker dies, his or her skills and experience are destroyed. (b) Firms and the government lose trained workers on both counts and must replace them. In particular, many teachers die prematurely of AIDS. (c) Substantial expenditure, public and private alike, may be required to treat and care for those who become sick. (d) Savings are also diverted out of net investment in physical and human capital into the treatment and replacement of workers who fall sick and die. (e) Lifetime family income is greatly reduced, and with it the family's means to invest. (f) Children lose the love, care, guidance, and knowledge of one or both parents, which plausibly weakens the transmission of knowledge and capacity from generation to generation. (g) The tax base shrinks. (h) Collateralization in credit markets becomes more difficult, and as a consequence credit markets function less well. (i) Social cohesion and social capital decline.

Their model explicitly takes into account the factors listed above in an overlapping generations model with human capital investment. They note some explicit facts about morbidity in South Africa (along with Zimbabwe). In 1990, 11% of 20-year-old males and 4% of 20-year-old females died before their fortieth birthday. By 2010, the proportions would be 36 and 54%. To put it differently, more than a third of all males aged 20 would die before 40 and more than half of females aged 20 would die before 40. To get an idea of the mortality impact of AIDS compared with other diseases, it is sufficient to remember that the number of death from AIDS would exceed the total number of deaths from all other diseases combined.

This rising mortality would imply that a third of the children in the country would have at least one parent die during their childhood and one in five would become an orphan. This would lead to a loss of human capital of unprecedented scale. The level of education would decline in the next generation.

Bell, Devarajan and Gersbach describe this process vividly:

> In the absence of support, [the children] do not attend school, and each will marry another uneducated individual. In the absence of support or compulsion, the offspring of these unions will also go uneducated, and so on. Observe that any premature adult mortality will produce a new crop of orphaned children in each period and that these lineages will fall into poverty and illiteracy, even if they were not in that condition before. Hence, as time progresses, a steadily increasing proportion of the whole population finds itself in poverty. Caring for orphans is not, of course, a new problem for humankind, and societies have devised various ways of dealing with it. Whether these arrangements can withstand the burden of an epidemic like AIDS, however, remains to be seen.

After calibrating the model to South African parameters, Bell, Devarajan and Gersbach proceed to work out the dynamics of the evolution of family income in the model under three scenarios. First, they calculate it for the case of "No AIDS". Then, they contrast it with two possible scenarios with different levels of human capital investment. In "AIDS (L)" case, they assume that human capital investment would taper off rapidly. In "AIDS (H)" case, they assume that human capital investment would taper off relatively slowly. These results are depicted in Figure 4.5.

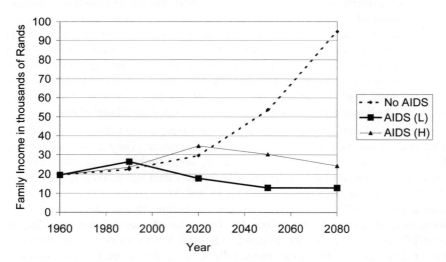

Fig. 4.5 Projection of family income in Bell, Devarajan and Gersbach model. Source: Bell et al. (2004)

Had there been no AIDS, the family income in real terms would have increased almost fivefold between 1960 and 2080. In the worst case scenario of AIDS (L), the family income declines by 40% by 2080. In the not-so-bad scenario of AIDS (H), the family income would show a modest rise of 20% by 2080.

4.5.4 Fertility, HIV/AIDS and Economic Growth

Young (2005) undertook a study to examine the impact of HIV/AIDS on the future welfare of the people who will survive it. The new element he introduced was the effect of HIV on fertility (see also Boldrin and Jones, 2002). He starts with the premise that this effect is strongly negative. Couples with one partner who is HIV-positive would have fewer children. He proceeds to generate projections of the South African population with and without the HIV epidemic (see also Doepke, 2005).

He first notes that, in the absence of the epidemic, the population would have grown to 110 million persons by 2050. With the epidemic, the combination of adult mortality, HIV infant mortality, the effects of HIV infection on fertility and the endogenous response of fertility to higher wages would keep the population below 50 million for almost 50 years (see also Chakraborty, 2004).

He argues that the positive effects of lower population growth are strong enough to counteract the most pessimistic forecasts of the human capital losses of orphaned children due to AIDS, thus implicitly endowing the economy with extra

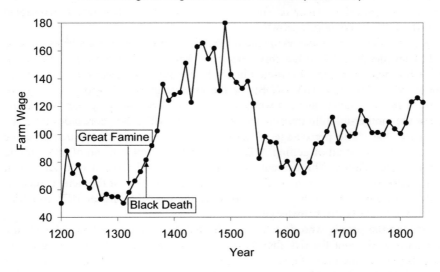

Fig. 4.6 Wages for farm workers in England 1200–1840 AD. *Source*: Clark (2005)

resources that can be used to extend the lifespan of the afflicted and still leave reserves to raise the per capita welfare of future generations (Ehrlich and Lui, 1991).

The argument of high wages in the post HIV/AIDS societies in sub-Saharan Africa relies on the following observation (see Fig. 4.6): For several centuries after the Black Death, real wages stayed high, while the population was halved between 1300 and 1400 in England.

In summarizing the argument, Young (2005) noted: "Regardless of the precise mechanism, it is clear that the Black Death, in a purely economic sense, was a boon to the generations which survived and succeeded it, who, for a sustained period of time, experienced living standards which were not seen again until the late nineteenth century." The implication for the unfolding pandemic of HIV/AIDS is clear. A similar effect would be observed over the next decades in sub-Saharan Africa.

In a separate paper, Young (2006) also tackles the question of the negative relationship between HIV and fertility. Using a series of Demographic and Health Survey (DHS) data, he shows that the relationship is indeed negative.

4.5.5 Fertility and Human Capital Accumulation

The Kalemli-Ozcan (2006) study contradicts the results of Young (2006). She asks the following question: What is the effect of HIV/AIDS on fertility and human capital accumulation in the aggregate data? With a panel data set of two decades from Africa she shows that (1) the HIV/AIDS epidemic affects the total fertility rates positively and (2) it affects the school enrollment rates negatively. She provides empirical evidence on specific mechanisms through which demographic transition affects economic growth.

Kalemli-Ozcan provides evidence on the risk perception of people who are at risk. Consider Fig. 4.7. It has three elements. For a number African countries, it gives information about: (1) women in 15–19 age group who consider themselves not to be at risk from HIV/AIDS; (2) the percentage of HIV-positive pregnant women in the country; and (3) women in the child-bearing age group who know about the mother-to-child transmission risk of HIV/AIDS. She concludes from the evidence that: "The percentage of sexually active women (15–19) that perceive not to be at risk at all of getting AIDS is rather high, with a mean of 48% among the countries shown. The percentage of 15–49 year old women who know that HIV can be transmitted from mother to child is also plotted for the same countries, with a mean of 58%. It does not seem to be the case that higher HIV countries necessarily have better knowledge."

Among the people who do not know the risk they face or people who are not well informed about the risk they face, behavior would not change. How would parents react in the face of uncertainty about a child's survival? They would have more children and provide each of them with less education.

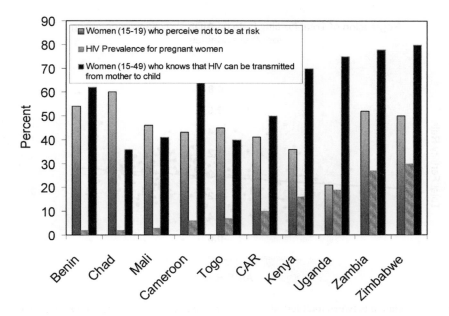

Fig. 4.7 Prevalence, risk perception and knowledge of women about HIV. *Source*: Kalemli-Ozcan (2006)

Figures 4.8 and 4.9 provide evidence of these two important relationships. Note that the two variables are not simply correlated by ignoring the effect of other factors. Rather, they exhibit the relationship after taking into account other factors.

How strong are these effects? Kalemli-Ozcan notes the following: "The empirical estimates predict that parents in a country with a high level of HIV/AIDS prevalence, such as Congo, have two more children compared to a country with a low level of HIV/AIDS prevalence, such as Madagascar. Botswana had a quadrupling of the prevalence of HIV/AIDS. It has had 1.5 more births per woman and 30% points lower primary school enrollment since 1985. The results imply lower economic growth and welfare for current and future African generations."

Juhn et al. (2007) followed up on Kalemli-Ozcan (2006) by examining directly the fertility response to HIV/AIDS. They used the latest rounds of the Demographic and Health Surveys linking an individual woman's fertility to her HIV-status based on testing. The data allows us to distinguish the effect of positive HIV status on fertility (which may be due to lower fecundity and other physiological reasons) from the behavioral response to higher mortality risk (measured by the local community's HIV prevalence). They found that the disease significantly lowered an infected woman's fertility. On the other hand, the local community's

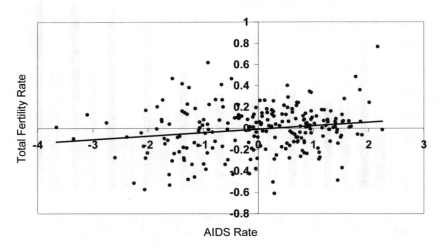

Fig. 4.8 Relation between total fertility rate and prevalence. Source: Kalemli-Ozcan (2006)

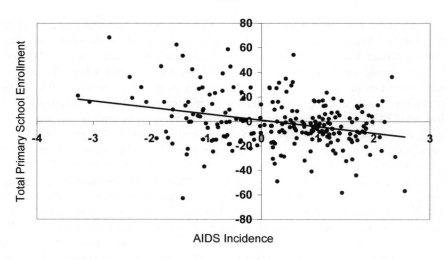

Fig. 4.9 Relation between education and prevalence. *Source*: Kalemli-Ozcan (2006)

HIV prevalence had no significant effect on non-infected women's fertility when they pooled all communities (see Table 4.5). However, HIV/AIDS had a significant positive effect on fertility in the sub-sample of communities with non-zero prevalence. This result kills the argument of a negative impact of HIV/AIDS posited by Young through empirical facts on the ground.

Table 4.5 Knowledge of status in Africa

Country	Year	Percent of men who knew status[a]	Percent of HIV+ men who knew status[b]	Percent of women who knew status[a]	Percent of HIV+ women who knew status[b]
Botswana	2005	10.3	17.4		
Cameroon	2004	9.7	25.1	13.9	23.6
Ethiopia	2005	3.8	4.9		
Ghana	2003	7.4	12.4	7.5	8.2
Kenya	2003	13.1	18.2	14.3	22.8
Lesotho	2004	12.0	16.8	9.1	16.2
Malawi	2004	12.9	15.0	15.1	20.0
Mozambique	2003	3.7	3.6		
Nigeria	2003	6.4	13.6		
Congo	2005	9.5	10.6		
Tanzania	2004	12.1	12.3		
Uganda	2004	12.7	23.5	10.8	15.0

Source: Demographic and Health Surveys, 2003–2005. Notes: [a]Percent distribution of men or women aged 15–49 years who were ever tested for HIV and received test results. [b]Percent distribution of HIV-positive men or women aged 15–49 years who were ever tested for HIV and received results of the last test before the survey

4.5.6 Summary of Reviewed Literature on Fertility and Human Capital

There are many channels of transmission of the impact of HIV/AIDS on macroeconomic variables. They do not necessarily move in the same direction. For example, theoretically speaking, a rising incidence of HIV/AIDS can lead to a rising or falling total fertility rate (Meltzer 1992). The empirical results depend on the strengths of each channel through which the fertility rate is affected. In sub-Saharan Africa, where even basic macroeconomic data can be spotty, it is not always possoble to get conclusive results. Thus, many economists have turned to microeconomic or sectoral studies, where conclusions are sharper but the results do not necessarily point to any macroeconomic outcomes (Lorentzen et al., 2004). Specifically, these studies do not give clear answers regarding the impact of HIV/AIDS on overall economic welfare in the form of changes in GDP.

4.6 Microeconomic and Epidemiological Models of Behavior

Microeconomic and epidemiological models try to answer questions about the behavioral response of people who are either at risk of or actually living with HIV/AIDS. For example, does the threat of HIV lead to less sex without condoms? What factors affect the behavior of people when they know about the risk of HIV/AIDS, given that there is no cure? Does the introduction of ARV drugs lead people to have more risky sex? Is it possible to set out policies that are aligned to the incentives of people to undertake activities to limit the propagation of HIV/AIDS? Answers to such behavioral questions are important. For example, the ABC policy (A for abstinence B for be faithful and C for condom), which is favored by the Bush Administration and implemented by PEPFAR in countries in Africa with high HIV/AIDS prevalence, emphasizes A and B and relies heavily on the behavioral response.

4.6.1 Do Ugandans Behave Differently?

Figure 4.10 provides a picture of the prevalence of HIV in the antenatal clinics in various African countries over a decade and a half. In Kenya, HIV/AIDS prevalence rose dramatically over this period. In the province of Kwazulu Natal, it rose

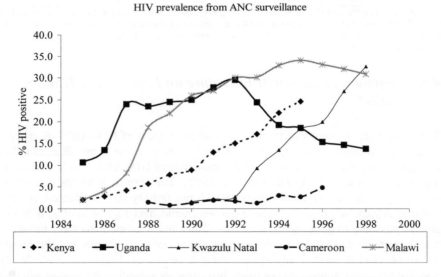

Fig. 4.10 HIV prevalence in antenatal clinics in Africa 1984–1999. *Source*: Mosley (2005)

spectacularly in 6 years, after starting from very low figures. The only country that stands out in this group is Uganda. Between 1985 and 1992, the figure rose, but then declined dramatically.

This effect is also clear for every site for which data on the HIV status of pregnant women are collected in various parts of Uganda, as Fig. 4.11 shows. All of the sites show a clear downward trend, without exception.

The Ugandan government has been using a three-pronged strategy: Abstinence (efforts to raise the age of sexual debut by young adults), Be Faithful (efforts to discourage more than one sexual partner) and Condom (efforts to increase the use of condoms) – the so-called ABC approach. The "success" of Uganda's ABC program attracted the attention of the US Agency for International Development (USAID) in 2001. It convened a group of policymakers from academia, various government bodies, such as the CDC, along with various charitable American organizations working in Africa. The point of this meeting was to hammer out the importance of different components of ABC.

When PEPFAR began planning its strategy, it clearly had Uganda in mind. For example, in testimony before Congress, Anne Peterson, Assistant Administrator for Global Health at USAID noted, "It is important that we highlight the successful interventions in Uganda so we can better apply them to other countries. The new Emergency Plan for AIDS Relief that President Bush announced in January in the State of the Union Address is based on one of these successful models" (Peterson 2003).

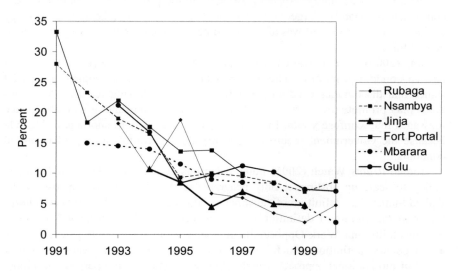

Fig. 4.11 Downward March of HIV prevalence in antenatal clinics in Uganda. *Source*: Mosley (2005)

One of the strongest ABC proponents was Dorothy Brewster Lee of Christian Connections for International Health. She noted that, in Cameroon, where faith-based organizations were marginalized because they would not support condoms, HIV infections among pregnant women continued to increase. She emphasized that interventions that have proven effective in Europe and North America should not be applied in African settings without consideration for indigenous culture, including views on recreational or casual sex. She noted that many African countries have higher rates than the United States of under-15-year-olds who have not had sex. She also argued that HIV prevention approaches have generally failed to provide fair and balanced recognition to abstinence and faithfulness. Instead, the reports and strategies of UNAIDS and other international organizations gave condoms much more attention and emphasis (USAID 2002).

It was clear from the outset that the policy prescription of PEPFAR would bring Uganda to the central stage. However, what was not clear at the time was that US policy would have, in turn, a big impact on the future course of Ugandan policy. Once the US government began spending large sums of money in Uganda, rewarding it as the role model, the official policy in Uganda changed considerably. It began to emphasize A and B and to downplay C, just as Dorothy Brewster Lee had proposed. Thus, we could characterize the new policy as ABc, rather than ABC, in which all three elements had played prominent roles.

In November 2004, Uganda claimed to have become the first country in the world to draft an official national policy on abstinence and fidelity. Titled the "Uganda National Abstinence and Being Faithful Policy and Strategy on Prevention of Transmission on HIV," the draft policy is described by its authors as a companion to the country's existing strategy on the promotion of condoms and a component of Uganda's larger "ABC" strategy. One of the coauthors of this strategy document (Edward Green) was also a founding member of PEPFAR (Kyomuhendo et al., 2004).

Gray (2005) noted a clear change in the Ugandan government position with respect to condom promotion. The government of Uganda has adopted an official stance that discourages condom promotion, for the following reasons: "(1) Condoms may promote promiscuity. (2) Promotion of condoms along with abstinence messages may confuse youth. In addition, there is a condom shortage in Uganda because the Government requires in-country quality control testing of imported condoms."

Human Rights Watch (2005) noted a curious coincidence. The new Ugandan policy to scale up abstinence-only programs is styled after those in use in the United States. The definition of "abstinence education" in the draft follows almost verbatim the eight-part definition of "abstinence education" in the US Personal Responsibility and Work Opportunity Reconciliation Act of 1996 (Section 912). The Ugandan definition which reads: "Abstinence education means an educational or motivational approach which: (1) Has as its exclusive purpose, teaching, supporting and empowering the social, psychological, and health gains to be relized by abstaining from premarital sexual activity; (2) Teaches abstinence from sexual activity outside marriage (or "faithfulness") as the expected standard; (3) Teaches that abstinence from sexual activity is the only certain way to avoid sexually transmitted diseases, and other associated health problems; (4) Teaches that a mutually faithful monogamous relationship in context of marriage is the expected standard of human sexual activity."

Dr. Alex Kamugisha, Uganda's minister of state for primary health care, was quoted in the newspaper saying, "We want to slowly move away from the condom. As a ministry, we have realized that abstinence and being faithful to one's partner are the only sure ways to curb AIDS. From next year, the ministry is going to be less involved in condom importation but more involved in awareness campaigns, abstinence and behavior change" (Kasyate 2005).

However, the policy of emphasizing abstinence and faithfulness was not based on hard research (Luke and Munshi, 2004). Regarding abstinence, longitudinal research results exist that use US data. Lipsitz et al. (2003) surveyed over 500 college students over period of time. They found that 16.3% had taken virginity pledges. The majority of pledgers (61%) broke their vows. Pledge-breaking virgins had their first sexual intercourse later but used condoms less. The results were consistent with earlier evidence found by Bearman and Brückner (2001). Abstinence, used as a policy instrument in Uganda, has had negative effects on the use of condoms in the United States.

On the issue of faithfulness, the data in Uganda itself is rather discouraging, as Figs. 4.12 and 4.13 show. In Fig. 4.12, we examine the number of non-marital partners 15–19 year old girls in Uganda had between 1995 and 2003. It shows an increasing trend.

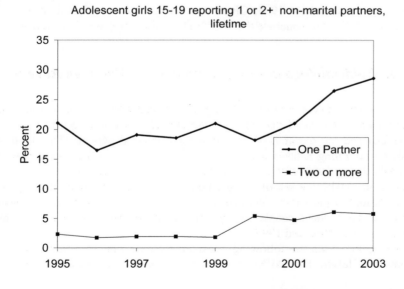

Fig. 4.12 Number of sex partners of adolescent girls in Uganda. *Source*: Gray (2005)

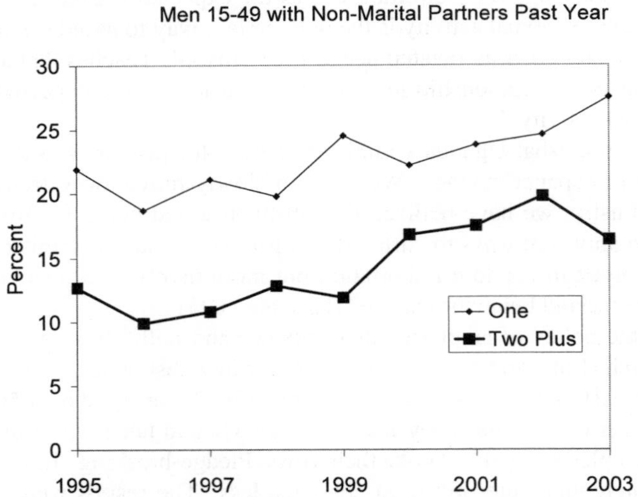

Men 15-49 with Non-Marital Partners Past Year

Fig. 4.13 Married men with one or more non-marital sex partners in Uganda. *Source*: Gray (2005)

In Uganda, it is common practice for married men to have sexual partners who are not their wives. Despite the campaign to be faithful to one wife (in Uganda, it is called "no grazing"), the data shows no reduction in the number of partners by married men since at least 1995. Given that nearly half the infected people are married, it is difficult to conclude that the "Be Faithful" campaign is a success.

4.6.2 An Epidemiological Interpretation of the Ugandan Results

The total number of people living with any disease in a population is a product of only two factors: the incidence rate (the number of new cases occurring in any time period) and the duration of disease among affected persons. The duration depends on how long it takes a patient to fully recover or to die. In the case of HIV/AIDS, during 1992–1999, when prevalence in Uganda fell substantially, full recovery from AIDS was out of the question. Moreover, increasing the length of survival through triple-combination therapy only became available in developed countries in 1997. Most people in Uganda would not have had access to this treatment between 1992 and 1999.

Mosley (2005) asks the following question: Can we find an epidemiological explanation of falling HIV/AIDS prevalence in Uganda? Prevalence at year t is defined as follows: $P(t) = I(t) + I(t-1) + \ldots + I(t-6)$ where $I(t)$ is the incidence during year t. Here, we confine the prevalence at time t, $P(t)$ to the accumulation of 7 years of incidence because the average longevity of a patient after becoming HIV-positive is 7 years in Africa without access to triple therapy. Thus, a falling value for $P(t)$ could simply be explained by higher incidence in the distant past that is causing the fall in the value for $P(t)$ at present. After examining the data from Uganda, Mosley (2005) concluded that the most likely explanation is exactly that. Of course, deaths due higher incidence in the past are not the only explanation. As Fig. 4.14 shows, the use of condoms substantially increased among the adolescents between 1998 and 2002.

Quantifying the effects, Mosley concluded that 6.2% of the decline in prevalence over a period of can be explained as follows: 5% of the decline can be explained by mortality and the rest for other reasons.

In order to claim that ABC worked for Uganda, we need evidence regarding how each component contributes to Uganda's plan.

For Abstinence, Gray (2005) notes the following facts for the Rakai District of Uganda. In 1995, the average age of first sexual contact for boys was 17.1 years. By 2002, the age has fallen to 16.2 years. For girls, during the same period, it had fallen from 15.9 to 15.5. He notes that while sexual abstinence before marriage is highly desirable, 14% of all girls have coercive first sex without condoms. Moreover, there is economic pressure to engage in paid sex (for example, to cover school fees). In addition, males in Uganda accept premarital sex as part of the local culture (Green 1994).

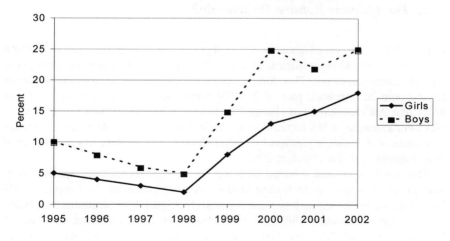

Adolescent Current Condom Use, Rakai 1995-2002

Fig. 4.14 Condom use among adolescents in Rakai district 1995–2002. *Source*: Gray (2005)

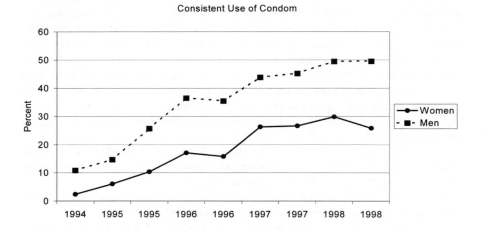

Fig. 4.15 Consistent use of condoms in Rakai, Uganda. *Source*: Gray (2005)

As we saw in Figs. 4.12 and 4.13, monogamy is neither rising for men nor for women. While 95.4% of married women are monogamous, only 55.1% of married men are monogamous. Thus, the "Be Faithful" slogan seems to have had very little effect in the population. The only part of the campaign that seems to have had any effect was the use of condoms (see Fig. 4.15 on the consistent use of condoms).

4.6.3 Do Africans Behave Differently?

Oster (2007a) has investigated whether there is something very peculiar about Africans. In sub-Saharan Africa, at least 90% of HIV infections are transmitted through heterosexual sex. Therefore, encouraging changes in heterosexual behavior has become an important part of the HIV prevention effort in that region. Oster notes that Africans have not changed their sexual behavior much in response to HIV. For example, a 1% increase in the HIV prevalence rate decreased the share of women with multiple partners by 0.4% points. For men, there was no change in this behavior (see also Haacker, 2002).

This result is in stark contrast with the big changes in behavior another high-risk group – gay men in the United States – exhibited when the first wave of HIV hit in the mid-1980s and no treatment was in sight. Figure 4.16 illustrates their behavioral response between 1984 and 1991. However, as we will see in Chap. 9, between 2001 and 2006, new HIV infections in gay men under 30 increased significantly in New York City and risky behavior continues to be a problem.

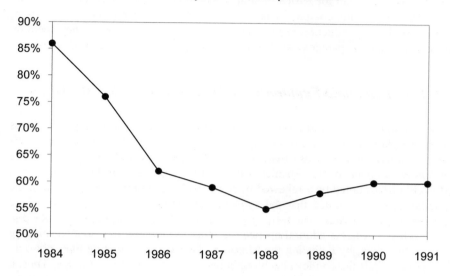

Fig. 4.16 Share of gay men with multiple partners in the United States 1984–1991. *Source*: MultiCenter AIDS Cohort Study Database

In theory, most people would adopt safer sexual practices in response to HIV risks (for example, monogamy). Oster examined African data to see if this theoretical relationship holds true in practice. Her results suggest a strong correlation between income, life expectancy and behavior change. Individuals with higher incomes and longer expected future life spans are more likely to respond to HIV risk by lowering their number of sexual partners. This alone goes a long way to explain the difference in behavioral response between Africa and the United States.

Oster also analyzed the effect of mortality risk on behavioral response, in a novel way. She compared regions in Africa with high malaria rates and low malaria rates. In areas with high rates of malaria, people already face a high risk of death from malaria. She argued that they would have little incentive to change their sexual behavior. This is exactly what she observed in the data; individuals who live in areas with high malaria prevalence have a lower behavioral response to HIV.

To evaluate the effect of different policy responses to the HIV epidemic, Oster developed a simulation model to track how the epidemic and sexual behavior evolve over time. Oster found that behavioral changes made little difference in the magnitude of HIV rates predicted by the model.

What are the policy implications? The implication of Oster's study is devastating for the ABC Plan for Africa. It simply would not work. However, a reduction in malaria risk, while completely unrelated to HIV risk, would have a big impact. We know that the reduction of malaria risk is inexpensive. Thus, money spent on preventing malaria, paradoxically, is a cost-effective way of reducing HIV risk.

4.6.4 An Economic Explanation of Why Ugandan Results Differ

It is well-known that migration, travel and trade are prime drivers of epidemics from one place to another. For example, in Chap. 1 we saw how air travel can affect the spread of infectious diseases like SARS and how trade routes and people movement converted the Spanish Flu of 1918 into a worldwide pandemic. McNeill (1976) noted how renewed trade networks spread the Black Death in the Middle Ages. He argued that the spread of Black Death was facilitated by the Mongol hordes in Asia. The turning point of the spread in Europe took place in 1291, when a Genoese admiral opened the Strait of Gibraltar to Christian shipping for the first time, by defeating the Moroccan forces. New shipping lines not only brought in goods faster; they also brought the plague to the rest of Europe. Thus, it is logical to see the spread of HIV/AIDS as a consequence of rising trade. That the geographical locations of trade routes have something to do with HIV/AIDS has been known for some time.

Klitsch (1992) was the first to note that, in Uganda, trade routes have had a clear relationship with HIV. He estimated that 62% of men and 30% of women in the main road trading centers had more than two sexual partners in the previous 5 years. Men were more likely to be seropositive if they lived in trading centers or villages. Compared with the rest of the population, men had three to five times more risk of being seropositive. Given the evidence, Klitsch deduced that "HIV transmission follows trade routes, and is probably linked to commercial sex. Rural trading villages may spread HIV to more rural villages."

Steinbrook (2007) examined the past evidence in India, and concluded, "India has perhaps five million truck drivers. About half drive long-distance routes that keep them away from home for a month or more; often they have a young male helper. Truckers are more likely than other men to be clients of sex workers, and sex work is common along major truck routes. The Golden Quadrilateral, an express highway that links India's four largest cities – New Delhi, Mumbai, Chennai, and Kolkata – traverses many areas where the rate of sexual transmission of HIV is high."

Okware (2007) noted that all the sites in Uganda that had showed a clearly declining trend in HIV/AIDS began to show a rise between 2003 and 2005 (see Fig. 4.17). Why did the prevalence in Uganda decline during 1993–2001 and why did it rise after that? Oster (2007b) found evidence that a large portion of such

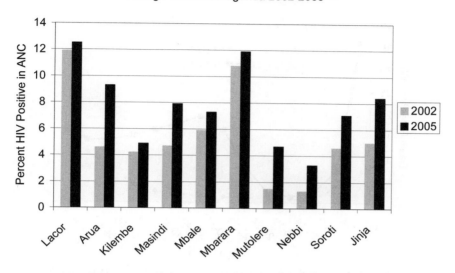

Fig. 4.17 Reversal of fortune in Uganda. *Source*: Okware (2007)

changes can be explained by changes in exports. This research confirmed the relationship between trade and the propagation of HIV that had been observed by other researchers, like Klitsch and Steinbrook.

Oster (2007b) wanted to relate new infections (incidence of HIV) with changing export values. Unfortunately, the incidence of HIV is rarely recorded in developing countries. If a person discovers that she has HIV in 1990, this does not mean she contracted it that year. Oster devised an indirect method. She argued that, given that contracting HIV in Africa was virtually a death sentence in Africa in the 1980s and in the 1990s, she could estimate the incidence by examining the excess mortality for different age groups in a given country by comparing it with a similar country that had not been affected by HIV/AIDS. She illustrates the theory behind the methodology in Fig. 4.18, which shows death rates for Egypt over the 1990s and Botswana in 2001 for different age groups. She argues that the pattern of death rates over the life cycle for Egypt is similar to Botswana, as expected for a country in its income level. Specifically, mortality is high in infancy and childhood, then low through the age of 40 and increasing after that – the typical U-shape we expect. In contrast, the pattern for Botswana produces a W shape, signaling significant AIDS mortality. Although death rates are similar to Egypt up to age 19, they are much higher after that, until late adulthood. This mortality pattern clearly reflects AIDS deaths, as virtually no other disease had this mortality path over the life cycle during the period of study. Thus, unlike the researchers who have been

Death Rate Per 1000 in Egypt (1995) and Botswana (2001)

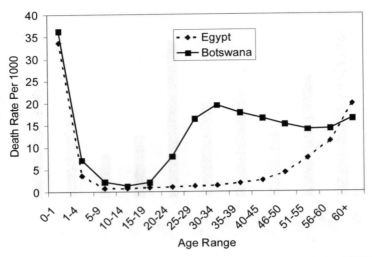

Fig. 4.18 Mortality rates Botswana versus Egypt. *Source*: Oster (2007b)

interested in the effect of HIV on mortality patterns, Oster is working the impact in reverse. By examining the mortality pattern, she reveals the HIV incidence.

There is one more adjustment to be made. Since HIV/AIDS death does not occur immediately after contracting the virus, Oster had to calculate the distribution of the time lag between the infection and the death. She uses mortality data for a number of years in a simultaneous equation framework with smoothing restrictions, and allows for a realistic path of death from the epidemic. She also makes a novel use of sibling mortality histories in the Demographic and Health Surveys to show that her estimates from the mortality calculated from the simulated tables seem to be a good match to actual mortality rates in areas where both are available.

Using this method, she recalculated the incidence and the corresponding prevalence in Oster (2006). In that paper, she correctly anticipated the overestimated HIV/AIDS prevalence that the UNAIDS acknowledged a year later (see Chap. 3 for a fuller discussion of this issue).

Oster (2007b) proceeds to build a model of the HIV epidemic, making explicit how HIV and economic activity may be linked. For the model, she notes: "The model builds on three observations. First, truck drivers and other migrants (i.e., those who spend time living or traveling away from home) tend to have more sexual partners than the average person. Second, the sexual partnerships these people have away from home tend to be higher risk than those they have at home, largely because their partners are more likely to be infected: for example, [they] are more

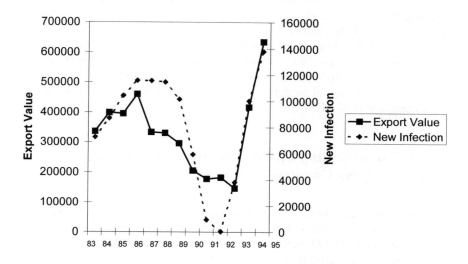

Fig. 4.19 Exports versus HIV incidence for Uganda. *Source*: Oster (2007b)

likely to be bar girls or commercial sex workers. Third, the partners (for the most part, wives) of those who travel may be more likely to have additional sexual partners while their spouses are away. These observations suggest that in times when there are more people traveling, there may be more HIV infections; that link is formalized in the model here. I begin by describing the model setup and then discussing the predictions. At the end of this section I provide evidence for the other necessary link here namely, a positive relationship between economic activity (exports) and the share traveling away from home. In addition to generating an overall connection between HIV and exports, the model also makes additional predictions about how this relationship should vary across groups and initial conditions."

She then applies the model to export data from Uganda. Ugandan exports are very closely tied to coffee. It was the principal export of Uganda in the 1980s and the 1990s. What she finds is a remarkable relation between exports and incidence for Uganda, illustrated in Fig. 4.19. In addition to Uganda, she applies the same methodology for Burkina Faso, Cameroon, Kenya, Malawi, Mali, Zambia and Zimbabwe. The results hold up for all countries, in varying degrees.

Oster (2007b) also notes the policy implications: "This result on Uganda has obvious, potentially important, policy implications. The connection between exports and HIV in general also suggests specific avenues of HIV prevention. In particular, the implication that truckers and other migrants is a very important driver of the overall epidemic supports targeting prevention activities at that group (similar to the targeting done of prostitutes in Thailand). In addition, if increases in economic activity make the HIV epidemic worse, it suggests that aid groups aiming to increase growth should do so in collaboration with those seeking to decrease HIV."

Oster's research (2006, 2007a, b) shows that economics plays a significant role in the propagation of HIV/AIDS in high incidence countries. Thus, policies based on simple epidemiological models may fall short of desired effects if we ignore the economics of HIV/AIDS.

4.7 The Cost of Scaling Up Prevention and Treatment in Developing Countries

Many researchers are concerned with how much it would cost to scale up prevention and treatment programs. For example, Stover et al. (2006) estimate that if an investment of USD 122 billion is made before 2015, in 125 low- and middle-income countries, targeted at sexual transmission and transmission among injection drug users, it would avert 28 million new infections. They estimate the cost at about USD 3900 to prevent each new infection, but that this would save USD 4700 in foregone treatment and care costs per person, thus justifying the cost.

Similarly, interventions in other forms have been investigated. The World Bank (2006) provided a comparison of various types of interventions. We report this in Table 4.6. It gives us a unique perspective on different types of interventions. For example, we find that by far the most cost effective interventions are achieved through sex workers and the management of sexually transmitted infections. Given our discussions about how trade routes and sex workers provided a potent combination for expanding the disease and that there is high correlation between different sexually transmitted diseases and HIV/AIDS, these results should not be surprising. Surprisingly, mother-to-child transmission intervention turns out to be very expensive in India. This is not a universal finding (see Chap. 9).

Data from India also provides another insight into the cost effectiveness of the scale of operation of HIV/AIDS projects. A study by Guinness et al. (2007) examines data from HIV/AIDS projects targeted at commercial sex workers in Andhra Pradesh and Tamil Nadu – two large southern states of India – during the financial year 2001–2002. Figure 4.20 illustrates their findings. It shows that costs go up as the coverage increases. The analysis of the data suggests a point of minimum efficient scale. This scale of operation is achieved when 1,500–2,000 persons are covered by the operation.

Table 4.6 Summary of cost-effectiveness analysis of HIV/AIDS program in India

	HIV infections averted after 5 years in millions	Infant HIV averted after 5 years	Program cost over 5 years in millions of dollars	Cost per HIV infection averted	Cost per DALY saved
Sex worker intervention	5.6	160,000	$298	$53	$2.66
STI management	3.2	90,000	$780	$47	$2.35
VCTC	3.5	110,000	$782	$199	$9.96
High risk men	5.6	160,000	$1,887	$308	$15.42
Youth interventions	3.5	110,000	$5,203	$1,324	$66.20
MCTC	0.3	350,000	$898	$2,568	$128.40

Source: World Bank (2006). *Notes*: *DALY* disability adjusted life years; *STI* sexually transmitted infections; *VCTC* voluntary counseling and testing center; *MCTC* mother to child transmission

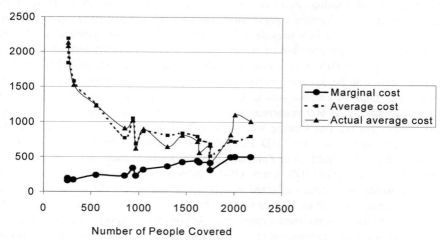

Fig. 4.20 Marginal and average cost of HIV/AIDS programs. *Source*: Guinness et al. (2007)

The findings from this study have clear policy implications for the planned scaling up of HIV/AIDS programs around the world. If prevention and treatment are to be scaled up, what should be the optimum size for each center? This study provides an idea. However, as the authors note, the findings are far from universal. Andhra Pradesh and Tamil Nadu show substantial differences. Thus, we would need to apply the results of this research with caution for other regions and other countries (Hellinger 1998).

4.8 Economic Tradeoffs

Economics is full of tradeoffs. Consider the simple case of a flat rate tax on individual incomes. A government might think of it as an endless source of revenue. If expenditure falls short of revenue, all it has to do is to increase the tax rate. Unfortunately, there is a tradeoff. The higher the rate, the higher is the incentive to hide the income or to hive it off to a low tax regime country. Thus, beyond a certain rate, the revenue will not rise any further. Here we will consider two such tradeoffs. One is a tradeoff between the influx of foreign money to fight HIV/AIDS against the destabilizing effect on the exchange rate. The other is the tradeoff between using each marginal dollar to combat one disease or another.

4.8.1 The Zambian Dilemma

In this subsection, we will follow McPherson (2007) to illustrate the problem using the example of Zambia. Zambia has a high-prevalence, generalized HIV/AIDS epidemic. In 2006, Zambia's population was 11.5 million and growing at the rate of 2.2% per year. The HIV prevalence rate among adults 15–49 years was 17%, an estimated 98,000 people died of AIDS, the number of children and adults (0–49 years) living with HIV was around 1.1 million and the number of AIDS orphans was estimated to be 710,000. Forty-six percent of the population was aged 0–15 years. The GDP of Zambia was USD 6.93 billion making the average per capita income around USD 600 in current dollars or USD 900 when adjusted for purchasing power parity. The income was not evenly distributed, so 64% of Zambians had expenditures below the USD 1 per day. At 46% of the total population, there are over 5 million children in Zambia. Of them, suppose there are 1 million children affected by HIV/AIDS. Then, USD 1 billion would be required to meet the welfare needs of children affected by HIV/AIDS. This would be equivalent to 14% of Zambia's GDP or 17% of total (public and private) consumption expenditure, 54% of total government expenditure, 48% of total imports of goods and services and 309% of international grants provided to the government. And this is not a one-time expenditure. Presumably an equal amount has to be spent every year.

The inflow of such a large amount of money, even if it came from foreign sources, would have a series of unwelcome side effects. First, inflation would likely rise. With the economy currently incapable of efficiently absorbing existing flows of foreign assistance and the government budget in deficit, any additional expenditure would add to the money supply, boosting the rate of inflation. Second, the balance of payments would deteriorate. The large inflows of resources would significantly raise the real value of the local currency. That would contribute to low economic growth, increasing international debt, accelerating imports and lowering exports. Third, the additional expenditures would crowd out private sector investment. It would raise the wages of the skilled professionals such as teachers, nurses, managers, administrators and child care specialists. This would feed into general labor input cost in the long run, making the private sector less competitive. Fourth, the economy would become significantly more dependent on aid and remain that way for the indefinite future. Thus, even when foreign aid is available to confront the issue of AIDS orphans, it is not an unmitigated blessing.

4.8.2 The Tradeoff Among Competing Needs

Any country has competing needs for money. For developing countries, the competition among needs is even more acute. Many needs are life and death issues for many citizens. Economists have developed the concept of biggest effect for the marginal dollar. The concept is simple. Suppose we have one extra dollar to spend on the welfare of the population. Which program should get it? If we assume that the lives of all citizens are equally valuable, then the marginal dollar should be spent where it saves the most lives.

Let us we examine the proposal of Stover et al. (2006) to invest in prevention programs targeted at sexual transmission and transmission among injection drug users, in order to avert 28 million new infections. Each additional life saved through HIV/AIDS prevention would cost USD 3,900. Compare that with the WHO (2005) proposal of extending maternal and newborn health coverage to 95% of the poorest countries in the world. The total 10-year cost of implementing this proposal is estimated at USD 39 billion. The number of lives saved would exceed 100 million. Thus, the cost of each life saved is USD 390 – about one-tenth of the cost of the life saved in the Stover et al., proposal. Bryce et al. (2005) come up with a different proposal for saving the lives of children. They estimate that USD 5.1 billion in new resources annually would save 6 million children's lives in the 42 countries responsible for 90% of child deaths in 2000. The average cost per child's life saved would be USD 887.

The question that arises is whether we can justify singling out HIV/AIDS for increased funding when the lives could be saved in other programs in a much more inexpensive fashion. Even among the different programs for HIV/AIDS, there are competing needs. Should the money be spent on mother-to-child transmission or should it be spent on needle exchange? Should money be targeted to sex workers or should it be targeted to men who have sex with men? Halperin (2007) has raised this issue (along with many other economists at earlier times).

There are a number of justifications for spending money on HIV/AIDS (and other infectious diseases). First, the reason for spending more on HIV/AIDS is the nature of the disease: it is infectious. Thus, prevention of the disease implies much more than just saving the life of that one person. In economic terms, such diseases have negative externalities. It is precisely for this reason that cholera, tuberculosis and other infectious diseases are a public health problem, not just another disease that affects people. Second, prevention through targeted groups (such as sex workers or truckers) is extremely cost effective, as they provide the largest conduit for disease propagation among other groups of people. Third, many targeted programs for HIV/AIDS do not simply go into the prevention and treatment of HIV/AIDS alone. The money is spent on general health care. One good example is the MAP program of the World Bank (which is discussed in Chap. 7).

4.9 The Economics of SARS

Severe acute respiratory syndrome (SARS) provides a glimpse into a set of policy responses from policymakers in the developed world. It jolted them to take many unprecedented steps, after an initial lack of response. SARS emerged in southern China in November 2002. It spread rapidly along international air routes in early 2003, as far away as Canada. Asian countries had the most cases (7,782) and deaths (729). SARS challenged Asian health care systems, disrupted Asian economies and tested the effectiveness of the International Health Regulations of the World Health Organization (WHO) (also see our analysis of the International Health Regulations in Chap. 8). Worldwide, there were 8,437 people infected and 813 deaths. Outside Asia, the country most affected by SARS was Canada. There were 250 infected people in Canada, resulting in 38 deaths.

The WHO implemented extensive actions to respond to SARS. Its response was delayed by an initial lack of cooperation from officials in China. The WHO activated its global infectious disease network. It deployed public health specialists to affected areas in Asia to provide technical assistance. The WHO also established international teams to identify the cause of SARS and to provide guidance for managing the outbreak. Its ability to respond to SARS in Asia was limited by its authority under the existing International Health Regulations.

Asian governments initially struggled to recognize the SARS emergency and to organize an appropriate response. They ultimately established control once the very negative economic impact SARS produced became clear. Their initial response was hindered by a number of problems: (1) poor communication; (2) ineffective leadership; (3) inadequate disease surveillance systems; and (4) insufficient public health capacity. Improved screening, rapid isolation of suspected cases, enhanced hospital infection control, and quarantine of close contacts ultimately helped to end the outbreak. The SARS outbreak added impetus to the process of revising the International Health Regulations. The WHO and its member states have since expanded the scope of required disease reporting to include all public health emergencies of international concern and devised a system for better cooperation with the WHO and other countries. It has also set up an emergency response system.

The SARS crisis temporarily dampened consumer confidence in Asia, costing Asian economies USD 11–18 billion. SARS had significant, but temporary, negative impacts on a variety of economic activities, especially travel, tourism and manufacturing.

The estimated impact of the short term effects of SARS can be split into three broad categories: the demand side effect, the effect of rising cost and the country risk effect. Lee and McKibbin (2003) estimated the impact. Their model is a general equilibrium model that has the virtue of taking into account compensatory effects. For example, if tourists shun Hong Kong as the preferred destination, they might go to Maldives, thereby compensating one country's loss by another country's gain. Not surprisingly, Hong Kong suffered the biggest loss (Table 4.7).

Table 4.7 Temporary shock of SARS as a percentage of GDP

	Total effects	Demand shift	Cost rise	Country risk
United States	−0.07	−0.01	−0.06	0.00
Japan	−0.07	−0.01	−0.06	0.00
Australia	−0.07	0.00	−0.06	0.00
New Zealand	−0.08	0.01	−0.08	0.00
Indonesia	−0.08	0.01	−0.09	0.00
Malaysia	−0.15	0.01	−0.16	0.00
Philippines	−0.10	0.04	−0.14	0.00
Singapore	−0.47	−0.02	−0.45	0.00
Thailand	−0.15	0.00	−0.15	0.00
China	−1.05	−0.37	−0.34	−0.33
India	−0.04	0.00	−0.04	0.00
Taiwan	−0.49	−0.07	−0.41	−0.01
Korea	−0.10	−0.02	−0.08	0.00
Hong Kong	−2.63	−0.06	−2.37	−0.20
OECD	−0.05	0.00	−0.05	0.00
OPEC	−0.07	−0.01	−0.05	0.00
Canada	−0.10	−0.09	−0.01	0.00

Source: G-Cubed (Asia Pacific) Model version 50n. Figures taken from Lee and McKibbin (2003)

There have been a number of single country studies as well. For example, Darby (2003) examines the case of Canada and concludes that Canadian losses amounted to 1.5 billion Canadian dollars or 0.15% of Canadian GDP, with the Toronto area being the hardest hit.

The entire episode of SARS lasted just a few weeks. It did not kill many people. Yet the negative economic impact was sharp and swift. This episode and the subsequent bird flu outbreaks in different parts of the world prompted the Congressional Budget Office to produce a potential impact study. It considered two scenarios: Mild (where 25% of the population is affected but not seriously ill, with 1.4% fatality) and Severe (where 30% of the population is affected and a third of them are seriously ill, with 2.5% fatality). They estimated that the supply side impact of a potential pandemic on GDP would be about 4.25% in the severe scenario and about 1% in the mild scenario (Congressional Budget Office 2006).

Box 4.1 Contrasting SARS with HIV/AIDS

SARS is a fast-moving disease, like most forms of influenza. The beginning of an epidemic to the end of the cycle lasts 3 months. The method of transmission of SARS is well-known. There are vaccines available to stop it and there are treatments available for persons with SARS. HIV/AIDS, on the other hand, is a slow-moving disease. In most cases, it stays undetected for years. Infected HIV patients stay outwardly healthy for years. Once somebody is infected with HIV, there is no cure. There is no vaccine to protect uninfected persons.

Infection with SARS and other similar diseases results from even minimal physical contact. Thus, with the help of modern transportation and large populations living in close quarters, it can rapidly spread from one corner of the globe to another in a matter of weeks, as the 2003 outbreak showed. Such diseases would take about a month to build up from a few to a thousand cases. Then it would take perhaps 2–4 weeks to spread from Asia to Europe and the Americas. It has been estimated by the UK health authorities that imposing a 90% restriction on air travel would delay the peak of a pandemic wave by only 1–2 weeks. A 99.9% travel restriction might delay a pandemic wave by 2 months. Thus, for SARS and similar diseases, travel restrictions would do very little to stop the spread of disease.

HIV propagation is slow. It has taken decades for the disease to spread from Western Africa to the rest of the world. This may suggest that it would be easy to stop its propagation. However, given the time it takes for people infected with HIV to show signs of full-blown AIDS, it is still difficult to stop HIV propagation through travel restrictions. For people moving legally from one country to another temporarily, for tourism or other purposes, it is all but impossible to detect an HIV-positive person without running a medical test (using either saliva or blood). It is still prohibitively expensive to run such tests for every single traveler with a sufficient degree of accuracy of the test to make it universal for all travelers. Thus, for all practical purposes, travel restrictions do not work. Of course, this has not stopped many countries from imposing legal barriers on travel and migration (see Chap. 9). Moreover, such restrictions are completely ineffective in the case illegal migration. Today, more than half of global migration takes place illegally.

4.10 Implications for Other Global Diseases

There is evidence that the substantial difference in the transmission rates between the United States and sub-Saharan Africa are due to untreated bacterial sexually transmitted infections. One implication of this evidence is that expanding treatment of other sexually transmitted infections may prove to be a cost effective way to reduce the incidence of HIV/AIDS. Another implication is that lower levels of economic development are not necessarily the root cause of higher rates of HIV/AIDS prevalence or vice versa. Poverty reduction is too broad a goal to constitute what might be termed an HIV/AIDS prevention strategy. Moreover, there is no clear evidence that reducing poverty and income inequality will necessarily reduce HIV/AIDS prevalence. These findings point to the importance of understanding reasons for differences in disease prevalence rates in order to ensure specific and cost effective interventions, a conclusion that applies equally to other diseases and pandemics.

It is difficult to predict the impact of HIV/AIDS on economic development. Since HIV/AIDS strikes the population at a productive age, it may reduce the labor force more than the entire population, and the labor participation rate would fall. However, a decline in the supply of labor would lead to a rise in capital per labor unit in the short run. Nevertheless, in the long run, the supply of capital may fall if rising HIV/AIDS leads to less saving and investment. In addition, falling life expectancy and rising mortality due to HIV/AIDS may lead to lower future economic growth. HIV/AIDS destroys human capital and reduces that transmission of human capital between generations, leading to declining levels of education. The slow-moving nature of HIV/AIDS produces higher costs of treatment and palliative care than epidemics that kill quickly. These additional costs can decrease GDP growth by reducing savings and investment. On the individual level, HIV/AIDS can reduce income and increase costs. However, it is difficult to determine the impact of HIV/AIDS on all macroeconomic variables. As a result, the impact of HIV/AIDS on overall economic welfare, in the form of changes to GDP, remains unclear. Since HIV/AIDS is a slow-moving epidemic, its economic impact will not likely be the same as for fast-moving epidemics.

Microeconomic and epidemiological models for Uganda show that promoting sexual abstinence before marriage and monogamy are less effective HIV/AIDS prevention strategies than condom promotion. Moreover, behavioral responses to HIV/AIDS risk depend on life expectancy. Reducing the risk of death from malaria would be a more effective strategy to increase incentives to change sexual behavior to reduce HIV risk. This finding demonstrates the importance of scientific investigation into the effectiveness of behavioral change strategies and is relevant to the issue of inducing behavioral change to minimize the impact of other diseases and pandemics.

Evidence from Uganda regarding the connection between exports and HIV suggest that targeting prevention at vulnerable groups, notably truckers, would be an effective strategy in generalized HIV epidemics. In addition, if increases in economic activity make the HIV epidemic worse, economic growth strategies need to incorporate HIV prevention strategies. In Chap. 1, we noted the impact of trade and people movement on the propagation of fast-moving epidemics. This highlights the importance of incorporating disease prevention in economic growth strategies in the case of other diseases and pandemics as well. However, as we will see in Chaps. 8 and 9, the need to prevent the spread of infectious diseases must be balanced against the economic importance of trade and people movement and must respect human rights as far as possible.

Another economic issue raised by HIV/AIDS is the side-effect of large increases in foreign aid to combat HIV/AIDS in high-prevalence, low-income countries. Where foreign aid increases the money supply, inflation may rise and the balance of payments may deteriorate. Large inflows of resources could significantly raise the real value of the local currency, thereby producing low economic growth, increased international debt, higher imports and lower exports. Additional expenditures would raise the wages of skilled professionals, making the private sector less competitive in the long run. The economy would become significantly more dependent on aid and remain that way for the indefinite future. Thus, foreign aid is not an unmitigated blessing. These findings apply equally to foreign aid that is targeted at other diseases and pandemics.

Another question is whether we can justify singling out HIV/AIDS for increased funding when lives could be saved in other, less expensive programs. There are a number of justifications for spending money on HIV/AIDS (and other infectious diseases). First, since HIV/AIDS is infectious, HIV prevention saves more than the life of the person who avoids HIV infection. Second, prevention targeted at vulnerable groups is a cost effective means to reduce disease propagation among the general population. Third, where HIV/AIDS funding is spent to strengthen general health care systems, the benefits are not limited to HIV/AIDS alone.

References

Acemoglu D, Johnson S (2005) Disease and Development: The Effect of Life Expectancy on Economic Growth. Mimeo, MIT, Cambridge

Ainsworth M, Over M (1995) AIDS and African Development. World Bank Research Observer 9:203–241

Bearman PS, Brückner H (2001) Promising the Future: Virginity Pledges and First Intercourse. American Journal of Sociology 106:859–912

Bell C, Devarajan S, Gersbach H (2004) Thinking About the Long-Run Economic Costs of AIDS. In: Haacker M (ed) The Macroeconomics of HIV/AIDS. IMF, Washington

Bils M, Klenow P (2000) Does Schooling Cause Growth? American Economic Review 90:1160–1183

Biswalo PM, Lie GT (1995) Hospital-Based Counselling of HIV-Infected People and AIDS Patients. In: Klepp KI, Biswalo PM, Talle A (eds) Young People at Risk: Fighting AIDS in Northern Tanzania. Scandinavian University Press, Oslo

Bleakley H (2003) Disease and Development: Evidence from the American South. Journal of European Economic Association 1:376–386

Bleakley H, Lange F (2005) Chronic Disease Burden and the Interaction of Education, Fertility and Growth. UCSD Mimeo

Bloom D, Mahal A (1997) Does the AIDS Epidemic Threaten Economic Growth. Journal of Econometrics 77:105–124

Bloom D, Mahal A (2001) HIV/AIDS and the Private Sector: A Literature Review. River Path Associates, American Foundation for AIDS, Washington, DC:

Boldrin M, Jones LE (2002) Mortality, Fertility, and Saving in a Malthusian Economy. Review of Economic Dynamics 5:775–814

Bonnel R (2000) HIV/AIDS: Does it Increase or Decrease Growth in Africa? Mimeo, World Bank, Washington

Botswana Sentinel Survey (2001) Botswana Government Publication, Gaborone, Botswana

Bryce J, Black RE, Walker N, Bhutta ZA, Lawn JE, Steketee RW (2005) Can the world afford to save the lives of 6 million children each year? Lancet 365:2193–2200

Chakraborty S (2004) Endogenous Lifetime and Economic Growth. Journal of Economic Theory 116:34–67

Chin (1994) A Beginner's Guide to EPIMODEL, Version 2.1, University of California, Berkeley

Clark G (2005) The Long March of History: Farm Laborers Wages in England 1208–1840. Working Paper, University of California-Davis

Cohen B (1998) The Emerging Fertility Transition in Sub-Saharan Africa. World Development 26:1431–1461

Cohen D (2002) Human Capital and the HIV Epidemic in Sub-Saharan Africa. World Bank, Washington

Congressional Budget Office (2006) A Potential Influenza Pandemic: Possible Macroeconomic Effects and Policy Issues. Congressional Budget Office, Washington, DC

Corrigan P, Glomm G, Mendez F (2005) AIDS Crisis and Growth. Journal of Development Economics 77(1):107–124

Darby P (2003) The Economic Impact of SARS. The Conference Board of Canada

David A (2007) Social Capital, HIV/AIDS, Economic Development. World Bank Policy Research Working Paper 4263

Doepke M (2005) Child Mortality and Fertility Decline: Does the Barro-Becker Model Fit the Facts? Journal of Population Economics 18:337–366

Ehrlich I, Lui FT (1991) Intergenerational Trade, Longevity, Intrafamily Transfers and Economic Growth. Journal of Political Economy 99:1029–1059

Gray R (2005) Lessons from Africa. Presentation at the International AIDS Society Conference, Rio de Janeiro

Green G (1994) The reproductive careers of a cohort of men and women following an HIV positive diagnosis. Journal of Biosocial Science 26:409–415

Guinness L, Kumaranayake L, Hanson K (2007) A Cost Function for HIV Prevention Services: Is There a 'U' Shape? Cost Effectiveness and Resource Allocation 5:5(1)

Haacker M (2002) The Economic Consequences of HIV/AIDS in South Africa. IMF Working Paper, IMF, Washington, DC

Halperin D (2007) AIDS Prevention: What Works? Washington Post 22 October 2007 A23

Hellinger F (1998) Cost and Financing of Care for Persons with HIV Disease. Health Care Financing Review 19:5–18

Holtgrave DR, Crosby RA (2003) Social Capital, Poverty, and Income Inequality as Predictors of Gonorrhea, Syphilis, Chlamydia and AIDS Case Rates in the United States. Sexually Transmitted Infections 79:62–64

Human Rights Watch (2005) The Less They Know, the Better: Abstinence-Only HIV/AIDS Programs in Uganda. March 17:4(A)

Husain IZ, Badcock-Walters P. Economics of HIV/AIDS mitigation: responding to problems of systemic dysfunction and sectoral capacity. In: Forsythe S, ed. State of the art: AIDS and economics. Washington, DC, Policy Project, 2002:84–95.

Juhn C, Kalemli-Ozcan S, Turan B (2007) HIV and Fertility in Africa: First Evidence from Population Based Surveys. Working Paper, December

Kalemli-Ozcan S (2006) AIDS, Reversal of the Demographic Transition and Economic Development: Evidence from Africa. Working Paper 12181, National Bureau of Economic Research

Kasyate S (2005) The Less They Know the Better: Abstinence Only HIV/AIDS Program in Uganda, Human Rights Watch, March 2005 Vol. 17, No. 4 (A)

Klitsch M (1992) Rural Ugandan Women's HIV Infection Rates SeemRelated to Truck Routes. International Family Planning Perspectives 18:79

Kyomuhendo S, Ssempa M, Lamulatu L, Langa S, Kiwanuka J, Green EC (2004) Uganda National Abstinence and Being Faithful Policy And Strategy On Prevention Of Transmission of HIV/AIDS. Uganda AIDS Commission, Kampala

Lee JW, McKibbin W (2003) Globalization and Disease: The Case of SARS. Working Paper No. 2003/16, Australian National University

Lipsitz A Bishop PD Robinson C (2003) Virginity Pledges: Who takes them and how well do they work? Poster presented at: 15th Annual Convention of the American Psychological Society May 31 Atlanta, Georgia

Lorentzen P, McMillan J, Wacziarg R (2004) Death and Development. Mimeo, Stanford University

Luke N, Munshi K (2004) New Roles for Marriage in Urban Africa: Sexual Activity and Labor Market Outcomes in Kisumu. Mimeo, Brown University

McNeill W (1976) Plagues and People. Doubleday Publishing Company, New York

McPherson MF (2007) Can a Developing Country Support the Welfare Needs of Children Affected by AIDS? Paper submitted to the Joint Learning Initiative on Children and AIDS

Meltzer D (1992) Mortality Decline, the Demographic Transition and Economic Growth. PhD Dissertation, University of Chicago

Moore M, Viscusi K (1988) Doubling the Estimated Value of Life: Results using New Occupational Facility Data. Journal of Policy Analysis and Management 7:476–490

Mosley H (2005) The ABC's of AIDS Prevention: What's the Controversy? Johns Hopkins University, CCIH Conference

Muntaner C, Lynch J (2002) Social Capital, Class Gender and Race Conflict, and Population Health: An Essay Review of Bowling Alone's Implications for Social Epidemiology. International Journal of Epidemiology 31:261–267

Okware S (2007) Opportunities and Challenges in HIVAIDS Prevention and Control. International Workshop on Strengthening Capacity for HIV/AIDS Treat-ment and Care in West and East Africa, Kampala

Oster E (2005) Sexually Transmitted Infections, Sexual Behavior, and the HIV/AIDS Epidemic. Quarterly Journal of Economics 120:467–514

Oster E (2006) Measuring the Magnitude of HIV in Africa," Working Paper, University of Chicago, November, 2006

Oster E (2007a) HIV and Sexual Behavior Change: Why not Africa? Working Paper, University of Chicago

Oster E (2007b) Routes of Infection: Exports and HIV Incidence in Sub-Saharan Africa. Working Paper, University of Chicago

Over M (1992) The Macroeconomic Impact of AIDS in Sub-Saharan Africa. World Bank Working Paper

Papageorgiou C, Stoytcheva P (2004) What Do We Know About the Impact of AIDS on Cross-Country Income So Far? Mimeo, LSU

Peterson A (2003) Testimony of Dr. Anne Peterson, USAID Assistant Administrator for Global Health before the Subcommittee on African Affairs, Committee on Foreign Rela-ations, http://www.usaid.gov/press/speeches/2003/ty030519.html. May 19, 2003

Poulin MA, Muula S (2007) Male Circumcision and HIV Infection: The Case of Malawi. Working Paper, Princeton University

Putnam RD (2000) Bowling alone: the collapse and revival of American community. Touchstone, New York

Steinbrook R (2007) HIV In India – A Complex Epidemic. New England Journal of Medicine 356:1089–1093

Stover J et al. (2006) The Global Impact of Scaling-Up HIV/AIDS Prevention Programs in Low- and Middle-Income Countries 2006 Mar 10, 311:1474–1476

US Personal Responsibility and Work Opportunity Reconciliation Act of 1996 http://frwebgate.access.gpo.gov/cgi-bin/getdoc.cgi?dbname=104_cong_bills&docid=f:h3734enr.txt.pdf. Accessed 30 December 2007

USAID (2002) The "ABCs" of HIV Prevention: Report of a USAID Technical Meeting On Behavior Change Approaches To Primary Prevention of HIV/AIDS US Agency for "ABC" Experts Technical Meeting, International Development, Washington

Werker E, Ahuja A, Wendell B (2006) Male Circumcision and the Economic Impact of AIDS in Africa. Mimeo, Harvard Business School

WHO (2005) Estimating the Cost of Scaling-up Maternal and Newborn Health Interventions to Reach Universal Coverage: Methodology and Assumptions. Technical Working Paper

World Bank (2006) Second National HIV/AIDS Control Project for India

Young A (2005) The Gift of the Dying: The Tragedy of AIDS and the Welfare of Future African Generations. Quarterly Journal of Economics 120:423–466

Young A (2006) In Sorrow to Bring Forth Children: Fertility Amidst the Plague of HIV. Mimeo, University of Chicago

5 The Political Economy of Patents and Global Health Threats

"There never did, there never will, and there never can, exist … any description of men, or any generation of men, in any country, possessed of the right or the power of binding and controlling posterity to the end of time."

Thomas Paine

HIV/AIDS raises the divisive issue of the distribution of costs and benefits between developed and developing countries in addressing global diseases, in particular with respect to patents for pharmaceutical products negotiated through the TRIPS Agreement. It is important to understand how and why the developing countries agreed to the terms and conditions of TRIPS during the negotiations of the final phase of the Uruguay Round of multilateral trade negotiations. Jagdish Bhagwati was an active participant in the negotiations. According to Bhagwati, there were four main reasons why the developing countries came to the table. First, the developing countries wanted to get concessions for their main exports: textiles and agricultural products. They believed that the business community in the developed countries would not support these concessions unless they supported TRIPS. Second, they feared that large nations like the United States would punish them by taking unilateral trade sanctions if they did not respect intellectual property rights. Third, many developing countries speculated that intellectual property protection would attract foreign investment and eventually technology transfer. Fourth, some of the (larger) developing countries (like India and Brazil) recognized that they were themselves in a position to create valuable intellectual property through their creative industries. Thus, they wanted to position themselves for these future benefits (Bhagwati 1994).

In Chap. 6, we will analyze the key TRIPS provisions regarding patents in greater detail. In this chapter, we focus on the political economy of national and international regulation of pharmaceutical patents. First, we examine the WTO negotiations to amend the TRIPS Agreement to facilitate access to pharmaceutical products in developing countries, which took place against the backdrop of the terrorist attacks of 11 September 2001 and the subsequent anthrax scare in the United States and Canada. Second, we examine how developed countries have applied political pressure to discourage developing countries from exercising their rights to suspend patents under compulsory licenses, in particular with respect to compulsory licensing in Thailand. Third, we examine how the United States has used free trade agreements to reverse the gains made by developing countries in the WTO negotiations on pharmaceutical patents. We then examine how the problem of national regulatory capture can lead to de facto international regulatory capture when the national government in question has disproportionate influence in international organizations or disproportionate bargaining power in international negotiations.

Finally, we analyze the economic rationale for patents in order to determine the extent to which patent laws reflect health, economic and political concerns.

5.1 The Political Economy of Compulsory Licensing

Patents are granted by governments on the national level, which means that they only have legal effect in the jurisdictions where the application for a patent has been granted. However, the TRIPS Agreement harmonizes the national patent laws of WTO Members by establishing minimum standards for the protection of patent rights. By virtue of TRIPS Articles 28 and 33, a patent gives its owner a 20-year monopoly on making, using, selling or importing a patented product. However, TRIPS Article 29 places conditions on patent applicants. An applicant for a patent must disclose the invention in a manner sufficiently clear and complete for the invention to be carried out by a person skilled in the art. In addition, an applicant may be required to indicate the best mode for carrying out the invention known to the inventor at the filing date. Governments may require an applicant for a patent to provide information concerning the applicant's corresponding foreign applications and grants as well. TRIPS Article 39 requires governments to protect undisclosed test or other data, submitted to obtain marketing approval for pharmaceutical products which utilize new chemical entities, against unfair commercial use. In addition, governments must protect such data against disclosure, except where necessary to protect the public, or unless steps are taken to ensure that the data are protected against unfair commercial use. However, governments have the right to grant a compulsory license, which permits the use of the invention without the patent holder's authorization. Under TRIPS Article 31, a government may issue a compulsory license authorizing the government or a third party to produce generic drugs without the authorization of the patent holder where negotiations fail to obtain authorization on reasonable commercial terms. However, the use of the patent must be "predominantly" to supply the domestic market and the patent holder must be paid adequate remuneration, based on the economic value of the license. The negotiation requirement may be waived in cases of national emergency, extreme urgency, or non-commercial public use. The beneficiary of a compulsory license can produce the patented product or import it from a country where it is not patented. To understand the issue of the political economy of compulsory licensing in both the national and international arenas, we will examine the relatively simple case of anthrax.

5.1.1 The Case of Anthrax

In October 2001, the first inhalational anthrax case in the United States since 1976 was identified in a media company worker in Florida. The other cases that followed came with threatening letters that mentioned 11 September 2001, denounced Israel and praised Allah. The US government initiated a national investigation to identify additional cases of possible exposure to *Bacillus anthracis*. From 4 October to 20 November 2001, 22 cases of anthrax (eleven inhalational and eleven cutaneous) were identified; five of the inhalational cases were fatal. Twenty patients were either mail handlers or were exposed to worksites where contaminated mail was processed or received. Initially, there were reports that some of them were "weaponized" versions of anthrax that were developed in Iraq. These reports were never substantiated. Instead, B. anthracis isolates from four powder-containing envelopes, 17 specimens from patients and 106 environmental samples were proven to be indistinguishable by molecular sub-typing. One case of possible anthrax contamination proved to be a hoax in January 2001 (Kournikakis et al., 2001). These highly publicized cases got the American and the Canadian governments scrambling to prepare for the worst.

As a reaction to the potential threat of anthrax as a bio-terrorist weapon, the United States and Canada used the threat of a compulsory license against German pharmaceutical company, Bayer, to lower the price of anthrax drugs (Lancet Editorial 2001). Following the appearance of anthrax in the United States, the Canadian government decided to acquire a stockpile of ciprofloxacin (Cipro) in case the same problem occurred in Canada (although not a single person died in Canada as a result of anthrax contact). At the time, Cipro was considered to be the most potent drug to fight anthrax infections. Health Canada, the national healthcare authority of Canada, ordered one million pills of Cipro from Canadian generic drug manufacturer Apotex, even though Bayer's patent would not expire until 2004. The Canadian Minister of Health claimed that he had placed the order with the generic manufacturer because Bayer was unable to fill the order. Bayer denied the claim.

Bayer and Canadian government later reached an agreement in which Bayer agreed not to sue the Canadian government for violating its own patent laws and to supply one million Cipro tablets within 48 hours of receiving an order. The less expensive generic drugs already purchased by the government would be held by Bayer, to be used in case Bayer was unable to fill an order. After the US government negotiated a price discount with Bayer on its purchase of Cipro, Bayer agreed to give Canada the same discount, which lowered the price to the same price charged by the generic manufacturer. Thus, while a compulsory license was actually issued, it was not given effect, in light of Bayer's commitment to supply the Canadian market.

In the United States, the Secretary of Health and Human Services negotiated a price reduction from the US retail price of USD 4–5 per pill (and the USD 1.75 per pill that Bayer offered to the US government) to just under USD 1 per pill. The Secretary had said he would consider going to Congress to seek a waiver of the patent and to allow production of a generic medication if Bayer did not lower its price. Nevertheless, the US Government openly denied its intention of issuing a compulsory license to produce Cipro, even though it seems reasonable to assume that they might have issued it if they needed to. However, the threat by itself succeeded in lowering the price.

While negotiations with Bayer were proceeding in North America, trade negotiators in Geneva were preparing for the WTO Ministerial Conference that would
take place in Doha, Qatar from 9–13 November 2001. In the words of a trade nego-
tiator from Brazil, the Canadian and American moves had provoked "a lot of talk
in the corridors." One trade delegate said there was a lot of anger that there was a
double standard at work. A group of developing countries began pushing harder
for a clarification to the patent rules in the WTO TRIPS agreement that would allow them to circumvent patents to protect public health.

Prior to the Doha Ministerial Conference, the United States took the position that there was no need to change the TRIPS Agreement and was backed by
Switzerland, Japan and Canada on this issue. However, the threats that Canada
and the United States had made against Bayer's patent on Cipro weakened their
bargaining position.

In preparation for the Doha meeting, two competing visions emerged. One
version, backed by the United States, proposed to acknowledge a right "to take
measures necessary to address public health crises, in particular to secure affordable access to medicines." The version backed by developing countries provided
that "nothing in TRIPS shall prevent members from taking measures to protect
public health." Going into the Doha meeting, the Director General of the WTO,
Mike Moore, declared that "this could well be the deal-breaker at this conference."

5.1.2 The WTO Declaration on the TRIPS Agreement and Public Health

At Doha, Brazil and India used their combined leverage in the WTO to champion
the cause of creating a clearer public health exception to the patent rules. By the
fourth day of the ministerial meeting, the negotiators had reached a tentative agreement stating that TRIPS "shall be interpreted and implemented in a manner supportive of WTO members' rights to protect public health and in particular to ensure
access to medicines for all." However, while developing countries were insisting
on the word "shall," some developed countries were insisting on the weaker "can
and should." While the final agreement that was reached contains many more provisions, the following paragraph represents the consensus reached on this point:

> 4. We agree that the TRIPS Agreement does not and should not prevent
> members from taking measures to protect public health. Accordingly, while
> reiterating our commitment to the TRIPS Agreement, we affirm that the
> Agreement can and should be interpreted and implemented in a manner
> supportive of WTO members' right to protect public health and, in par-
> ticular, to promote access to medicines for all.
>
> In this connection, we reaffirm the right of WTO members to use, to
> the full, the provisions in the TRIPS Agreement, which provide flexibility
> for this purpose.

The severity of the HIV/AIDS crisis in many parts of the developing world, combined with the duplicitious policy of Canada and the United States regarding patent rights, contributed to a North–South divide at the Doha Ministerial Conference over the issue of drug patents and threatened to derail global trade negotiations. There was also a North–North divide with respect to this issue. The European Commission and Norway took fairly flexible positions regarding the developing countries' positions. In addition, important sectors of civil society within developed countries shared the same concerns as those of developing countries, as abundantly displayed in international public opinion during the pre-Doha debate. The result was the TRIPS Declaration, which clarified the application of TRIPS provisions to public health crises, including HIV/AIDS, malaria and tuberculosis. Seven months later, the TRIPS Declaration led to the *Decision of the Council for TRIPS of 27 June 2002* (the Transition Period Decision) and a Waiver delaying the application of TRIPS patent obligations for pharmaceuticals in the least-developed countries until 2016. However, as the discussion in the next part shows, this was insufficient to provide least-developed countries that lack manufacturing capacity with the same access to pharmaceuticals that those with manufacturing capacity enjoy.

5.1.3 The Problem Identified in Paragraph 6 of the TRIPS Declaration

The ability to manufacture drugs under compulsory license provides developing countries with significant bargaining power to extract price concessions for patented drugs or to issue compulsory licenses when those price negotiations fail. The TRIPS Declaration further enhances that bargaining power by clarifying the circumstances in which a patent may effectively be revoked to deal with public health crises. However, this bargaining power applies only to countries that have the capacity to produce generic drugs under compulsory licenses issued to government laboratories or private generic producers (for example, see the case of Brazil in Chap. 2). Many developing countries do not have the capacity to manufacture generic drugs. This weakens their bargaining position substantially unless they can import generic drugs from another country that has issued a compulsory license on their behalf or that has not granted a patent on the drug in question. Since most countries with pharmaceutical manufacturing capacity are WTO Members, and are required to grant 20-year patents by virtue of TRIPS, the latter option is less likely to be available. To serve as an effective bargaining chip, the threat to issue a compulsory license must be credible.

The TRIPS Declaration recognized this problem in paragraph 6:

> 6. We recognize that WTO members with insufficient or no manufacturing capacities in the pharmaceutical sector could face difficulties in making effective use of compulsory licensing under the TRIPS Agreement. We instruct the Council for TRIPS to find an expeditious solution to this problem and to report to the General Council before the end of 2002.

What is the extent of the problem identified in Paragraph 6? Let us consider two examples of circumstances in which TRIPS might allow WTO members to export part of their generic production to countries in need.

1. When Argentina fell into its economic crisis in 2001–2002, patients who relied on the Argentine government to provide medicine were put at risk (including diabetics and HIV-positive patients on drug therapy). Brazil sent emergency supplies of generic HIV/AIDS drugs to Argentina. Brazil supplied these drugs to Argentina on a non-commercial basis. On the same basis, Brazil has also supplied small amounts of drugs to a few African countries (such as Kenya) and some other Latin-American countries. In principle, such exports should meet the requirements of TRIPS Article 31 (see Chap. 6). The destination (Argentina) is a developing country. Argentina may accept the donations of drugs from Brazil, since its economic crisis (and the resulting lack of medicine for patients whose lives depend on it) qualifies as a situation of national emergency, extreme urgency, or non-commercial public use under TRIPS Article 31. The Brazilian exports are likely to meet the requirements of Article 31(f) because Brazilian production is used to serve predominantly the Brazilian market. The head of Brazil's HIV/AIDS program has stated that the limited capacity of the state laboratory, combined with a limited health budget, puts Brazil in no position to provide generic drugs (in large scale) to other countries. Doctors Without Borders buys small quantities of generic medicine from Brazil to provide free triple-therapy treatment to a limited number of patients in South Africa. Moreover, such operations seem to be less likely to be challenged by pharmaceutical companies than the substantial price cuts offered by Indian companies, such as in example (2) below.

2. Cipla Ltd. of India, a major manufacturer of generic drugs, offered to supply triple-therapy drug "cocktails" (a triple-combination of anti-retroviral drugs (ARV): *stavudine* (d4T) + *lamivudine* (3TC) + *nevirapine* (NVP)) for USD 350 a year per patient to Doctors Without Borders. The doctors' group, which won the Nobel Peace Prize in 1999, would distribute the Cipla drugs for free in Africa. Cipla also offered to sell the drugs to larger government programs for USD 600 a year per patient, about USD 400 below the price offered by the companies that held the patent.

There had been a dramatic drop in the price of the ingredients of HIV/AIDS drugs. This is illustrated in Table 5.1. The drop in price for AZT between 1998 and 2001 was slightly over 20%. For the other three drugs, D4T, 3TC and *nevirapine*, the drop in price was in the order of 90%.

Table 5.1. Global prices for active ingredients for HIV/AIDS drugs

Price of	AZT	D4T	3TC	Nevirapine
Midyear 1998	800	10,000	10,000	10,000
Midyear 1999	750	2,500	5,000	7,000
Midyear 2001	650	1,000	750	1,500

Note: Prices are expressed in dollars per kilo. *Source*: James Love, Consumer Project on Technology, Washington, DC. Available at http://lists.essential.org/pipermail/ip-health/2001-March/001087.html

The fall in price documented above is a clear result of the introduction of generic drugs. This effect is illustrated vividly in Fig. 5.1. The patented version of the drug cocktail sold for USD 10,439 (up to September 2000). Brazil's government laboratories produced and sold to the government-sponsored programs in Brazil the same cocktail for USD 2,767 in June 2000. Cipla started selling the cocktail for USD 800 in September 2000. By October 2000, the patented version sold for USD 931. In February 2001, Cipla upped the ante by selling the drug cocktail for USD 350. This action prompted a reduction in the price of the patented version to USD 727 by April 2001. Later, two more Indian companies brought the price down further to USD 209 (Aurobindo in April 2002) and then to USD 201 (Hetero in January 2003) (Doctors without Borders 2003). The offers from Cipla, Aurobindo, Hetero and Ranbaxy – all Indian generic pharmaceutical manufacturers – has had the effect of motivating patent holders to lower the price of the patented versions in the same markets. By June 2007, the originators had lowered the price to USD 343 in response to Ranbaxy's offer of USD 99. At the end, the price war had produced a 99% price reduction for 3TC/d4T/NVP.

In the case of the price cuts offered by Indian companies, the destination countries are primarily least-developed countries. TRIPS allowed least-developed countries and developing countries to delay providing patent protection for pharmaceuticals. Least-developed countries could delay intellectual property protection generally until 2006, while developing countries could do so until 2000. With respect to patents however, developing countries could delay protection until 2005 if they did

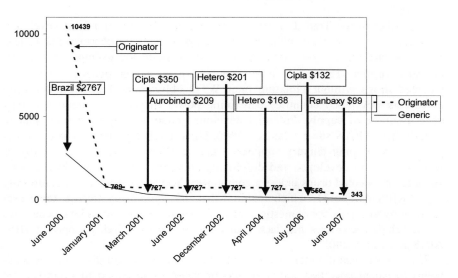

Fig. 5.1. Price of triple therapy 2000–2007. *Source*: Médicins sans Frontières

not provide patent protection for a particular area of technology when TRIPS obligations came into effect in 1995. Less than 20 developing countries fit this description, but they included Brazil and India. However, the affected WTO members still had to permit patent applications to be submitted during this transition period for pharmaceutical products (the so-called mailbox provision). If the country later approved the sale of the product, and a patent has been filed and granted in another WTO member after 1 January 1995, the patent applicant had to be given "exclusive marketing rights" for 5 years even though there was no patent. These obligations have been in force since 1 January 1 1995. In a WTO dispute involving India, the WTO Appellate Body found that India had not complied with its obligations under TRIPS Articles 70.8(a) and 70.9 because these articles came into effect 1 January 1995 and India had not introduced legislation to implement them (India – Patent Protection for Pharmaceutical and Agricultural Chemical Products, WTO Appellate Body, 1997).

The TRIPS Declaration provides, "We also agree that the least-developed country members will not be obliged, with respect to pharmaceutical products, to implement or apply Sects. 5 and 7 of Part II of the TRIPS Agreement or to enforce rights provided for under these Sections until 1 January 2016...." Section 5 applies to patents and Sect. 7 applies to the protection of undisclosed information. The TRIPS Transition Period Decision formalizes paragraph 7 of the TRIPS Declaration, using the same language. While this suspension of obligations takes the form of a Decision, the effect is to waive these obligations for least-developed countries for the stated period of time. The TRIPS Waiver provides, "The obligations of least-developed country Members under paragraph 9 of Article 70 of the TRIPS Agreement shall be waived with respect to pharmaceutical products until 1 January 2016."

The effect of the Transition Period Decision and Waiver, for least developed countries, is to waive their obligations to provide patents for pharmaceuticals and exclusive marketing rights until 2016, at which point the exemptions may be extended further. Thus, they may manufacture or import generic versions of patented drugs without violating their WTO obligations. However, this only gives least-developed countries bargaining power in price negotiations if they have a source of supply. Potential developed countries suppliers have had to comply with TRIPS since 1 January 1996. Since 1 January 2005, India and other potential developing country suppliers (such as China) have had to comply as well. Thus, both developed and developing countries could not produce generic versions of patented drugs unless a compulsory license were issued in conformity with TRIPS Article 31, which required that the compulsory license serve predominantly to supply the domestic market. Where would least-developed countries and developing countries that lack manufacturing capacity find a supply of HIV/AIDS drugs after 2005?

Uncertainty regarding the scope of TRIPS Article 31 would discourage amendments to patent laws that authorize generic suppliers to export to countries that lack manufacturing capacity. Even if national governments chose to authorize such exports, the legal uncertainty regarding the WTO consistency of such measures would increase the risk to the generic drug producers disproportionately in comparison to the attractiveness of the mostly small and poor country markets that would be the destination of the exports. The importance of even relatively minor obstacles to generic entry in such markets has been pointed out by Lanjouw (2003). These are the issues that lay at the heart of the problem identified in Paragraph 6. The solution was the Paragraph 6 Decision of 2003, and the subsequent amendment to TRIPS Article 31 of 2005, which allow a WTO Member with the necessary manufacturing capacity to issue a compulsory license to export medicine to another WTO Member, within the parameters set out in the decision. No formal restriction on the countries that are eligible to import exists under the Paragraph 6 system, but several WTO Members have made a commitment not to use the Paragraph 6 system as importers and some WTO Members have committed to use the system as importers only in situations of national emergency or extreme urgency (see Chap. 6).

5.1.4 Abbott in Thailand

As we noted in Chap. 2, in January 2007, the Thai government announced that it would issue a compulsory license to produce lower-cost generic versions of Abbott Laboratories' antiretroviral Kaletra. Thailand, like other members of the WTO, has a right to issue compulsory licenses for domestic use of patented products by virtue of TRIPS Article 31 or under the Paragraph 6 Decision. Thailand made no commitment to restrict its use of the Paragraph 6 Decision. Nevertheless, the Thai move proved to be controversial. The United States placed Thailand on a priority watch list of countries, citing the Thai government's decision as "further indications of a weakening of respect for patents" (USTR 2007a, p 27). The European Union's Trade Commissioner Peter Mandelson sent a letter lamenting Thailand's disregard for Abbot's intellectual property.

One day after Abbott Laboratories and Thailand failed to reach an agreement on the price of Abbott's antiretroviral drugs Aluvia and Kaletra, the Thai Health Minister offered to not issue compulsory licenses if the pharmaceutical companies offered prices lower than those charged by generic drug makers. Aluvia is a heat-stable version of Kaletra that eliminates the need for refrigeration and doesn't need to be taken with food, both advantages in a tropical developing country such as Thailand. Abbott offered to sell Aluvia in Thailand for USD 1,000, per person annually on the condition that the country agree not to allow generic versions of the drug into the market, that Thailand not to seek compulsory licensing for Aluvia and that the price of Aluvia could not be reduced any further. Indian generic drug maker Matrix Laboratories offered to sell a generic version of Aluvia to Thailand for USD 695, per person annually. Abbott had reduced its price for Kaletra in Thailand to USD 2,200 per patient per year in 2006.

Abbott threatened to not register the patent for Aluvia in Thailand and to not sell it in Thailand, in order to block the option of compulsory licensing. By not registering the patent, Abbott would not have to disclose to the Thai government its patented process for making Aluvia and there would be no Thai patent for which to issue a compulsory license under the TRIPS Article 31 exception. Thus, Abbott's strategy would undermine the credibility of Thailand's threat to issue the compulsory license on Aluvia (though not on Kaletra) and strengthen Abbott's negotiating power with respect to the price for Aluvia in Thailand.

However, Thailand would still have the option of issuing a compulsory license to import Aluvia from a country where the patent has been registered, using the Paragraph 6 system, provided that another country would be willing to do so. There are two problems with this approach. First, it is not clear whether the patent would have to be registered in Thailand in order for Thailand to use the Paragraph 6 Decision to import a generic version from a country where the patent is registered. Second, even if the lack of registration in Thailand were not an obstacle to using the Paragraph 6 Decision, it is likely that the United States (and possibly the European Union) would pressure other countries not to issue a compulsory license to export a generic version of Aluvia to Thailand.

The Paragraph 6 system has only been used once (see Chap. 6). In 2007, Canada issued a compulsory license to export generic drugs to Rwanda, following efforts by Médicins sans Frontières (MSF) to test the new system. Initially, MSF could not find an eligible developing country that was willing to issue the corresponding license to import generic drugs under the Paragraph 6 system, because no developing country government it worked with was willing to do so, possibly because of the political pressure that had been applied to Brazil and Thailand after they had used compulsory licenses (Hestermeyer 2007).

The pressure applied to Thailand over its use of compulsory licensing and the difficulty of finding countries that are willing to use the Paragraph 6 system both demonstrate that, despite the changes that have been made to the WTO patent rules, the politics of patents still remain an obstacle to access to medicine in developing countries.

5.1.5 Foreign Aid, Foreign AIDS and Regulatory Capture

There is another obstacle that stands in the way of effectively implementing the TRIPS Paragraph 6 solution – the spending power of the US government. Countries that rely on American foreign aid are reluctant to use the Paragraph 6 system for fear of losing that aid. For example, Central American governments reportedly continue to use more expensive patented AIDS drugs, rather than cheaper generic versions that would increase the availability of treatment, to avoid irritating the US government. Moreover, US aid for AIDS during the George W. Bush Administration came with strings attached that promote less effective AIDS strategies that are designed to cater to religious conservatives and to favor the interests of the US pharmaceutical industry (see Chaps. 4 and 8). There are two incentives for the US government to use its spending power to induce the adoption of less effective AIDS programs in developing countries: (1) campaign contributions from the US pharmaceutical industry and (2) votes from religious conservatives.

If a small developing country, such as Guatemala, buys patented AIDS drugs for 1,000 patients at a cost of USD 10,000 per year, the pharmaceutical company gets USD 10 million to supply drugs whose marginal cost is extremely low. If the pharmaceutical company donates USD 1 million of that to political parties as campaign contributions, it is left with a substantial profit. The US government can then tax those profits, generating revenue that can be channeled into foreign aid programs that induce the developing country government to restrict the use of generics. The US government wins, the political parties win and the pharmaceutical industry wins. The Guatemalan government wins because it gets more money to spend. But the people with HIV/AIDS in Guatemala lose, because fewer people have access to treatment. If a country like Canada offers to supply cheap generic drugs under the Paragraph 6 system, the offer does no good unless the government of a country that needs the drugs requests them. As we noted above, most developing country governments have been unwilling to do so.

In countries with federal systems of government, such as the United States and Canada, constitutional jurisdiction to legislate is divided between a federal government and states or provinces. Federal governments use their power to tax and spend in order to induce states or provinces to adopt particular policies that fall within the jurisdiction of the latter. At the global level, there is no world government with the power to tax and spend. The US government has taken advantage of its spending power to use this strategy at the global level to induce poor countries to adopt particular policies with respect to AIDS and other issues. This use of spending power undermines the international rule of law to the extent that it induces governments to avoid exercising the rights that are available to them in international agreements such as TRIPS.

In Fig. 5.2, we explain the process through which the regulatory capture process takes place at the international level. The WTO sets international rules regarding the national laws that govern trade between Member countries and that govern intellectual property protection. Here, we use the example of the US government as a developed country. The same logic would apply to many other developed countries as well. The dotted boxes connect the US government and a developing country through the market access that is facilitated by WTO rules. This process benefits traders in both the countries. However, the pharmaceutical industry adds another element to the equation.

The preference of the US pharmaceutical industry is to sell patented drugs to the developing country. However, the TRIPS Agreement allows the developing country to use compulsory licensing get generic drugs at a lower cost from other sources, or to take advantage of parallel imports. Because US pharmaceutical companies make the largest donations to elected officials among all industries in the

United States, they are able to apply pressure to the US government to draft laws and regulations that benefit the US pharmaceutical industry, such as foreign aid regulations. A good example is PEPFAR, through which the US government pays for the HIV/AIDS drugs that are supplied to developing countries. PEPFAR regulations do not permit the purchase of WHO-approved drugs, but only drugs approved by the US FDA and some other national regulatory agencies (see Chap. 8). The regulations governing other US foreign aid programs can also be designed to require that the money be used to purchase the products of US companies, rather than less costly alternatives. In addition to formal regulations, the policies and practices of the US government can be influenced by the pharmaceutical industry. Thus, through the national regulatory process, the US pharmaceutical industry is able to extract regulatory concessions in exchange for campaign donations.

This process can be described as the regulatory "market" that operates inside the United States. The US government can use the leverage of foreign aid to induce the developing country to adopt the policy preferred by the US pharmaceutical industry, which is to purchase their patented drugs. Moreover, even when the US government is not directly providing foreign aid, it can influence the laws and policies of the developing country through bilateral trade negotiations (see the next section). The US government can also influence the policies of multilateral organizations, such as the World Bank and the International Monetary Fund, because it is one of the largest donors to these organizations. In Sect. 5.2, we explain precisely the mechanism by which such a regulatory capture occurs in the international arena.

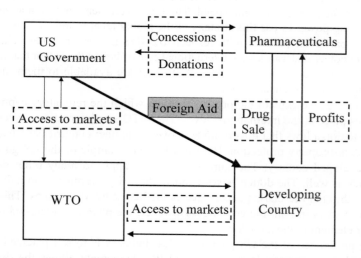

Fig. 5.2. Indirect influence of pharmaceutical companies. Source: Elaboration of the authors

In the absence of a world government that can tax and spend in the interests of all people, the US government is able to act as a de facto world governor that uses its spending power to serve more narrow interests. So what is the solution? A global authority with the power to tax and spend more benignly than the US government would be one solution. The Global Fund aims to fulfill this role for developing country diseases, but through donations rather than taxation. A variation on the proposed Tobin tax provides an alternative means of financing the Global Fund. But the US government is unlikely to agree to create a competitor that would take its funding strings away. This explains why the Bush administration prefers to channel the bulk of its AIDS funding bilaterally, rather than through the Global Fund (see Chap. 7).

5.1.6 Undermining TRIPS in Free Trade Agreements

Beginning with its free trade agreement with Jordan in 2000, the United States has been using free trade agreements to introduce "TRIPS plus" obligations on patent protection for pharmaceuticals that increase the cost of medicines in developing countries and undermine the progress made in making TRIPS provisions more balanced in this regard (Oxfam 2007). Under international law, the patent provisions in these free trade agreements would prevail over TRIPS provisions in the event of any inconsistency. A recent example of this policy is the Central America-Dominican Republic-United States Free Trade Agreement (CAFTA-DR), which was signed on 5 August 2004, a free trade agreement between the United States and Costa Rica, the Dominican Republic, Guatemala, Honduras, Nicaragua and El Salvador.

CAFTA-DR Articles 15.9 and 15.10 contain patent obligations that do not exist in TRIPS. Article 15.9 (6) (a) requires governments to adjust the term of a patent to compensate for "unreasonable delays that occur in granting the patent." Article 15.9 (6) (b) requires the restoration of the patent term for pharmaceutical products to compensate the patent owner for "unreasonable curtailment of the effective patent term resulting from the marketing approval process related to the first commercial marketing of the product in that Party." Under TRIPS there is no obligation to extend the period of patent protection to compensate for the period of time required to approve pharmaceutical products for sale (see Chap. 6). Article 15.10 requires governments to not permit third parties to obtain authorization or to market a pharmaceutical product for 5 years based on information on safety and efficacy of a product that was disclosed by the patent owner in order to obtain marketing approval. In effect, Article 15.10 creates an obstacle to issuing compulsory licenses during the first 5 years that a pharmaceutical product is approved for marketing in the CAFTA-DR countries, whether or not the patent has expired, by preventing generic manufacturers from relying on clinical test data from brand-name companies. No such obstacle exists in TRIPS. A report by the Government Reform Committee Minority Staff (2005) concluded that that CAFTA-DR would impede access to safe and affordable prescription drugs for patients throughout the Central American region, delaying the introduction of generics even longer than in the United States.

In spite of criticism of the "TRIPS plus" approach taken in CAFTA-DR, the Bush Administration went on to require Guatemala, as a condition for allowing the agreement to enter into force, to enact intellectual property reforms that went beyond even the requirements in CAFTA-DR, in order to expand the scope of what is considered a new product, to increase the regulatory requirements for generics to gain marketing approval and to allow for patents or data protection for new clinical applications for existing medicines (Kucinich et al., 2006). Criticism of the CAFTA-DR approach led to a bipartisan agreement on intellectual property provisions in free trade agreements that sought to integrate more flexibility into the free trade agreements between the United States and Peru, Colombia and Panama, including a commitment to the 2001 Doha Declaration on TRIPS and Public Health (USTR 2007). However, it is unclear what impact this bipartisan agreement will have on intellectual property provisions in future US trade agreements with developing countries. It has not been applied to the Korea-United States Free Trade Agreement, which has the same type of TRIPS-plus provisions as CAFTA-DR (Flynn and Palmedo, 2007).

Because TRIPS does not contain an exception for free trade agreements, but does contain a Most-Favored-Nation obligation, where a country provides greater intellectual property protection by virtue of a TRIPS-plus FTA, it must provide that same treatment to nationals of all WTO Members, not just nationals of the FTA members. Thus, for example, if Guatemala agrees to provide TRIPS-plus protection for patents in its FTA with the United States, that same patent protection must be extended to patent owners from other WTO Members, such as the European Union and Switzerland. This means that FTAs may serve as a vehicle for increasing intellectual property protection on a global scale, without having to negotiate in the WTO (Frankel 2008).

5.2 Regulatory Capture of the Patent System

State regulation (in the narrow sense) implies control of monopolies. Regulatory capture is the process through which regulated monopolies end up manipulating the state agencies that are supposed to control them. Here, we will discuss regulatory capture in the context of monopolies granted by the state in the form of patents. At the end of this section, we will argue that the multinational pharmaceutical companies have effectively captured the regulators at the national level and, through this regulatory capture, have been able to strongly influence the content of international intellectual property regulation in TRIPS, free trade agreements and in other countries.

If we think of regulation as a market, there are two sides to this market – the supply of and the demand for regulation. The demand for regulation would require that the group of beneficiaries have two features. First, the number of beneficiaries cannot be large. If it is, each potential beneficiary has an incentive to shirk his obligations in the common lobbying effort. After all, lobbying is costly. Second, the group has to have a big stake in regulation. Big stakes would mobilize group members and give them an incentive to demand regulation. On the supply side, the public sector responds to political pressures. Stigler (1971) viewed politicians as potential suppliers of regulation who pursue two selfish objectives: staying in power and the desire to augment that power. Power depends on money and votes. If the politicians relied solely on the money, they could lose votes because the electorate might see them as corrupt politicians. Stigler noted one factor that could mitigate this cost – many voters are only marginally affected by regulation. These voters would have low incentives to be well informed about the regulation in question. In addition to a desire to stay in power, there are other incentives for regulators. If it is understood that taking a soft stance on regulation while in power would create potential jobs in the regulated industry once the regulator leaves office, there is an additional incentive for the regulators to give into the demands of the industry while they are in power. If people from the industry come to power, coming from an industry may induce regulators to make pro-industry decisions because the regulator has been "socialized" in an industry (this is known as the "Revolving Door Argument").

In the case of patents for drugs, the demand for regulation that benefits the industry is clear. There are a small number of companies involved in the pharmaceutical industry. Any new entry to the industry would be deterred by the large fixed cost required to enter the market. The pharmaceutical industry also has a big stake in patent regulation because losing patent protection would cost pharmaceutical companies a lot of money. The supply side equation is also clear in the context of the politicians and pharmaceutical companies. In the United States, the largest political contributions for both the Republicans and the Democrats come from the pharmaceutical industry.

5.2.1 Regulatory Capture of National Patent Law

The domestic political process of the United States has allowed patent owners to exert undue influence on the regulation of pharmaceutical patents, creating a problem of regulatory capture by the pharmaceutical industry at the national level. The pharmaceutical lobby provided nearly USD 60 million in funding in the 2002 mid-term US elections, helping the Republicans win key seats in their successful bid to retake control of the senate. This is the evidence on the demand side of the existence of regulatory capture. The industry has 625 registered lobbyists, of whom more than half are former members of Congress, their staff or government employees. This provides evidence of a revolving door for regulatory capture. One hundred thirty four lobbying firms are retained. The industry spent a reported USD 197 million on lobbying and campaign contributions in 1999–2000. The money absorbed by elected officials is evidence of the existence of a supply side for the regulatory capture market.

In a discussion of the evolution of Canadian patent laws, Bronwyn H. Hall argues that, once strong intellectual property laws are introduced, they only get stronger because of regulatory capture. Thus, she concludes, "because it is sometimes difficult to get the genie back into the bottle, it may be advisable to move slowly in expanding and strengthening IP rights" (Hall 2001, p. 5).

5.2.2 Regulatory Capture of International Patent Law

Generally speaking, the United States exercises disproportionate influence in global trade negotiations, due to the power of its market. In 2006, the United States accounted for 20.5% of global merchandise imports and 11.5% of global merchandise exports (excluding intra-EU (25) trade) (WTO 2007a). In the same year, the United States accounted for 11.6% of imports in world trade in commercial services and 14.1% of exports in world trade in commercial services (excluding intra-EU (25) trade) (WTO 2007b). These figures should be considered in perspective. The United States has 4% of world population and accounts for 27% of world GDP (data from the CIA Factbook, for the years 2006, available at www.cia.gov). It also accounts for 50% of the value of stocks and 44% of the value of bonds in the world (Walter 2003). It is an even bigger importer of capital. More than 70% of the world capital is imported by the United States. Therefore, it is difficult for global trade negotiations to advance without the participation of the United States, particularly with respect to intellectual property, because the United States produces more than 70% of the world's patents.

Intellectual property rights disproportionately benefit the firms of wealthy countries that produce most of the world's intellectual property. For example, UNDP (1999) reports that the proportion of patents held in the developed countries account for 97% of all patents granted in the world. This state of affairs created a problem for an international organization that aims to promote economic development in poor countries, many of which have been ravaged by AIDS and other diseases.

Regulatory capture by the pharmaceutical industry in the United States has translated into a problem of regulatory capture at the global level. The history of negotiation and lobbying suggests that the United States Trade Representative (USTR) was captured by the patent and copyright lobbies and ended up negotiating the TRIPS Agreement on their behalf during the Uruguay Round (Scotchmer 2004).

It has been widely argued that the expansion of intellectual property rights under TRIPS extended intellectual property rights beyond what is optimal, because US trade negotiators were captured by the US industry (Scotchmer 2003a). This problem of international regulatory capture has continued, as evidenced by the Paragraph 6 Decision, where the US pharmaceutical industry exerted considerable influence on the negotiations. The United States refused to accept the agreement on Paragraph 6 that was accepted by all the other members of the WTO until it was amended to address the concerns of the US pharmaceutical industry. The power of the pharmaceutical lobby was demonstrated by the way even the wording the USTR used in trade negotiations was influenced by the lobby group, as the following quote from Hamburger (2003) shows:

So the drug companies turned to their allies in Washington to help squelch the broader interpretation, which they said would set a dangerous precedent and erode the value of their patents world-wide. Their lobbyists asked lawmakers to contact Mr. [Robert] Zoellick's office, even suggesting specific language delineating the diseases and countries that would be affected. 'It should be clear that only truly disadvantaged countries, such as those in sub-Saharan Africa, be the beneficiaries of changed rules,' the letter suggested. As it happened, those were precisely the words that appeared in individual and group letters that 34 lawmakers signed and sent to Mr. Zoellick. One signatory was Republican Rep. Nancy Johnson of Connecticut, who survived a pivotal House race last November with help from more than $204,817 of drug-industry spending, according to the Center for Responsive Politics. Another senior Republican lending a hand was Senate Judiciary Committee Chairman Orrin Hatch of Utah, who received $387,824 for his re-election campaign in the year 2000. So did Senate Finance Committee Chairman Charles Grassley of Iowa, who received nearly $100,000 of pharmaceutical-industry donations in 2000. To be sure, some prominent Democrats sprang to the industry's aid as well. Outgoing Senate Finance Committee Chairman Max Baucus of Montana, who received $124,372 of industry-related contributions in his successful 2002 re-election bid, endorsed the industry's interpretation of Doha. Five members of the Congressional Black Caucus signed letters containing the language suggested by the industry. Yet the industry has provided roughly three–fourths of its largess in recent campaigns to Republicans, who now control both Congress and the White House.

The episode makes one fact of American political life undeniably clear: After spending millions of dollars on campaign help in recent years, the pharmaceutical industry has accumulated powerful friends it can turn to in a pinch.

In the following section, we analyze the economic rationale for patents in order to determine the extent to which patent laws reflect health, economic and political concerns.

Box 5.1 PhRMA: Marketing vs. innovation

In the 1950s, a US Senate Committee began to conduct hearings on the state of the pharmaceutical industry. The chairman of that committee proposed a bill to reduce the patent holder's exclusive control to 3 years, to require generic names on labels, to require federal licensing of drug firms and to require a demonstration of the drugs' effectiveness and safety prior to marketing approval. On 12 April 1961, after several years of hearings, Senator Estes Kefauver introduced Senate Bill 1552, which proposed these provisions. The evidence that was presented through testimony at the hearings filled 13 volumes and covered 12,885 pages.

Kefauver found that after a particular company had developed a new drug, it would then modify the chemical structure slightly, patent the result with a new trade name and then market this as a new drug. Kefauver recommended that combinations and modifications of existing drugs be patentable only if their effects had been proved to be therapeutically better than the previous versions. Kefauver made recommendations to curtail the marketing and promotional practices of the brand name pharmaceutical corporations. The multinationals mounted an attack on Bill S-1,552, and vowed "...to fight to the death [of the bill]." Eventually, the bill was defeated on the Senate floor.

Five decades later, the same debate goes on.

The pharmaceutical industry is still facing the same charges – that they spend too little on innovation and too much on marketing. Gagnon and Lexchin (2008) have produced the latest research on this battle. During 2004, these researchers estimated various components of the cost structure of the pharmaceutical industry, based on the systematic collection of data directly from the industry and doctors. They show that the US pharmaceutical industry spent 24.4% of their revenues on promotion and only 13.4% for research and development, as a percentage of US domestic sales of USD 235.4 billion.

5.3 The New Economics of Patents

It has long been argued that granting patents is necessary for innovation. Specifically, it is said that without patent protection, new drugs will not appear in the market, thus hurting consumers. Giving monopoly rights to patent holders for a limited time has been seen by economists as a way to strike a balance between incentives and equity. It is seen as a necessary evil – monopolies lower economic welfare, but if we do not give monopoly rights, there will be no future incentives to invent new goods. However, it would be very wrong to conclude what the Economist (2001) does: A patent is *the way* of rewarding somebody for coming up with a worthy commercial idea (quoted by Boldrin and Levine 2002). We discuss more fully the arguments developed in Boldrin and Levine (2008) below.

5.3.1 Two Centuries of Patent Protection in Europe and the United States

Article 1, Sect. 8 of the US Constitution clearly sets out the goal for patent and copyright protection in the following terms: "To promote the progress of science and useful arts, by securing for limited times to authors and inventors the exclusive right to their respective writings and discoveries." In practice, the US government recognizes two distinct forms of patent: (1) the process by which a drug is produced and (2) the chemical formula for the drug. Until 1984, US patent law treated medical discoveries no differently from any other innovation. The Hatch–Waxman Act of 1984 produced a separate line for pharmaceuticals to compensate for the delay in the introduction of new drugs, thus increasing the effective length of patent protection for pharmaceuticals by 5 years (Boldrin and Levine, 2008).

For two centuries, Continental Europe only allowed patent protection for the process of producing a drug, but not the product itself. In France, after a law was introduced in 1844, new chemicals could not be patented. France did allow the patenting of processes. The ban on patenting drugs was lifted in 1978. Germany introduced patents for both chemical and pharmaceutical processes in 1877, but products were explicitly excluded. Starting in 1891, Germany extended patent protection to products obtained *only through a patented process.* General patentability of chemical and pharmaceutical products in Germany came into effect in 1967. In Switzerland, the constitution explicitly prohibited patents for chemical and pharmaceutical products. Under German pressure, Switzerland adopted very restrictive patents for processes in 1907. In 1977, Switzerland introduced patents for products.

Italian laws also prohibited pharmaceutical patents. In 1978, the Supreme Court ruled in favor of 18 foreign pharmaceutical companies that had requested the enforcement of foreign patents on medical products in Italy. Despite this complete lack of patent protection, Italy had developed a strong pharmaceutical industry; by the end of the 1970s it was the fifth world producer of pharmaceuticals and the seventh exporter. Spain had regulation since 1931 that prohibited patenting substances but allowed process patenting. A new law for product patenting came into effect only after Spain joined the European Community in 1992 (Boldrin and Levine, 2008).

In summarizing the patent rules for Continental Europe, Boldrin and Levine (2008) observe the following: "It is worth pointing out that under E.U. patent law, programs for computers together with scientific discoveries and theories, mathematical methods, aesthetic creations, schemes, rules and methods for performing mental acts, playing games or doing business, and presentations of information are expressly not regarded as inventions and therefore cannot be patented. Since there is a large degree of ambiguity as to what a scientific theory or discovery is, it is unclear of the extent to which a new medicine, or a new biologically engineered product is or is not independent of the underlying chemical and biological model that explains it. Through this ambiguity medical products and treatments have been increasingly patented in the E.U. in ways altogether similar to the US".

In the matter of copyrights, Americans were in exactly the opposite camp of the Europeans. Europeans vigorously adhered to the inalienable rights of the authors. Americans, on the other hand, not only refused to adhere to international copyright treaties but also engaged in piracy of copyrighted foreign works for a century, not just in literature, but in other forms of arts as well. This was done under the guise of mass literacy and public education (Khan 2006).

It is interesting to note an ongoing dispute at the WTO between the European Communities and the United States regarding the failure of the United States to comply with TRIPS obligations regarding copyright. In United States – Section 110(5) of US Copyright Act, in 2000 a WTO Panel ruled that the US Copyright Act violated TRIPS by allowing a substantial majority of eating and drinking establishments and close to half of all retail establishments to amplify music broadcasts without authorization and without payment of a fee to copyright owners. As of 7 December 2007, the United States had not complied with this ruling.

5.3.2 Innovation and Patents

Paragraph 3 of the TRIPS Declaration makes reference to the effect of patent rights on research incentives as follows: "We recognize that intellectual property protection is important for the development of new medicines. We also recognize the concerns about its effects on prices." In terms of research incentives, there are two principal areas of concern for pharmaceutical companies with respect to patent rights in developing countries. The first issue is the effect of price discounts on patented medicine in developing countries on incentives to fund research for predominantly developing country diseases. A second issue concerns the impact of parallel imports of discounted patented medicine on price discrimination strategy. We discuss them in turn.

5.3.2.1 The Effect of Price on Research Incentives

Pharmaceutical companies argue that the actions allowed by TRIPS exceptions, as clarified by the TRIPS Declaration, increase the risk of investing in research for HIV/AIDS, tuberculosis and malaria (and other diseases that might be covered by the TRIPS Declaration), as it would reduce the financial incentives of pharmaceutical companies to invest in research for these diseases. This claim is false for the reasons given below.

First, both tuberculosis and malaria have been with humanity for a long time, killing millions of people. Yet, we do not see a rush by the pharmaceutical companies to invest large amounts of money to develop treatments for those diseases. Why? Pharmaceutical firms have high fixed costs (for research and development) but very low marginal costs for developing a new drug. Therefore, they will not be able to make profits if price is based solely on marginal cost. But this is precisely the kind of pricing that will be required in the developing countries (otherwise, they will not be able to afford the drug). In general, we observe apathy on the part of pharmaceutical companies to develop drugs for developing country diseases. Between 1975 and 1999, of 1,393 new chemical entities marketed, only 16 were for tropical diseases and tuberculosis (Trouiller et al., 2002). Of the annual health-related research and development worldwide, only 0.2% is for pneumonia, diarrhoeal diseases and tuberculosis, even though these account for 18% of the global disease burden (UNDP 1999). The industry developed HIV/AIDS drugs to serve the *developed* country markets. They *still* serve those markets primarily. It is estimated that 98% of the revenue for drugs for combating HIV/AIDS come from the OECD countries (Lanjouw 2001).

Second, the pharmaceutical companies are not alone in investing in research and development (R&D) for new drugs. For example, in 1998 total US private sector pharmaceutical R&D spending was USD 17.2 billion, while the federal government spent over USD 11 billion in medical and biological research. Research shows that there is a good degree of complementarity between the private and public investment in pharmaceutical research (Book 2002). Book argues on the basis of time series regression analysis that in the short run, government spending crowds out private sector R&D expenditure. He also shows that in the long run, government expenditure on R&D spurs more private sector R&D expenditure (Book 2002). Moreover, what the pharmaceutical industry classifies as R&D may contain dubious elements. For example, if a pharmaceutical company buys a chair, and if it is used (even partly) by a researcher who is counted as part of the R&D department, the chair will be classified under R&D and not common expenditure. The problem is that quite often in many countries, the tax code allows for more generous deduction of R&D expenditures than normal expenses. Therefore, there is always an incentive for a firm to include as much as the tax authorities will allow as R&D.

Third, what do we observe with respect to the development of vaccines? We do not observe a rush by the pharmaceutical companies to develop vaccines for most diseases. A common argument one hears is that it is more profitable for a pharmaceutical company to develop drugs to keep a patient alive than try to find a cure (Smetter 2005). Without getting into the question of morality, plain economics suggests that this is a faulty argument. Theoretically, the value of a vaccine would be at least as valuable to the present value of the treatment to the consumer. Therefore, a vaccine should be very valuable to the pharmaceutical company. The problem with this line of reasoning is that it presupposes that the potential consumers of the vaccine do not have any inter-temporal budget constraint. In other words, if the present value of the vaccine is USD 10,000 right now, the consumer will be willing and able to pay that amount right now. If capital markets were perfect then the consumers could potentially buy state contingent assets in all
world, and therefore, get around their inter-temporal budget constr

because of moral hazard and adverse selection, such contingent markets do not exist. Therefore, such budget constraints in real life drastically reduce the potential value of the vaccine. To put it differently, many potential customers will not be able to pay for it unless it can be paid over a number of years in installments. Such markets do not exist except for a few things like housing or credit card debt. To put it yet another way, it is difficult for people with low incomes to borrow against their future potential income. Most low-income people are in developing countries. If there were fortunes to be made in third-world disease eradication, we should have seen greater advances by now. One clear indication of this lack of interest is the lack of research efforts by pharmaceutical companies in the so-called "neglected diseases," such as malaria, tuberculosis, human African trypanosomiasis (sleeping sickness), South American trypanosomiasis (Chagas disease), Buruli ulcer, dengue fever, leishmaniasis, leprosy, lymphatic filariasis and schistosomiasis. A survey by Doctors without Borders concluded that the pharmaceutical industry had virtually no drugs under development for neglected diseases (DND Working Group 2001).

Fourth, HIV/AIDS straddles both the developed world and the developing world. The types of HIV infection found commonly in the developing and the developed worlds are not the same (Doherty 2005). There are many subtypes of HIV-1 (the most commonly occurring HIV infection in humans). The major HIV-1 subtypes accounting for most infections in Africa are subtype C in southern Africa, subtypes A and D in eastern Africa, and circulating recombinant form 02_AG (CRF02_AG) in west-central Africa (Peeters and Sharp 2000). On the other hand, the most commonly occurring form of HIV-1 in North America (and in Europe) is of subtype B. The first HIV/AIDS vaccine ever to reach Phase III trial (the last phase before it is approved for general use) was for subtype B. The gp120 vaccine (called AIDSVAX and developed by the VaxGen company of Brisbane, California) reached large-scale phase III efficacy testing in North America, the Netherlands, and Thailand. Preliminary results from the North American and Dutch trials in June 2003 showed that the vaccine was not effective. In the case of HIV/AIDS, we see a clear pattern of development of potential vaccines not in the subtypes where the needs are the greatest but in the area where the biggest monetary rewards are expected.

Fifth, the industry's argument would have greater force were patent interventions to occur frequently, particularly in developed countries. If they do not, their argument weakens considerably. The fact is, despite the events surrounding anthrax and HIV/AIDS, most governments have not invoked TRIPS exceptions to issue compulsory licenses for any other drugs that save lives in large numbers. We have not witnessed many governments issuing compulsory licenses for drugs to lower cholesterol level even though it is well known that it will save millions of lives. A less prominent virus than HIV is hepatitis C, which afflicts 170 million people worldwide and causes acute hepatitis and chronic liver disease, such as cirrhosis and liver cancer. However, the cost of treatment (a combination of interferon and ribavirin) is about USD 30,000 per patient per year. Still, we do not observe many governments threatening to use compulsory licenses to force down the prices of these drugs. TRIPS Article 31 permits governments to issue compulsory licenses for non-commercial public use. Thus, governments may issue compulsory licenses to lower the cost of treatment for such diseases if they wish to do so in the context of a public health-care scheme, as Thailand has done.

Sixth, if patent protection induces more innovation, we would see new drugs with new chemicals coming to the market. Instead, we see that many of the patents are offered to "me too" drugs where the "innovation" is either in dosage (e.g., 100 mg instead of 500 mg) or the shape of the pill (e.g., oval ones instead of round ones) or the color of the pills (e.g., pink ones instead of white ones). In Table 5.2, we report the results of one such study of all the patented drugs in the United States between 1980 and 2000. It shows that nearly two thirds of all the patented new drugs "may be a new molecule but is superfluous because it does not add to the clinical possibilities offered by previous products available. In most cases it concerns a me-too product."

Seventh, Continental Europe, until the 1970s, did not allow patents for products, but only processes. Yet, the pharmaceutical industry flourished in Switzerland and Germany. In fact, Bayer was a pioneer (with the invention of aspirin) and a pharmaceutical giant even though Germany was not giving them any product protection (only process protection). Of course, it did not prevent them from seeking product protection wherever they could (such as in the United Kingdom or the United States).

Table 5.2. Assessment of new drugs introduced between 1981 and 2000

Category	Number	Percent
Major therapeutic innovation in an area where previously no treatment was available	7	0.31
Product is an important therapeutic innovation but has certain limitations	67	2.96
Product has some value but does not fundamentally change the present therapeutic practice	192	8.51
Product has minimal additional value, and should not change prescribing habits except in rare circumstances	397	17.59
Product may be a new molecule but is superfluous because it does not add to the clinical possibilities offered by previous products available. In most cases it concerns a me-too product	1427	63.23
Product without evident benefit but with potential or real disadvantages	58	2.57
Editors postpone their judgments until better data and a more thorough evaluation of the drug is available	109	4.83

Source: Prescrire International (www.prescrire.org)

In summary, decisions by pharmaceutical companies to develop expensive new drugs should not be affected by the ability of developing countries to extract price concessions for HIV/AIDS drugs. Expensive drugs are beyond the reach of potential users in developing countries. Their greater concern should be with the economic reasons why governments must intervene to develop vaccines for such diseases. Why? If a successful vaccine is developed, the disease will disappear and so will the profits from a patented drug that treats it. Pharmaceutical companies are driven by profit motives. The market for vaccines that will largely be used in developing countries provides little financial incentive for the pharmaceutical companies to develop them. Therefore, the incentive to develop vaccines will have to come from governments. For example, governments could develop the vaccines themselves or make a commitment to buy the vaccines from pharmaceutical companies that develop them (Kremer 2001) (also see Chap. 9).

There is a more pragmatic argument as to why we do not observe pharmaceutical companies from developed countries expending resources to invent drugs for "developing country diseases"; until recently, their patents were not protected in developing countries. Therefore, even if some could afford to pay a monopoly price for such drugs in developing countries, there was no incentive for the pharmaceutical companies from developed countries to develop such drugs.

Scherer and Watal (2001) have developed a strictly economic argument based on discriminatory pricing (also called Ramsey pricing). They show, under certain conditions, to maximize profits, pharmaceutical companies should charge lower prices in lower income countries and higher prices in higher income countries. This economic argument is congruent with the "fairness" principle that the poor should pay less. However, empirical evidence muddles the picture. In a summary of the empirical evidence, Scherer and Watal (2001) wrote, "[These] unsystematic variations would appear to suggest that the pricing of HIV/AIDS drugs by multinational pharmaceutical companies conforms at best poorly to the Ramsey strictures we [Scherer and Watal 2001] have suggested." This may reflect the indirect influence of differential pricing on demands for lower prices in rich country markets. However, in the past few years, the price of patented HIV/AIDS drugs has come down drastically in developing countries, particularly in sub-Saharan Africa (where low-cost generics have increased price competition).

5.3.2.2 The Effect of Parallel Imports on Price Discrimination Strategies

For pharmaceutical companies with monopoly rights, price discrimination between markets is an important strategy for maximizing profits. When they have a monopoly over certain drugs, they charge the price that will maximize their total profits. As long as they own the patents, the legal protection provided in each market permits them to "set the price" and to seek compensation for their investment. However, if governments allow parallel imports, they have the potential to undermine a firm's price discrimination strategy. Parallel imports involve products sold by the patent owner in one market that are then imported into another market without the patent owner's approval.

Is this a real threat? At present, the European Union (EU) permits parallel trade within the EU but *does not* permit importation of on-patent drugs from countries outside the EU (European Union 2001). In many countries, especially in the EU, there are universal national health schemes. Therefore, in those countries it is possible for the government to act as a monopsony (single buyer in the market). Hence, the governments can negotiate drug prices directly with the pharmaceutical companies rather than depend on the pricing strategy of the pharmaceutical companies alone. Consideration for political economy may undermine some of these processes. For example, it has been proven theoretically (using economic models of monopoly) that the prohibition of parallel imports is more likely to emerge (where it would not otherwise) the more the government cares about lobby contributions and the greater profits from price discrimination are (Knox and Richardson 2002).

Under a system of national exhaustion, a patent holder can prevent parallel importation of her product from a foreign country. Under a system of international exhaustion, as soon as the product is put on the market of any country, by the patent holder, she can no longer block the importation of that product into any other country (Barfield and Groomridge 1999).

During the Uruguay Round negotiations, WTO members were unable to reach agreement on how to deal with the issue of exhaustion of intellectual property rights. TRIPS Article 28 requires that patents grant patent holders the exclusive right to prevent third parties from making, using, selling or importing their product without consent. However, under a system of international exhaustion of patents, the patent owner cannot prevent the importation of his own product from a foreign country once it has been sold there. By virtue of TRIPS Article 6, exhaustion of patent rights cannot be raised in a WTO dispute, leaving each WTO Member free to establish its own regime regarding exhaustion of patent rights. This raises the risk that patented drugs sold at a discount in developing countries could be imported to a developed country market. This could threaten differential pricing strategies used by pharmaceutical companies unless they prevent the buyers of discounted drugs from offering them for resale.

As long as developed countries maintain a policy of national exhaustion, the primary source of profits remains secure. Thus the issue is not the price charged in developing countries, but rather the policies maintained in developed countries. The patent owners are primarily located in developed countries. Industrial countries hold 97% of all patents worldwide, and 80% of patents granted in developing countries belong to residents of industrial countries (Pollock Allyson and David Price 2003). In 1995, over half of global royalties and licensing fees were paid to the United States, mostly from Japan, the United Kingdom, France, Germany and the Netherlands (UNDP 1999). Therefore, developed country governments have an incentive to support prices through a system of national exhaustion. It is thus a North–North issue more than a North–South issue.

When companies agree to price discounts in negotiations with government purchasers, for example in Brazil and the United States, the companies should negotiate a contractual obligation to prevent the resale in other markets and monitor compliance. That will protect the profits in other markets and provide economic incentives to fund research into treatments. As long as the discounted drugs sold in developing countries do not make their way back to the developed countries, their price strategy in the developed world is secure.

5.3.2.3 Revisionist Views of Current Legal Treatment of Intellectual Property Rights

The theoretical foundation for TRIPS in general, and patents in particular, lies in the economic argument that these monopoly rights are the sine qua non of innovation in the pharmaceutical field. In essence, this argument states that, without patents, the invention of new pharmaceuticals would cease, making the issue of affordable access to medicine a moot point. We have demonstrated above that this argument weakens considerably when it comes to incentives to invent treatments for poor country diseases. Moreover, we have shown that the incentives for inventing treatments for HIV/AIDS come from the developed country markets, not developing or least-developed country markets, and that owners of patents for existing HIV/AIDS drugs have no incentive to develop a cure, at least for the kind of HIV-1 strains that are virtually nonexistent in the developed world. Beyond these critiques of the underlying economic premise for patents, however, there is an emerging view that questions the conventional view regarding the impact of patents on innovation. In some circumstances, patent rights may be used (or abused) so as to stifle innovation. The notion that competition spurs innovation and reduces prices to consumers is another theoretical underpinning of international trade. Patents, by granting monopolies, stifle competition. For this reason, their duration is limited. The tension that exists between patents and competition points to the importance of achieving the correct balance, in order to maximize social welfare and to minimize economic deadweight loss and regulatory capture.

In economic literature, the standard argument for pricing in a perfectly competitive market says that the socially desirable outcome (in economic jargon, Pareto efficient) is to have the price equal to the marginal cost of production of a good. This argument applies only when the cost of bringing a good to the market is relatively low. In many information intensive products, this is not so. For these products, the cost of producing the first unit is extremely high whereas the cost of producing subsequent units is very low. For example, it is expensive to produce working software. However, copying the same software is essentially free. The same applies for movies, data and pharmaceuticals.

For such goods, if feasible, the producer will charge different prices in different markets. Barton (2001, pp. 476–478) provides a good example:

> When the movie goes onto the market, the production costs are sunk costs, and the cost of showing the movie to each additional viewer is small. If the producer must choose a single price, he or she might choose the price at which marginal cost equals marginal revenue. But this leaves

profits on the table for the benefit of the viewers. The producer would rather maximize his or her profits through price discrimination. To accomplish this, the producer first shows the movie at a high-price first-run theater, followed by discount theaters, and on down to post-midnight TV showings and remaindered videocassettes. By doing so, the producer can achieve a higher overall return....If, however, the movie is easily reproduced and distributed by third-parties in taped or internet form, a portion of the movie maker's market will be lost from the lost rents.

A similar argument is normally used to make the case by pharmaceutical companies for any drug:

> Innovators in all industries rely on patents to ensure that their inventions are protected and that they will be given an opportunity to recover their research investments. Strong intellectual property protection is essential for the preservation and growth of the research-based pharmaceutical industry – and thus for the continuing development of new and better medicines for patients. The reason is simple: no company would be able to invest the huge amount of time and money it takes to discover and develop a new medicine if the drug could be immediately copied and marketed at a greatly reduced cost by a competitor with no R&D expenses to recover (PhRMA 2003).

In particular, this argument has been put forward for HIV/AIDS drugs. The argument of the pharmaceutical industry goes as follows. Given that the marginal cost is very low or zero, there is a temptation to force the price to the level of the marginal cost or sell it at zero price. In economic terms, this outcome will be Pareto efficient. A Pareto efficient outcome is one where it is impossible to make anybody better off without making somebody worse off. If an outcome is Pareto inefficient, there is room for improvement by reallocation. It is then possible to make some economic agents (producers or consumers) better off without making anybody else worse off. However, note that Pareto efficiency does not guarantee a "fair" or "just" outcome in any sense. For example, it is quite possible that one economic agent has all the resources in the economy whereas others have none and yet the outcome is Pareto efficient. Thus, in some sense, Pareto efficiency is a necessary but insufficient condition for a "good" outcome. If pharmaceutical companies are forced to charge near zero prices after a new drug is invented, simply because the marginal cost of production is near zero, in the long run it will have a negative impact on how future developments of the same product take place. Thus, long-term efficiency (in economic terms, dynamic efficiency) for society will require that the additional value to the society is bigger than the development cost. The pharmaceutical industry has long claimed that new drug development is precisely in this category – each new drug requires enormous additional investment.

How much does the development of a new drug cost? DiMasi et al. (1991) provided the first such study. Their conclusion was that it costs 318 million dollars to bring a new drug to the market (converted in 2001 dollars). DiMasi et al. (2001) replicated this study 10 years later. They report that the cost had risen to 802 million dollars (measured in 2001 dollars). The pharmaceutical industry has forcefully used these two studies to make a case that long tailed patent protection (that is, patents with many years of full protection) is required to keep up the incentives of the pharmaceutical companies. However, there are a number of critiques regarding the approach of DiMasi et al.

First, the analysis of dynamic efficiency, which claims that we require compensation for development costs, assumes that the development of each drug is independent of any other. Thus, it assumes the development of each drug can have an easily identifiable cost structure. In reality, this is not so. Quite often, the fixed cost of producing different types of drugs can be spread across different products (for example, the same machines can be used for analyzing different drugs in the same laboratory). Thus, the so-called "out of pocket expenses" of pharmaceutical companies can easily be overstated.

Second, to strengthen the critique, let us consider all the drugs that were introduced in the US market between 1989 and 2000. An analysis shows that only 35% of these drugs were New Molecular Entities (NMEs). NMEs are medicines containing active ingredients that have never before been approved for the market and must be subjected to a lengthy process of testing in animals and humans, in order to prove their safety and efficacy, prior to approval (National Institute for Health Care 2003). Some 11% contained *exactly* the same material as before. The "innovative" aspect of these drugs was that they had different modalities of applications, as slow release globules. Thus, the cost analysis by DiMasi et al., is dubious. They do not account for these differences in patents that come from the NMEs and the incrementally modified drugs, which contain the same active ingredient as an approved product, and which account for 65% of all new patents.

For products that contain the elements of a public good, the dynamic efficiency argument of patent protection weakens considerably. The evidence points to the overwhelming preponderance of "downstream patenting" in the context of pharmaceuticals. Boldrin and Levine call this phenomenon "intellectual monopoly." They explain their idea as follows:

> "Intellectual property" has come to mean not only the right to own and sell ideas, but also the right to regulate their use. This creates a socially inefficient monopoly, and what is commonly called intellectual property might be better called "intellectual monopoly." When you buy a potato you can eat it, throw it away, plant it or make it into a sculpture. Current law allows producers of a CDs and books to take this freedom away from you. When you buy a potato you can use the "idea" of a potato embodied in it to make better potatoes or to invent french fries. Current law allows producers of computer software or medical drugs to take this freedom away from you." (Boldrin and Levine 2002, p. 210)

Boldrin and Levine argue that the cost of developing a new drug (or new software) is a sunk cost and not simply a fixed cost. Fixed cost is the cost that does not vary with the level of output. Suppose a company has two employees: a janitor and a director. The cost of having the director is fixed. It does not vary with the level of output produced. But the cost of the janitor is variable. If the company does not produce anything, it would have no cleaning expenses. Hence, the janitor is not necessary. Sunk cost, on the other hand, is the portion of fixed costs that is not recoverable. For example, consider an investment in new technology. It is only necessary once. Thus, unlike the salary of the director, it does not have to be incurred every period. Note that in a one-period model, there is no difference between a fixed cost and a sunk cost. In a model with multiple time periods a fixed cost is incurred each period (but the cost does not vary with output) while a sunk cost is incurred only once (at the first period). A simple example of sunk cost is the opportunity cost of writing a paper. Once the time cost is incurred writing the paper, it cannot be avoided, eliminated or reduced no matter whether the paper is eventually published or not. In the above example of the janitor and the director, if the company ceases to exist, the director can be fired and the company does not incur the cost of paying the director.

Boldrin and Levine further note that "As far as we know there is no organized movement to provide producers of potatoes, or any other commodity involving sunk costs, with a government monopoly" (Boldrin and Levine, 2002, p. 210). They go on to argue the following:

> On the patent front, more time and energy seems to be spent on nuisance and defensive patenting of the obvious or well-known than is spent on actually innovating new ideas. Individuals exploit the relative ignorance of patent examiners by patenting ideas already in wide-spread use in hopes of collecting licensing fees, or at least greenmail, from a few large companies; large corporations patent and cross-license everything imaginable both to protect themselves against greenmail, and to suppress entry into their industry. That cross-licensing and "protection of intellectual property" can be instrumental in promoting collusion within an industry seems transparent. (Boldrin and Levine 2002, p. 211)

The importance of the Boldrin–Levine model cannot be overstated. For example, Quah provides an extension of the Boldrin–Levine model with the following comment: "The Boldrin–Levine analysis is an important and profound development. It seeks to overturn nearly half a century of formal economic thinking on intellectual property, suggesting instead that perfectly competitive markets in intellectual assets function in the usual Arrow–Debreu way and therefore lead to socially efficient outcomes." (Quah 2002)

Boldrin and Levine (2008, Chap. 9) provide the following evidence about the rate of innovation with and without patent protection for Italy, which provided a natural experiment for patent protection after their Supreme Court Decision of 1980: "During the period 1961–1980 a total of 1,282 new active chemical compounds was discovered around the world. Of these, a total of 119 came from Italy

(9.28%). During the period 1980–1983 a total of 108 compounds were discovered. Of these, 8 came from Italy (7.5%)."

Even the sunk cost (the one time only cost of producing new drugs) is shared by the governments (and, by implication, the consumers as taxpayers). It is estimated that in 2000, some USD 70 billion was spent on research on pharmaceuticals. Of this amount, approximately USD 30 billion was spent by governments (Survey 2003). Book (2002) cites a slightly different set of numbers.

The argument that strong patent rights are essential to provide incentives to invest in innovation has been used to support a balance between the rights of patent holders and users that favors the former. However, the Boldrin–Levine model demonstrates that such an "intellectual monopoly" approach to patent rights has the effect of stifling innovation because it provides an incentive to patent holders to invest in legal action to extend the life of their patents and to prevent others from developing new innovations. In economic terms, patents provide rights to the person first in the door of the patent office. This is an inefficient way of allocating economic resources.

In summary, we need to choose between two opposing stories of what patent rights really do. One view claims that patent rights spur innovation, and innovation leads to economic growth. The opposite view is that patent rights, as they stand today, lead to monopoly. The monopoly itself is undesirable in economic terms as it is inefficient. This has led many economists to believe that there is no inherent reason for patent protection. For example, Scotchmer (2003b) notes that there is no economic rationale for protecting inventors *per se*.

Historical evidence seems to favor the latter view. For example, Boldrin and Levine (2008, Chap. 1) show how James Watt (of the steam engine fame) managed to set back the clock of the industrial revolution by lobbying for and getting his monopoly extended.

5.4 Implications for Other Global Diseases

The global expansion of patent rights for pharmaceutical products under the TRIPS Agreement has led to an increasingly inefficient allocation of economic resources. Despite the considerable time and effort taken to negotiate an amendment to TRIPS to facilitate the export of medicine under compulsory license, the Paragraph 6 system remains little used. Moreover, ongoing political pressure from the governments of the major pharmaceutical companies continues to discourage the use of compulsory licensing to increase affordable access to medicine in developing countries, even after the TRIPS Declaration clarified the right of all governments to use compulsory licensing for this very purpose. In addition, the regulatory capture of the US government by the pharmaceutical industry has resulted in yet more favorable patent regulation in free trade agreements that undermine the progress made in WTO negotiations to address the imbalance between the rights of producers and users of patented products.

There are serious consequences for other diseases and pandemics of strengthening patent rights for pharmaceutical products. First, the political interests of politicians in developed countries, and the economic interests of the pharmaceutical companies that support them, have taken precedence over the health interests of the majority of the world's population. Second, the limited resources available to reduce the global disease burden will be allocated inefficiently. Third, the lack of affordable access to medicines for developing country diseases will continue to be an issue for the foreseeable future. Fourth, global pandemics are likely to leave developing countries that lack the capacity to produce pharmaceuticals without access to medicine to address such health crises. In the next chapter, we will explore ways to correct the current imbalance in the global patent regime.

References

Barfield CE, Groomridge MA (1999) Parallel Trade in the Pharmaceutical Industry: Implications for Innovation, Consumer Welfare and Health Policy. Fordham Intellectual Property Media and Entertainment Law Journal 10:185–265

Barton JH (2001) The Economics of TRIPS. The George Washington International Law Review 33:473–501

Bhagwati J (1994) Comment on Bernard Hoekman, Liberalizing Trade in Services. In Collins S, Bosworth BP (eds) The New GATT: Implications for the United States, The Brookings Institution, Washington, DC

Boldrin M, Levine D (2002) The Case against Intellectual Property. The American Economic Review 92:209–213

Boldrin M, Levine D (2008) Against Intellectual Property. Cambridge University Press, Cambridge

Book RA (2002) Public Research Funding and Private Innovation. PhD thesis, University of Chicago. home.uchicago.edu/~rbook/Book_PharmInnov.pdf. Acces-sed 2 June 2005

DiMasi JA, Hansen RW, Grabowski HG, Lasagna L (1991) Cost of Innovation in the Pharmaceutical Industry. Journal of Health Economy 10:107–142

DiMasi JA, Hansen RW, Grabowski HG (2001) The Price of Innovation: New Estimates of Drug Development Costs. Journal of Health Economy 22:167

DND Working Group (2001) Fatal Imbalance: The Crisis in Research and Development for Drugs for Neglected Diseases. MSF Access to Essential Medicines Campaign 171

Doctors without Borders (2003) A Progress Report on TRIPS. http://www.doctorswithoutborders.org/publications/reports/2003/cancun_report.pdf. Accessed 5 May 2004

Doherty P (2005) Interview, St. Jude Children's Research Hospital, Memphis, TN

European Union (2001) http://www.europarl.eu.int/meetdocs/committees/juri/20010514/437115en.pdf. Accessed 5 July 2003

Flynn S, Palmedo M (2007) PIJIP Comments on the Korus FTA Pharmaceuticals and IP Chapters. http://lists.essential.org/pipermail/ip-health/2007-May/011282.html. Accessed 10 September 2007

Frankel S (2008) The Legitimacy and Purpose of Intellectual Property Chapters in FTAs. In: Buckley R, Lo VI, Boulle L (eds) Challenges to Multilateral Trade: The Impact of Bilateral, Preferential and Regional Agreements. Kluwer, The Hague

Gagnon MA, Lexchin J (2008) The Cost of Pushing Pills: A New Estimate of Pharmaceutical Promotion Expenditures in the United States. PloS Medicine 5(1): e1 doi: 10 1371/journal.pmed.0050001

Government Reform Committee Minority Staff (2005) Trade Agreements and Access to Medications under the Bush Administration. http://www.democrats. reform.house.gov. Accessed 11 September 2007

Hall BH (2001) The Global Nature of Intellectual Property: Discussion. Mimeo, Toronto IP Conference, May 2001

Hamburger T (2003) US Flip on Patents Shows Drug Makers' Growing Clout – Political Donors Get Help in Reversing Policy On Poor Nations' Access to Cheaper Medicine, Wall Street Journal, 6 February 2003, A4

Hestermeyer HP (2007) Canadian-Made Drugs for Rwanda: The First Application of the WTO Waiver on Patents and Medicines, ASIL Insight 11:28

Khan ZB (2006) The Democratization of Invention: Patents and Copyrights in American Economic Development, 1790–1920. Cambridge University Press, Cambridge

Knox D, Richardson M (2002) Trade Policy and Parallel Imports. European Journal of Political Economy 19:133

Kournikakis B, Armour SJ, Boulet CA, Spence M, Parsons B (2001) Risk Assessment of Anthrax Threat Letters. Defence R&D Canada. Technical Report DRES-TR-2001-048, September 2001

Kremer M (2001) Creating Markets for New Vaccines, parts I and II. Mimeo, Harvard University

Kucinich, Michaud, Grijalva, Lee, Waters, Brown, Evans, Stark, Allen (US Congress Representives) (2006), Letter to USTR Concerning CAFTA Implementation in Guatemala. http://www.cptech.org/ip/health/trade/cafta/representatives04072006.pdf. Accessed 11 September 2007

Lancet Editorial (2001) Patent Protection Versus Public Health. The Lancet 358:1563

Lanjouw J (2001) A Patent Policy Proposal for Global Diseases. The Brookings Institution, http://www.brook.edu/views/papers/lanjouw/20010611.htm. Accessed 11 September 2004

Lanjouw J (2003) The Dialogue Continues, Latin American Advisor, 5 September 2003, www.thedialogue.org. Accessed 8 September 2003

National Institute for Health Care Management Research and Educational Foundation (2003) Changing Patterns of Pharmaceutical Innovation. www.nihcm.org/innovations.pdf. Accessed 15 November 2007

Oxfam (2007) All Costs, No Benefits: How TRIPS-Plus Intellectual Property Rules in the US-Jordan FTA Affect Access to Medicines. Oxfam Briefing Paper #102. http://www. oxfam.org/en/files/bp102_jordan_us_fta.pdf/. Accessed 25 November 2007

Peeters M, Sharp PM (2000) Genetic Diversity of HIV-1: The Moving Target. AIDS 14: S129–S130

PhRMA (2003) The PhRMA Industry Profile. www.phrma.org/publications / publications/profile02/chapter3.pdf, p 30. Accessed 17 February 2003

Pollock Allyson M, David Price (2003) New Deal from the World Trade Organisation May not Provide Essential Medicines for Poor Countries. British Medical Journal 327:572

Quah D (2002) 24/7 Competitive Innovation. econ.lse.ac.uk/staff/dquah/p/0204-247-2pp.pdf. Accessed 15 November 2004

Scherer FM, Watal J (2001) Post-TRIPS Options for Access to Patented Medicines in Developing Countries. Commission on Macroeconomics and Health, Working Paper WG4-1

Scotchmer S (2003a) The Political Economy of the Intellectual Property Treaties. National Bureau of Economic Research, Working Paper.

Scotchmer S (2003b) Political Economy of Intellectual Property Rights, Working Paper, National Bureau of Economic Research, Working Paper.

Scotchmer S (2004) Intellectual Property in the Global Economy. In: Scotchmer S (ed) Innovation and Incentives. MIT Press, Cambridge

Stigler G (1971) The Theory of Economic Regulation. Bell Journal of Economics and Management Science 2:3-21

Smetter K (2005) Interview at Wharton School, University of Pennsylvania

Survey of Private Sector Drug Research and Development (2003) www.neglecteddiseases.org/4-1.pdf. Accessed 5 June 2004

The Economist (2001) Patently Absurd? Economist 359/8227:40

Trouiller P, Olliaro P, Torreele E, Orbinski J, Laing R, Ford N (2002) Drug Development for Neglected Diseases: A Deficient Market and a Public-Health Policy Failure. The Lancet 22:2188-2194

UNDP (1999) Human Development Report. www.undp.org. Accessed 6 May 2001

USTR (2007) Bipartisan Agreement on Trade Policy: Intellectual Property Provisions. http://www.ustr.gov/assets/Document_Library/Fact_Sheets/2007/asset_upload_file312_112 83.pdf. Accessed 10 November 2007

USTR (2007a) 2007 Special 301 Report, http://www.ustr.gov/assets/ Docu-ment_Library/ Reports_Publications/2007/2007_Special_301_Review/asset_upload_file230_11122. pdf. Ac-Accessed 10 November 2007

Walter I (2003) Global Financial Stability Report. Market Developments and Issues, International Monetary Fund, Washington DC

WTO (2007a) International trade statistics 2007, Table I.9, Leading exporters and importers in world merchandise trade (excluding intra-EU (25) trade), 2006. http://www.wto. org/english/res_e/statis_e/its2007_e/its07_world_trade_dev_e.htm. Accessed 15 November 2007

WTO (2007b) International trade statistics 2007, Table I.10, Leading exporters and importers in world trade in commercial services, 2006. http://www.wto.org/english/res_e/ statis_e/its2007_e/its07_world_trade_dev_e.htm. Accessed 15 November 2007

6 Global Diseases, Global Patents and Developing Countries in WTO Law

"It is becoming ever more apparent that the patent system isn't working."

The Economist, 13 November 2004

Special and differential treatment of members is a controversial subject at the World Trade Organization (WTO) and nowhere is the debate more pronounced than in the context of life-saving medicines and patent protection. However, concerns have been raised in WTO negotiations regarding how to ensure that special and differential treatment targets developing countries' trade, financial and development needs, without prejudicing the rights of other WTO members. In 2003, the WTO adopted a decision to amend the Agreement on Trade-Related Aspects of Intellectual Property Rights (TRIPS) in order to enhance access to essential medicines in developing countries. In 2004, the World Intellectual Property Organization (WIPO) adopted an agenda to further the development of countries by considering different intellectual property regimes appropriate to the circumstances of a particular country or region. The WTO and the WIPO are the two major entities working to develop international patent law, and one of the objectives of TRIPS is to establish a mutually supportive relationship between the two. The application of TRIPS to developing countries has become even more important with the full entry into force of their patent obligations on 1 January 2005.

The current willingness to take individual circumstances into account is a significant development. However, while there is recognition of the need to adapt special and differential treatment to the individual circumstances of WTO members, the negotiations in the WTO Committee on Trade and Development have not made much progress in determining the criteria that should be applied. The rationale for introducing greater flexibility in the application of special and differential treatment is that differentiation amongst developing country Members is necessary if special and differential treatment is to be made effective and targeted. The issue of how to define developing countries has also been raised in this context, although there has been disagreement regarding whether this falls within the negotiating mandate for the Doha Round of WTO negotiations. Paragraph 44 of the Doha Ministerial Declaration, which reaffirmed that "provisions for special and differential treatment are an integral part of the WTO Agreements" and directed that "all special and differential treatment provisions shall be reviewed with a view to strengthening them and making them more precise, effective and operational," established the mandate for negotiations on special and differential treatment for the Doha Round. In WTO negotiations in the Committee on Trade and Development, introducing the concept of "situational flexibility" or "member-specific flexibility" into special and differential treatment of developing countries has become a matter of debate. In the context of TRIPS, the concept of situational flexibility is particularly relevant to the issue of extending the transition periods during which least-developed countries are not required to implement patent obligations and striking the appropriate balance between the rights of producers and users of intellectual property. Least-developed countries in particular want to strengthen special and differential treatment measures in TRIPS.

In this chapter, several WTO mechanisms for implementing special and differential treatment in TRIPS with respect to pharmaceutical patents are analyzed. We challenge conventional economic views regarding the relationship between international intellectual property law and research incentives to invent medicines to treat global diseases in developing countries. In our analysis of the economics of pharmaceutical patents, we will distinguish between global diseases (which occur in both developed and developing countries) and neglected diseases (which occur overwhelmingly in developing countries, rather than in developed countries). In other parts of our analysis, we will use the term developing country diseases to refer to both neglected and global diseases.

We present a new analytical framework for determining differential treatment of developing and least-developed countries and apply this framework in the context of TRIPS. We propose that the balance of legal rights between producers and users of patents be determined on a market-by-market basis, rather than on a global basis, and that criteria for doing so be developed.

In this chapter, we provide an overview of key TRIPS obligations and exceptions relating to patents, as amended to date by the Doha Round negotiations. Part III analyzes how WTO provisions on special and differential treatment of developing countries should be applied to TRIPS law and policy, taking into account the 2004 Appellate Body ruling in European Communities – Tariff Preferences for Developing Countries. Part IV analyzes the consistency of global patent rights with the economic and developmental objectives of the WTO and shows how strong patent rights in developing countries contradict these objectives. Part V then analyzes whether TRIPS is amenable to an interpretation that would achieve a more appropriate balance between the rights of producers and users of patented pharmaceuticals and shows that an amendment to TRIPS to facilitate the use of compulsory licensing in developing and least-developed countries is a second-best solution. Rather, the best solution is to grant waivers for developing countries and extensions of the transition period for least-developed countries. This chapter proposes a set of measurable criteria to implement special and differential treatment of countries with respect to pharmaceutical patents on a market-by-market basis using these two mechanisms. Equal access to life-saving medicines requires equal access to legal rights that affect that access.

6.1 Key TRIPS Exceptions Relating to Patents

Patents are granted by governments on the national level, which means that they only have legal effect in the jurisdictions where the application for a patent has been granted. TRIPS established minimum standards for the protection of intellectual property rights in the national laws of WTO Members. TRIPS Article 28.1

requires patents to provide patent owners with the exclusive right to prevent third parties from making, using, selling or importing a patented product without the owner's consent. Articles 30 and 31 authorize exceptions to these rights. These two articles thus play a key role in balancing the rights of patent owners against the needs of consumers of patented products, whether they are pharmaceuticals or other patented products. The ability to manufacture drugs under compulsory license provides developing countries with bargaining power to extract price concessions for patented drugs or to issue compulsory licenses when negotiations fail. However, this bargaining power applies only to countries that have the capacity to produce generic drugs under compulsory licenses issued to government laboratories or private generic producers. Countries that lack domestic manufacturing capacity would need to be able to import generics manufactured under compulsory licenses in other countries in order to enjoy a comparable level of bargaining power. This section will discuss Article 30 first, followed by Article 31, and consider how effective these articles are in ensuring that governments can issue compulsory licenses to meet national needs, including with respect to public health problems.

6.1.1 TRIPS Article 30

TRIPS Article 30 permits "limited exceptions" to patent rights. Academic opinions diverge over whether Article 30 can be interpreted to permit generic exports. If one accepts the interpretation of Article 30 in Canada – Patent Protection of Pharmaceutical Products, Article 30 does not permit such exports. However, if one rejects that interpretation, there is nothing in the wording of Article 30 to prevent such an interpretation.

Article 30 establishes three criteria, each of which must be satisfied in order to qualify for the exception: (1) the exception must be "limited"; (2) the exception must not "unreasonably conflict with the normal exploitation of the patent"; and (3) the exception must not "unreasonably prejudice the legitimate interests of the patent owner, taking into account the legitimate interests of third parties." The panel ruled that each of the three must be presumed to mean something different from the other two or else there would be redundancy.

In Canada – Patent Protection of Pharmaceutical Products, the panel considered whether the Canadian Patent Act violated TRIPS by permitting generic manufacturers to infringe patent rights (1) to develop submissions for regulatory approval in Canada or a foreign country (the regulatory review exception) and (2) to manufacture and stockpile a patented product during the final 6 months of the patent in preparation for sale after the patent expired (the stockpiling exception). The panel's decision thus examined the legality under TRIPS of two well-recognized exceptions to patent protection. The panel accepted the argument of the European Communities that both exceptions violated the "exclusionary" patent rights set out in TRIPS Article 28. Canada defended both exceptions under TRIPS Article 30. The panel ruled that the regulatory review exception passed the Article 30 test but the stockpiling exception did not.

In rejecting the stockpiling exception, the panel ruled that any exception that entirely removes the right to exclude making and using the patented product cannot be considered a "limited exception" under Article 30. In contrast, the regulatory review exception created a minimal reduction in the legal rights of the patentee and therefore qualified as a "limited exception." The regulatory review exception allowed a generic manufacturer to produce a limited quantity of patented drugs to submit to a national regulatory review process. The regulatory review exception was confined to conduct needed to comply with the requirements of the regulatory review process, and no commercial use was made of the products resulting from the production runs. Thus, the acts permitted would be small and narrowly bounded. The economic impact of this regulatory review exception could be considerable. Since it could take generic producers several years to develop the generic product and to obtain regulatory approval, permitting these activities during the course of the patent could significantly reduce the length of time that the patent owner would enjoy a monopoly in the market and thereby reduce profits. However, the panel reasoned that the first condition of Article 30 addresses the impact on legal rights, not economic impact.

The panel further reasoned that the regulatory review exception did not conflict with the normal exploitation of patents. The regulatory review process is an unintended consequence of the conjunction of patent laws with product laws, not a normal consequence of enforcing patent rights. Unlike many other kinds of patentable products, pharmaceuticals are subject to rigorous government scrutiny due to their potential to cause serious harm to human health through unintended side effects. Thus, patent owners cannot claim a "legitimate interest" in the economic benefits caused by the length of time required to get regulatory approval for generic drugs. While a number of governments had extended the patent term to compensate for the delays in obtaining approval, several others had not. Therefore, the interest claimed was neither so compelling nor so widely recognized that it could be regarded as a "legitimate interest." Moreover, the issue of regulatory review exceptions was well known before the TRIPS negotiations, but was not addressed in the recorded agenda of the negotiations. Does this interpretation of the Article 30 exception stand in the way of issuing compulsory licenses on HIV/AIDS drugs exclusively for export or would that be too great an intrusion on patent rights to qualify as a limited exception? Such a license would not affect the economic interests of the patent holder in the market in which it is issued. Nor would it affect its legal rights or economic interests in the export market if that market is a least-developed country that will not provide patent protection until 2016. However, if one follows the reasoning of the panel, it would abrogate entirely the right to exclude making and using the patented product in protected markets and therefore fail the first test under Article 30 for the same reason as the stockpiling exception.

In addition to the panel interpretation, there are other reasons to conclude that Article 31, not Article 30, is the appropriate provision with respect to compulsory licenses to address public health problems. First, with the decision to amend Article

31 (discussed below), the WTO members have rejected the interpretation of Article 30 as a means to resolve the issue of compulsory licensing for countries that lack adequate manufacturing capacity. Second, the negotiating history of TRIPS indicates that Article 31 was intended to govern compulsory licensing. Finally, interpreting Article 30 to resolve compulsory licensing issues would be problematic. While it would provide greater certainty regarding the rights of WTO members, it would introduce a new element of uncertainty regarding the correct interpretation of Article 30 in other circumstances and the relationship between Articles 30 and 31.

6.1.2 TRIPS Article 31

Under Article 31, a government may issue a compulsory license authorizing the government or a third party to produce generic drugs without the authorization of the patent holder where negotiations fail to obtain authorization on reasonable commercial terms. However, the use of the patent must be "predominantly" to supply the domestic market and the patent holder must be paid adequate remuneration, based on the economic value of the license. The negotiation requirement may be waived in cases of national emergency, extreme urgency, or non-commercial public use. Members are not obliged to comply with the negotiation requirement or to predominantly serve the domestic market where the use is permitted to remedy anti-competitive practices.

The TRIPS provisions relating to compulsory licensing strengthen a government's position in price negotiations with patent holders by permitting the government to issue a compulsory license to manufacture drugs, rather than purchase them from the patent owner. For example, where a government provides drugs to patients through a public health care scheme, it meets the necessary conditions to halt price negotiations because generic versions manufactured under compulsory license would serve a non-commercial public use and predominantly supply the domestic market. Since the term "adequate remuneration" is not defined, patent owners cannot predict with certainty what compensation they will receive if a government abandons negotiations. The specific manner in which compensation is determined may vary from one WTO member to the next, as may the principles that apply to judicial review or its equivalent in each legal system. Calculating compensation for compulsory licenses is likely to be an uncertain process in any legal system. This gives the patent owners an incentive to determine the price through negotiation.

Many developing countries do not have the capacity to manufacture generic drugs. This weakens their bargaining position substantially unless they can import generic drugs from another country that has issued a compulsory license on their behalf. To serve as an effective bargaining chip, the threat to issue a compulsory license to government or private pharmaceutical manufacturers must be credible. TRIPS Declaration Paragraph 6 acknowledged the difficulties countries with inadequate manufacturing capacity would face with respect to compulsory licensing:

6. We recognize that WTO members with insufficient or no manufacturing capacities in the pharmaceutical sector could face difficulties in making effective use of compulsory licensing under the TRIPS Agreement. We instruct the Council for TRIPS to find an expeditious solution to this problem...

6.1.3 The Paragraph 6 Decision

In order to implement Paragraph 6, the WTO General Council agreed to amend Article 31(f) and 31(h) by means of a Decision that sets up a new set of rights and obligations, adding to the pre-existing rights and obligations set out in the TRIPS agreement. We shall refer to this Decision of 30 August 2003 as the "Paragraph 6 Decision" and the new set of rights and obligations as the "Paragraph 6 system."

The Paragraph 6 Decision aims to increase the availability of pharmaceutical products needed to address public health problems in developing and least-developed countries, especially those resulting from HIV/AIDS, tuberculosis, malaria and other epidemics. Because the text of TRIPS Article 31(f) was clear, WTO members had to agree to an amendment in order to facilitate access to essential medicines in developing and least-developed countries that have inadequate manufacturing capacities. It was not possible to solve the problem through treaty interpretation.

The Paragraph 6 Decision waives an exporter's Article 31(f) obligation to supply predominantly the domestic market, enabling any country with manufacturing capacity to issue a compulsory license to produce generic drugs for export to countries that have insufficient or no manufacturing capacity, subject to several conditions. TRIPS Article 31(h) requires the issuer of a compulsory license to compensate the patent holder. The amendment clarifies that in the situation where the license is issued to serve an export market under the Paragraph 6 system (as opposed to serving the domestic market), the exporting country, not the importing country, must pay compensation. The compensation takes into account the economic value in the importing country. No formal restriction on the countries that are eligible to import exists under the Paragraph 6 system. However, the Paragraph 6 Decision creates four categories of importing members. Least-developed countries are eligible to import without formal notification to the WTO. All other members are required to notify the Council for TRIPS of their intention to use the system set out in the Paragraph 6 Decision, although the notification is not subject to WTO approval. Two further categories consist of countries that have made a commitment not to use the Paragraph 6 system as importers (Australia, Austria, Belgium, Canada, Denmark, Finland, France, Germany, Greece, Iceland, Ireland, Italy, Japan, Luxembourg, Netherlands, New Zealand, Norway, Portugal, Spain, Sweden, Switzerland, United Kingdom, United States of America, the Czech Republic, Cyprus, Estonia, Hungary, Latvia, Lithuania, Malta, Poland, Slovak Republic and Slovenia) and countries that have committed to using the system as importers only in situations of national emergency or extreme urgency (Hong Kong

China, Israel, Korea, Kuwait, Macao China, Mexico, Qatar, Singapore, Chinese Taipei, Turkey, and the United Arab Emirates). Countries making the latter commitment have agreed, in effect, not to use the system for non-commercial public use. For example, they have agreed not to use the system simply to lower the general cost of purchasing medicine for public health care systems. These commitments resolve an issue of concern to the pharmaceutical industry – that countries that lacked manufacturing capacity, but could afford to pay the full price of patented medicine, would import cheaper generic versions instead. The fourth category consists of the members that do not fall into the first three categories.

In order to ensure that imports occur only within the parameters set out in the Paragraph 6 Decision and that medicines supplied under this system do not make their way back to markets that have been carved out of the system under these commitments, members must have laws in place to prevent the diversion of medicine supplied under the system. The Paragraph 6 Decision also requires all importing countries, regardless of their development status, to take "reasonable measures within their means, proportionate to their administrative capacities and to the risk of trade diversion" to prevent the re-export of the products they import under this system. The types of measures that they must take are not specified. Where developing countries and least-developed countries experience difficulty implementing this provision, developed countries must provide technical and financial assistance to facilitate its implementation. However, WTO members are free to determine whether to permit parallel imports without these laws being subject to WTO dispute settlement procedures. Parallel imports involve products sold by the patent owner in one market and then imported into another market without the patent owner's approval.

No restrictions exist regarding the countries that are eligible to export. However, exporters are required to follow a series of procedural requirements and conditions, in addition to the compensation requirement noted above. Moreover, the obligations under Article 31(f) are waived only "to the extent necessary for the purposes of production of a pharmaceutical product(s) and its export to an eligible importing Member(s)." A further necessity test requires that the license restrict the authorization to "only the amount necessary to meet the needs of the eligible importing Member(s)."

Under the Paragraph 6 system, with the exception of least-developed countries, importing countries must specify the names and quantities of the products needed in their notification to the WTO. They must also confirm that they have granted or intend to grant a compulsory license in accordance with TRIPS Article 31. Finally, they must establish that they have no or insufficient manufacturing capacity in the pharmaceutical sector for the product in question in one of two ways. Either they have no manufacturing capacity in the pharmaceutical sector at all, or they have examined this capacity (excluding that owned or controlled by the patent holder) and found it to be insufficient to meet their needs. The Paragraph 6 system will no longer apply once it is established that the capacity has become sufficient to meet its needs.

The Paragraph 6 system does not apply to countries that have sufficient manufacturing capacity to issue compulsory licenses to meet the needs of their own populations. The question in a given case is whether the importing country has manufacturing capacity for the pharmaceutical product in question. For example, countries like China, India and Brazil could use the Paragraph 6 system as importers if they lack capacity for a particular medicine, importing drugs from generic manufacturers in other countries. However, where developing countries do have manufacturing capacity, they will have to determine whether and how to use compulsory licensing to reduce the cost of providing treatment by issuing licenses to their own generic manufacturers. When a country issues a compulsory license to its own generic drug manufacturers to serve its own market, the Paragraph 6 Decision will not apply. In order to strike the right balance between the rights of producers and users of patented drugs, the country must rely on TRIPS Article 31 exceptions, which continue to operate in this situation, unchanged by the Paragraph 6 Decision. Many of these exceptions are more ambiguous than paragraph 31(f), thus raising the issue of whether they need clarification or amendments to enhance access to essential medicine in these countries. The focus of the remainder of this chapter is on the application of TRIPS Article 31 to compulsory licenses issued in developing countries that have sufficient generic manufacturing capacity to meet their own needs without importing generic drugs under the Paragraph 6 system. All developing countries are required to comply fully with TRIPS as of 1 January 2005.

6.1.4 Implementation and Use of the Paragraph 6 Decision by WTO Members

By a decision of the General Council on 6 December 2005, the WTO adopted an Amendment of the TRIPS Agreement regarding the implementation and use of the Paragraph 6 Decision by WTO Members (WTO 2005). The Protocol amending the TRIPS Agreement that was attached to this Decision was to be open for acceptance by Members until 1 December 2007 and was to take effect for the Members that have accepted the amendment upon acceptance by two thirds of the Members and thereafter for each other Member upon acceptance by it, in accordance with paragraph 3 of Article X of the Agreement Establishing the WTO (WTO 2005). As of November 2007, 39 out of 151 WTO Member countries had formally accepted the amendment: United States (17 December 2005); Switzerland (13 September 2006); El Salvador (19 September 2006); South Korea (24 January 2007); Norway (5 February 2007); India (26 March 2007); Philippines (30 March 2007); Israel (10 August 2007); Japan (31 August 2007); Australia (12 September 2007); Singapore (28 September 2007); China (28 October 2007); and the European Union (19 November 2007). This was the first time that the WTO had used the amendment procedure, which has since been criticized for being too slow.

The Paragraph 6 Decision provides a right, subject to certain conditions, rather than establishing an obligation. WTO Members have some flexibility with respect to the manner in which they implement this right. While they can not make access to compulsory licensing under this system less restrictive than the conditions established in the Decision, they can make access more restrictive and design the implementation of the Decision in a manner that is consistent with their existing legal system.

The Paragraph 6 Decision was implemented in Canada by an Act to Amend the Patent Act and the Food and Drugs Act (The Jean Chrétien Pledge to Africa Act), of 2004 (http://laws.justice.gc.ca/en/showdoc/cs/P-4/bo-ga:s_21_01//en). The Canadian law imposes conditions for obtaining a compulsory license for export in addition to those contained in the Paragraph 6 Decision. It only applies to products listed in Schedule 1 of the Canadian Patent Act. Since Schedule 1 of the Canadian Patent Act originally did not include fixed-dose combinations, it had to be amended in September 2005 (Hestermeyer 2007). This embellishment slows down the approval process for any existing drugs that are not listed in Schedule 1 and any future drugs that might become available. The Canadian law also requires that the generic manufacturer certify that it has sought a voluntary license from the patent owners to manufacture and sell the pharmaceutical product and that such efforts have not been successful. In the first use of the Canadian law, negotiations between the generic manufacturer and the patent owners delayed the process. A further condition, which requires a review of the drug under the Canadian Food and Drugs Act, introduces additional delays. The Canadian law provides only a 2-year term for the compulsory license, which can be renewed once only if the quantities of the pharmaceutical product authorized to be exported were not exported before the initial 2-year term expired. Any country that is not a WTO Member and that is named on the Organization for Economic Co-operation and Development's list of countries that are eligible for official development assistance can only use the Canadian version of the Paragraph 6 Decision in a national emergency or other circumstances of extreme urgency, which excludes the use of the system for non-commercial public use.

On 19 September 2007, Canada's Commissioner of Patents granted a compulsory license to Apotex, Inc., to supply Rwanda with a fixed dose combination tablet of *lamivudine* (150 mg), *nevirapine* (200 mg) and *zidovudine* (300 mg). Rwanda had filed a related notification, dated 17 July 2007 (IP/N/9/RWA/1). Canada notified the WTO regarding the compulsory license 4 October 2007 (WTO 2007). The information on the shipment (quantities and distinguishing features) was to be posted on the licensee's website (www.apotex.com/apotriavir/abouttriavir.asp). The compulsory license was issued solely for purposes directly related to the manufacture of 15,600,000 of these fixed dose combination tablets, for a period of 2 years and to sell it for export to Rwanda only (WTO 2007). The Rwandan and Canadian notifications were the first received by the WTO from an importing country and an exporting country, respectively.

Attaran has criticized the Canadian law as too complex and not user-friendly. Applications must be filed and processed on an individual basis. It would be more simple and efficient if applicants could file jointly. The limited duration of the compulsory license means that the application process must be repeated when the license expires. These national and temporal restrictions have been criticized for being out of step with the global and chronic nature of the HIV/AIDS pandemic. However, another argument that has been made to explain the lack of use of the Canadian law is that it is not that necessary, for two reasons. First, many drugs have not been patented in the least-developed countries. Second, the cost of manufacturing generic drugs is higher in Canada than in developing countries (such as India), making Canada a less cost-effective source for generic drugs. Another reason the Canadian law has been little used is the lack of requests from the developing countries themselves (Attaran 2007).

6.2 Special and Differential Treatment in WTO Law

Special and differential treatment of developing countries is a concept that finds expression throughout WTO law. This section proposes three tests to determine whether WTO law – and TRIPS patent provisions in particular – achieves its stated objective(s) with respect to developing countries. The first test is based on the development needs of WTO members. The second test is based on the economic impact of WTO provisions on developing countries. The third test asks whether the interpretation or design of the law is effective. Applying this analysis to TRIPS supports the view that the balance to be struck between producers and users of patented medicine should shift in favor of developing and least-developed countries when they are the users under consideration.

The conventional view of treaty interpretation is that legal rights and obligations must be interpreted in a uniform manner for all of the parties to the treaty. However, this view does not prevent taking the individual circumstances of member States into account where the text of the treaty supports such an interpretation. The Decision of 28 November 1979 on Differential and More Favorable Treatment, Reciprocity and Fuller Participation of Developing Countries (the Enabling Clause) introduced special and differential treatment as an integral part of the GATT system. The Uruguay Round of Multilateral Trade Negotiations then incorporated several more provisions regarding special and differential treatment into WTO law. The legal effect of WTO provisions referring to special and differential treatment for developing countries varies with their wording and the context in which they appear. Nevertheless, special and differential treatment for developing countries is a concept that now finds expression throughout WTO law and supports the view that economic inequality can and should be taken into account in the design or interpretation of WTO rights.

In European Communities – Conditions for the Granting of Tariff Preferences to Developing Countries (the Tariff Preferences case), the WTO Appellate Body interpreted the Enabling Clause in light of the recognition in the preamble to the

WTO Agreement of the "need for positive efforts designed to ensure that developing countries, and especially the least developed among them, secure a share in the growth in international trade commensurate with the needs of their economic development". The Appellate Body further noted the recognition in the preamble that WTO Members' "respective needs and concerns at different levels of economic development" may vary according to the different stages of development of different Members. Responding to the needs of developing countries – the existence of which must be assessed according to an objective standard such as broad-based recognition by international organizations – could thus entail treating different developing-country beneficiaries differently.

In the Tariff Preferences case, the Appellate Body also recognized that the equal application of certain obligations, regardless of economic status, could impede rather than facilitate the WTO objective of promoting economic development through trade. Switzerland has expressed a similar view in the Doha Round negotiations on special and differential treatment, arguing that equal treatment of Members with fundamental differences of starting positions does not promote the economic development of those who need it most.

The Vienna Convention requires contextual WTO rule interpretation. Article 31 requires that the ordinary meaning be given to the terms of the treaty in their context and in the light of its object and purpose. The approach taken by the Appellate Body has been to first examine the context of the provision in which the language is expressed, then examine the context of the particular agreement in which the provision is found, and, lastly, examine the context of the Uruguay Round Agreements as a whole. Although it provides no binding right or obligation, the WTO preamble sets out the object and purpose of the trade agreements and provides an overall context in which to interpret trade obligations and exceptions, including those found in TRIPS. It thus directly affects interpretation as part of the single combined operation of Article 31. In Japan – Taxes on Alcoholic Beverages, the Appellate Body reasoned that WTO rules should be interpreted flexibly in order to be effective in real cases in the real world. The asymmetries of economic development that exist among the member States need to be addressed in order to ensure the effectiveness of special and differential treatment in WTO law. These need to be taken into account not only in the design of the rules but also with respect to their interpretation.

The preamble of the WTO Agreement indicates that the objective of special and differential treatment for developing countries is "to ensure that developing countries, especially the least developed among them, secure a share in the growth of international trade commensurate with the needs of their economic development." According to the preamble, achieving this objective requires a consideration of their "respective needs and concerns at different levels of economic development." This objective applies to all of the covered agreements. Therefore, the provisions in the WTO preamble inform the interpretation of TRIPS. The following analysis develops a framework for analyzing special and differential treatment provisions, including the references in the WTO preamble, before considering how the preamble should inform the interpretation of specific TRIPS provisions.

The Appellate Body's decision in European Communities – Conditions for the Granting of Tariff Preferences to Developing Countries recognizes that the references to the needs of developing countries in the WTO Agreement preamble support the view that they may have different needs according to their levels of development and particular circumstances. However, variation in levels of development is only one factor to take into account in determining the legal and economic effects of special and differential treatment provisions. The needs of developing countries and the impact of special and differential treatment on their development both vary depending on the economic context of each WTO agreement. Likewise, Vienna Convention Article 31 requires that variations in the interpretative context of special and differential treatment provisions be taken into account in determining their legal effect in different agreements. Thus, the legal and economic effects of special and differential treatment provisions will vary with the legal and economic context of each agreement.

For example, the central thrust of GATT is to reduce tariffs and other barriers to trade (the legal context) in order to stimulate economic growth through specialization in areas of comparative advantage (the economic context). GATT seeks to remove barriers to competition. In contrast, TRIPS promotes intellectual property rights (the legal context) in order to stimulate economic growth through innovation (the economic context). TRIPS seeks to protect monopoly rights. In the context of GATT, economic development is based on market access for products in which developing countries enjoy a comparative advantage. In the context of TRIPS, economic development is based on access to technology. The nature of the rules and their underlying economic theories are different in these two agreements.

Since the legal and economic contexts of GATT and TRIPS are not the same and all developing countries are not the same, there cannot be special and differential treatment that is universally appropriate (1) for all covered agreements or (2) for all developing countries. Moreover, the context of special and differential treatment varies within each of the covered agreements. For example, both the legal and economic contexts in TRIPS will vary between different types of intellectual property right (for example, patents vs. geographical indications) and within categories of intellectual property right (for example, patents for medicine vs. patents for computer technology).

This raises the issue of how to determine the appropriate level of special and differential treatment and the correct interpretation and application of special and differential treatment provisions from one agreement to the next. The basic purpose of special and differential treatment is to stimulate sustainable economic development in accordance with the needs of developing countries. Thus, both the needs of developing countries and the economic impact of special and differential treatment on their development should be taken into account (1) when interpreting special and differential treatment provisions and (2) when assessing the appropriateness of special and differential treatment as a policy. Applying the needs test and the economic impact test produce different results in different agreements and in different economic contexts.

Both the needs test and the economic impact test involve economic analysis. For example, determining the needs of developing countries in the context of pharmaceutical patents requires an analysis of disease prevalence and purchasing power. Determining the economic impact of compulsory licenses for pharmaceuticals involves an assessment of the value of the market to the patent holder. Both tests also involve legal analysis. Both spring from the treaty text. How they play out will vary with the wording and the context of each provision that is analyzed. For example, paragraph 3(c) of the Enabling Clause specifies the developing country needs that are to be taken into account when developed countries design preferential schemes. In order to determine the economic impact of a particular provision, its legal effect must be determined. Thus, the correct interpretation of a particular WTO provision will require a combination of legal and economic analysis.

Special and differential treatment rules are not the only WTO provisions in which the needs of developing countries can be taken into account. A closely related issue is how the uniform application of other WTO rules may produce different results depending on the level of economic development enjoyed by a particular WTO member. Does the uniform application of WTO rules, irrespective of variations in development, give effect to the rules in a way that meets the needs of developing countries? Put another way, do variations in development levels need to be taken into account in order to ensure that WTO rules are effective in achieving the objective(s) of a given rule (which may encompass more that just the objective of economic development in developing countries)? Must all WTO rules be effective for all WTO members?

Applying an effectiveness test, in addition to the needs test and the economic impact test, is consistent with the rules of treaty interpretation. The rule of effective treaty interpretation is a corollary of the general rule of treaty interpretation in Vienna Convention Article 31. According to the rule of effective treaty interpretation, an interpreter is not free to adopt a reading that would result in reducing whole clauses or paragraphs of a treaty to redundancy or inutility. Put another way, a treaty must be interpreted harmoniously in a way that gives effect to all of its provisions. A logical extension of this rule of interpretation is that the interpretation must give effect to the provision for not just some members, but for all of them. It is reasonable to conclude that the parties to a treaty intend its provisions to be effective for all. Thus, if the text supports an interpretation that makes a provision effective for all, then that interpretation should be preferred over one that does not. Thus, testing the interpretation of an ambiguous provision for its effectiveness in achieving special and differential treatment objectives is in accordance with customary rules of interpretation of public international law that apply to the interpretation of the WTO agreements.

Thus, there are three factors that should be taken into account in interpreting or designing special and differential treatment provisions to make them operational and effective. The first two factors reflect the objectives of the WTO Agreement preamble and TRIPS, while the third springs from a customary rule of interpretation of public international law.

1. Development needs (TRIPS preamble and WTO Preamble)
2. Economic impact (TRIPS Article 7 and WTO Preamble); and
3. Effectiveness.

Taken together, these three factors or tests create an interdisciplinary approach to the analysis of WTO law and policy. What these tests share in common is that they all seek to answer the same fundamental question – does the law, as interpreted or designed, achieve its stated objective(s) in both the legal and economic contexts?

The objectives of TRIPS must be understood in light of the overall objectives of the WTO Agreement relating to developing countries. The relationship between these two sets of objectives should be harmonious, in light of the principle of effective treaty interpretation and the presumption against conflicts in international law.

Two core objectives of TRIPS are to achieve a balance between the rights of producers and users of intellectual property and to promote development. There are a number of TRIPS provisions that support an approach to balancing TRIPS rights and obligations that differs with the level of development of the member in question. The objectives in TRIPS Article 7 promote "technological innovation...to the mutual advantage of producers and users...in a manner conducive to social and economic welfare, and to a balance of rights and obligations." According to TRIPS Article 8, WTO members may "adopt measures necessary to protect public health...provided that such measures are consistent with [TRIPS]." The TRIPS preamble seeks "effective and adequate protection of intellectual property rights," while recognizing the developmental objectives of intellectual property protection and the special needs of least-developed countries for "maximum flexibility in the domestic implementation of laws." These provisions reflect the concerns of developing countries in the Uruguay Round negotiations that earlier drafts of TRIPS did not adequately address the questions of the balance of the rights and obligations of rights holders, developmental concerns and public policy objectives. These concerns were reflected in the preamble so that they could be taken into account in the interpretation of the agreement.

Article XI of the WTO Agreement provides that: "The least-developed countries recognized as such by the United Nations will only be required to undertake commitments and concessions to the extent consistent with their individual development, financial and trade needs or their administrative and institutional capabilities." Article 1 of The Decision on Measures in Favor of Least-Developed Countries leaves no doubt that this aspect of differential treatment applies to TRIPS and repeats the language from above: "if not already provided for in the instruments negotiated in the course of the Uruguay Round, notwithstanding their acceptance of these instruments, the least-developed countries... will only be required to undertake commitments and concessions to the extent consistent with their individual development, financial and trade needs or their administrative and institutional capabilities." The WTO Agreement preamble also makes special reference to the needs of developing countries, "especially the least developed among them." The reference to sustainable development in the WTO Preamble provides further support for the view that TRIPS should be interpreted in a manner that supports the development needs of the developing and least-developed countries. While the term sustainable development has received a great deal of attention with respect to its role in balancing trade and environmental protection, economic development is also an important aspect of sustainable development.

These provisions support the view that the balance to be struck between producers and users should shift in favor of developing and least-developed countries when they are the users under consideration. While the Uruguay Round negotiations on TRIPS rejected country-by-country transition periods, several members were of the view that the balance of rights between producers and users of intellectual property should take the needs of developing countries into account and that transition periods alone were not enough to meet their needs. Moreover, the promotion of innovation through the intellectual property regime was not an objective in and of itself but rather was a means of attaining other economic and social objectives. Existing international intellectual property conventions respected this and the fact that the relative costs and benefits of the protection on intellectual property rights varied from country to country depending on the level of economic development. In order for special and differential treatment to be effective in meeting the needs of developing countries, the correct balance must differ from one market to the next, rather than be universally applicable without regard to the conditions existing in each market. The absence of internationally agreed criteria that determine the needs of each country at different levels of economic and technological development makes this difficult to achieve. However, the context of specific provisions and agreements provide guidance regarding the criteria that would be appropriate.

When read together, the objectives of TRIPS and of the WTO Agreement integrate into TRIPS the twin themes of balancing intellectual property rights against development needs and providing differential treatment based on the level of development of WTO members. There is no inherent conflict between the objectives of the WTO Agreement and the specific objectives of TRIPS.

TRIPS permits flexibility in the manner in which its provisions are implemented in domestic legal systems. TRIPS Article 1 provides that "Members shall be free to determine the appropriate method of implementing [TRIPS] provisions within their own legal system and practice." The appropriateness of a particular legal system in a given market depends on the conditions prevailing in that market (Arruñada and Andonova 2005). In the following section, we argue that patent laws, like legal systems in general, will be more effective in promoting innovation and economic development where their design, interpretation and implementation take into account prevailing conditions on a market-by-market basis.

6.3   The Economic Impact of Patents and their Effect on Development Needs

In the context of drug patents, striking the right balance between the rights of producers and users requires an analysis of development needs and economic impact
to determine whether patent rights (the rights of producers) or compulsory licensing rights (one of the rights of users) are more effective in promoting innovation
that meets the needs of developing countries. This raises economic issues regarding the effect that patents have on innovation and economic development and
whether drug patents are conducive to social and economic welfare.

The argument for patent rights in developing countries is based on several
assumptions regarding the general economic impact of patents and the specific
economic impact of patents in developing countries: (1) technological innovation
promotes economic growth; (2) patent rights are necessary to provide research
incentives to spur technological innovation; (3) patents in developing countries
will provide research incentives to create technological innovations that serve the
needs of developing countries; (4) patent rights in developing countries are necessary to promote the transfer of technological innovations from firms in developed
countries and to promote technological innovation in developing countries; and (5)
technology transfer to developing countries promotes economic growth in developing countries.

The theoretical foundation for drug patents lies in the economic argument that
monopoly rights are necessary to spur innovation in the pharmaceutical field. In
essence, this argument states that, without patents, the invention of new pharmaceuticals would cease, making the issue of affordable access to medicine a moot
point. This argument is normally used by pharmaceutical companies to make the
case for any drug. In particular, the argument has been put forward for HIV/AIDS
drugs.

However, the economic issues are different for global diseases (diseases that
are prevalent in both developed and developing countries, such as HIV/AIDS) and
neglected diseases (developing country diseases that are not prevalent in developed countries, such as malaria). This is because the markets for drugs that treat
the diseases are different.

In some cases, it may be difficult to determine whether a disease is global or
neglected. For example, HIV/AIDS straddles both the developed world and the
developing world, which suggests that it is best characterized as a global disease.
However, the types of HIV infection found commonly in the developing and the
developed worlds are not the same. There are many subtypes of HIV-1 (the most
commonly occurring HIV infection in humans). The major HIV-1 subtypes
accounting for the most infections in Africa are subtype C in southern Africa, subtypes A and D in eastern Africa, and a circulating recombinant form 02_AG
(CRF02_AG) in west–central Africa (Peters and Sharp, 2000). On the other hand,
the most commonly occurring form of HIV-1 in North America (and in Europe)
is subtype B. The drugs developed are more effective against HIV-1 subtype B.

Thus, the sub-types prevailing in developing countries can be characterized as neglected diseases. Moreover, HIV/AIDS drugs primarily serve the developed country markets. It is estimated that 98% of the revenue for drugs for combating HIV/AIDS come from the OECD countries (Lanjouw 2003).

In the following sections, we consider various economic arguments for and against the use of patents to stimulate innovation in treatments for neglected and global diseases. The focus of our analysis in this section is on the issue of whether global pharmaceutical patents are necessary to create research incentives to treat neglected and global diseases in developing countries. It is important to note that this issue is distinct from the issues of whether global patent rights lead to differential pricing (Ramsey pricing) and how regulatory capture affects research incentives.

6.3.1 Are Global Patents Necessary to Provide Research Incentives for Neglected Diseases?

One of the reasons proffered for having global patents is that a global patent system will provide research incentives for the development of drugs for neglected diseases. According to this view, the reason these diseases have been "neglected" by the pharmaceutical industry is due to the general absence of effective patent protection in developing countries prior to the implementation of TRIPS.

Another argument is that the risk of compulsory licensing makes developing countries unattractive for the pharmaceutical industry, even with global patent rights in place. The risk of losing the entire potential profits in developing countries makes it unattractive for the pharmaceutical companies to develop drugs for any disease – in particular for neglected diseases. However, WTO rules – and national legislation in markets such as the United States – permit compulsory licensing. The risk of compulsory licensing in the United States has not deterred investment in the US market. Moreover, WTO rules require compensation for the patent holder when compulsory licenses are issued.

There are several arguments against global patents. Even with patent protection in developing countries, their markets lack the purchasing power needed to spur private investment in treatments for neglected diseases. Of the 1,393 new chemical entities marketed between 1975 and 1999, only sixteen were for tropical diseases and tuberculosis, i.e. diseases no longer found in developed countries (Trouiller et al., 2002). Of the annual health-related research and development worldwide in 1999, only 0.2% was for pneumonia, diarrheal diseases and tuberculosis – yet these account for 18% of the global disease burden (UNDP 1999). These statistics indicate that the advent of TRIPS has not created adequate research incentives by itself. Only time will tell whether this trend will continue.

Nevertheless, there is another argument against the necessity of global patents. Patents do not provide an incentive for innovation even where there is adequate purchasing power in the market (Boldrin and Levine, 2002). An "intellectual monopoly" approach to patent rights has the effect of stifling innovation because it provides an incentive to patent holders to invest in legal action to extend the life of their patents and to prevent others from developing new innovations. In economic terms, patents provide rights to the person first in the door of the patent office. This is an inefficient way of allocating economic resources. This has led many economists to believe that there is no inherent reason for patent protection (Scotchmer 2003). Historical evidence favors this view (Khan 2005).

6.3.2 Are Global Patents Necessary to Provide Research Incentives for Global Diseases?

The argument in favor of global patents for global diseases is as follows. Developed country markets will be undermined through parallel imports unless patents are global, even if developed countries prohibit parallel imports. Prohibitions on illegal recreational drugs (such as cocaine or marijuana) are not effective in preventing their import and sale on black markets. The same would be true for pharmaceutical products.

However, drugs to treat potentially fatal diseases are not the same as recreational drugs. Fake recreational drugs (most often) do not harm the user's life. Fake drugs for HIV/AIDS (or other diseases) will. Most patients will not be willing to risk their lives buying pharmaceuticals on the black market that have potentially lethal consequences. We do not see drug dealers selling in HIV/AIDS drug cocktails on the street corners of the United States, even though generic HIV/AIDS drug cocktails can be bought in developing countries for the tenth of the price that one has to pay in developed countries. Black markets for parallel imports of pharmaceuticals are unlikely.

An argument against global patents is that developed country markets provide sufficient incentives to invent drugs to treat global diseases, thus making developing country patents unnecessary. The case of treatments for HIV/AIDS supports this view. Global patents were not necessary to create research incentives to invent treatments, but global patents have impeded affordable access to treatment in developing countries. TRIPS Article 6 permits WTO members to determine whether to allow parallel imports. Therefore, patent laws in developing countries should focus on increasing affordable access to treatment, not research incentives. Global patents impede affordable access by reducing price competition.

Moreover, global patents have stifled innovation in HIV/AIDS treatment regimens. In markets served by patented drugs, the regimen requires a large number of pills taken three times a day. In contrast, in markets served by generic drugs, both the number of pills and the number of daily doses have been reduced. This innovation on the part of the generic manufacturers has simplified treatment for patients in countries where the patents are not in force, in addition to lowering the price of treatment considerably. This provides further support for the argument against global patents, whether for neglected or global diseases.

We conclude that global patents are neither necessary for the development of drugs for global diseases nor for neglected diseases. The effect that patents have on innovation and economic development in developing countries is not conducive to their social and economic needs. Thus, uniform application of TRIPS obligations regarding drug patents is unlikely to be effective in promoting innovation that meets the needs of developing countries. This argument, which was originally put forth by Condon and Sinha (2005), has been strongly endorsed by Cahoy (2007) who notes: "Given that innovation costs are the primary industry argument against compulsory licensing, this [argument of Condon and Sinha] appears logical."

6.4 Making Patents Effective in Achieving Economic and Development Objectives

Drug patents have neither a positive economic impact on developing countries nor meet their development needs. They have the opposite effect. The lack of affordable and effective access to medical treatment has a negative impact on development. Several measures of development are affected by HIV/AIDS, including GDP per capita, economic growth, education, life expectancy, and health. Indeed, Peter Piot, the executive director of the United Nations HIV/AIDS program, has stated that countries with high rates of HIV infection, such as Botswana, risk becoming "undeveloping" countries because of HIV/AIDS. Thus, if patents decrease access to life-saving medicines in developing countries facing an HIV/AIDS epidemic, the impact on their development needs will be negative and defeat the objectives of the WTO.

The result is that TRIPS obligations regarding patent rights are not effective in meeting the objectives of the WTO Agreement and TRIPS. There are two possible solutions to this problem. The second-best solution is to use the exceptions in TRIPS to achieve a better balance between the rights of users and producers until the patent obligations can be eliminated. This might be achieved through an interpretation or an amendment to Article 31. The first part of this section will examine specific Article 31 exceptions in that context. The best solution is to eliminate the obligation of developing countries to provide patent rights for pharmaceutical products, through waivers for developing countries (whose transition period has ended under TRIPS Article 65) and extending transition periods for least-developed countries (an option that is contemplated in TRIPS Article 66). This solution has been partly achieved for least-developed countries, whose obligations to protect pharmaceutical patents have been delayed until 2016. The second part of this section will propose an index that can be used to determine the circumstances in which patent obligations should be waived for developing countries whose obligations are already in force or to extend transition periods further for least-developed countries. Both are needed as part of the solution proposed in this chapter because TRIPS contemplates extending the transition period for least-developed countries, but not for developing countries. Moreover, the transition period for developing countries has ended, leaving waivers as the mechanism to use to suspend their patent obligations.

Another option is to advocate an interpretation through the dispute settlement process of the WTO. However, this option is unappealing for three reasons. First, it would require waiting for a dispute to come before the dispute settlement body that raises the right issues. Second, even if this were to occur and the WTO panel or Appellate Body were to adopt the advocated interpretation, the interpretation would be legally binding only for the parties to the dispute. Third, ambiguous treaty language should not be used to resolve a normative policy issue that is still a matter of unresolved political debate. Thus, other WTO decision-making mechanisms are preferable.

6.4.1 Solving the Problem Through Interpretation or Amendment

Where TRIPS provisions are sufficiently ambiguous to be susceptible to an interpretation that resolves the issue of special and differential treatment, an official interpretation would be feasible. However, where there is insufficient ambiguity, reforms are better addressed through the amendment process. This section briefly considers the degree of ambiguity in Article 31 in this context, rather than engage in a detailed analysis. There is already a great deal of literature addressing how TRIPS Article 31 can be interpreted in ways favorable to developing countries. This section is limited to the point that interpretation is not the best route to follow in order to introduce objective criteria for applying situational flexibility to compulsory licensing exceptions.

In the context of patent provisions in TRIPS, the rights conferred on patent owners in Article 28.1 and 33 are expressed in unambiguous terms. The lack of ambiguity in this treaty text makes it difficult to take special and differential treatment into account through interpretation. As noted earlier, Articles 30 and 31 authorize exceptions to TRIPS patent rights, and while Article 30 permits "limited exceptions," Article 31 is broader and provides a right to make other use of the subject matter of the patent without the authorization of the right holder.

Article 31 permits WTO members to allow "other use of the subject matter of the patent," and covers compulsory licensing of patents. The term "other use" means "use other than that allowed under Article 30." The language in this provision is more ambiguous than the language in Articles 28 and 33. Thus, the rule of effective treaty interpretation might be applied to take the circumstances of the WTO member invoking Article 31 rights into account to ensure that the right is effective for that member in a specific case. Subsection (a) of Article 31 requires that a given authorization "be considered on its individual merits."

Subsection (b) provides that other use may only be permitted if "the proposed user has made efforts to obtain authorization from the right holder on reasonable commercial terms and conditions and that such efforts have not been successful within a reasonable period of time." This provision contains sufficient ambiguity to be open to different interpretations. The needs of a developing country in a particular case might be taken into account to determine whether (1) the efforts are adequate, (2) whether the commercial terms and conditions are reasonable, and (3) what constitutes a reasonable period of time. Interpreting these three conditions in light of the objectives of the WTO Agreement and TRIPS means that the standard could vary with the level of economic development of the country invoking the right and the circumstances in which the right is invoked. For example, if the right is invoked to increase the affordability of medical treatment for a developing country disease (which could be a neglected disease or a global disease), the development needs of the country and the economic impact of expanding access to treatment should be taken into account to make access to the right effective. A similar analysis can be applied to the scope and duration of the use under subsection (c) and what constitutes adequate remuneration under subsection (h).

Given the ambiguity of several subsections in Article 31 and arguments that support taking into account the needs of developing countries, an official interpretation might be used as the vehicle. However, given the need to negotiate criteria and the proviso that interpretations not be used to amend an agreement, it is a less satisfactory alternative than an amendment.

However, an amendment to Article 31 that would facilitate the use of compulsory licensing in developing and least-developed countries is a second-best solution. The aim of such an amendment would be to make Article 31 sufficiently flexible to vary the balance between the rights of producers and users of patented drugs on a market-by-market basis. This solution is problematic. It would be difficult to implement situational flexibility in a manner that would provide both certainty and flexibility, particularly with respect to the issue of what would constitute adequate compensation for the patent holder in specific cases. Moreover, the adequacy of compensation is a complex issue that is addressed in national courts, not the WTO (see Box 2.1 in Chap. 2). Determining whether compensation is adequate through litigation is an uncertain and expensive process. In contrast, eliminating patent obligations for drugs altogether through waivers or the extension of the transition period on a market-by-market basis provides legal certainty and is far easier to implement on a case-by-case basis. In the following section, we propose a set of criteria to be applied to determine the circumstances in which obligations should be suspended for pharmaceutical patents in a given market for a given medicine.

6.4.2 Eligibility for Exemption from Patent Obligations

Determining the correct balance between producers and users of patented products using the current breakdown of WTO members into the three categories of developed, developing and least-developed countries is overly simplistic and inappropriate in the context of pharmaceutical patents. This chapter proposes a more sophisticated categorization of the WTO membership in the form of an index that can be used to achieve a more equitable balance between the rights of producers and users on a market-by-market basis. This proposal is grounded on economic considerations and takes into account the need to apply a systematic international standard to determine the particular needs of developing countries. This section offers a step by step guide for permitting a country to waive or delay patent protection using a multidimensional approach. The method recognizes the needs of a country not just based on its level of poverty, but also on a threshold level of infection rate of a particular disease.

A difficult issue is how to determine the cut-off point with respect to economic development in the case of developing countries. There are no WTO definitions of "developed" and "developing" countries. Members can announce for themselves whether they are developing countries. However, this does not automatically provide rights. Other members can challenge the announcement, and this has sometimes happened in the area of intellectual property. This challenge can then lead to negotiations to clarify the position. For countries that joined the WTO after 1995, their status depends on the terms agreed in their accession negotiations.

The WTO recognizes as least-developed countries those countries that have been designated as such by the United Nations. There are currently 50 least-developed countries on the UN list. A country like Brazil does not qualify as a least-developed country. Nevertheless, a country's level of development will affect the balance between research incentives and affordable access even in the case of a developing country like Brazil because the value of its market influences the evaluation of the impact of compulsory licenses on research incentives. For this reason, we propose a more sophisticated approach to balancing the rights of producers and users.

Least-developed countries are officially designated as such by the United Nations General Assembly on the basis of a number of criteria, including: low national income (per capita gross domestic product (GDP) under USD 900 million for countries now joining the list); low levels of human development (a combined health, per capita income and education index); and economic vulnerability (a composite index based on indicators of instability, inadequate diversification and the handicap of small size). The population of countries that meet all the other criteria for admission to the category must not exceed 75 million inhabitants.

This definition provides an inadequate measure for determining the correct balance between producers and users of patented drugs. Consider the case of HIV/AIDS. Using above criteria, a middle-income country with a high rate of HIV/ AIDS infection, such as South Africa, would not qualify for the most favorable level of treatment. Therefore, we propose that a different index be used (somewhat similar to the Human Development Index) to categorize countries and to determine the correct balance between TRIPS rights and obligations regarding pharmaceutical patents on a market-by-market basis.

It is important to emphasize that we are not proposing that this index be used regarding other forms of intellectual property or other WTO agreements. Nor are we proposing that this index be used to justify the erosion of core non-discrimination obligations. Rather, we propose that this index be used for the narrow purpose of achieving equality among WTO members with respect to access to medicine to address the HIV/AIDS pandemic and other public health problems. Finally, while the legal rights and obligations that flow from the concept of special and differential treatment for developing countries are far from clear, and the current means of defining developing and least-developed countries in international law are inadequate, we are by no means suggesting this index as the appropriate solution to these highly controversial issues.

There are three specific ingredients to the construction of the index: (1) disease prevalence; (2) per capita income; and (3) poverty rate.

6.4.2.1 Disease Rate

First, a disease has to be above some threshold rate that will be determined by a world body. Once a country is above that threshold rate for the specific disease, it will qualify for a waiver (developing countries) or an extension of the transition period (least-developed countries) with respect to patent obligations for treatments for that disease. The reason developing countries would require a waiver is that the TRIPS Agreement does not contemplate an extension to the transition period for developing countries, which expired 1 January 2005.

Because this has to be done impartially on a global scale, we need to decide which world body should decide on the threshold. It seems logical that the World Health Organization (WHO) would be the right forum for making such a decision. After all, the WHO is authorized to adopt regulations on international health matters. But the reality of the WHO makes it the wrong forum for the following reason. It has not made much progress in setting standards for health related matters in the past (see Chap. 8). Therefore, we could not rely on an international body that moves at glacial speed on matters that require urgent and speedy decisions. Eric Stein notes that "WHO activities have been carried out primarily by consensus through nonbinding and less formal procedures such as recommendations, resolutions, and promulgation of technical standards" (Stein 2001). He also notes that the WHO has failed to set up a dispute settlement procedure. In fact, the WHO has been very politicized. The decision-making processes at the WHO have been anything but transparent. Therefore, our recommendation is to have the TRIPS Council decide on the threshold. This raises the obvious objections that the WTO mandate should be limited to trade-related matters and should not be expanded further to public health issues. However, this objection seems weak, given the relationship between patents and public health and the work that has already been done in this area under the purview of TRIPS. Indeed, the issue of adopting criteria to implement special and differential treatment in WTO agreements is already the subject of negotiations in the Doha Round. Moreover, there is a precedent for the WTO to negotiate a threshold for addressing the special and differential treatment of developing countries in the WTO Subsidies Agreement.

Suppose the disease rate in a country is denoted by r. Suppose also one has agreed upon a threshold of the infection rate of the disease t(r). The criterion used would be as follows. A country would qualify if the actual rate of infection prevailing in the country is larger than the agreed upon threshold value (in symbols, a country would qualify if $r > t(r)$ regardless of the economic development or any other criterion). A high rate of infection would override every other criterion. The rationale for using this method is simple. It does not exclude countries that may not qualify because of otherwise mitigating factors such as a relatively high level of per capita income. How should the threshold be determined? This should depend on the disease in question. For infectious diseases, the threshold should be determined by a level such that with a higher rate, the disease would rapidly spread. A paper by Romualdo Pastor-Satorras and Alessandro Vespignan gives us clues as to how to determine the threshold. Roughly speaking, the threshold is determined by the number of "nodes" that allow the spread of the disease. If there are many nodes, the spread speeds up. In the case of HIV/AIDS, the identifiable nodes are commercial sex workers and truck drivers (Pastor-Satorras and Vespignan, 2002).

6.4.2.2 Per Capita Income

Second, one needs to include a country if the income level is low. This requires a threshold value below which a country would qualify for a waiver. Once again, the threshold would be determined by a world body (in this case, the suitable organization would be the World Bank). If a country has a per capita income below some threshold, it would automatically qualify. Here we have left the exact method of determining the value of per capita income open. Usually, to get comparable per capita income across countries, we convert per capita income from local currencies (which are not comparable across countries) into some fixed currency (usually in US dollars) on the basis of the exchange rate on a given day. However, the current exchange rate does not necessarily reflect the purchasing power of a certain income in a given country. One way of adjusting for it is the so-called Purchasing Power Parity (PPP) method. The idea for the PPP adjustment is to create an index by calculating how much a fixed basket of goods and services would cost in different countries (in local currency) and then adjusting the "value" of one unit of that currency in terms of US dollars. We are recommending a purchasing power adjustment for per capita income but not for determining the poverty level threshold. The reason is the following: the general well being of the population in a given country is determined by how much money can buy in the country. The use of the poverty level index is meant to capture the affordability of medicine in the international market as it is likely that they have to be imported. If the average purchasing power parity adjusted income is high, such as in South Africa or in Brazil, the people who need it but cannot afford it will be captured by the threshold measure of poverty of USD 1 a day income.

The per capita income is denoted by pci and the corresponding threshold per capita income by t(pci). Expressed in symbols, the criterion is written as follows: If the per capita income $pci < t(pci)$, then the country automatically qualifies.

6.4.2.3 Poverty Rate

Third, we need to have a mechanism to take into account the poverty level in the country. One possible candidate could be the average level of income in the country. Unfortunately, the average income does not do the job because it papers over the inequality in income among the population. (There is an ancient joke that says if you put your head in the oven and your feet in the freezer, you are comfortable on the average).

There are different measures of inequality that are potential candidates. One commonly-used measure is the Gini coefficient. The most common geometric definition of the Gini coefficient is based on the Lorenz (or concentration) curve. It represents cumulative income share as a function of cumulative population share. If a population share is always exactly equal to a share in overall income then there is a situation of perfect equality. However, the Gini coefficient is not affected by a multiplicative factor. If everyone's income increases by ten-fold, the Gini coefficient is not affected. Technically, the Gini coefficient is a relative measure of inequality. To take a concrete example, Uganda and the United States have approximately the same Gini coefficient of income distribution. Both are around 38%. The lower the number, the more equal the income. Conversely, the higher the number is the higher the inequality will be. Thus, a zero (percent) Gini coefficient means everybody in the economy has the same income. On the other hand, a 100% value the Gini coefficient implies that one person has all the income in the country and everyone else has zero income. Of course, in real life, neither extreme is observable. In real life, it ranges from around 25% (for countries such as Belgium, Finland and the Czech Republic) to over 60% (such as Brazil or Sierra Leone). Thus, the Gini coefficient would be meaningless as a measure of inequality that can be compared across countries at a given point in time.

A more appropriate measure of inequality is to include people who are poor in the country in absolute terms. One possibility would be to consider a threshold of some proportion of people who are below some absolute measure of poverty level. The rationale is simple. If there are many people below some absolute poverty level, they cannot afford treatment. A simple measure (available for most countries around the world) is the proportion of people in the country who live on USD 1 or less a day. So, the criterion would be the following: if the proportion of population (p) with USD 1 income exceeds some threshold t(p), then the country would automatically qualify. In symbols, if $p > t(p)$, then a country automatically qualifies for a waiver.

Thus, there are three possible indices that could be used for determining the countries that qualify. The three are combined to arrive at a single criterion. If a country qualifies using any of the above threshold criteria, it should qualify. The following criterion, which includes all three measures using a compact notation, can be used: If maximum $\{r - t(r), t(pci) - pci, p - t(p)\} > 0$, the country qualifies. This criterion ensures that: (1) if the disease rate (r) is above the pre-determined threshold (t(r)), then the country qualifies; (2) if the per capita income (pci) is below the predetermined threshold (t(pci)), then the country qualifies; and (3) if the proportion of population (p) is above certain threshold (t(p)), then the country qualifies.

Although the measure above is useful, it is not entirely satisfactory. Suppose a country has all the above problems but it fails each threshold criterion by some amount and therefore fails to qualify. Clearly, we will need a method of "adding" each "score" to come up with an aggregate value that reflects the issue in all three dimensions. There are two ways of achieving this, which are discussed below.

Let max(r) be the country with the maximum infection rate. Let min(pci) be the country with minimum per capita income. Let max(p) be the country with the maximum proportion of people below USD 1 per day per capita income. We construct the following absolute index (Absolute Component Summed Index or Absolute CSI):

$$\text{Absolute CSI for a country} = [r/\max(r) + \min(pci)/pci + p/\max(p)]/3$$

The rationale for the formula is as follows. If a country hits the maximum infection rate, minimum income level and maximum number of poor people in the pool of all countries, the CSI will hit a maximum of 1. We can set a predetermined value of the Absolute CSI such that any country with the value of the index above that level would qualify for a waiver.

Since this measure will never hit zero, some people might consider this measure unsatisfactory. We can adjust that by considering a modified version that measures different dimensions in relative terms. Thus, we construct the Relative Component Summed Index:

$$\text{Relative CSI for a country} = [I(r) + I(pci) + I(p)]/3$$

where, $I(r) = [r - \min(r)]/[\max(r) - \min(r)]$, $I(pci) = [\max(pci) - pci]/[\max(pci) - \min(pci)]$ and $I(p) = [p - \min(p)]/[\max(p) - \min(p)]$.

To see why we take such ratios, consider the first one: $I(r)$. If, for a given country, the infection rate r is the highest among all countries, then the index $I(r) = 1$. On the other hand, if the infection rate r is the lowest among all countries, $I(r) = 0$. Similarly, if the per capita income (pci) is the lowest among all countries, then the index $I(pci) = 1$. On the other hand if the per capita income pci is the highest among all countries, then the index $I(pci) = 0$. If the USD 1 a day population p is the highest among all the countries in question, then $I(p) = 1$ whereas if it is the lowest, then $I(p) = 0$. Thus, the relative CSI is a measure bounded by 0 and 1 as two extremes. By construction, the relative CSI could touch the limits for the best (in that case, it will touch 0) and the worst (in that case, it will touch 1) case scenarios. It should be noted that the worst outcome country in terms of Absolute CS Index may not be the worst outcome country in terms of the Relative CS Index. Thus, it is quite probable that in the list of all countries we will never observe the extreme value 1 for the Relative CS Index. Similarly the best outcome country in the RCSI measure may not be the best outcome country in the ACSI measure. Thus, we might not observe the extreme value 0 in a sample of countries.

With the Relative CSI (RCSI), the criterion should specify a threshold (t): if the RCSI > t, the country should qualify under the composite measure for the most favorable level of treatment available. To incorporate this measure into our overall criterion, we propose the following:

If maximum $\{r - t(r), t(pci) - pci, p - t(p), RCSI - t\} > 0$, then a country should qualify for the most favorable level of treatment.

This measure for determining economic needs is quite consistent with the long run interest of the pharmaceutical companies. Consider the case of Botswana. It was called the "miracle country" of Africa until the early 1990s. The real GDP of Botswana grew at a rate of 8–9% per year for more than a decade. However, with the devastating effects of HIV/AIDS, the country is slowly sinking. The life expectancy at birth has fallen by 20 years (see Table 4.4 in Chap. 4). HIV/AIDS is reversing much of the economic gains of the past decades. If the pharmaceutical industry insists on protection of its drug patents, it will generate very little profit now. Worse, the pharmaceutical industry will have to forego all the future growth in profits it might have generated in the future. Botswana will recede into the backwaters of economic development.

The use of our index allows these types of countries to return to economic growth. That process should eventually push them over the threshold value of the index so that they no longer qualify for the waiver. Without such measures, these countries will be caught in a vicious circle and, therefore, will never generate the level of purchasing power needed to create a market for the pharmaceutical industry.

The index allows us to redress this balance of incentives through a mechanism that uses objective standards recognized by international bodies that represent all interested parties. The index serves to promote affordable access to medicine using criteria that are tailored to address the specific circumstances surrounding global or neglected diseases, which is more appropriate than the UN measure of least-developed or developing countries. The index can also be used to determine differential pricing strategies for drugs (see Chap. 9).

Tsai (2007) has proposed using a modified version of our Relative CSI to determine the priority of countries that would benefit from incentives to promote technology transfer from institutions and enterprises in developed countries to developing countries, under TRIPS Article 66.2.

6.5 Implications for Other Global Diseases

The HIV/AIDS epidemic has sparked a broader debate over the right balance to strike between the rights of patent holders and the needs of developing countries. Pharmaceutical companies are concerned about the precedent that may be set for intellectual property rights as a result of the measures taken to address HIV/AIDS. We conclude that their concerns are largely unfounded.

TRIPS established uniform minimum standards for the protection of intellectual property rights. At the same time, however, both the WTO Agreement and TRIPS recognized that vastly different levels of economic development warranted differential treatment of WTO members, based on their level of development. The TRIPS Declaration represents a partial acknowledgement that the differential treatment that was initially set out in TRIPS was inadequate, by extending the transition period for least-developed countries and recognizing that WTO members did not enjoy equal access to patent exceptions due to the lack of manufacturing capacity in the pharmaceutical sector. The Paragraph 6 Decision further refines how differential treatment is to operate in practice with respect to compulsory licensing for export. However, it conditions access to legal rights on the level of economic development in a manner that does not resolve the fundamental issue of equal access to legal rights and the access to medicine that these imply.

Conditioning special and differential treatment in TRIPS based on the categorization of countries as developed, developing and least-developed, and determining membership in the latter category based on the UN method, is inappropriate when it comes to patents for medicines. This chapter has proposed two alternative methods for rectifying this problem: the first based on an amendment and the second based on the adoption of objective criteria to make decisions regarding waivers and extensions of transition periods. The second option is the better of the two. In the context of global and neglected diseases, uniformity of TRIPS obligations relating to patented medicine impose unnecessarily high costs on users and poor distribution of costs and benefits among producers and users of intellectual property. Uniform rules can have disparate effects that worsen inequalities rather than correct them. To achieve the correct balance between the rights of producers and users of patented medicine, a broader range of factors must be taken into account than are currently used in the WTO and UN contexts.

This chapter (along with the previous chapter) has questioned the underlying premise of TRIPS that strong global patent rights are necessary to ensure innovation. Even if one accepts the premise that patents rights are necessary in every WTO member, regardless of the member's level of development, the proposed index shows that the UN classification of countries is an inappropriate basis for achieving an equitable balance between the rights of patent owners and users. The UN classification was not meant for handling a complex issue such as HIV/AIDS, which encompasses epidemiological issues (incidence of infection of the disease in the population). The proposals set out in this chapter take into account the objectives of the WTO Agreement and TRIPS and provide a systematic basis for incorporating member-specific flexibility into TRIPS. It is hoped that these proposals will move the current WTO negotiations forward in the area of special and differential treatment for developing countries and dispel the notion that member-specific flexibility is unworkable in practice.

The applicability of the CS Index to other diseases and pandemics depends on the speed at which the disease spreads. In the case of other slowing-moving global diseases, such as tuberculosis and diabetes, the Index is applicable because the disease rate can be determined. In the case of a fast-moving global disease, such as

SARS or Avian Influenza, or the use of biological agents in war or terrorism, such as anthrax, governments may wish to stockpile medical treatment before the disease occurs. Following the terrorist attacks of 11 September 2001, Canada and the United States acquired stockpiles of Bayer's antibiotic ciprofloxacin in case of a terrorist attack involving anthrax. Similarly, in 2005 many governments made stockpiling of vaccines and anti-viral drugs part of their risk management strategy to address the threat of a global Avian Influenza pandemic. In these circumstances, the disease rate cannot be determined before the government needs to acquire the necessary medical treatment. However, WTO members can exercise their right to issue compulsory licenses to address a national emergency or other circumstances of extreme urgency under TRIPS Article 31 or the Paragraph 6 system or use the threat of a compulsory license to expand production or to lower the cost of the drugs that they need to stockpile.

References

Arruñada B, Andonova V (2005) Market Institutions and Judicial Rulemaking. In: Ménard C, Shirley M (eds) Handbook of New Institutional Economics. Springer, Berlin Heidelberg New York

Attaran A (2007) A Tragically Naive Canadian Law for Tragically Neglected Global Health. http://www.cmaj.ca. Accessed 20 April 2007

Boldrin M, Levine D (2002) The Case Against Intellectual Property. The American Eco-nomy Review 209

Cahoy D (2007) Confronting Myths and Myopia on the Road from Doha. Georgia Law Review 42:131–192

Condon B, Sinha T (2005) Global Diseases, Global Patents and Differential Treatment in WTO Law: Criteria for Suspending Patent Obligations in Developing Countries, North-western. Journal of International Law and Business 26:1–35

Hestermeyer HP (2007) Canadian-made Drugs for Rwanda: The First Application of the WTO Waiver on Patents and Medicines. ASIL Insight 11:28

Khan BZ (2005) The Democratization of Invention: Patents and Copyrights in American Economic Development. Cambridge University Press, Cambridge

Lanjouw J (2003) A Patent Policy Proposal for Global Diseases. The Brookings Institu-tion, http://www.brook.edu/views/papers/lanjouw/20010611.htm. Accessed 5 July 2005

Pastor-Satorras R, Vespignan A (2002) Epidemic Dynamics in Finite Size Scale-Free Networks. http://arxiv.org/abs/cond-mat/0202298. Accessed 25 July 2004

Peters M, Sharp, PM (2000) Genetic Diversity of HIV-1: The Moving Target. AIDS 14:S129–S130

Scotchmer S (2003) The Political Economy of Intellectual Property Treaties. National Bureau of Econ Research, Working Paper No. 9114

Stein E (2001) International Integration and Democracy: No Love at First Sight. American Journal of International Law 95:489–534

Trouiller P, Olliaro P, Torreele E, Orbinski J, Laing R, Ford N (2002) Drug Develop-ment for Neglected Diseases: A Deficient Market and a Public-Health Policy Failure. The Lancet 359:2188–2194

Tsai J (2007) Not Tripping Over the Pebbles. Michigan State University Journal of Medicine and Law 11:427–450

UNDP (1999) Human Development Report. http://www.undp.org

WTO (2005) Amendment of the TRIPS Agreement, Decision of 6 December 2005, General Council, WT/L/641. http://www.wto.org/english/tratop_e/trips_e/wtl641_e.htm. Accessed 5 June 2006

WTO (2007) Notification under Paragraph 2(c) of the Decision of 30 August 2003 on the Implementation of Paragraph 6 of the Doha Declaration on the TRIPS Agreement and Public Health, Council for Trade-Related Aspects of Intellectual Property Rights, IP/N/10/CAN/1. http://www.wto.org/english/tratop_e/trips_e/public_health_notif_export_e.htm. Accessed 5 July 2004

7 Bilateral and Multilateral Financing of HIV/AIDS Programs: The World Bank, the International Monetary Fund, the Global Fund, Bilateral Donors and the Private Sector

"While much of the surge in HIV funding is attributable to a highly successful lobby including UNAIDS, some results from donor frustration at the lack of reform in government organisations. At least, donors say, we can save some lives through investing directly in prevention and treatment. Unfortunately, disease-specific funding such as that for HIV is making things worse by creating policy, programming and financing in parallel with those for basic health services. Funding for preventing mother-to-child transmission, for example, is not strengthening maternal and child health services including antenatal care, where the testing of pregnant women must become part of normal business if transmission is to be reduced. More-over, there are opportunity costs: high spending on HIV is attracting staff away from other programmes."

Veronica Walford, August 14, Financial Times

This chapter examines the operations of the World Bank (a multilateral development institution), the International Monetary Fund (a multilateral financial institution) and the Global Fund to Fight AIDS, Tuberculosis and Malaria (a multilateral fundraising and financing institution) to fight HIV/AIDS. We also examine the role of bilateral donors and the private sector in financing the fight against HIV/AIDS. We examine the relationships among bilateral donors and international organizations, what distinguishes their roles in the global HIV/AIDS pandemic and the extent to which their activities overlap. In addition, we consider how funding strategies and parameters may affect the effectiveness of AIDS funding in preventing transmission and providing treatment.

7.1 Overview of HIV/AIDS Funding

During the past two decades, funding has grown exponentially – especially since 2001. In 1986, global donor funding for HIV/AIDS was less than one million US dollars. By 2007, the funding had grown to USD 10 billion. As Fig. 7.1 shows, the three largest donors are the US President's Emergency Plan for AIDS Relief (PEPFAR), the Global Fund to Fight AIDS, Tuberculosis and Malaria, and the World Bank Multi-Country HIV/AIDS Program for Africa (MAP), in that order. The activities of PEPFAR are analyzed in Chap. 8. Figure 7.2 charts the growth of total annual resources available over this period of time. Figure 7.3 projects the funding required to achieve universal access by 2015.

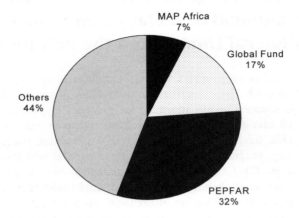

Fig. 7.1 Global funding for HIV/AIDS. *Source*: Oomman et al. (2007)

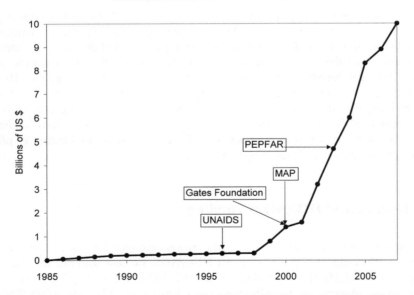

Fig. 7.2 Flow of resources to combat HIV/AIDS 1986–2007. *Source*: Financial resources required to achieve universal access to HIV prevention, treatment, care and support, UNAIDS, 26 September, 2007

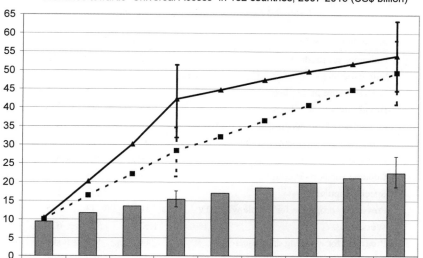

Scenarios towards "Universal Access" in 132 countries, 2007-2015 (US$ billion)

Projected trends using current scale-up   - ■ ·Phased scale-up   —▲—Universal Access by 2010

Fig. 7.3 Scaling up towards universal care. Source: financial resources required to achieve universal access to HIV prevention, treatment, care and support, UNAIDS, 26 September, 2007

The following series of Tables (7.1–7.7) show the funding requirements for HIV/AIDS and break down those requirements by area in which the funding is needed. Table 7.8 contrasts the actual funding available and the funding gap. (In Chap. 4, we considered the potential economic impact on recipient countries of achieving HIV/AIDS funding requirements).

Table 7.1 AIDS funding requirements for low- and middle-income countries in USD billion

Item	2006	2007	2008	2006–2008
Prevention	8.4	10.0	11.4	29.8
Care and treatment	3.0	4.0	5.3	12.3
Support for orphans	1.6	2.1	2.7	6.4
Program costs	1.5	1.4	1.8	4.6
Human resources	0.4	0.6	0.9	1.9
Total	14.9	22.1	55.1	18.1

Source: UNAIDS

Table 7.2 Funding required for prevention

Prevention activities	2006–2008	2007	2008
Universal precautions	5,838	1,944	2,303
Safe injections	2,690	897	897
Post-exposure prophylaxis	5	2	2
Blood safety	685	228	231
Prevention of mother-to-child transmission	794	264	324
Improving management of STI	2,154	718	764
Condom provision	4,506	1,501	1,625
Condom social marketing	525	175	190
Special populations	654	252	252
Prevention programs for people with HIV	103	33	48
Workplace	1,573	523	628
Programs for injecting drug users	443	149	180
Programs for men who have sex with men	1,218	407	499
Programs on sex workers and clients	1,663	552	682
Youth out of school	2,838	945	1,126
Youth in school	313	104	108
Voluntary counseling and testing	1,710	569	690
Community mobilization	1,830	608	772
Mass media	299	100	109
Total	29	11	840

Source: UNAIDS

Table 7.3 Funding required for treatment and care to achieve the coverage targets shown

Year	People on ART (millions)	ART coverage of urgent cases (%)	Total Funding (USD million)
2006	3.0	55	2,986
2007	4.8	67	4,029
2008	6.6	75	5,250
2009	8.3	79	–
2010	9.8	80	–

Source: UNAIDS

Table 7.4 Distribution by activity of the funding required for treatment and care

Treatment and care (USD million)	2007	2008	2006–2008
Palliative care	302	295	905
Provider initiated testing	79	109	254
Opportunistic infections treatment	703	707	2,096
Opportunistic infections prophylaxis	403	510	1,200
Antiretroviral therapy	2,482	3,624	7,748
Laboratory testing	79	104	237
Total	4,048	5,349	12,440

Source: UNAIDS

Table 7.5 Funding required for activities supporting orphans and vulnerable children

Orphan support (USD million)	2006	2007	2008	2006–2008
Education	193	287	443	923
Health care and support	145	174	200	519
Family/home support	971	1,255	1,604	3,830
Community support	14	18	25	57
Organization costs	246	322	422	990
Total	3,043	4,048	5,349	12,440

Source: UNAIDS

Table 7.6 Funding required for program support and infrastructure support

Program activities (USD million)	2007	2008	2006–2008
Management	376	390	1,251
Advocacy and communications	111	111	340
Monitoring and evaluation	138	146	432
Operations research	7	7	25
Training	136	231	439
Logistics and supply	259	304	868
Supervision and patient tracking	68	92	257
Drug resistance surveillance	68	68	205
Construction of new health centers	23	167	250
Infrastructure upgrading	185	236	542
Total	1,371	1,753	4,610

Source: UNAIDS

Table 7.7 Funding required for building human resource capacity

(USD million)	2007	2008	2006–2008
Education	89	123	262
Nurses' wage supplements	261	370	784
Doctors' wage supplements	258	366	776
Total	608	859	1,822

Source: UNAIDS

Table 7.8 Actual funding and funding gap

Billions of US dollars	2006	2007
Available resources	$8.9	$10
Funding gap (2005–2007)	At least $18 billion	

Source: UNAIDS. Resource needs for an expanded response to aids in low and middle income countries. Presented to the Program Coordinating Board. Seventeenth Meeting, Geneva, 27–29 June 2005

While the increase in funding for HIV/AIDS is a positive development, the multiplicity of donors has created problems regarding overlapping actions and conflicting conditions attached to the aid. In 2005, over one hundred Ministers, Heads of Agencies and other Senior Officials endorsed the Paris Declaration on Aid Effectiveness, an international agreement to increase efforts in harmonization, alignment and managing aid for results with a set of monitorable actions and indicators (OECD 2005). Also in 2005, the UNAIDS Global Task Team on Improving AIDS Coordination Among Multilateral Institutions and International Donors (GTT) published a set of recommendations on how countries and multilateral institutions can streamline their AIDS-related activities. Many of these recommendations are aimed at improving the coordination of the AIDS-related activities of multilateral organizations and minimizing overlap. The recommendations build upon the principles of the "Three Ones" – the three principles for coordinated response at the country level: (1) one agreed HIV/AIDS action framework that provides the basis for coordinating the work of all parties; (2) one national AIDS coordinating authority, with a broad based multi-sector mandate; and (3) one agreed country level monitoring and evaluation system (UNAIDS 2005). According to a 2006 UNAIDS report, more than 40% of national AIDS plans were not serving as the framework for contributions by donors (UNAIDS 2006). More than 40% of national AIDS plans were not evaluated for cost or provided sufficient clarity on inputs and outputs, with the result that donors preferred to engage more directly with countries (Sidibe et al., 2006).

Poor alignment of donor strategies with national efforts and poor harmonization among donor procedures for aid management are significant impediments to achieving universal access to treatment for HIV/AIDS, because of the number and diversity of organizations that have become involved in addressing the pandemic. Duplication of work and high transaction costs by individual agencies, together with the absence of important learning exchanges, economies of scale and synergies, impedes the speed, quantity, and quality of the response to the pandemic (Sidibe et al., 2006). Thus, while pursuing affordable access to medicine and expanding medical services infrastructure are both essential elements for expanding access to treatment, they form a two-legged stool. The harmonization of donor and governance processes represents a key third element in the efforts to expand access to information and treatment.

Donald Kaberuka, President of the African Development Bank, has noted that in the late 1980s, 22 members of the Development Assistance Committee of the OECD (OECD/DAC) accounted for 95% of total aid to developing countries. Twenty years later, aid to developing countries is delivered through more than 150 multilateral agencies, 33 bilateral members of the OECD/DAC and at least 10 non-DAC governments. As a result, some developing countries have more than 700 active projects and receive more than 400 missions a year, each with its own specific requirements. In theory, this proliferation of donors should bring new perspectives, more resources, greater innovation and competition, which could reduce costs and improve program delivery. However, this has not been the result thus far (Kaberuka 2007). Figure 7.4 shows the sources of the estimated and projected funding for the AIDS response from 2005 to 2007.

In this regard, national leadership in recipient countries is important for ensuring a coordinated, multi-sectoral approach (that is, coordination across several government ministries, not just the health ministry) (Patel 2004). However, even where the host government has donor coordination mechanisms in place, coordination is made more difficult when individual donors come with pre-established priorities, without involving host countries in the setting of priorities (Dekay 2004). One clear example is PEPFAR. It has established abstinence-only as a priority, and denied funding for needle exchange programs, which are priorities for the US government that do not necessarily coincide with the priorities of host governments (see Chap. 8 for details).

In addition to the multiplicity of players, donors and host governments with different interests, ideologies, demands and expectations make coordination more difficult for host countries. When donors are driven by their own national ideologies and interests, at the expense of scientifically proven approaches, they undermine coordination and local leadership. Moreover, when donors focus on civil society, they may undermine adherence to a national HIV/AIDS framework (Mwale 2004).

There has also been a proliferation of recipients. Figure 7.5 shows the distribution of entities that participated in the preparation of funding proposals for Round Four of the Global Fund.

With respect to the lack of donor coordination, some argue that the source of the problem is the host government, which may fear losing control over the agenda to a well-coordinated group of donors, rather than the donors themselves.

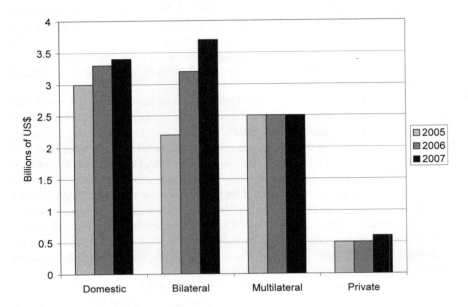

Fig. 7.4 Sources of the estimated and projected funding for the AIDS response from 2005 to 2007. *Source*: UNAIDS

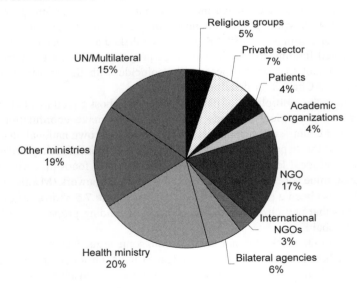

Source: The Global Fund to Fi‿ht AIDS, Tuberculosis and Malaria

Fig. 7.5 Country coordinating mechanisms: entities participating in preparation of round four proposals. *Source*: Global Fund

Donor commitments and disbursements can diverge. Table 7.9 shows that, in the case of some bilateral donors, commitments have exceeded disbursements, while for others the reverse is true. In most cases, the actual disbursements lag commitments (OECD 2006).

Table 7.9 Bilateral commitments and disbursements of DAC members in 2004 (USD Millions)

Country	Bilateral commitments	Imputed multilateral commitments	Total HIV commitments	Bilateral disbursements
Australia	3.7	12.2	15.9	22.8
Austria	1.2	3.6	4.8	0
Belgium	30.4	21.4	51.8	11.5
Canada	134.3	26.2	160.4	73.6
Denmark	9.2	22.7	31.9	5.4
Finland	4.7	7.3	12	
France	11.1	135.3	146.4	3.6
Germany	84.5	35.9	161.3	27.1
Greece	0.6	2.1	2.7	0.6
Ireland	5.8	5.5	11.3	5.8
Italy	2.4	16.9	19.3	3.6
Japan	3.1	86.8	83.7	7.3
Luxembourg	3.6	2.1	5.7	3.8
Netherlands	90.5	83.6	174.1	50
New Zealand	0.7	1.4	2.1	0.6
Norway	15.4	42.7	58.1	27.4
Portugal	0.1	2.1	2.2	0.1
Spain	7.5	23.1	30.6	7.5
Sweden	58.2	52.9	111.1	46.5
Switzerland	7.8	10	17.7	6.5
United Kingdom	120.8	76.5	197.3	134.7
United States	1,107.4	326.5	1,433.8	9,01.3
Total DAC countries	1,702.9	1,031.6	2,734.5	1,338.5
EC	67.4	29.9	95.7	10.8
Total DAC members	1,770.3	1,031.5	2,801.8	1,349.4

Source: OECD

The Center for Global Development has analyzed the policies and practices of PEPFAR, the Global Fund and the World Bank's MAP in Mozambique, Uganda and Zambia, and compared these systems against six key funding practices that can help donors support the national AIDS response in a manner consistent with the aid effectiveness principles of the Paris Declaration. These best practices are:

working with the government; building local capacity; keeping funding flexible; selecting appropriate recipients; making the money move; and collecting and sharing data. This study made the following recommendations to all three donors to increase the effectiveness of aid: (1) Jointly coordinate and plan activities to support the National AIDS Plan; (2) Assist the host government in tracking total national AIDS funds; (3) focus on building and measuring capacity; (4) develop strategies with host governments and other donors to ensure financial sustainability; and (5) strengthen financial data collection and disclosure. The study also offered specific recommendations for how each donor can improve its own program to increase the effectiveness of aid (Oomman et al., 2007). These specific recommendations are addressed further below.

7.2 The World Bank: A Development Institution

Since its foundation since the end of the World War II, the World Bank has grown in size and importance. In 2008, it provides financial and technical assistance to developing countries through two development institutions owned by 185 member countries – the International Bank for Reconstruction and Development (IBRD) and the International Development Association (IDA). The World Bank's current mission is to reduce global poverty and to improve living standards. The IBRD focuses on middle income and creditworthy poor countries, while IDA focuses on the poorest countries. Together they provide low-interest loans, interest-free credit and grants to developing countries for education, health, infrastructure, communications and other development programs. The World Bank's traditional loan package integrates loans with analytic and advisory services. The World Bank's research program supports studies on a range of development issues (http://web.worldbank.org).

7.2.1 Nature of World Bank Operations Related to HIV/AIDS

The World Bank provides loans to national governments to assist in the implementation of national HIV/AIDS programs. The Bank also does research and provides assistance to make national AIDS programs more effective. The World Bank's first HIV/AIDS-related project was in 1988. Between 1988 and 2005, the Bank loaned over USD 2.5 billion to finance national HIV/AIDS programs.

The World Bank organizes its AIDS-related activities globally, through its "Global HIV/AIDS Program of Action" and six regional HIV/AIDS programs: (1) Sub-Saharan Africa, (2) East Asia and the Pacific, (3) Europe and Central Asia, (4) Latin America and the Caribbean, (5) Middle East and North Africa, and (6) South Asia. The purpose of this organizational structure is to have a global focus that takes regional differences into account and to define the World Bank's role in relation to other multilateral and international actors. The overall goals of these programs are prevention and treatment, taking into account local transmission patterns and sources of infection, in order to avoid a mismatch between funding and infection patterns in national programs (World Bank 2005a).

The World Bank's programs seek to focus support where national programs need it the most. The World Bank has adopted the "Three Ones principles", noted above. The World Bank monitors and evaluates its programs to ensure HIV/AIDS programs are context-specific. The World Bank also seeks to integrate HIV/AIDS issues into the broader development planning process. The World Bank recognizes the need to make all of the key players part of each national strategy – governments, the private sector, community and civil society organizations, people living with HIV/AIDS, NGOs and international organizations (World Bank 2005a).

The Bank's Program of Action focuses on five areas: (1) Sustained funding for HIV/AIDS programs and health systems; (2) Better national HIV/AIDS planning, focused on high-risk groups and locations; (3) Accelerating implementation of national HIV/AIDS plans by overcoming administrative constraints that delay the use of new funding; (4) Building country monitoring and evaluation systems and capacity to collect, analyze and use data; and (5) Improving and applying knowledge through impact evaluations and analysis (World Bank 2005a).

7.2.1.1 The Need for Sustained Funding

Sustained funding is crucial. Once people with HIV begin taking medication, they need a reliable supply of medication and their response to the medication needs to be monitored on an ongoing basis. If the underlying funding is not sustained, and medication and laboratory work get suspended, individuals with HIV will become more infectious and develop drug-resistant viruses. Thus, the suspension of treatment is not only inhumane, but also makes prevention and treatment more difficult.

7.2.1.2 Focus on High-Risk Groups and Locations

The need to focus on high-risk groups and locations flows from the fact that resources are limited and need to be used effectively. Targeting tripartite prevention-treatment-human rights strategies at high-risk groups has proved effective in countries like Brazil (see Chap. 2). Targeting high-risk groups is a key component of an effective national HIV/AIDS strategy, particularly when those groups have been marginalized through discrimination.

Figure 7.6 shows the mismatch between most affected groups and funding in Ghana. It is important to note that the transmission patterns for HIV/AIDS in Ghana are not representative. However, the mismatch between the most affected groups and the allocation of funding in Ghana highlights the importance of matching funding to prevailing prevalence and transmission patterns in a given country or region.

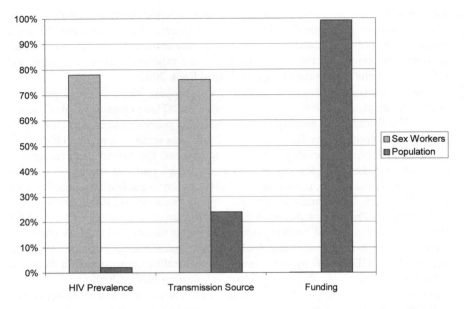

Fig. 7.6 Mismatch between funding and affected groups in Ghana. *Source*: Wilson (2007)

7.2.1.3. Accelerated Implementation of Funding

While funding for HIV/AIDS programs has increased, there remains an "implementation gap" between the available funding and its deployment. This is due to impediments to quick implementation: a lack of skilled personnel; unpredictable or conditional funding; burdensome disbursement and procurement processes; government reluctance to contract out implementation to civil society or the private sector; and multiple systems of management, monitoring and evaluation to meet different donor requirements. To address this problem, the World Bank is simplifying its own processes and procedures, strengthening its Implementation Advisory Service and coordinating UN, Global Fund and World Bank actions through the Global Joint Problem-Solving and Implementation Support Team (GIST) (World Bank 2005a).

7.2.1.4. Country Monitoring and Evaluation Systems and Data Capacity

The Global AIDS Monitoring and Evaluation Support Team (GAMET) seeks to build a well-functioning monitoring and evaluation system in each country, to enhance the impact of national programs. GAMET provides field support to build country systems and capacity, as well as training and guidelines (World Bank 2005a).

7.2.1.5. Impact Evaluation and Analysis to Improve Program Impact

The World Bank's main focus has shifted from getting resources to countries to ensuring that more impact evaluations are done of Bank-supported HIV/AIDS programs, including prospective evaluations that are begun ahead of project implementation. The regional and country strategies include plans for analytical work, to be complemented by analysis of cross-cutting and cross-country issues to highlight good practices (World Bank 2005a).

Most HIV Monitoring and Evaluation (M&E) systems – the 3rd of the Three Ones – are not fully functional. For example, in 2006 the M&E plans in 13 countries out of 20 in East and Southern Africa had yet to be implemented (Kasheeka et al., 2006).

7.2.2 Scope of World Bank Operations

The scope of the World Bank's operations is quite wide, covering a wide range of development issues in a large number of countries, in addition to its work related to HIV/AIDS. Table 7.10 shows the distribution of World Bank lending by theme and sector from 2001 to 2006. Figure 7.7 shows the distribution of World Bank lending by region.

Table 7.10 World bank lending by theme and sector in millions of dollars

Theme	2001	2002	2003	2004	2005	2006
Economic management	895	1,408	777	428	594	213
Environmental and natural resource management	1,354	924	1,102	1,304	2,493	1,387
Financial and private sector development	3,940	5,055	2,882	4,176	3,862	6,137
Human development	1,134	1,756	3,374	3,079	2,951	2,600
Public sector governance	2,053	4,247	2,464	3,373	2,636	3,820
Rule of law	410	273	530	503	303	757
Rural development	1,822	1,600	1,910	1,507	2,802	2,215
Social development, gender, and inclusion	1,469	1,385	1,003	1,557	1,285	1,094
Social protection and risk management	1,651	1,086	2,324	1,577	2,437	1,891
Trade and integration	1,059	300	566	1,212	1,079	1,610
Urban development	1,458	1,482	1,576	1,358	1,860	1,911
Total	17,250	19,519	18,513	20,079	22,307	23,641

Source: World Bank, 2006 Annual Report

As of 24 June 2004, the World Bank had 72 approved and active HIV/AIDS projects with an HIV/AIDS component of more than USD one million, in 60 countries. These projects include health sector support and reform, prevention and control programs, human resources development and education and national AIDS programsupport. (http://siteresources.worldbank.org /INTHIVAIDS/ Projects/20385466/ Financing06-24-04.xls) Some of these projects are conducted as part of the World Bank's regional initiatives. For example, the World Bank's Africa MAP was designed to help countries intensify and expand their multi-sector national responses to the HIV epidemic, to dramatically increase access to HIV prevention, care, and treatment (World Bank 2007). Below, we look at the example of Rwanda's MAP project.

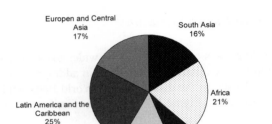

Total IBRD-IDA Lending by Region

Fig. 7.7 Proportion of total lending of the World bank by region. *Source*: World Bank, 2006 Annual Report

7.2.2.1 The Africa Multi-Country HIV/AIDS Program (MAP) in Rwanda

In Rwanda the World Bank used MAP community grants for HIV Initiatives to fund over 100 civil society organizations to provide preventive, medical and support services for people living with HIV. In 2002, Rwanda was among the ten countries most severely affected by HIV and had recently emerged from a genocide/war. The USD 30.5 million grant became effective on 11 August, 2003 and was fully committed and almost fully disbursed by the end of 2006. The World Bank Board of Directors approved additional financing of USD 10 million on 2 February 2007 to consolidate gains from the initial investments and plan for their sustainability.

As Table 7.11 shows, about 30% of the World Bank's funds went to poverty mitigation combined with HIV prevention messages. Roughly 17% paid for prevention activities, such as social mobilization, advocacy, condom promotion and HIV testing. About 19% of the funds were used for institutional support, capacity building, and monitoring and evaluation of programs. Just over 10% paid for HIV/AIDS treatment and care. The costs of administering this project were roughly 6% of the total grant over the life of the project (World Bank 2007).

Table 7.11 Rwanda HIV/AIDS multi-sectoral project, distribution of world bank funds (in millions of USD)

Activity	Funds	Percent (%)
HIV/AIDS treatment and care	3.1	10
General health systems support	3.1	10
Home based care	2.1	7
HIV/STI prevention	5	17
Mitigation	8.8	30
Multi-sectoral capacity building	5.6	19
Project management	1.9	6

Source: World Bank 2007

Female Sex Workers in Rwanda

One part of this project was to help female sex workers to find different sources of income. Several factors contributed to the success of this project. First, the project engaged local champions to mobilize people (in this case, the deputy mayor in charge of social welfare on the district HIV/AIDS commission became personally engaged in designing the program design). Second, to break the AIDS-poverty cycle, poverty mitigation accompanied preventive measures (in this case, new sources of income provided a basis for further, community-based economic development projects). Third, the project sought to empower women to benefit the whole family (in this case, empowering them to provide better education and health care for their children). Fourth, ongoing support was provided to sustain the success of the project (in this case, to prevent the women returning to prostitution when challenges arise) (World Bank 2007). However, as we will see in Chap. 9, programs for sex workers that focus on alternative employment have been criticized for contributing to their stigmatization and failing to address the needs of those who continue to earn their income from sex work.

Orphans and Vulnerable Children in Rwanda

Another part of the Rwanda MAP project provided orphans and vulnerable children with sewing machines and training as tailors so that they could start a clothes-manufacturing association. This program combined information about HIV and AIDS, reproductive health and life skills with income generating activities. The children then served as role models and sources of information on HIV and AIDS for other vulnerable children. The experience with this program suggests three key factors for success. First, establish solidarity among participants, in this case by bringing the children together to find solutions to their problems and design their own interventions. Second, enable beneficiaries to be role models for behavioral change. Third, address poverty and vulnerability in order to make AIDS prevention effective (World Bank 2007).

HIV Awareness and Testing for Youth in Rwanda

In yet another part of the MAP project, the Rwanda National Youth Council (CNJR) created a voucher system for expanding access to HIV testing for youths aged 10–24 (almost 40% of the population). The rationale behind promoting testing is that enabling people to learn their HIV status is a first critical step in changing behavior. The CNJR trained 230 peer educators in behavioral change communication and reached out to youth through anti-AIDS clubs and sports and cultural activities. The voucher system enabled youths to go to local health facilities on designated days, minimizing waiting times. The MAP funding was used to pay for these services. This approach was more cost-effective (USD 2 per person) than using mobile units to reach these youths (USD 10 per person). It also enhanced the returns on Global Fund investments in facility-based services. In the first 4 months almost 70,000 youths were tested. About 6% tested HIV positive. The three main lessons from the CNJR campaign were (1) HIV testing is critical to modifying sexual behavior and expanding condom use; (2) better knowledge leads to greater empathy and solidarity with people living with HIV; and (3) awareness campaigns foster a culture of responsibility, trust and faithfulness among young couples (World Bank 2007).

Expanding Access to Anti-Retroviral Treatment in Rwanda

The Rwandan government developed a treatment plan with the support of the Clinton Foundation. A user fee policy with a sliding scale results in most Rwandans receiving free care because they live below the poverty line. The Rwandan government, the World Bank, the Clinton Foundation, the Global Fund, US Centers for Disease Control and Prevention (CDC) and the US Government/PEPFAR worked together to design, implement and monitor the treatment program. Different sites were funded by different donors (the World Bank, the Global Fund and the US Government/PEPFAR). Patients receiving treatment increased from 870 patients at seven sites at the end of 2002 to roughly 32,000 patients at 130 sites nationwide in the first half of 2007 (over 50% of those who need care). Using the national procurement system, the World Bank and the Global Fund finance generic drugs and the US Government/PEPFAR pays for brand name drugs. The Clinton Foundation has helped to lower the prices paid for drugs and diagnostics. PEPFAR funded the "TRACNet" system, which uses mobile phones to transmit information. It tracks the number of patients on treatment and the drugs dispensed nation-wide, to manage the treatment program and supplies efficiently and to avoid drug shortages that would lead to interruptions in treatment. Interruptions in treatment could diminish the effectiveness of treatment by creating resistance to the drugs being used and raise costs by requiring the use of other drugs and medical treatments. Performance-based contracting and bonuses for health care staff expanded key HIV services rapidly in a relatively short time (for example, the number of HIV tests performed by staff) (World Bank 2007).

7.2.2.2 Central America and the Need for Human Rights Protection

The World Bank has also addressed the HIV/AIDS epidemic in Central America on a regional basis. Four of the six countries in Latin America with the highest HIV prevalence are in Central America. Two Central American countries have prevalence rates above 1%, which is a key threshold for an HIV epidemic to run out of control unless prevention efforts are improved among high-risk groups, such as commercial sex workers, men who have sex with men and prisoners (see Chap. 2). The adult HIV prevalence rates are as follows (in alphabetical order): Costa Rica (0.6%); El Salvador (0.6%); Honduras (1.6%); Guatemala (1%); Nicaragua (0.2%) and Panama (0.9%). By 2010, the adult HIV prevalence rate may reach 2% in the region. HIV transmission in Central America is primarily associated with heterosexual sex (with the exception of Costa Rica), as in Africa and the Caribbean (World Bank 2006). The World Bank has developed a model to help governments to allocate resources efficiently to prevent the maximum number of new infections (World Bank 2003). In Central America, the World Bank also studied the extent of discrimination and stigmatization and identified areas where changes in general legislation or HIV/AIDS laws are necessary (World Bank 2006).

7.2.3 The Effectiveness of the World Bank

Economist Jagdish Bhagwati has taken the World Bank to task for not having a sufficiently narrow focus. In particular, he has opined that the world does not need a global think tank staffed by 8,500 people and that the World Bank should not be involved in intellectual programs for countries, like India, that have sufficient resources to handle their own affairs. Thus, in his view, the World Bank should be cut to 300 staff to focus on a good intellectual program for countries that need it (BBC News 2007a).

Easterly (2006) has accused the World Bank of wasting resources on inefficient bureaucracies and for having a late response to the HIV/AIDS epidemic (it had only implemented one project by 1993 and only completed ten by 1998). In a comparative study of US and World Bank funding for HIV/AIDS between 1995 and 1999, Smith (2007) found that, although there is a positive correlation between the incidence of HIV/AIDS and poverty and the likelihood of receiving aid from the World Bank, the US government is more responsive to the incidence of HIV/AIDS and poverty with its foreign aid donations. Moreover, the World Bank allocates more money to countries with political systems that are less likely to use the funds for public goods like education, treatment and health care, and does not do as well as the United States in targeting aid to countries most in need of funding (Smith 2007).

It is difficult to assess the success of the World Bank's HIV/AIDS programs, since they are ongoing, diverse and numerous. However, the World Bank's current programs have incorporated several features that suggest that they will be effective: following "the three ones", ongoing support, monitoring and evaluation of programs for effectiveness, sharing information regarding the factors that contribute to the success of individual projects and working with other multilateral and bilateral donors to reduce overlap.

The World Bank has undertaken or commissioned three reviews of its HIV/AIDS work (World Bank 2005a). The "Interim Review of the Multi-Country HIV/AIDS Program for Africa", was done in early 2004. This review listed the following key barriers and challenges: (1) Many national HIV/AIDS plans are not strategic, and are poorly prioritized; (2) Prevention, care and treatment efforts are too small, and coverage is too low; (3) Management and implementation constraints hamper action; (4) Health systems are weak and overwhelmed, particularly with efforts to expand access to treatment; (5) The effort to expand antiretroviral (ARV) treatment raises difficult issues of equity, sustainability and adherence; (6) Prevention remains inadequate, regardless of the stage of the epidemic in a given country; (7) Stigma and discrimination, denial and silence persist, to the point that some people would rather die than let others know they are HIV positive; and (8) Donors sometimes create additional problems for countries, for example in Tanzania, where program managers spend more time meeting the needs of visiting donors than implementing the programs.

The World Bank's Operations Evaluation Department (OED) has assessed the development effectiveness of the World Bank's country-level HIV/AIDS assistance (defined as policy dialogue, analytical work and lending to reduce the scope or impact of the AIDS epidemic) (World Bank 2005b). The OED's assessment found that the World Bank's assistance has induced governments to act earlier or in a more focused and cost-effective way. It has helped raise political commitment, create or strengthen AIDS institutions, enlist NGOs, and prioritize activities. The OED's assessment also found that political commitment and capacity had been overestimated and needs continuous assessment. Moreover, failure to reach people with the highest risk behaviors likely had reduced the efficiency and impact of assistance. The effectiveness of the national response had been hampered by weak monitoring and evaluation and the failure to ensure that country-based research is focused on priorities areas.

As a result of its assessment, the OED made several recommendations for the future work of the World Bank in the HIV/AIDS epidemic. First, it should help governments use human and financial resources more efficiently and effectively. Second, the World Bank should help governments to be more strategic and selective, and to prioritize activities that will have the greatest impact. Third, it should work to strengthen national institutions for managing and implementing the long-run response, particularly in the health sector. Fourth, it needs to improve the local evidence base for decision-making and create incentives to ensure that program decisions are guided by relevant local evidence and rigorous analytical work.

Wilson has concluded that the World Bank's MAP programs must place far greater emphasis on improved surveillance, research and analysis in order to design more intelligent MAPs that take into account prevalence and transmission patterns, the distinction between generalized and concentrated epidemics, the effect of stigma and community values on treatment programs and the role of political leadership in national AIDS strategies. The money must follow the epidemic by focusing primarily on normative and behavioral change in the general population in generalized epidemics and on high coverage of vulnerable groups in concentrated epidemics. In generalized epidemics, emphasis must shift from knowledge and awareness to normative change. In more concentrated epidemics, the World Bank needs greater focus on groups and areas where transmission is occurring (Wilson 2007).

A 2007 survey revealed that more than a third of patients on HIV medication in sub-Saharan Africa die or discontinue their treatment within 2 years of starting; only 61.6% of all patients were still receiving medication. The study found that many were too late taking up ARV drugs and died within a few months of commencing treatment. For some it was impractical to travel to distant clinics. The researchers also found evidence that, in cases where patients had to pay for ARVs, some stopped treatment. Some people also suffered from stigma: in some workplaces, people are not able to carry their ARVs and take their ARVs freely at workplaces. Retention rates between individual ARV programs varied widely across Africa. One program in South Africa retained as many as 85% of their patients after 2 years while another in Uganda retained only 46% of patients after the same period of time (BBC News 2007b).

The World Bank was a member of the GTT. The agreements reached by the GTT, including the division of labor, are reflected in the World Bank's Program of Action (World Bank 2005a). However, as noted above, more work is needed to resolve the problems created by the proliferation of donors.

In its 2007 study of funding practices, the Center for Global Development made the following recommendations to the World Bank regarding MAP: (1) focus resources on building government capacity; (2) become a knowledge bank, with a focus on prevention; (3) make the transition to the use of existing government systems; (4) increase individual disbursement amounts; and (5) publicly disclose data (Oomman et al., 2007).

7.3 The International Monetary Fund (IMF): A Multilateral Financial Institution

Dominique Strauss–Kahn, who became the director general of the IMF on 1 November 2007, has noted the need for the IMF to adapt to a new global economic order (to better reflect the rise of emerging market economies and the interests of less developed ones, plus the need to better regulate globalization) and to downsize or die. In Strauss–Kahn's view, the IMF needs to reach out to other multilateral organizations, in particular the World Bank. The IMF also needs to mend fences in a meaningful way with regions of the world that felt hard done by during past crises. In this regard, he said, "My first priority is to cross (Washington DC's) 19th street and go to the other side where there's the World Bank. My second priority is to cross the equator to Latin America and my third priority is to cross the Pacific to Asia." Clearly this means he does not believe there is enough communication between the IMF and the World Bank, despite the physical proximity of their offices. This drives home the need for more coordination among international institutions (Love and Pattanaik, 2007).

7.3.1 Nature of IMF Operations

The IMF is an international organization that was established to promote international monetary cooperation, exchange stability and orderly exchange arrangements; to foster economic growth and high levels of employment; and to provide temporary financial assistance to countries to help ease balance of payments adjustment. It has 185 member countries.

The IMF is to be guided in all its policies and decisions by the purposes set forth in Article I of the Articles of Agreement of the International Monetary Fund. Article I sets out these purposes as follows:

> 1. To promote international monetary cooperation through a permanent institution which provides the machinery for consultation and collaboration on international monetary problems.
>
> 2. To facilitate the expansion and balanced growth of international trade, and to contribute thereby to the promotion and maintenance of high levels of employment and real income and to the development of the productive resources of all members as primary objectives of economic policy.
>
> 3. To promote exchange stability, to maintain orderly exchange arrangements among members, and to avoid competitive exchange depreciation.
>
> 4. To assist in the establishment of a multilateral system of payments in respect of current transactions between members and in the elimination of foreign exchange restrictions which hamper the growth of world trade.
>
> 5. To give confidence to members by making the general resources of the Fund temporarily available to them under adequate safeguards, thus providing them with opportunity to correct maladjustments in their balance of payments without resorting to measures destructive of national or international prosperity.
>
> 6. In accordance with the above, to shorten the duration and lessen the degree of disequilibrium in the international balances of payments of members.

Since inception the IMF's purposes have remained the same, but its operations have developed over time, particularly with respect to surveillance of public expenditure management systems, financial assistance and technical assistance.

7.3.2 Scope of IMF Operations

The IMF focuses on three kinds of operations. First, surveillance operations monitor economic and financial developments and provide policy advice, aimed especially at crisis prevention. Second, the IMF also lends to countries with balance of payments difficulties, to provide temporary financing and to support policies aimed at correcting the underlying problems. Loans to low-income countries are also aimed at poverty reduction. Third, the IMF provides countries with technical assistance and training. The IMF also conducts economic research and gathers statistics related to these three types of operations. An IMF loan usually stipulates the specific policies and measures a country has to implement to resolve its balance of payments problem. Low-income countries may borrow at a concessional interest rate through the Poverty Reduction and Growth Facility and the Exogenous Shocks Facility. Non-concessional loans are subject to the IMF's market-related interest rate, which is revised weekly to take account of changes in short-term interest rates in major international money markets. Large loans carry a surcharge. The IMF also provides emergency assistance to support recovery from natural disasters and conflicts, in some cases at concessional interest rates (http://www.imf.org).

The IMF can allocate additional spending to HIV/AIDS as part of national poverty-reduction strategies. The IMF also provides advice to countries on the macroeconomic impact of HIV/AIDS and how to manage inflows of foreign aid. Country-level HIV prevention and treatment programs form part of many Poverty Reduction Strategy Papers, which provide the operational basis for IMF and World Bank loans to low-income countries and for debt relief under the Heavily Indebted Poor Countries (HIPC) Initiative (IMF 2005).

Unlike development banks, the IMF does not lend for specific projects. Thus, unlike the World Bank and the Global Fund, the IMF does not have projects specifically aimed at HIV/AIDS. Rather, HIV/AIDS issues are addressed as part of the IMF's general operations. The research of the IMF on HIV/AIDS has been focused primarily on its macroeconomic impact.

7.3.3 Effectiveness of the IMF

With respect to HIV/AIDS, IMF (and World Bank) policies have been criticized for not considering the impact of structural adjustment requirements (austerity measures) on the spread of HIV/AIDS. The IMF has also been criticized for making debt repayment a higher priority than health care, thereby undermining the ability of national governments to finance health care.

Peter Lurie et al. (1995) argued that export-oriented, structural-adjustment policies were undermining HIV/AIDS control by contributing to social changes that favor the spread of HIV in the developing world, through increased mobility, migration, urbanization and dislocation of family units.

Hanlon (1999) noted that the IMF required the Mozambican Government and other African governments to reduce spending in the 1990s without decreasing repayments of its debts, thereby contributing to cuts in spending on health services that increased corruption in hospitals. The international community later recognized that much of Africa's debt could not be paid and agreed to cancel some debts. This led to the HIPC Initiative in 1996. However, Hanlon reported that with the HIPC Mozambique would still be paying back USD 100 million a year, because the World Bank and IMF agreed to cancel only the part of the debt that Mozambique was not paying. The HIPC only canceled the uncollectable debt. Thus, Mozambique was paying USD 275,000 per day in debt service, but only USD 100,000 per day for its entire health service.

In 2003, African Ministers of Finance, Planning and Economic Development warned that the enhanced HIPC Initiative was not delivering long-term debt sustainability. They recommended that the IMF impose fewer structural conditions and provide for outcomes-based conditions where appropriate. The Ministers also urged the IMF and World Bank, bilateral partners and the African Development Bank to avoid "cross-conditionalities" that impede access to resources. They recommended that to provide greater fiscal flexibility, the IMF should also analyze the linkages, trade-offs and policy choices required to attain the Millennium Development Goals (which include addressing the HIV/AIDS pandemic). They also proposed that evaluating exogenous shocks should be a standard feature of IMF discussions with member states, and that access to loans should be extended to countries suffering from exceptional exogenous shocks such as the onslaught of new communicable diseases. On HIV/AIDS specifically, the Ministers urged the IMF and World Bank to consider revising the eligibility criteria for assistance to middle-income countries affected by the AIDS epidemic, and to find ways of ensuring that countries could expand expenditure on health and social welfare without violating conditions that impose limits on public spending (ECA 2003).

The IMF restricted aid to Mozambique's budget in order to control inflation and required donors' aid to fund more projects outside the state budget, contrary to the policy of many donors (Hanlon 2006). The IMF Resident Representative Mozambique argued that it was difficult for the government to be certain about the level of donor payments in the medium term, and it might not be prudent to make medium term expenditure commitments (such as the hiring of health personnel) given the uncertainty about whether the money would still be available over the next budget cycle.

The IMF Representative recognized the need to improve the design of the IMF fiscal target taking into account that donor aid has increasingly moved away from lending to support capital investment projects, and toward direct budget support for hiring personnel and purchasing medicine (Perone 2006). This story highlights the ongoing importance of policy coordination on the ground between the IMF, donors and national governments and the need for sustainable funding from donors.

7.4 The Global Fund: A Fundraising and Financing Institution

The Global Fund was created to raise and disburse additional private and public sector funds for the fight against AIDS, tuberculosis and malaria. As of October 2007, the Global Fund had committed USD 8.4 billion in 136 countries. It provides around two thirds of all international financing for tuberculosis and malaria and close to a quarter of the global resources for AIDS. As we saw in Chap. 4, malaria prevention is a cost-effective means to prevent HIV/AIDS in areas with high malaria prevalence, because of the impact of life-expectancy on incentives to change sexual behavior to reduce the risk of HIV/AIDS. The prevalence of HIV/AIDS also has a direct impact on the spread of extensively drug-resistant tuberculosis (XDR-TB). People living with AIDS are especially susceptible to XDR-TB because of their depressed immune systems, increasing the risk that XDR-TB will spread rapidly in sub-Saharan Africa (Picard 2007). In turn, an XDR-TB epidemic could reduce life expectancy, thereby hampering HIV/AIDS prevention. Thus, it is important to attack all three diseases together.

There are two key differences between the Global Fund and the World Bank. First, the Global Fund is a hands-off operation that focuses on financing rather than implementation, whereas the World Bank is very involved in the implementation of its programs. Second, the Global Fund has a much narrower scope of operations with respect to the issues that it tackles, being restricted to AIDS, tuberculosis and malaria. The World Bank has a much broader development agenda, albeit one that incorporates health care in general, and HIV/AIDS in particular, into its development programs.

7.4.1 Nature of Global Fund Operations

Section II of the Framework Document of the Global Fund sets out its purpose in the following terms:

> The purpose of the Fund is to attract, manage and disburse additional resources through a new public-private partnership that will make a sustainable and significant contribution to the reduction of infections, illness and death, thereby mitigating the impact caused by HIV/AIDS, tuberculosis and malaria in countries in need, and contributing to poverty reduction as part of the Millennium Development Goals (Global Fund 2003).

Section II of the Framework Document clarifies that the Fund's mandate is to finance prevention, treatment, care and support in an integrated and balanced way, not to implement such programs. The Framework Document provides further that the Global Fund "should make use of existing international mechanisms and health plans". In making its funding decisions, the Global fund is to focus on best practices and performance, linking resources to the achievement of clear, measurable and sustainable results. Another focus is on the creation, development and expansion of government/private/NGO partnerships. The Global Fund is required to support programs that reflect "national ownership", by focusing upon the technical quality of proposals, while leaving the design of programs and priorities to partners within recipient countries.

"Country Coordinating Mechanisms" (CCMs) are country-level partnerships that develop and submit grant proposals to the Global Fund based on priority needs at the national level. After grant approval, they oversee progress during implementation. CCMs include representatives from the public and private sectors, including governments, multilateral or bilateral agencies, non-governmental organizations, academic institutions, private businesses and people living with the diseases.

The proposals that are supported by the Global Fund must be consistent with international law and agreements, respecting intellectual property rights laws, such as TRIPS. At the same time, the programs should encourage efforts to make quality drugs and products available at the lowest possible prices and give priority to the most affected countries and communities, and to those countries most at risk. The Framework Document provides specifically for programs that aim to eliminate the stigmatization of and discrimination against those infected and affected by HIV/AIDS, especially for women, children and vulnerable groups.

The Framework Document requires the Global Fund to use, wherever possible, existing monitoring and evaluation mechanisms. Monitoring at the country level is country-driven, but also linked to the Fund's monitoring and evaluation system at a global level. Grantees need to be: (1) accountable to donors for the use of funds and achievement of results; (2) responsive to developing countries; and (3) responsive to the needs of those infected and directly affected by the three diseases. The Framework Document contemplates the following options for who oversees the process of monitoring both global and local program progress on behalf of the Global Fund Board: Global Fund Secretariat; Ad hoc monitoring and evaluation working group; the World Bank's Operations Evaluation Department; a UN agency; existing mechanisms (UNAIDS, Stop TB, Roll Back Malaria); an independent monitoring and evaluation oversight committee appointed by the Global Fund Board; or a third party (for example, an accounting firm or university).

The World Bank serves as the Trustee for the Global Fund. The Trustee has primary responsibility for financial accountability, including: (1) collection, investment, and management of funds; (2) disbursement of funds to national-level entities, on the instruction of the Global Fund Board; (3) reporting to stakeholders on the financial management of the Fund and the allocation of Fund resources; and (4) independent audits.

Local Funding Agents are organizations (mainly multinational audit firms) that the Global Fund contracts to provide the Secretariat with the information used to make decisions regarding grant management. KPMG and PriceWaterhouseCoopers act as Local Funding Agents in 80% of the 136 countries involved and are responsible for 83% of approved funds. Local Funding Agents verify, assess and report on the capacity of the agencies that implement funded programs and on program results and make recommendations regarding future funding. The outsourcing of fiduciary risk management to Local Funding Agents obviates the need for Global Fund offices in the relevant countries, thereby enabling the Global Fund to have a leaner administration and to set up more rapidly in a country (Euro Health Group 2007).

7.4.2 Scope of Global Fund Operations

The Framework Document requires the highest priority to be given to proposals from countries and regions with the greatest need, based on the highest burden of disease and the least financial resources. These are identified as including sub-Saharan Africa, currently the region most affected, as well as some countries within the Caribbean, Asia-Pacific, Latin America and Central and Eastern Europe. The criteria for identifying these proposals include: (1) disease burden for HIV, TB and/or malaria; (2) poverty indicators, such as per capita GNP and the UN Human Development Index; (3) potential for rapid increase in disease, based on indicators such as recent disease trends, size of population at risk, prevalence of risk factors, extent of cross-border and internal migration, conflict, or natural disaster; (4) political commitment, as indicated by contribution to the financing of the proposal, public spending on health, existence of supportive national policies or the presence of a national counterpart in the proposal; (5) existence of a country coordination mechanism, which consists of an inclusive collaborative partnership, with all relevant partners engaged in planning, decision-making and implementation. Figures 7.8 and 7.9 show the Global Fund's distribution of funds, by disease and by country income level. Figure 7.10 shows the Global Fund's expenditure targets for products and services. Figures 7.11 and 7.12 show the Global Fund's distribution of funds, by region and by sector of recipients.

The Framework Document requires the Global Fund to provide grants to public, private and non-governmental programs for the prevention, treatment, care and support of the infected and directly affected, which may include: increased access to health services; provision of critical health products (for example, bed nets; condoms; antiretroviral, anti-TB and anti-malarial drugs; treatment for sexually transmitted infections; laboratory supplies and materials; and diagnostic kits); training of personnel and community health workers; behavioral change and outreach; and community-based programs, including care for the sick and orphans.

Technical Review Panels, made up of independent, impartial teams of experts appointed by the Global Fund Board, review grant proposals, based on criteria set by the Board, and make recommendations to the Board for final decision.

Funding by Diseases

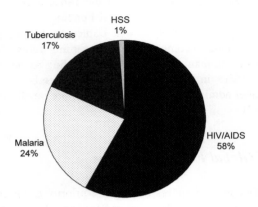

Fig. 7.8 Global fund's distribution of funds by disease (2001–2006). *Source*: Global Fund

Distribution by Country Income

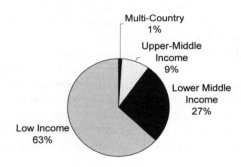

Fig. 7.9 Funding by Country Income Levels (2001–2006). *Source*: Global Fund

7.4.3 Effectiveness of the Global Fund

The Global Fund's Technical Evaluation Reference Group (an independent advisory body) was charged with overseeing a Five-Year Evaluation on the operations of the Global Fund, during 2006–2008. The first area of evaluation is "organizational efficiency", which analyzes whether the Global Fund is efficient and effective in fulfilling its core principles, including acting as a financial instrument rather than implementation agency and furthering country ownership. The second area of evaluation is "partnership environment", which considers how effective

Expenditure Target

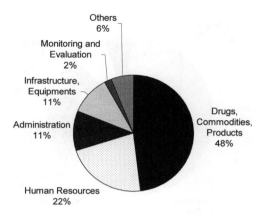

Fig. 7.10 Global fund expenditure targets for products and services. *Source*: Global Fund

Expenditure by Region

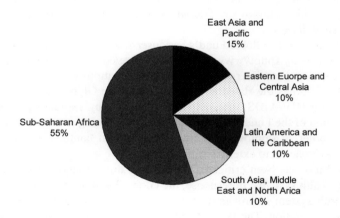

Fig. 7.11 Global fund expenditure by region. *Source*: Global Fund

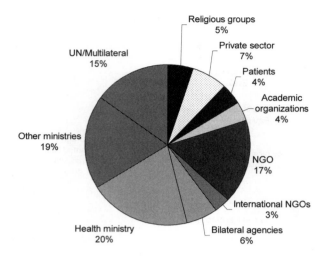

Source: The Global Fund to Fi_ht AIDS, Tuberculosis and Malaria

Fig. 7.12 Global fund, sector of recipients (2001–2006). *Source*: Global Fund

and efficient the Global Fund partnership system is in supporting HIV, malaria and TB programs at the global and country level. The third area of evaluation is "health impact", which studies the Global Fund's contribution to reducing the burden of the three diseases.

A striking feature of the Global Fund's very user-friendly web site is the Global Fund Evaluation Library (http://www.theglobalfund.org/en/links_resources/ brary/). This web page makes both internal and external evaluations of the Global Fund readily available and has the stated aim of improving the Global Fund's delivery of key services for HIV/AIDS, tuberculosis and malaria by stimulating open debate and evaluation of the Fund. This novel method of inviting and inciting critical evaluations, in order to improve performance, stands in contrast to the World Bank and IMF approaches to external criticism.

The Global Fund has been criticized for funding drugs without strengthening the underlying health systems. In response, the Global Fund opened the possibility of funding health system improvements, but this was not used often and rarely covered staff remuneration. The World Bank has proposed leaving the strengthening of health systems up to the World Bank, in order to avoid overlap. However, the World Bank itself has been criticized for poor performance in supporting and reinforcing public health services, particularly given its role, together with the International Monetary Fund, in maintaining limits on public health expenditures and wages. The Global Fund, with its narrow funding mandate, has also been criticized for not placing more conditions on the use of the resources provided and for giving into technical advisors from the World Bank and bilateral donors who oppose the exceptional nature of AIDS (Philips 2007).

The Global Fund evaluates program performance after 2 years. The Center for Global Development analyzed data on 134 of the first 140 Global Fund grants evaluated in 2006. Due to the subjective nature of the evaluation process, this analysis should be seen as an analysis of evaluation scores rather than of the actual performance of the programs. Moreover, the results were not intended to be used to influence the distribution of funding, but rather to allocate resources for oversight and risk management. The programs that scored lowest had government agencies as principal recipients, had a large amount of funding, were focused on malaria, had weak initial proposals or were evaluated by the accounting firm KPMG. Countries with a high number of doctors per head, high measles immunization rates, few health-sector donors and high disease-prevalence rates had higher evaluation scores. Poor countries, those with small government budget deficits and those that have or have had socialist governments also received higher scores. Programs in which a government was the principal recipient received significantly lower scores than those with civil society, private sector or multilateral recipients. Malaria programs were 12.9% less likely than HIV/AIDS or tuberculosis programs to receive an A. In addition, evaluation scores were slightly higher in countries with higher prevalence rates for the target disease of the program (Radelet and Siddiqi, 2007).

Countries with stronger health systems and larger numbers of trained health workers were more likely to have successful programs. This suggests that the Global Fund needs to ensure greater oversight in countries with weaker systems and capacity, and underscores the importance of building strong health systems rather than focusing narrowly on short-term targets. However, evaluation scores were lower in programs where there were many other donors. This may have been due to the greater administrative and management burden placed on recipients when there are multiple donors. Alternatively, it may indicate that the incentives for strong performance are weaker when recipients have many funding alternatives (Radelet and Siddiqi, 2007).

The Global Fund's country coordination mechanism has been criticized for focusing on government actors and not including people with HIV/AIDS (Gonzalves 2004; McKai 2004). Faith-based organizations in host countries have also not been included in country coordination mechanisms to the degree that they would like, often due to a lack of information from governments, a lack of access to guidelines for funding proposals and a need for assistance in preparing funding proposals (Lee et al., 2002).

The Center for Global Development convened a high-level independent Working Group to help the new Executive Director of the Global Fund define the major tasks that require attention, and provided specific recommendations for action. The Working Group consisted of 21 members, including relevant experts in government, civil society organizations, foundations, academia, private sector companies and disease-based partnership initiatives. Some of the Working Group's key recommendations were: (1) Convene a "Heads of Agencies Group" with the Director General of the WHO, the Executive Director of UNAIDS, and the President of the

World Bank to jointly tackle key problems in technical assistance, procurement, monitoring, evaluation and other key issues; (2) Work with other agencies to develop an information market for technical assistance, building on existing mechanisms with UNAIDS, the Stop TB Partnership and Roll Back Malaria; (3) Provide early warning information on country programs to recipients, CCM members, governments, international partners and key NGO groups so that actions can be taken quickly to get programs back on track; (4) Commission a management audit of the Secretariat, consider hiring additional Portfolio Managers and consider shifting from one portfolio manager per country to teams of two or three working across countries; (5) Hire a full-time professional fund raising team, led by a senior professional and comprised of experts with diverse skills to work with traditional, non-traditional and private sector donors; (6) Make the Executive Director a non-voting member of the Board so that the experiences and insights of the Executive Director and the Secretariat are more fully reflected in Board discussions (Radelet 2006).

In its 2007 study of funding practices, the Center for Global Development made the following recommendations to the Global Fund: (1) keep the focus on funding gaps; (2) re-examine strategies to build local capacity; (3) simplify procedures for good performers; and (4) publicly disclose data (Oomman et al., 2007).

A 2007 external evaluation of the Global Fund's Local Funding Agent system concluded that the system should be maintained, but needs to be improved. The evaluation found that the system needs: (1) greater emphasis on health program skills (since few Local Funding Agents have staff with health backgrounds); (2) to implement a quality assurance system to verify the adequacy of Local Funding Agent methods (for example, with respect to documentation of audits); (3) to provide more complete capacity assessments of the organizations that implement programs; (4) to increase the use of in-country partnerships; (5) to implement a comprehensive performance evaluation system for Local Funding Agents; and (6) to create an operational manual or handbook to govern the Local Funding Agent management process (Euro Health Group 2007).

An internal evaluation made similar findings: (1) that there were gaps in Local Funding Agent documentation that failed to meet professional auditing standards; (2) adherence to specific auditing standards needed to be integrated as a requirement in the tendering process; (3) a lack of a consistent management approach; (4) that the Global Fund Secretariat should introduce a systematic performance evaluation system for Local Funding Agents and a handbook; (5) that capacity assessment should extend to sub-recipients, not just principal recipients of funding; (6) the health program skills and experience of Local Funding Agents was inadequate; and (7) that Local Funding Agents needed to develop partnerships with other health-sector players through networking, to have greater access to health sector intelligence and improve coordination with other players (Technical Evaluation Reference Group 2007).

The United States Government Accountability Office (GAO) also conducts reviews of the Global Fund, since the United States contributes funds. In 2007, the GAO review of 80 grant disbursements and 45 grant renewal decisions found that they were well documented and that documentation had improved since 2005. The GAO also noted that the Global Fund has begun developing a risk assessment framework to improve the identification of risks that may affect grant implementation, having found that an earlier risk assessment model was inadequate. However, the GAO also found that the lack of a mandatory system of Local Funding Agent performance assessment limits the Global Fund's ability to determine the quality of Local Funding Agent monitoring and reporting (GAO 2007).

7.5 Bilateral Donors

Bilateral governmental donations are an important source of financing for HIV/AIDS programs. In 2005, the resources available from all sources totaled USD 8.3 billion, out of which G7/EC and other donor government commitments for HIV/AIDS totaled roughly USD 4.3 billion. Of these donor government commitments, USD 3.5 billion were bilateral commitments and USD 810 million were contributions to the Global Fund. The G7/EC commitments were 85% of the total donor government commitments for HIV/AIDS (Kates and Lief, 2006).

As we noted earlier, commitments and disbursements are not the same thing. For example, while the United States accounted for 54.4% of bilateral commitments, it only accounted for 40.6% of bilateral disbursements in 2005 (see Figs. 7.13 and 7.14).

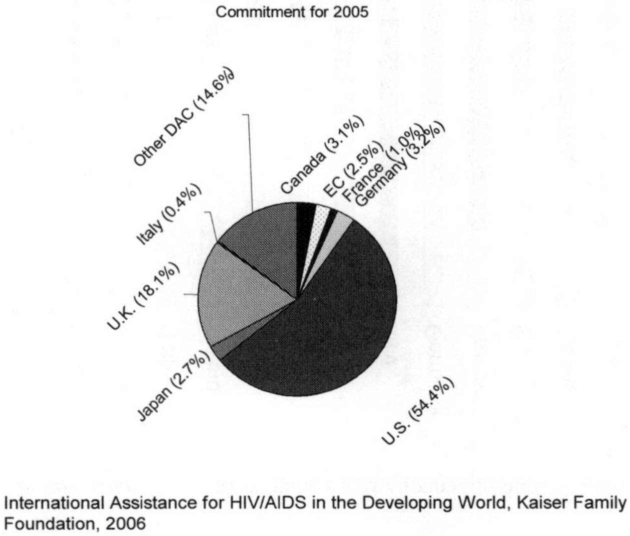

Commitment for 2005

Other DAC (14.6%)
Canada (3.1%)
EC (2.5%)
France (1.0%)
Germany (3.2%)
Italy (0.4%)
U.K. (18.1%)
Japan (2.7%)
U.S. (54.4%)

International Assistance for HIV/AIDS in the Developing World, Kaiser Family Foundation, 2006

Fig. 7.13 Origin of resources committed. Source: Kaiser Family Foundation

Disbursement in 2005

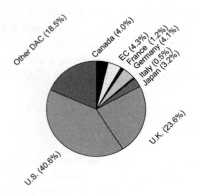

International Assistance for HIV/AIDS in the Developing World, Kaiser Family Foundation, 2006

Fig. 7.14 Actual spending of resources. *Source*: Kaiser Family Foundation

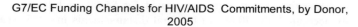

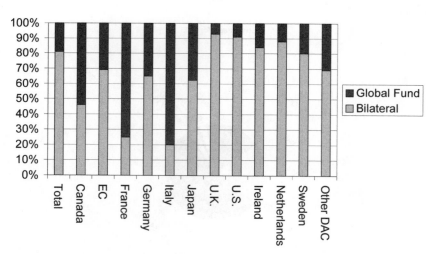

Fig. 7.15 Funding commitments by rich countries for HIV/AIDS. *Source*: Kates and Lief (2006)

Many donors prefer to channel funding through bilateral programs (81% of G7/EC commitments), rather than the multilateral channel (19% of G7/EC commitments). However, preferences vary from one donor country to the next. For example, at on end of the spectrum, the UK made 93% of its commitments through bilateral channels and 7% through the Global Fund. At the other end of the spectrum, Italy made 20% of its commitments through bilateral channels and 80% through the Global Fund. Canada was in the middle, with 46% of its commitments through bilateral channels and 54% through the Global Fund (see Fig. 7.15) (Kates and Lief, 2006).

7.6 The Role of the Private Sector in Funding Prevention and Treatment

Engaging the private sector in HIV/AIDS prevention and treatment is increasingly becoming a major focus for governments, advocates and public health practitioners. The private sector, through domestic firms or the foreign direct investment of multinational firms, is a significant source of financing for the prevention and treatment of HIV/AIDS. Private charitable foundations have also become an important source of funding in the fight against HIV/AIDS.

Two issues regarding private sector donors provoke controversy. One is the issue of donations of goods and services in kind by the private sector. Critics argue that such donations impede the ability of recipient governments to build their own infrastructure. Supporters argue that such donations give a boost to local efforts to build infrastructure, provided they take place in close cooperation with recipient governments. A second issue is donor reliability and sustainability, particularly with respect to donations from the private sector (although this issue is also raised regarding other sources of funding). Here, the concern is that host governments will be unwilling to integrate funding for HIV/AIDS into general revenues that support the overall health infrastructure (for example, salaries for medical personnel) unless there is some assurance that the funding will be ongoing (McKinnell 2004).

While the participation of the private sector in addressing the HIV/AIDS pandemic is very important, its efforts need to be coordinated with the other players (governments, donors and NGOs) and the roles of the various players need to be well defined. For example, Oxfam has criticized developed countries and the World Bank for undermining governments' ability to deliver public services by advocating inappropriate private sector projects in health. Oxfam acknowledges that the private sector has a role to play, but argues the private sector cannot provide services on the necessary scale, geared to the needs of all citizens (Oxfam 2006).

7.6.1 Incentives for Companies to Invest in HIV/AIDS Programs

Companies have an incentive to invest in HIV/AIDS programs due to the impact of the pandemic on enterprise performance. This impact depends on worker attrition due to sickness and death, the corresponding costs to the firm for providing health and sickness benefits, replacement costs to obtain new workers and the impact of HIV/AIDS on worker productivity (Ramachandran et al., 2005). At the same time, the health of a country's population may affect inflows of foreign direct investment to low- and middle-income countries (Alsan et al., 2004). The HIV/AIDS pandemic thus creates a catch-22 situation.

HIV/AIDS has clear effects on a company's workforce and its customer base. The literature suggests that skilled workers are most likely to contract the virus, and that these are extremely difficult to replace. Customers, suppliers and investors in a company are also likely to be affected by HIV/AIDS, and this effect is expected to increase as the virus spreads (Bloom et al., 2001). However, a PriceWaterhouseCoopers survey found that only 39% of organizations in Eastern Africa had HIV/AIDS policies in place (PriceWaterhouseCoopers 2003).

On an individual basis, firms can have a tremendous impact in promoting prevention among employees and their families and providing access to treatment. For example, in Botswana an early and innovative program by Debswana, a diamond mining company that is the country's largest non-government employer, made it the first company to provide free anti-retroviral treatment to employees and their spouses (Center for Global Development 2005). However, as with multilateral organizations such as the World Bank, the IMF, the Global Fund and the UN, it is important to have an overarching framework in order to ensure the adoption of best practices by individual firms and to minimize overlap between the private sector and the other players that are involved in addressing the pandemic. In this regard, there have been some important national and global initiatives. An example of a national initiative is the Commercial Market Strategies (CMS) project, which was a 5-year USAID-funded project (1998–2003). CMS's AIDS treatment brochure articulated the business case for providing ARVs to employees as part of their health care benefits. The key global initiative is the Global Business Coalition on HIV/AIDS (GBC), which has 220 members, headquartered in thirty countries, employing over eleven million people in more than 200 countries and is supported almost entirely by its member companies.

The GBC and Booz Allen Hamilton conducted a baseline survey and interview program to establish a basis to look at the scope and depth of the response being made by the global business community. The study highlighted variations in business response by region, industry and enterprise scale. The study found that business increasingly sees HIV/AIDS as a strategic as well as a social responsibility issue, and manages programs and resources based on bottom line impact (GBC and Booz, Allen, Hamilton 2006).

The data source was the expertise and experiences of 75 GBC member companies across 17 industries that were surveyed in April 2006 and 30 companies who participated in a detailed interview program. The baseline showed business response in the form of an index, on a scale of 0–10. The index was calculated from the number of companies active in each of 10 global business HIV/AIDS categories of Best Practice AIDS Standard (BPAS), each with five levels of action. The

75 surveyed companies had an average index score of 4.5. This was equivalent to being active in more than 8 of 10 categories with two actions underway in each. The most active 25% scored 7.5 and the least active 25% scored 1.4. This variation was primarily due to perceived business needs and the length of time the companies had been addressing the HIV/AIDS issue. Of the 10 BPAS categories there are two in which the business response was particularly strong – prevention initiatives and community and government partnerships. Companies had the most difficulty in engaging business associates and suppliers (see Fig. 7.16). The most active industry groups were Food/Beverages, Mining and Minerals and Energy (gas and oil) (GBC and Booz, Allen, Hamilton 2006).

The survey found that developing and implementing a company HIV/AIDS program requires about 3 years to move from concept and strategy to fully operational across the business. Of the surveyed companies, 82% provided workplace information on HIV/AIDS. However, only 41% conducted surveys and assessments, suggesting that program design and follow up could be enhanced. With respect to prevention programs, 60% of the companies had trained peer educators in place and 55% had expanded prevention programs to the community. Companies

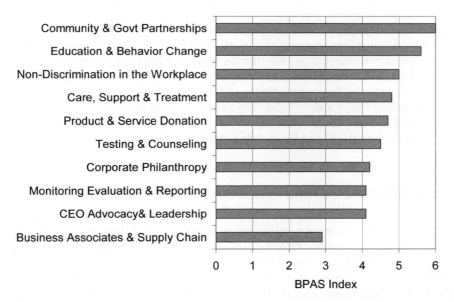

Fig. 7.16 GBC and Booz, Allen, Hamilton survey of company HIV/AIDS programs. *Source*: GBC and Booz, Allen, Hamilton (2006)

were twice as likely to fully subsidize treatment for employees in high prevalence areas. In parts of Africa with high HIV prevalence, more than 70% of the companies surveyed were fully subsidizing staff access to HIV treatment. Globally, 36% of surveyed companies fully subsidize treatment for direct employees and 45% provided access to treatment for all dependents (GBC and Booz, Allen, Hamilton 2006).

The GBC survey had several key findings regarding ways to improve the global business community's response to HIV/AIDS. First, there is a need to develop strategies to work closely with suppliers and business associates to expand the network of business engagement. Second, there is a need to partner with NGOs, community, and local government to develop and fund programs and initiatives with greater reach. Third, companies should extend confidential testing and treatment programs, including monitoring of testing participation rates, access to viral load tests and, in high prevalence areas, treatment for dependents and post employment. Fourth, companies should focus on balanced prevention and treatment programs that target behavior change in conjunction with treatment. Fifth, there is a need to increase the role of business in advocacy and to extend programs into emerging markets. In particular, CEOs and senior management should provide leadership to dispel myths and stigma, break down workplace barriers and influence community change. In this regard, the GBC study concluded that the private sector can enhance their response to HIV/AIDS by treating it like any other disease and integrating responses into broader packages supporting health and well-being. Employment contracts and health benefits packages should include HIV as a normal component rather than an exception. Rather than isolating HIV/AIDS, interventions should be part of a comprehensive health system for employees and the broader community (GBC and Booz, Allen, Hamilton 2006).

The GBC study recommends that an HIV/AIDS response be a core component of an overall business strategy, whether the response takes the form of cause-related marketing, co-investments with governments on HIV programs or comprehensive workplace policies. Proactive action on AIDS can help position a company as an overall market leader and will also help sustain markets and serve a need in countries like India and China, with rapidly growing young, sexually active middle-class populations (GBC and Booz, Allen, Hamilton 2006).

7.6.2 Market-Based Initiatives to Increase Private Sector Funding

In addition to direct company participation in prevention and treatment programs, there have been efforts to create market-based incentives for the private sector to donate more funds to combating HIV/AIDS. The most notable example is Product RED, an economic initiative designed to deliver a sustainable flow of private sector money to the Global Fund to Fight AIDS, Tuberculosis and Malaria. This initiative was announced at the World Economic Forum Annual Meeting in 2006 by Bono and Bobby Shriver. With Product RED, the world's leading companies made a commitment to channel a portion of their profits from sales of specially-designed products to the Global Fund to support AIDS programs for women and children in Africa.

Another market-based initiative for the private sector is "social marketing". Population Services International (PSI), a nonprofit organization based in Washington, DC., created a comprehensive Corporate AIDS Prevention Program for companies seeking to fight HIV/AIDS in the workplace. PSI, a large aid contractor, uses commercial marketing strategies to promote health products, services and healthy behavior in low-income and vulnerable populations in 70 developing countries. Products and services are sold at subsidized prices rather than being provided free of charge. The logic behind social marketing is that charging money will enhance the perceived value of products and services, increase the likelihood of use, and motivate commercial sector involvement. However, the notion that fee needs to be charged for HIV treatment in order for the recipients to see "value" in the drugs has been discredited.

Arata Kochi, the director of the World Health Organization's malaria program, has concluded that the social marketing approach is not an effective means to expand the use of mosquito nets to prevent malaria. Using the social marketing approach, mosquito nets were sold through local shops at subsidized prices, with donors underwriting the losses and paying consultants to come up with brand names and to advertise the nets. The social marketing approach was also used to distribute condoms and oral rehydration salts. However, it was revealed that the United States Agency for International Development (USAID) was spending 95% of its malaria budget on consultants and 5% on goods like nets, drugs and insecticide. Experiences in Kenya helped to persuade the WHO to change its policy. A 5-year study of 40 health districts revealed that a PSI social marketing scheme for malaria nets only increased coverage from 7% of the population to about 21% between 2002 and 2006. In contrast, when the health ministry got a grant from the Global Fund that allowed it to hand out 3.4 million free nets in 2 weeks, coverage rose to 67%, and distribution became more equitable. Under social marketing, the richest of the poor had 38% coverage, while the poorest of the poor had only 15%. After the distribution of free nets, they were about equal and deaths of children dropped 44%. Free distribution was also cheaper. With consultant fees, transportation, advertising and shipping, social marketing added about USD 10 to the cost of each net beyond the USD 5 to USD 7 that manufacturers charged. Even with payments to volunteers, the added cost of free distribution was only about USD 1.25 per net (Kyama and McNeil, 2007).

Médecins Sans Frontières (MSF) has criticized donors for proposing to continue having patients make a financial contribution to the cost of ARV treatment in populations where incomes are barely adequate for people to feed themselves (Médecins Sans Frontières 2005). AIDS patients need to receive treatment their entire lives without interruption in order to avoid death or creating drug-resistant mutations of HIV. Requiring patients (who do not have enough money for food) to pay for treatment reduces the effectiveness of ARV treatment, reduces adherence and decreases survival rates. Even where ARV treatment is free of charge, where countries define AIDS care narrowly many direct treatment costs must be covered by patients. For example, the high cost of laboratory tests can deter patients from monitoring the effectiveness and side effects of ARV treatment. A related problem is the cost of treatment for opportunistic infections (such as pneumonia), which may bankrupt patients before they even start ARV treatment. Other costs, such as consultation or hospital fees, can also constitute a barrier to treatment for patients in developing countries. As a result, MSF has recommended that major international donors such as the Global Fund, PEPFAR, and the World Bank should require recipients to provide ARV treatment and other essential elements of AIDS care without patient contributions, and to slightly increase funding to include these complementary costs (Philips 2007).

The World Bank President, former US trade representative Robert Zoellick, has called on the bank's 185 member nations to give the private sector a bigger role in development (Reuters 2007). With respect to the World Bank's AIDS programs, as well as other health-related issues, careful thought will have to be given to the appropriate role for the private sector, particularly the failure of social marketing to achieve adequate and equitable coverage in poor populations.

The experience of the private sector thus far indicates that the business response to the AIDS pandemic needs to be standardized and coordinated with the activities of other players, notably national governments, NGOs and multilateral institutions. While some companies limit their response to donations of money, goods and services, others have taken a more proactive approach by implementing prevention and treatment programs for their employees and, in some cases, the dependents of employees. This proactive approach is particularly useful in areas with high prevalence rates and poor public health care infrastructure.

Global multinational companies are in a position to use their influence with suppliers and other business associates to expand the use of best practices, particularly with respect to prevention and treatment programs. In this regard, the GBC plan to review the state of business and AIDS annually and to use the results of these assessments to adapt the Best Practice AIDS Standard is to be commended. The GBC study notes that companies have addressed child labor, wage equity and occupational safety through their supply chains, including distributors, business associates and small and medium enterprises. However, this network of global suppliers has been a weak link in the AIDS response. If tapped, the reach of employee and community networks could make a tremendous impact in mobilizing communities around HIV prevention and treatment. Similarly, enhanced supply chain practices promoting youth education and gender equity can help to address underlying social factors that contribute to the spread of HIV/AIDS (GBC and Booz, Allen, Hamilton 2006).

The further standardization of best practices would be a useful next step. The International Standards Organization (ISO) certification process that is currently used to improve business processes could serve as a model. The ISO has specific standards for the automotive industry and has specific standards for environmental processes. While these standards are voluntary, many multinational companies require their suppliers to be ISO-certified. The creation of specific ISO standards for HIV/AIDS policies, or for company health policies more generally, would be a useful vehicle for standardizing best practices and expanding the adoption of best practices to suppliers. As with ISO, the standards could be voluntary, but major multinationals could require their suppliers to get certified in order to qualify as suppliers.

7.6.3 Funding from Private Charitable Foundations

Private charitable foundations have become a significant source of funding, research and political leadership in fighting HIV/AIDS. In this section, we examine the HIV/AIDS activities of three US foundations: the Bill & Melinda Gates Foundation, the Kaiser Family Foundation and the William J. Clinton Foundation. It is notable that these foundations have largely avoided overlap in the nature of their operations related to HIV/AIDS, by specializing in addressing different needs. The first two foundations have also collaborated closely.

7.6.3.1 Bill & Melinda Gates Foundation

As of 31 December 2006, the Bill & Melinda Gates Foundation had net assets totaling USD 30 billion, which it uses to fund global development and global health initiatives. The mission of the foundation's Global Health Program is to encourage the development of lifesaving medical advances and to help ensure they reach the people who are disproportionately affected. The foundation is guided by the belief that all lives, no matter where they are lived, have equal value. With respect to global health, the foundation focuses its funding in two main areas: (1) access to existing vaccines, drugs and other tools to fight diseases common in developing countries; and (2) research to develop health solutions that are effective, affordable and practical. In developing countries, the foundation supports efforts to prevent and treat diseases and conditions that meet three criteria: (1) they cause widespread illness and death in developing countries; (2) they represent the greatest inequities in health between developed and developing countries; and (3) they receive inadequate attention and funding. HIV/AIDS is one of the foundation's priority diseases. To slow the global spread of HIV, the foundation supports the development of vaccines and other tools and strategies with the potential to prevent tens of millions of infections and deaths. The foundation also funds comprehensive initiatives that include both prevention and treatment (http://www.gatesfoundation.org/GlobalHealth/).

The Bill & Melinda Gates Foundation's primary focus with respect to HIV/AIDS is on prevention. Illustrative examples of the programs funded by the foundation are: (1) Avahan (which means Call to Action in Sanskrit), an AIDS prevention initiative established in India in 2003, to which it has committed USD 258 million;

(2) the Global HIV Prevention Working Group, an international panel of experts; and (3) the Global HIV Vaccine Enterprise. Through the Avahan program, the foundation is working to expand access to effective prevention in the six states with India's highest infection rates and along the nation's major trucking routes. The Working Group is an international panel of more than 50 leading public health experts, clinicians, researchers and people affected by HIV/AIDS. It is co-convened by the Henry J. Kaiser Family Foundation and the Bill & Melinda Gates Foundation. The Global HIV Prevention Working Group has developed reports and other materials about critical HIV prevention issues, such as scaling up the combined use of proven prevention strategies (male circumcision, AIDS education, condoms, HIV testing and prevention of mother-to-child transmission) in order to cut the number of projected new infections to 2015 in half (Global HIV Prevention Working Group 2007).

The Global HIV Vaccine Enterprise is an international alliance of independent organizations dedicated to accelerating the development of an HIV/AIDS vaccine through collaborative research efforts. The Bill & Melinda Gates Foundation serves as interim chair and funds vaccine research. In July 2006, the Bill & Melinda Gates Foundation funded 16 grants totaling USD 287 million to create an international network of collaborative research consortia focused on accelerating the pace of HIV vaccine development (http://www.gatesfoundation.org).

7.6.3.2 Henry J. Kaiser Family Foundation

The Kaiser Family Foundation is a non-profit, private operating foundation focusing on the major health care issues facing the United States, but has a growing role in global health. The foundation has an endowment of over half a billion dollars and an operating budget of over USD 40 million per year. Unlike grant-making foundations, Kaiser develops and runs its own research and communications programs, sometimes in partnership with other non-profit research organizations or major media companies. This foundation focuses on three areas of activity: (1) Producing policy analysis and research; (2) Operating a large-scale health news and information service on the web and a series of specialized websites; and (3) Developing and helping to run large-scale public health information campaigns in the United States and around the world, through direct partnerships with major media companies. The current focus of the latter is on HIV/AIDS, with an emphasis on reaching young people (http://www.kff.org/about/index2.cfm).

7.6.3.3 William J. Clinton Foundation

The William J. Clinton Foundation is President Bill Clinton's vehicle for strengthening the capacity of people in the United States and throughout the world to meet the challenges of global interdependence. One of the foundation's main initiatives is focused on HIV/AIDS. In 2007, the foundation helped to negotiate major price reductions for 66 developing countries for 16 medicines critical to fighting HIV/

AIDS, in an agreement with pharmaceutical manufacturers (see Chap. 9). These countries together have 90% of AIDS cases in the developing world. The foundation's HIV/AIDS Initiative (CHAI) has also involved political leadership from President Clinton to reduce fear and ignorance of the disease and to discourage discrimination. Donations are the primary source of revenue for the foundation, making up USD 109,730,002 of the USD 112,687,167 in revenue for 2006 (http://www.clintonfoundation.org).

The Clinton Foundation also funds access to treatment and information. It has committed USD 38 million to fund a 3-year program to ensure all HIV-positive children in Kenya receive treatment. The funds would pay for a public awareness campaign and purchase anti-retroviral drugs to rapidly scale up the number of infected children under treatment from 2009 to 2010. Half all HIV-positive children in Kenya die before their second birthday; 50% of those die because they are not provided with treatment. Anti-retroviral therapy would increase the life expectancy to 27 years. Of an estimated 102,000 HIV-positive children, 60,000 are in need of treatment and only 13,000 are on life-saving anti-retroviral therapy. A survey commissioned by the Kenyan Ministry of Medical Services showed that 61% of mothers and caregivers were unaware of the availability of HIV testing for children and that only 12% had taken their children for HIV testing (Ndegwa 2007).

7.6.3.4 Private Sector Collaboration

There is also collaboration among private firms, private foundations and host governments. For example, an innovative model for fighting HIV/AIDS in Africa is being piloted in Botswana through a public-private partnership involving the government of Botswana, the Bill & Melinda Gates Foundation and Merck & Co., Inc. The partnership is intended to help Botswana achieve an "AIDS-Free Generation by 2016" by expanding prevention, supporting treatment, increasing counseling and testing and empowering communities (Center for Global Development and Merck 2007).

7.7 Implications for Other Global Diseases

The main focus of this chapter has been on multilateral financial institutions. However, it is important to note the role of other financial donors, notably bilateral governmental arrangements. Private actors and NGOs also make significant contributions to addressing the global AIDS pandemic. As important as it is to marshal the resources of numerous governmental and non-governmental agencies, the multiplicity of donors involved in the AIDS epidemic, together with a multiplicity of donor requirements, is a significant issue in seeking to expand prevention and treatment programs.

National political leadership is a crucial part of any HIV/AIDS strategy. In many countries, statements made by politicians who make decisions on resource allocation have been appalling. In South Africa, Tshabalala-Msimang, the health minister, shares South African President Mbeki's rejection of the international scientific consensus that AIDS is caused by the HIV. The health minister has also criticized the use of standard anti-retroviral drugs to treat AIDS, recommending instead that South Africans with AIDS follow a diet of beetroot, garlic, olive oil and African potato. In a recent South African population survey, a quarter of the population said they didn't believe in a link between HIV and AIDS (Wilson 2007). Figure 7.17 reveals the impact of misinformation on South Africans perceptions regarding the sources of HIV transmission.

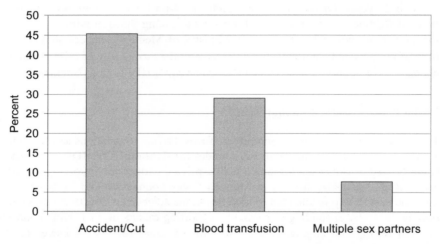

Fig. 7.17 Confusion in South Africa regarding sources of HIV transmission. *Source*: Wilson (2007)

The head of the Catholic Church in Mozambique, Maputo Archbishop Francisco Chimoio, has told the media he believes some European-made condoms are infected with HIV deliberately. He has also claimed some anti-retroviral drugs were also infected "in order to finish quickly the African people". The Catholic Church opposes any use of condoms, advising instead fidelity within marriage or sexual abstinence. About 17.5% of Mozambicans are Catholic and roughly 16.2% of Mozambique's population is HIV positive (BBC News 2007a). These lapses in political leadership highlight the need to incorporate political leadership into AIDS programs that are funded by multilateral, bilateral and private sector donors.

Multilateral institutions, such as the World Bank, the IMF and the Global Fund, and bilateral donors, including NGOs and national governments, need to coordinate and harmonize their policies and financing conditions further in order to reduce the administrative burden on recipients and in order to avoid imposing conflicting conditions on recipients. Donors also need to be careful with respect to the role assigned to the private sector in delivering aid, in order to avoid the unnecessary diversion of funds away from the core goal of health care. In this regard, the experience to date suggests that social marketing is less effective and less equitable than the free provision of goods and services. Particularly in the case of fast-moving infectious diseases, equitable and effective distribution should be paramount, since such diseases are unlikely to respect socio-economic boundaries, as the experience with HIV/AIDS and malaria has demonstrated. In particular, donors should not impose requirements to use patented medicines in place of cheaper, generic alternatives.

The global business community has an important role to play in addressing global diseases. There are several key lessons that arise from the GBC's experience with HIV/AIDS. First, it is important to integrate health issues into overall business strategy, particularly since it takes about 3 years to fully implement such strategies. Second, there is a need to standardize best practices on a more systematic basis and to create incentives for those best practices to be adopted by suppliers and business partners of global companies. In this regard, the creation of ISO standards for company health policies would be extremely useful, particularly for fast-moving global infectious diseases that have the potential to cause widespread economic damage and human suffering, such as avian influenza and SARS.

The global response to the HIV/AIDS pandemic has highlighted the need to strengthen health care infrastructure in developing countries. There is a concern that the high profile given to the HIV/AIDS pandemic may have diverted funds away from other important health issues (England et al., 2007). In Chap. 4 we concluded that the focus on HIV/AIDS is justified, but it is important to address the HIV/AIDS pandemic in a way that strengthens the ability of national governments and multilateral organizations to address health concerns more generally. The following chapter examines the role of global health organizations in the HIV/AIDS pandemic, with a particular focus on the World Health Organization, which is the multilateral institution that is charged with addressing global health issues.

References

Alsan M, Bloom DE, Canning D (2004) The Effect of Population Health on Foreign Direct Investment. NBER Working Paper No. 10596, http://papers.nber.org/papers/w10 596. Accessed 15 August 2005

BBC News (2007a) Shock at Archbishop Condom Claim. http://news.bbc.co.uk/2/hi/africa/7014335.stm. Accessed 26 September 2007

BBC News (2007b) HIV Treatment 'Failing' in Africa. http://news.bbc.co.uk/2/hi/africa/7046545.stm. Accessed 16 October 2007

Bloom DE, Mahal A, River Path Associates (2001) HIV/AIDS and the Private Sector – A Literature Review. http://www.psp- one.com/content/resource/detail/2612/. Accessed 5 June 2006

Center for Global Development (2005) Private Sector Responses to HIV/AIDS: The Case of Debswana, Botswana's Diamond Company. http://www.cgdev.org/content/calendar/detail/4258/. Accessed 15 June 2006

Center for Global Development and Merck (2007) Can Public-Private Partnerships Help Stop AIDS in Africa? Lessons from Botswana. http://www.cgdev.org/content/calendar/detail/13758/. Accessed 5 September 2007

Dekay S (2004) Funding the Response to AIDS: Why are Donors not Working Together? 15th Annual International AIDS Conference, Bangkok http://www.kaisernetwork.org/health_cast/uploaded_files/071204_ias_funding.pdf. Accessed 5 June 2006

Easterly W (2006) The White Man's Burden. Penguin, New York

ECA Press Release (2003) African Ministers Pronounce on Aid, Trade, Debt, IMF, HIV/AIDS. http://www.uneca.org/eca_resources/press_releases/2003_ pressreleases/pressrelease0803.htm. Accessed 25 June 2007

England R, de Lay P, Greener R, Izazola JA(2007) Are we spending too much on HIV? British Medical Journal 334:344–345

Euro Health Group (2007) Global Fund to Fight AIDS, Tuberculosis and Malaria: Evaluation of the Local Fund Agent System. http://www.theglobalfund.org/en/files/links_reesources/library/studies/specific_evaluations/GFATM_Evaluation_of_LFA_ Report. pdf. Accessed 7 January 2008

GAO (2007) Global Fund to Fight AIDS, TB and Malaria Has Improved its Documentation of Funding Decisions but Needs Standardized Oversight Expectations and Assessments. http://www.theglobalfund.org/en/files/links_resources/library/studies/integrated_evaluations/d07627.pdf. Accessed 7 January 2008

GBC and Booz, Allen, Hamilton (2006) The State of Business and HIV/AIDS. http://www.businessfightsaids.org/atf/cf/%7B4AF0E874-E9A0-4D86-BA28-96C3BC31180A%7D/The%20State%20of%20Business%20and%20HIVAIDSFINAL.pdf. Accessed 19 October 2007

Global Fund (2003) The Framework Document of the Global Fund to Fight AIDS, Tuberculosis and Malaria. http://www.theglobalfund.org/en/files/publicdoc/Framework_uk. pdf. Accessed 5 October 2007

Global HIV Prevention Working Group (2007) Bringing HIV Prevention to Scale: An Urgent Global Priority. http://www.globalhivprevention.org/pdfs/PWG-HIV_prevention_report_FINAL.pdf. Accessed 15 November 2006

Gonzalves G (2004) Funding the Response to AIDS: Why are Donors not Working Together? 15th Annual International AIDS Conference, Bangkok, 12 July 2004, http://www.kaisernetwork.org/health_cast/uploaded_files/071204_ias_funding.pdf. Accessed 5 June 2006

Hanlon J (1999) Pound of flesh: Joseph Hanlon Reports on How Local People have Wised up to a Huge International Hoax. New Internationalist, March 1999, http://findarticles.com/p/articles/mi_m0JQP/is_310/ai_30471475. Accessed 6 October 2007

Hanlon J (2006) Donor Concern over IMF Cap on Aid Increases. http://www.open.ac.uk/technology/mozambique/. Accessed 6 October 2007

IMF (2005) The IMF's Role in the Fight Against HIV/AIDS. http://www.imf.org/external/np/exr/facts/hivaids.htm. Accessed 16 October 2007

Kaberuka D (2007) The New International Aid Architecture: New Players, New Challenges, Old Problems? http://www.ideas4development.org/the-new-international-aid-architecture-new-players-new-challenges-old-problems/en/. Accessed 20 October 2007

Kasheeka EB, Bicego G, Gorgens-Albino M, Kemerer V, Nzima M (2006) Strengthening Partnerships in HIV Monitoring and Evaluation: How Joint Missions Build and Strengthen Partnerships to Support the Realization of National M&E systems. World Bank Working Paper, http://www-wds.worldbank.org. Accessed 5 August 2007

Kates J, Lief E (2006) International Assistance for HIV/AIDS in the Developing World: Taking Stock of the G8, Other Donor Governments, and The European Commission. Kaiser Family Foundation, Center for Strategic and International Studies/UNAIDS, data. unaids.org/pub/BaseDocument/2006/20060731-KFF-international-assistance_en.ppt. Accessed 6 November 2007

Kyama R, McNeil DG Jr (2007) Distribution of Nets Splits Malaria Fighters. www.nytimes.com. Accessed 9 October 2007.

Lee C et al. (2002) Global Fund Responsiveness to Faith-based Organizations. http://www.aidspan.org/documents/other/gfo33.pdf. Accessed 19 October 2007

Love B, Pattanaik S (2007) IMF must Adapt and Downsize or die, New Boss Says. Reuters, 2 October 2007

Lurie P, Hintzen P, Lowe RA (1995) Socioeconomic obstacles to HIV prevention and treatment in developing countries: The roles of the international monetary fund and the World bank. AIDS 9:539–546

McKai R (2004) Funding the Response to AIDS: Why are Donors not Working Together? 15th Annual International AIDS Conference, Bangkok, 12 July 2004, http://www.kaisernetwork.org/health_cast/uploaded_files/071204_ias_funding.pdf. Accessed 2 October 2007

McKinnell H (2004) Funding the Response to AIDS: Why are Donors not Working Together? 15th Annual International AIDS Conference, Bangkok, 12 July2004, http://www.kaisernetwork.org/health_cast/uploaded_files/071204_ias_ funding.pdf. Accessed 8 October 2007

Médecins Sans Frontières (2005) Access to Healthcare, Mortality and Violence in Democratic Republic of the Congo. http://www.doctorswithoutborders.org/publications/reports/2005/drc_healthcare_11-2005.pdf. Accessed 20 October 2007

Mwale B (2004) Funding the Response to AIDS: Why are Donors not Working Together? 15th Annual International AIDS Conference, Bangkok, 12 July 2004, http://www. kaisernetwork.org/health_cast/uploaded_files/071204_ias_funding.pdf. Accessed 19 October 2007

Ndegwa A (2007) Kenya: Clinton Foundation Provides $38M for Children Living with HIV/AIDS. East Africa Standard, 16 October 2007, http://www.eastandard.net/archives/index.php?mnu=details&id=1143976044&catid=159&PHPSESSID=8bf8ad663240a5985ae1e314fcb6c0f3. Accessed 23 October 2007

OECD (2005) The Paris Declaration. http://www.oecd.org/document/18/0, 2340,en_2649_3236398_35401554_1_1_1_1,00.html. Accessed 3 October 2007

OECD (2006) Measuring Aid in support of HIV/AIDS control. http://www.oecd.org/dataoecd/35/52/37266050.pdf. Accessed 23 October 2007

Oomman N, Bernstein M, Rosenzweig S (2007) Following the Funding for HIV/AIDS: A Comparative Analysis of the Funding Practices of PEPFAR, the Global Fund and the World Bank MAP in Mozambique, Uganda and Zambia. http://www.cgdev.org/content/publications/detail/14569/. Accessed 29 October 2007

Oxfam (2006) In the Public Interest: Health, Education, and Water and Sanitation for all. http://www.oxfam.org/en/policy/briefingpapers/bp_public_internest. Accessed 14 October 2007

Patel P (2004) Funding the Response to AIDS: Why are Donors not Working together? 15th Annual International AIDS Conference, Bangkok, 12 July 2004, http://www.kaisernetwork.org/health_cast/uploaded_files/071204_ias_funding.pdf. Accessed 12 October 2007

Perone P (2006) A Response to Joseph Hanlon's Recent Article, Donor Concern Over IMF Cap on Aid Increases. 7 February 2006, http://www.imf.org/external/np/vc/2006/020706.htm. Accessed 15 October 2007

Philips M (2007) Making AIDS patients pay for their care: Why evidence does not change anything in international donor policies? In: Medicins sans Frontieres (ed) AIDS: Free Access to Treatment, a Public Health Necessity or an Economic Heresy?

Picard A (2007) Quarantine Sought for Harsh TB strain: Variant Poses 'Extreme Risk,' Scientists Say. Globe and Mail, 23 January 2007

PriceWaterhouseCoopers (2003) HIV/AIDS: What is Business Doing? A Survey of the Business Community's Response to HIV/AIDS in Kenya, Tanzania, Uganda and Zambia. http://www.psp-one.com/content/resource/detail/2250/. Accessed 24 October 2007

Radelet S (Chair) (2006) Challenges and Opportunities for the New Executive Director of the Global Fund: Seven Essential Tasks. Center for Global Development, http://www.cgdev.org/content/publications/detail/10948/. Accessed 19 October 2007

Radelet S, Siddiqi B (2007) Global Fund grant programmes: an analysis of evaluation scores. Lancet 369:1807–1813

Ramachandran V, Shah MK, Turner G (2005) HIV/AIDS and the Private Sector in Africa: Evidence from the Investment Climate Survey Data. http://rru.worldbank.org/documents/PSDBlog/AIDSpaperOct28.pdf. Accessed 19 October 2007

Reuters (2007) World Bank Chief Calls For New Direction For Lender. 21 October 2007

Sidibe M, Ramiah I, Buse K (2006) Alignment, harmonisation, and accountability in HIV/AIDS. Lancet 368:1853–1854

Smith M (2007) To End an Epidemic: A Study of Foreign Aid and HIV/AIDS. International Relations Thesis, New York University

Technical Evaluation Reference Group (2007) Summary Paper on the Evaluation of the Local Fund Agent System. http://www.theglobalfund.org/en/files/links_resources/library/studies/specific_evaluations/TERG_Summary_Paper.pdf. Accessed 7 January 2008

UNAIDS (2005) Final Report, Global Task Team on Improving AIDS Coordination Among Multilateral Institutions and International Donors (GTT). UNAIDS, Geneva

UNAIDS (2006) Effectiveness of Multilateral Action on AIDS: Harmonized Support to Scaling up the National Response. Report for 18th meeting of the UNAIDS Program Coordination board. UNAIDS, Geneva

Wilson D (2007) The Evolving HIV Epidemic: What Have We Learned Since the MAP Began? powerpoint presentation, 10 June 2007

World Bank (2003) HIV/AIDS in Central America: The Epidemic and Priorities for its Prevention. World Bank, Washington

World Bank (2005a) The World Bank's Global HIV/AIDS Program of Action. World Bank, Washington

World Bank (2005a) Committing to Results: Improving the Effectiveness of HIV/AIDS Assistance, An OED Evaluation of the World Bank's Assistance for HIV/AIDS Control. http://siteresources.worldbank.org/EXTIEGHIVAIDS/Resources/hiv_complete_report.pdf. Accessed 3 October 2007

World Bank (2006) Reducing HIV/AIDS Vulnerability in Central America: regional HIV/ AIDS situation and response to the epidemic. Working Paper, http://www-wds.worldbank.org/ external/default/WDSContentServer/WDSP/IB/2007/02/02/000020953_20070202121215/ Rendered/PDF/385440ENGLISH01nalOverview01PUBLIC1.pdf. Accessed 1 October 2007

World Bank (2007) Rwanda Multi-Country Aids Program (MAP): Em-powering Communities, Harmonizing Approaches, Working Paper. http://www-wds.worldbank.org/ external/default/WDSContentServer/WDSP/IB/2007/09/07/000310607_20070907114625/ Rendered/PDF/406520RW0MAP0communities01PUBLIC1.pdf. Accessed 15 October 2007

World Bank (2007a) Our Commitment: The World Bank's Africa Region HIV/AIDS Agenda for Action 2007-2011. http://siteresources.worldbank.org/EXTAFRREGTOPHIVAIDS/ Resources/WB_HIV-AIDS-AFA_2007-2011_Advance_Copy.pdf. Accessed 19 October 2007

8 The Successes and Failures of Global Health Organizations: The World Health Organization, UNAIDS, Médicins sans Frontières and PEPFAR

"Eight million people die every year for the price of going out with your friends to the movies and buying an ice cream. Literally for about $30 a head per year, you could save eight million lives. Isn't that extraordinary? Preventable disease – not calamity, not famine, nothing like that. Preventable disease – just for the lack of medicines. That is cheap, that is a bargain."

Bono, Lead Singer of U2.

Chapter 7 examined the operations of multilateral, bilateral and private donors in financing the fight against HIV/AIDS. This chapter examines the operations of five organizations that focus more directly on addressing HIV/AIDS health issues on the ground: the World Health Organization; UNAIDS; Médicins sans Frontières (Doctors without Borders); the US President's Emergency Plan for AIDS Relief (PEPFAR); and the US Centers for Disease Control and Prevention. The first two form part of the United Nations (UN) system, the third is a private, non-profit non-governmental organization that relies on volunteers to deliver medical services and products in developing countries that are facing health crises and the fourth and fifth are a US government program and agency, respectively. The UN has won the Nobel Peace Prize a number of times: UN Middle East mediator (1950); UNHCR, the UN refugee agency (1954); UN Secretary-General (1961); UNICEF (1965); ILO, the UN labor agency (1969); UNHCR, the UN refugee agency (1981); UN peacekeeping (1988); and UN Secretary-General and the UN, jointly (2001). There are several bodies inside the UN that also have won the Nobel Peace Prize, such as the International Atomic Energy Agency (2005) and Director Mohamed El-Baradei and the Intergovernmental Panel on Climate Change (2007). In addition, the prime minister of Canada, Lester Bowles Pearson, won Nobel Peace Prize for his work with the UN (1957). Médicins sans Frontières has won the Nobel Peace Prize once (1999).

8.1 The World Health Organization: A Multilateral Health Institution

The World Health Organization (WHO) is charged with directing and coordinating health within the United Nations system. The WHO Constitution came into force on 7 April 1948. The WHO is responsible for providing leadership on global health matters, shaping the health research agenda, setting norms and standards, articulating evidence-based policy options, providing technical support to countries and monitoring and assessing health trends (http://www.who.int/en/). These core functions of WHO in public health for the 10-year period from 2006 to 2015 are set out in the "11th General Programme of Work" (http://whqlibdoc.who.int/publications/2006/GPW_eng.pdf). Article 2 of the WHO Constitution only authorizes assistance to governments and emergency aid upon request. Article 2 also specifically charges the WHO with stimulating and advancing work to eradicate epidemic, endemic and other diseases.

The World Health Assembly governs decision-making for the WHO's 193 Member States and appoints the Director General. Each Member has one vote. It meets annually at the headquarters in Geneva. An Executive Board, composed of 34 members technically qualified in the field of health that are elected for 3-year terms, implements the decisions and policies of the Health Assembly and provides advice to facilitate the work of the Health Assembly (http://www.who.int/governance/en/). The Director General and the secretariat, staffed by almost four thousand health and other experts, play a significant role in making proposals and influencing the agenda and outcomes of the WHO (Stein 2001).

Article 19 of the WHO Constitution authorizes the Health Assembly to adopt conventions or agreements, by a vote of two-thirds of the Assembly, with respect to any matter within the competence of the WHO. If the WHO adopts agreements, they come into force for each member when adopted according to its national constitutional processes. In practice, the WHO takes decisions primarily by consensus through nonbinding and less formal procedures such as recommendations, resolutions, and the promulgation of technical standards or guidelines drawn up by expert bodies (Stein 2001).

Article 21 authorizes the Health Assembly to adopt regulations regarding sanitary and quarantine requirements and other procedures designed to prevent the international spread of diseases, as well as standards for biological, pharmaceutical and similar products moving in international commerce. Article 22 provides that these regulations come into force for the members upon due notice of their adoption by the Health Assembly, unless the Members notify their rejection to the Director General with the period of time stated in the notice. The WHO adopted only two regulations in its first 50 years: Regulation No. 1, Unification of Statistical Classification of Morbidity and Mortality (1948, revised several times); and Regulation No. 2, International Sanitary Regulations (1951) (Stein 2001).

Article 23 authorizes the Health Assembly to make recommendations to Members with respect to any matter within the competence of the WHO. Chapter XIV of the WHO Constitution requires Members to provide annual reports on action taken to improve the health of its people (Article 61) and with respect to WHO recommendations, conventions and agreements (Article 62), and to report health laws, regulations and statistics (Article 63) and to provide statistical and epidemiological reports (Article 64). The International Court of Justice has jurisdiction to interpret the WHO Constitution should disputes arise, unless the relevant parties agree otherwise (Article 75).

8.1.1 Nature of WHO Operations Related to HIV/AIDS

The WHO HIV/AIDS Department forms part of the WHO Cluster for HIV/AIDS, TB and Malaria. The HIV/AIDS department provides technical support to WHO Member States to help them scale up treatment, care, and prevention services within the context of the overall health sector. It is made up of the following seven teams: (1) Prevention in the Health Sector; (2) Antiretroviral Treatment and HIV Care; (3) Operational and Technical Support; (4) Health Systems Strengthening; (5) Strategic Information and Research; and (6) the Office of the Director (ODH) that responds on policy coordination, advocacy communications, resource mobilization and program management (http://www.who.int/hiv/aboutdept/en/index.html).

8.1.2 Scope of WHO Operations Related to HIV/AIDS

The work of the WHO with respect to HIV/AIDS has been largely limited to prevention and treatment issues. The WHO has produced global guidelines for various aspects of prevention and treatment. It has also participated in advocacy, notably with respect to the expansion of access to antiretroviral treatment and other forms of health care for HIV-positive people. It publishes an annual update on the epidemic with UNAIDS.

In addition to the Department of HIV/AIDS, more than 30 other WHO departments have HIV-related functions, as part of WHO global HIV/AIDS program, including the following: (1) Child and Adolescent Health (prevention of mother-to-child HIV transmission, infant feeding, care and management of children with AIDS, integration of HIV/AIDS into the Integrated Management of Childhood Illness guidelines, HIV/AIDS prevention, treatment and care among young people, surveillance and strengthening of adolescent health services and policy development and advocacy); (2) Gender, Women and Health (equitable access to services and treatment for HIV-positive women, integration of gender issues into HIV programs and violence against women within the context of HIV); (3) Immunization, Vaccines and Biologicals (promotion of the development and availability of preventive HIV vaccines); Making Pregnancy Safer (integration of HIV into maternal and neonatal care services); (4) Reproductive Health and Research (integration of HIV into sexual and reproductive health services, prevention and control of sexually transmitted infections, research on standards and quality assurance of male and female condoms and research on male circumcision for HIV prevention, microbicides and hormonal contraceptives for HIV); (5) Medicines Policy and Standards (HIV medicines policies, prequalification, selection and rational use of medicines, intellectual property rights and prices and sources of HIV medicines); (6) Technical Cooperation for Essential Drugs and Traditional Medicine (technical cooperation with countries, development of national HIV medicines policies and strengthening of procurement and supply management systems related to HIV); (7) Essential

Health Technologies (blood transfusion safety, HIV diagnostics, laboratory monitoring of ART and laboratory technology, procurement of diagnostics and laboratory equipment, injection safety, health care worker protection and surgical and clinical procedure safety); (8) Equity in Health (social determinants of health relating to HIV, equity and HIV and equitable access to HIV/AIDS treatment and care); (9) Health Systems Financing, Expenditure and Resource Allocation (donor funding for HIV, HIV accounts within the framework of National Health Accounts, health spending and policies for risk protection and sustainable financing for HIV and financing strategies to enable free access to HIV services); (10) Health Policy, Development and Services (service delivery models for HIV, management of resources and integration of HIV into general health and development policies); (11) Human Resources for Health (country health workforce assessments that focus on HIV, country policies and plans for sustainable workforce development, strengthening of nursing, midwifery and other health worker capacity and performance); (12) Knowledge Management and Sharing (knowledge management strategies and knowledge sharing on HIV); (13) Measurement and Health Information Systems (HIV/AIDS surveillance and estimates, health services mapping, health system metrics and methodologies for monitoring HIV/AIDS scale up in countries, country capacity building for HIV/AIDS surveillance, monitoring and evaluation and ART scale up monitoring); (14) Stop TB Department (management of HIV/TB co-infection, integration of HIV into TB services, integration of TB into HIV services and collaboration with The Global Fund); (15) Global Malaria Program (management of HIV/malaria co-infection, collaboration with Roll Back Malaria Partnership and collaboration with The Global Fund); (16) Public Health Mapping and Geographic Information (application of global strategic information and mapping systems to monitoring of HIV/AIDS services, partners, resources and risks); (17) Control of Neglected Tropical Diseases (HIV and tropical diseases, HIV/leishmania co-infection and disease control in humanitarian emergencies); (18) Epidemic and Pandemic Alert and Response (HIV within the context of strengthening the capacity of countries to prepare for and respond to epidemics and implementation of the International Health Regulations); (19) Nutrition for Health and Development (infant feeding in paediatric HIV/AIDS, nutritional needs of people living with HIV/AIDS, integration of nutrition into HIV policies and programs and integration of HIV into nutrition policies and programs); (20) Mental Health and Substance Abuse (mental health and HIV, including integration of mental health issues into HIV policies and programs, management of mental health and neurological disorders related to HIV, quality of life of people living with HIV/AIDS and prevention and management of substance dependence); (21) Ethics, Trade, Human Rights and Health Law (ethical aspects of equitable access to services, HIV testing and counseling, human rights and HIV, health laws related to

HIV and impact of trade and globalization on HIV); (22) Health Action in Crisis (integration of HIV into humanitarian emergency responses); and (23) Commission on Intellectual Property Rights, Innovation and Public Health (health research and development, particularly HIV medicines, microbicides and vaccines, and implications of intellectual property rights) (http://www.who.int/en/).

8.1.2.1 AIDS Medicines and Diagnostics Service

The AIDS Medicines and Diagnostics Service (AMDS) is a network of technical partners, hosted by the WHO HIV/AIDS department, that support countries' procurement and supply management of HIV commodities. The AMDS collects and disseminates information on prices, availability and the regulatory status of antiretroviral medicines, technical information of HIV diagnostics and condoms through the AMDS website and by other means of communication (http://www.who.int/hiv/amds/about/en/index.html). The WHO also disseminates information on dosage recommendations for ART (http://www.who.int/hiv/treatment/en/index.html).

8.1.2.2 HIV Drug Resistance Prevention, Surveillance and Monitoring

The WHO and its HIV ResNet group of experts and organizations have developed a Global Strategy for HIV Drug Resistance Prevention, Surveillance and Monitoring, to investigate the scale of HIV drug resistance and to prepare countries to respond should drug-resistant HIV epidemics emerge. HIV is able to mutate in order to become resistant to antiretroviral drugs. Drug resistance results in treatment failure, increases health costs due to second-line treatment for patients, leads to the spread of resistant strains of HIV and creates the need to develop new anti-HIV drugs (http://www.who.int/hiv/drugresistance/en/index.html).

8.1.2.3 Prequalification Program for Medicinal Products

In 2001, the WHO created the Prequalification Program to evaluate medicinal products based on unified standards of acceptable quality, safety and efficacy, including those used for HIV/AIDS. The Prequalification Program also engages in capacity building and training of staff from national regulatory authorities, quality control laboratories and manufacturers and certifies quality control laboratories of pharmaceuticals. The WHO list of prequalified medicinal products is used principally by UN agencies to guide their procurement decisions but is also used by other organizations involved in bulk purchasing of medicines (http://mednet3.who.int/prequal/). A notable exception is PEPFAR (see below).

8.1.2.4 Guidelines for Prevention and Care

In 2007, the WHO, with support from the US National Institutes of Health and the US Centers for Disease Control, published guidelines on prevention and care for people living with HIV. Given the continuing gap between the need for antiretroviral treatment (ART) and the number of people who have access to treatment, the WHO developed these guidelines for people living with HIV who are not yet candidates for ART or who do not have access to ART. The focus of the guidelines is to promote health (for example, through nutrition guidelines), prevent transmission (through promotion of safe sex and safe drug use and testing and counseling, for example) and address diseases that have a great impact on the health of HIV-positive people, by preventing opportunistic infections (such as bacterial infections, pneumonia and tuberculosis) and other diseases (such as malaria) (http://www.who.int/en/). The WHO has also prepared guidelines for preventing HIV transmission among injection drug users, guidelines for expanding testing and counseling in health facilities and guidelines for the prevention of mother-to-child transmission of HIV. The WHO and UNAIDS also are developing specific policy recommendations for expanding and promoting male circumcision as a method of HIV prevention.

8.1.2.5 Safety of Blood Products

In May 1975, the Twenty-eighth World Health Assembly passed a resolution that recognized the risk of transmitting diseases through human blood products, especially when donors are paid, and urged Member States to promote voluntary, non-remunerated blood donations, especially in developing countries (http://www.who.int/bloodsafety/en/WHA28.72.pdf).

In January 1987, the Executive Board of the WHO passed a resolution on the rational use of blood products, but it made no mention of AIDS (http://www.who.int/bloodsafety/en/EB79.R1.pdf). In May 1987, the Fortieth World Health Assembly endorsed the WHO global strategy for the prevention and control of AIDS and the establishment of a special program on AIDS. It recognized that information and education on the modes of transmission and the availability of safe blood and blood products were still the only measures available to prevent the spread of AIDS. The Health Assembly also described AIDS as an emergency, urged Member States to make contributions in cash and in kind to implement the global strategy and appealed to bilateral and multilateral agencies to support the worldwide fight against AIDS (http://www.who.int/bloodsafety/en/WHA40.26.pdf). Nevertheless, as noted in Fig. 7.1 in Chap. 7, the total annual resources available to combat AIDS did not increase significantly until 1999, remaining well below USD 1 billion per year from 1986 to 1998. As Fig. 8.1 shows, between the establishment of the WHO AIDS strategy in 1987 and 2005, the estimated number of infections grew from about two million cases to almost forty million.

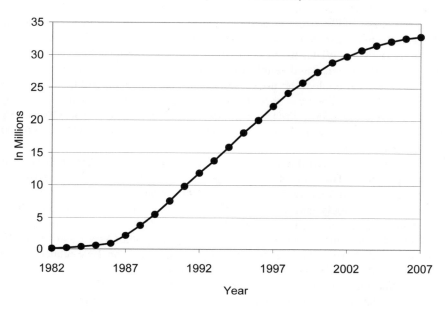

Fig. 8.1. Global tide of HIV/AIDS after the 2007 revision. *Source*: UNAIDS, Avert.org, and own calculations

The risk of AIDS infection through the use of blood products was recognized as early as 1982 (http://epe.lac-bac.gc.ca/100/200/301/hcan-scan/commission_blood_final_rep-e/vol1-e.pdf). However, as late as January 1987, the WHO passed a resolution on blood products that made no mention of AIDS. Moreover, countries were slow to adopt measures to ensure the safety of the blood supply, as shown in Table 8.1. In October 1986, the US FDA recommended that blood donor screening (through "confidential unit exclusion," a questionnaire to identify high-risk donors) be implemented throughout the United States. In Canada, confidential unit exclusion was not implemented nationally until the autumn of 1988. The Canadian Commission of Inquiry on the Blood System in Canada (known as the Krever Commission) found that the Canadian Red Cross could have done much more to reduce the risk of AIDS transmission through blood products and could have reduce the incidence of transfusion-associated AIDS significantly had it taken more vigorous action based on the available knowledge (http://epe.lac-bac.gc.ca/100/20 0/301/hcan-scan/commission_blood_final_rep-e/vol1-e.pdf). France was also slow to adopt effective measures for preventing transfusion-associated AIDS, with the result that France became the Western European country with the highest incidence of AIDS resulting from the use of blood products, between 1985 and 1993. In 1985, the national centre for blood transfusion had made a decision to distribute blood products that were known to be contaminated with HIV (http://epe.lac-bac. gc.ca/100/200/301/hcan-scan/commission_blood_final_rep-e/vol3-e.pdf).

In the early 1990s, Chinese health authorities began to establish commercial blood collection centers and promoted blood-selling by poor farmers, despite warnings from the WHO, based on a belief that only foreign blood was unsafe. The blood fractionation and re-injection process – in which blood from villages was collected and pooled, the useful blood products separated and the remainder re-injected into the donors – spread HIV efficiently to villages across China. In 2000, in Shangqiu county in Henan province, one report found that 62% of 155 people tested for HIV were HIV-positive, while another found that 84% of 100,000 people tested positive.

It has been estimated that there are one million people infected with HIV in Henan province. The Chinese authorities closed commercial blood collection centers and started heat-treating plasma in 1995, when the first HIV infections from the blood supply emerged. Nevertheless, illegal underground blood collection centers have continued to operate. In 2007, new HIV infections through hospital blood transfusions continued to be reported in China (Asia Catalyst 2007). As Table 8.2 shows, China is not the only country with an HIV-related blood scandal. We discuss the special case of Libya in Chap. 9, Box 9.2.

In addition to infection via blood products, there is a risk of HIV infection via organ transplants. In 2007, four Chicago transplant recipients contracted HIV and hepatitis C from a single organ donor, which marked the first incidence of HIV infection contracted from organ donation in the US since 1986, according to the US Centers for Disease Control and Prevention. The organs came from a high-risk donor. Standard tests failed to pick up the infections, likely because they occurred too close to the donor's death for the tests to detect. About 9% of the 22,000 organ transplants in the United States involve high-risk organs (Steenhuysen 2007).

Table 8.1 National adoption of measures to ensure the safety of blood products 1981–1989

Country	First reported	Reportable to public health authorities	First reported AIDS in hemophiliacs	First reported transfusion transmission of HIV/AIDS
Australia	April 1983	May 1983	May 1985	July 1984
Canada	March 1982	May 1983	March 1983	May 1985
France	August 1981	June 1986	June 1983	May 1983
Germany	November 1982	September 1987	April 1983	Unknown
Japan	July 1983	February 1989	July 1983	Late 1984
Netherlands	Autumn 1981	Never	1987	Unknown
United Kingdom	December 1981	Never	August 1983	Unknown
United States	June 1981	May 1983	July 1982	December 1982

Source: Canadian Commission of Inquiry on the Blood System in Canada

Table 8.2 Estimated HIV/AIDS infections due to contaminated blood

Country	Number of victims
China	69,000
United States	11,384
France	6,000
Germany	3,000
Japan	2,000
Mexico	1,844
Canada	1,400
UK	1,341
Libya	426
Australia	206
Netherlands	320
Kazakhstan	100
Iran	70
Tunisia	64
Morocco	36
Saudi Arabia	35
Iraq	34

Source: http://www.asiacatalyst.org/AIDS_blood_scandals_rpt_0907.pdf

8.1.3 The 2005 WHO International Health Regulations

The WHO Constitution envisages the use of binding international health regulations (Article 21) and the promotion and adoption of treaties (Article 19) in order to harmonize national behavior through international standards based on scientific and public health principles (Fidler 1998). Nevertheless, between 1948 and 1998, WHO never used its international legal authority under Article 19 and only adopted two regulations under Article 21. The WHO only adopted its first international treaty in 2003 (the Framework Convention on Tobacco Control) (Fidler 1998). The 1951 International Sanitary Regulations, which consolidated the nineteenth century International Sanitary Conventions, were renamed the International Health Regulations (IHR) in 1969 (von Tigerstrom 2005). The IHR were not updated until 2005, after the 2003 SARS outbreak and the threat of H5N1 influenza added a sense of urgency to a process that began in 1995 (von Tigerstrom 2005).

The IHR (2005), which came into force on 15 June 2007, aim to contain health emergencies at the source, not only at national borders, and apply to all diseases and health events that may constitute a "public health emergency of international concern" (http://www.who.int/features/qa/39/en/index.html). The previous IHR (1969) focused on the control at borders and relatively passive notification and control measures. The limited scope of the IHR (1969), which dealt only with cholera, plague, yellow fever and smallpox, made them irrelevant and ineffective with respect to more recent global public health crises, including HIV/AIDS, SARS and the threat of an influenza pandemic. Moreover, the WHO member states often did not comply with the IHR (1969), by failing to notify the WHO of cases of diseases and applying excessive health measures beyond those permitted by the IHR (1969). The IHR (1969) also limited the WHO's ability to respond to new outbreaks of disease by requiring the WHO to rely on official state notifications, rather than other sources (von Tigerstrom 2005). For example, the Chinese government proved to be a less timely source of information on the SARS outbreak than email and the internet. While the response to SARS was successful, it highlighted the ineffectiveness of the IHR (von Tigerstrom 2005). The key changes to the IHR are with respect to disease coverage, notification requirements, sources of information that the WHO can use and provisions regarding confidentiality of information provided to the WHO. The IHR (2005) also set standards for public health responses to the international spread of disease, but leave States with considerable discretion regarding their implementation at the national level.

The preamble of the IHR (2005) describes the IHR as the "key global instrument for protection against the international spread of disease" and makes reference to natural occurrence, accidental release or deliberate use of chemical and biological agents and radionuclear material that affect health and SARS. While the preamble is not a source of obligations by itself, it is relevant to the interpretation of the IHR (2005), by virtue of Article 31 of the Vienna Convention on the Law of Treaties. Article 2 establishes the purpose and scope of the Regulations in the following terms: "to prevent, protect against, control and provide a public health response to the international spread of disease in ways that are commensurate with and restricted to public health risks, and which avoid unnecessary interference with international traffic and trade." Article 1 defines "public health risk" as "a likelihood of an event that may affect adversely the health of human populations, with an emphasis on one which may spread internationally or may present a serious and direct danger." Article 3 sets out the principles of the Regulations, which include their implementation with full respect for the dignity, human rights and fundamental freedoms of persons and the recognition that States have the sovereign right to legislate and to implement legislation in pursuance of their health policies.

The objective of avoiding unnecessary interference with international traffic and trade reflects the concerns of countries regarding the negative economic impact of disproportionate responses to public health risks that lack scientific justification. There have been many such cases. Following an outbreak of cholera in Peru in 1991, even though the WHO and the US Centers for Disease Control found that there was no basis for travel or trade restrictions, the European Community and other countries imposed import bans on fish and other perishable foods, inspection requirements and restrictions on travelers from Peru. In 1994, after India reported a suspected outbreak of plague in one city, even though the WHO had advised that no travel or trade restrictions were appropriate other countries canceled flights, closed borders to goods and people, and issued travel advisories (von Tigerstrom 2005). Such responses explain the past reluctance of countries to report public health threats. While World Trade Organization (WTO) rules prohibit trade restrictions on food and plants that are not based on scientific evidence, when countries impose unjustified trade restrictions it may take a few years to resolve the matter through the dispute settlement system of the WTO, by which point the economic damage has already occurred. However, in the age of internet, email and mobile telephones, it has become difficult for countries to suppress information on outbreaks of disease.

Article 6 of the IHR (2005) requires States to notify the WHO of all events which may constitute a public health emergency of international concern within its territory and any health measure that has been implemented in response to those events. Article 1 defines "public health emergency of international concern" as an extraordinary event which constitutes a public health risk to other States through the international spread of disease and potentially requires a coordinated international response. "Health measure" is defined as a procedure applied to prevent the spread of disease or contamination, but excludes law enforcement or security measures. According to Annex 2, events must be notified if two of the answers to the following questions are affirmative: (1) Is the public health impact serious? (2) Is the event unusual or unexpected? (3) Is there is a significant risk of international spread? (4) Is there a significant risk of international travel or trade restrictions? Annex 2 lists some diseases that must always be notified (smallpox, poliomyelitis due to wild-type poliovirus, human influenza caused by a new subtype and SARS) and other diseases that must be analyzed under the four criteria in order to determine whether notification is necessary (cholera, pneumonic plague, yellow fever, viral haemorrhagic fevers (such as Ebola, Lassa, Marburg), West Nile fever and other diseases that are of special national or regional concern, such as dengue fever, Rift Valley fever and meningococcal disease). Article 1 defines "disease" as an illness or medical condition, irrespective of origin or source, which presents or could present significant harm to humans.

Article 9 allows the WHO to take into account reports from sources other than notifications or consultations from the affected State, but requires the WHO to consult with and attempt to obtain verification from the State in whose territory the event is allegedly occurring before taking any action based on such reports. Other States can inform the WHO of a public health risk identified outside their territory that may cause international disease spread. Notifications are encouraged by making all information received by the WHO under notification and consultation obligations confidential initially. If the affected State does not accept the WHO's offer of collaboration, the WHO may share the information with other States, when justified by the magnitude of the public health risk (Article 10). Article 11 authorizes the WHO to share information confidentially with all States when it is necessary to enable States to respond to a public health risk. However, the WHO must not make the information generally available to other States until: (1) the event is determined to constitute a public health emergency of international concern; (2) information evidencing the international spread of the infection or contamination has been confirmed by WHO; (3) control measures against the international spread are unlikely to succeed or the State Party lacks sufficient operational capacity to prevent further spread of disease; or (4) the nature and scope of the international movement of travelers, baggage, cargo, containers, conveyances, goods or postal parcels that may be affected by the infection or contamination requires the immediate application of international control measures.

The IHR (2005) establishes an Emergency Committee to give the Director General its views to on the existence and termination of a public health emergency of international concern and on any proposed temporary recommendations. Once the Director General determines that a public health emergency of international concern exists, the Director General will issue temporary recommendations regarding measures to be taken by the affected State or other States to prevent or reduce the international spread of disease and avoid unnecessary interference with international traffic. Article 17 requires that health measures recommended by the Director General be determined on the basis of a risk assessment appropriate to the circumstances, not be more restrictive of international traffic and trade and not more intrusive to persons than reasonably available alternatives that would achieve the appropriate level of health protection. The language of Article 17 echoes some of the legal criteria applied in WTO law to trade-restrictive health measures in order to determine whether they can be justified under the general exceptions of GATT Article XX (b) or permitted under the WTO Agreement on Sanitary and Phytosanitary Measures.

The IHR (2005) also contain provisions regarding health measures applied to travelers. However, the Regulations do not preclude States from requiring medical examination, vaccination or other prophylaxis or proof of vaccination or other prophylaxis: (1) when necessary to determine whether a public health risk exists; (2) as a condition of entry for any travelers seeking temporary or permanent residence; (3) as a condition of entry for any travelers, provided that States base their determinations upon scientific principles, available scientific evidence of a risk to human health and any available specific guidance or advice from the WHO; or (4) to ascertain if there was any travel in or near an affected area or other possible contacts with infection or contamination prior to arrival. However, States are entitled to implement health measures in response to specific public health risks or public health emergencies of international concern, which achieve the same or greater level of health protection than WHO recommendations. If a traveler fails to consent to health measure or refuses to provide the required travel information or health documents, a State may deny entry to that traveler. If there is evidence of an imminent public health risk, the State may compel the traveler to undergo the least invasive and intrusive medical examination that would achieve the public health objective, vaccination or other prophylaxis or additional established health measures that prevent or control the spread of disease, including isolation, quarantine or placing the traveler under public health observation. However, States are required to treat travelers with respect for their dignity, human rights and fundamental freedoms and minimize any discomfort or distress associated with such measures. In Chap. 9, we examine the issue of travel restrictions applied specifically to people living with HIV/AIDS.

The IHR (2005) provide that health measures not be applied to goods in transit without transhipment, other than live animals, unless authorized by applicable international agreements. Container and container loading areas are required to be kept free from sources of infection or contamination.

The foregoing review of the IHR (2005) reveals that their primary focus is on reporting outbreaks of fast-moving diseases and providing recommendations regarding appropriate health measures. While the definition of what constitutes a public health emergency of international concern is no longer limited to a short list of diseases, the lists of diseases in Annex 2 indicate that the Regulations are not primarily concerned with slow-moving diseases, such as HIV/AIDS, endemic diseases, such as malaria, or even common contagious diseases, such as tuberculosis. The central obligation of countries is to report outbreaks of disease, broadly defined, to the WHO. Given modern communication technologies, countries now have an incentive to report disease outbreaks to the WHO, in order to ensure the accuracy of the report and to trigger WHO recommendations. Modern communication technologies (mobile telephones, email and internet) make it very difficult for countries to suppress information regarding outbreaks of contagious diseases. Once the existence of an outbreak becomes known, the level of the public health risk and the effectiveness of the affected country's response will influence the responses of other countries (trade and travel restrictions) and the economic consequences of those responses. The WHO's assessment of the public health risk and the appropriate measures to take will carry more weight than the affected country's assessment of the situation.

Once the outbreak has been reported, the affected country has an incentive to comply with WHO recommendations regarding appropriate responses (see Box 8.1 on incentive compatibility mechanisms), in order to minimize the risk of disproportionate responses on the part of other countries. Failure to comply with WHO recommendations, or under compliance, would have a negative impact on the affected country's effort to persuade other countries to avoid imposing trade and travel restrictions. Given the economic incentives, there is no need for mandatory compliance with WHO recommendations. The key obligation is to report the outbreak, at which point the risk of negative economic consequences becomes real. Compliance with reporting obligations by the affected country is enhanced by modern communications technologies, obviating the need for legal mechanisms to enforce this legal obligation.

Likewise, there is no need for the IHR (2005) to provide enforceable legal obligations to regulate the use of disproportionate trade restrictions in response to a reported outbreak, since those obligations are addressed in WTO law. The key role of the WHO in this regard is to provide an objective risk assessment and to make recommendations regarding appropriate responses based on scientific evidence, both of which are provided for in the IHR (2005). As we noted above, Article 17 requires that health measures recommended by the WHO Director General be determined on the basis of a risk assessment appropriate to the circumstances, not be

---

Box 8.1 Incentive compatible designs

In mechanism designs, a process is said to be incentive compatible if all of the participants get the best "value" when they truthfully reveal any private information the mechanism seeks. In economics, incentive compatible designs are commonplace. One such example is the Vickrey–Clarke–Groves (VCG) auction, in which the highest bidder wins but pays the second highest price. Variants of such mechanisms are used in the sale of US Treasury Securities, stamps on eBay and setting online advertising rates for Google, among others.

In the context of infectious diseases, such as bird flu, the question about incentive compatibility arises because there are two relevant game forms we can consider. First, it is a game between the chicken farmers and the local/national health authorities. Second, it is a game between the national health authorities of the country and international organizations.

In the first game, once livestock on a farm has been infected with influenza, it is not incentive compatible for the farmer to reveal that information to the local or national health authorities. If the farmer does, his birds will be destroyed. Most often, the farmer would not be compensated for the loss. Even if he is, there will be huge disruption in the business. For the local authority, diseased birds in one farm create the risk of contagion in other farms in the area. Because of this externality, the local authority has an incentive to destroy the birds to save the entire community from disaster.

In the second game, the national authorities have an incentive to quickly disseminate information in order to minimize the risk of disproportionate responses on the part of other countries. At the beginning of the SARS outbreak (discussed in Chaps. 2 and 4), the Chinese government tried to minimize the risk of SARS by simple denial. SARS had a big negative impact on China (along with Hong Kong). Trade with and travel to those countries suffered disproportionately. Had the governments acted quickly, they could have reduced the negative impact on trade and travel, along with the deaths and human suffering that SARS caused directly. In the age of the Internet and cellular phones, it is now all but impossible to suppress such information anywhere in the world.

more restrictive of international traffic and trade and not more intrusive to persons than reasonably available alternatives that would achieve the appropriate level of health protection. The WHO's determinations on these issues will be relevant to determine whether trade-restrictive health measures can be justified under the general exceptions of GATT Article XX (b) or permitted under the WTO Agreement on Sanitary and Phytosanitary Measures. Evidence from the WHO has played a role in WTO cases regarding the compatibility of trade-restrictive health measures with GATT and WTO law (Thailand – Restrictions on importation of and internal taxes on cigarettes (1990); European Communities – Measures Affecting Asbestos and Products Containing Asbestos (2001)).

Disproportionate responses that affect the international movement of people still remain within the discretion of national governments and the WHO does not have the authority to interfere with that discretion. Rather, unjustifiable restrictions on the movement of people are more likely to be addressed under international trade agreements that regulate trade-related movement of people, such as the North American Free Trade Agreement. The WTO has not yet negotiated this category of legal provisions, but is likely to be the forum in which such rules will be negotiated on a global basis. Intellectual property rights that affect access to patented medicines are also regulated by the WTO, not the WHO. Thus, it seems both unlikely and unnecessary to extend the mandate of the WHO any further to the regulation of the international movement of goods and people or intellectual property rights, since the WTO regulates these issues at the international level.

8.1.4 The Effectiveness of the WHO

The WHO has had some success in fighting infectious diseases, most notably the eradication of smallpox. However, its health research has focused disproportionately on diseases of concern to developed countries and its narrow focus has led to other agencies entering the health field, such as the World Bank (Stein 2001). The WHO has been criticized for its substantive policies, for its failure to cooperate with the private sector, for excessive or inadequate control of the six regional offices by the headquarters, for weak leadership, cronyism, antiquated management structure and a lack of outreach (Turner 1997). The WHO also suffers from a lack of funding. Its own guidelines provide that funds may not be sought or accepted from commercial enterprises that have a direct commercial interest in the outcome of a project, such as the pharmaceutical industry (Day 2007).

In particular, the WHO has been criticized for not paying sufficient attention to HIV/AIDS (Fidler et al., 1997). The failure of bilateral and multilateral donors to increase funding for AIDS in the 1990s, the failure of national governments to slow the spread of AIDS and the general lack of response to 1987 World Health Assembly recommendations for the prevention and control of AIDS all point to the ineffectiveness of the WHO in implementing its global AIDS strategy and the lateness of its response to the pandemic, particularly the risk of HIV infection through the use of blood products. While limited by its Constitution in its ability to enforce its resolutions in Member States, it is likely that the WHO could have done more to induce countries to respond more quickly and effectively to the AIDS pandemic.

Fidler (1998) analyzed the failure of the WHO to develop and apply health regulations and conventions in response to global health issues and to the HIV/ AIDS pandemic in particular. In Fidler's view, the WHO's lack of interest in international law was anomalous, given the historical use of international law in international health cooperation from 1851 to 1940 (Fidler 1998). Accelerating globalization has changed the context in which the WHO works, and has also hastened the spread of infectious diseases. Moreover, the multiplicity of players involved in tackling global health issues has increased the need for global leadership to convene and coordinate activities related to international health. However, as we noted above, the new International Health Regulations focus on fast-moving diseases, provide binding obligations where necessary (reporting outbreaks) and provide recommendations that do not need to be binding, given the economic incentives for affected countries and the WTO's role in regulating the trade-related responses of other countries. The IHR (2005) are not designed to address diseases like HIV/AIDS, malaria and tuberculosis. However, as we saw in Chap. 7, several other international organizations focus on these diseases, including the World Bank and the Global Fund, that are seeking long-term solutions, such as financing and strengthening health infrastructure and services. The role of the WHO in these diseases is limited to its areas of expertise, which is a sensible approach, given the need to avoid overlap in the activities of international organizations.

Ruger argued that global advocacy for health, bio-ethical and human rights instruments, disease surveillance and application of standards urgently needed strengthening, and that the WHO must reassert its role in integrating, coordinating and advancing the worldwide agenda on health (Ruger 2005). The 2005 International Health Regulations address the concerns regarding disease surveillance and the application of standards to a certain extent, but these activities remain under national control. The area of public health-related human rights is a complex subject, which we address in Chap. 9. The IHR (2005) call for the observance of human rights in responses to public health threats and provide standards in this regard with respect to the application of travel-related measures.

Fidler (1998) has argued that the WHO needs to expand its approach beyond its traditional narrow focus on medical and technical issues, in order to address global health issues in a multidisciplinary fashion. In particular, Fidler has argued that the WHO needs to increase its international legal activity beyond the revised International Health Regulations and the tobacco control convention and to address the diverse areas of international law that relate to its global health mission. These areas include: (1) international trade law; (2) international human rights law; (3) international environmental law; (4) international law on biological, chemical, and nuclear weapons; (5) international maritime law; (6) international labor law; (7) international civil aviation law; (8) the law of the sea; (9) international telecommunications law; (10) international humanitarian law; (11) international intellectual property law; and (12) international law on bioethics. Fidler has proposed the creation of an international legal office at the WHO to service the needs of WHO staff members working on diverse global health questions. While any WHO international legal strategy might face political obstacles, such obstacles do not justify what Fidler has described as "international legal paralysis" at the WHO. However, as we have argued above, the IHR (2005) have been drafted in a way that avoids unnecessary regulation and that focuses on the core competencies of the WHO. Indeed, the IHR (2005) reflect a sophisticated understanding of the role of economic incentives in achieving effective regulation, use language that is compatible with WTO law and avoid overlap with the activities of other international organizations.

However, despite the multiplicity of public and private actors in international health law, Taylor (2004) argued that centralizing international health law-making functions at the WHO is neither feasible nor desirable. The WHO lacks experience and resources for international law-making and member States are unlikely to surrender their national autonomy by granting the WHO greater jurisdiction over international health law. In addition, the WHO has no binding authority over the health-related activities of other international organizations, such as other UN agencies or the WTO. However, as we noted above, the IHR (2005) contain provisions that are compatible with the health-related aspects of WTO law and are likely to influence the determination of the WTO compatibility of trade-related health measures.

8.2 UNAIDS: A Specialized Multilateral Agency

UNAIDS is the Joint United Nations Program on HIV/AIDS that is cosponsored by ten UN system organizations: UNHCR, UNICEF, WFP, UNDP, UNFPA, UNODC, ILO, UNESCO, WHO and the World Bank (http://www.unaids.org). UNAIDS was established in 1994 by a resolution of the UN Economic and Social Council and launched in January 1996. It is guided by a Program Coordinating Board with representatives of 22 governments from all geographic regions, the UNAIDS cosponsors, and five representatives of nongovernmental organizations, including associations of people living with HIV/AIDS (http://www.unaids.org). It has been headed since its creation by Executive Director and Under Secretary-General of the United Nations, Dr. Peter Piot.

8.2.1 Scope of UNAIDS Operations

UNAIDS has five focus areas: (1) leadership and advocacy; (2) strategic information and technical support; (3) tracking monitoring and evaluation; (4) civil society engagement; and (5) mobilization of resources (http://www.unaids.org/en/Coordination/default.asp). It is responsible for developing policy guidance on HIV and serves as the chief advocate for worldwide action against AIDS (http://www.unaids.org).

8.2.1.1 Leadership and Advocacy

UNAIDS provides leadership on the global AIDS agenda and pushes for political commitment from inter-governmental bodies, governments, the broader UN system and other key partners to respond to the evolving epidemic. For example, the World AIDS Campaign advocates for the fulfillment of the UN Declaration of Commitment on HIV/AIDS and subsequent policy commitments on AIDS (http://www.unaids.org). The Global Coalition on Women and AIDS works to lessen the impact of AIDS on women and girls. The Agenda for Action on Women and AIDS urges leaders to address the social, cultural and economic factors that intensify the impact of AIDS on women and girls, advocating stronger protection for women's rights, more funds for AIDS programs that address the needs of women and greater involvement for women's organizations (http://womenandaids.unaids.org/). UNAIDS also publishes an annual report on the global AIDS epidemic, together with the WHO.

Stephen Lewis, the former UN Special Envoy for AIDS, is an articulate and effective advocate for action on AIDS. In 2003, 3 weeks after the decision of the Members of the WTO to change the patent rules in TRIPS to allow the export of pharmaceuticals under compulsory license to developing countries that lack manufacturing capacity, he pushed for action in the following terms:

> [T]he rich world, annually, spends 600 times as much on defense as Africa has for AIDS, and 350 times as much on subsidies as Africa has for AIDS. My use of the phrase 'grotesque obscenity' ... may sound strong, but it wilts in the face of those numbers.... It's time for one of the major industrial countries, in particular, one of the G7 countries, to announce the manufacture and export of generic drugs to Africa. I would wish it to be my country, Canada....

After Lewis' statement, the Canadian government announced plans to change the Canadian patent law to permit the manufacture and export of generic HIV drugs under the new WTO rules. In 2007, Canada became the first country to agree to supply antiretroviral treatment under the amended WTO rules, to Rwanda (see Chap. 5). While it is unfortunate that Canada's internal political process took 4 years to achieve this action, the advocacy of Stephen Lewis was effective in motivating the Canadian government to act.

8.2.1.2 Strategic Information and Technical Support

UNAIDS generates and disseminates data, information and analysis on global, regional and country trends in the HIV/AIDS epidemic to support advocacy and inform policy and strategy formulation by its partners. For example, in 2005, when the first study on male circumcision demonstrated a greater than 60% reduction in HIV acquisition among men who received circumcision, UNAIDS began to develop a United Nations Male Circumcision Work Plan, with WHO, UNICEF, UNFPA, the US National Institutes of Health, the French Agence Nationale de Recherche sur le Sida and the Bill and Melinda Gates Foundation. This plan includes: (1) development of rapid assessment tools to determine male circumcision prevalence, rates of side effects and acceptability; (2) development of programmatic tools; (3) development of a surgical manual; (4) guidance on training, regulatory and licensing issues; (5) assessment of resource needs; (6) methods for estimating the potential impact on the epidemic; and (7) consideration of human rights.

UNAIDS has developed policy papers to define the actions needed to arrest the spread of new HIV infections (UNAIDS 2005a), the resource needs for an expanded response to AIDS in low- and middle-income countries and coverage of selected services for HIV/AIDS prevention, care and support in low- and middle-income countries (UNAIDS 2005b).

8.2.1.3 Tracking, Monitoring and Evaluation

UNAIDS works to harmonize monitoring and evaluation approaches at the global, regional and country levels. It also monitors the progress on the 2001 UN General Assembly's Declaration of Commitment on HIV/AIDS, which sets out concrete, time-bound commitments for a comprehensive and effective global response to the epidemic. In this regard, UNAIDS issued national guidelines for monitoring the implementation of the Declaration of Commitment and prepares a progress report on implementation for review and discussion at UN General Assembly. The Country Response Information System monitors and evaluates national responses to HIV/AIDS. The Resource Tracking and Projections system monitors and evaluates the flow of financial resources from funding sources to actual expenditure. UNAIDS also collects data quantifying HIV/AIDS financing in low- and middle-income countries in order to provide estimates of available financing, to track progress toward meeting resource requirements and to monitor progress against the financing goals set out in the 2001 declaration. The UNAIDS Secretariat also works to define and project the developing world's HIV/AIDS financing needs. UNAIDS collects both global and national data. The National AIDS Spending Assessment calculates the financial gap between resources available and resources needed (http://www.unaids.org).

8.2.1.4 Engagement and Partnerships

UNAIDS facilitates the involvement of civil society, people living with HIV and high-risk groups in global, regional and national partnerships in policy and program decision-making, including UNAIDS itself, based on the following principles: (1) full involvement of people living with HIV and their organizations; (2) human rights and gender sensitivity; (3) involvement of all key populations in planning and implementation of actions that have an impact on them; (4) encouragement, support and resources for appropriate actions in the changing epidemic; (5) replicating strategic partnerships and applying lessons learned; (6) applying the Three Ones principle (the three principles for coordinated response at the country level: (i) one agreed HIV/AIDS action framework that provides the basis for coordinating the work of all parties; (ii) one national AIDS coordinating authority, with a broad based multi-sector mandate; and (iii) one agreed country level monitoring and evaluation system); (7) focus on efficiency and accountability; (8) building capacity of all parties; and (9) seeking opportunities to learn and move the AIDS response forward (http://www.unaids.org).

UNAIDS engages diverse civil society organizations, including: (1) organizations and networks of people living with HIV; (2) AIDS-focused NGOs; (3) faith-based organizations; (4) development and humanitarian organizations and agencies; (5) advocacy organizations; (6) labor; (7) business and private sector coalitions; and (8) private philanthropic organizations and foundations (http://www. unaids.org).

8.2.1.5 Mobilization of Resources

UNAIDS seeks to mobilize increased human, technical and financial resources to meet priority needs in the response to the epidemic and to maximize the effective and efficient use of available resources. Together with leaders from donor and developing country governments, civil society, UN agencies and other multilateral and international institutions, UNAIDS formed a working group to review and revise the assumptions behind the financial resource needs for AIDS (http://www. unaids.org).

8.2.2 Effectiveness of UNAIDS

In the case of UNAIDS, the issue of effectiveness relates more to the effectiveness of the UN system, rather than just the effectiveness of the UNAIDS secretariat in particular. The very creation of UNAIDS suggests that the existing institutions of the UN were not effective in addressing the HIV/AIDS pandemic. In particular, the creation of UNAIDS highlights the ineffectiveness of the WHO in addressing the HIV/AIDS pandemic, which already had a mandate to address global health issues. While there is a need for political leadership and advocacy to address

HIV/AIDS, as well as a need to incorporate HIV/AIDS issues into the operations of various organs of the UN, the WHO could have been charged with these tasks. Indeed, the creation of UNAIDS, while it is a potentially useful coordinating mechanism, creates further risks of duplication and overlap between the activities of multilateral institutions with respect to HIV/AIDS, a problem discussed in Chap. 7. While the creation of UNAIDS serves to highlight the importance of HIV/AIDS, this precedent raises concerns about the ability of the UN system to effectively address similar global diseases that already exist or that are likely to emerge in the future. The creation of new UN agencies to address specific global diseases as they arise is a less desirable strategy than improving the effectiveness of existing institutions.

Médecins Sans Frontières has noted the increasing politicization of the international system of aid, in particular the UN system, and urged that the UN improve the effectiveness of relief actions by upholding and implementing humanitarian principles by the operational agencies of the UN in order to strengthen the impartiality and independence of humanitarian action and to respond more quickly and effectively to humanitarian disasters (Dubuet and Tronc 2006).

The former UN Special Envoy for AIDS, Stephen Lewis, has characterized UNAIDS' 2007 Epidemic Update as a symbol of insufficient leadership within the United Nations against the AIDS pandemic (we critique the UNAIDS methodology in Chap. 3). In particular, he has been a severe critic of UN inaction with respect to women, who constitute 61% of HIV infections in Africa, and called for action on the High-Level Panel on UN Reform that recommended the creation of a new international agency for women. He has also urged the UN to intensify HIV prevention, to focus on high-risk groups, to speed up male circumcision, to overcome ambivalence on harm reduction strategies for injection drug users, to stop neglecting mother-to-child transmission and to pursue the quest for a microbicide and a vaccine (Lewis 2007).

8.3 Doctors Without Borders (Médicins sans Frontières)

Médecins Sans Frontières (MSF) is an international humanitarian aid organization that has provided volunteer emergency medical assistance since 1971, currently in more than 70 countries. In countries where health structures are insufficient, MSF collaborates with local authorities to provide assistance. MSF also works in rehabilitation of hospitals and dispensaries, vaccination programs, water and sanitation projects and provides training of local personnel, with the objective of rebuilding health structures to acceptable levels. MSF seeks to raise awareness of crisis situations. MSF also seeks to address human rights violations encountered by field teams, by confronting the responsible actors, by mobilizing the international community and by issuing information publicly. MSF maintains neutrality and independence from individual governments and seeks to raise money for its work directly from the general public (http://www.msf.org).

8.3.1 Operations Related to HIV/AIDS

MSF has been caring for people living with HIV/AIDS since the mid-1990s. In 2001, the organization started offering ARV treatment to patients in Cameroon, Thailand and South Africa. A sharp decrease in prices caused by generic competition and the simplification of treatment protocols, including the use of three-in-one fixed-dose combinations (which combine triple combination therapy in one pill) has enabled MSF to rapidly increase the number of patients using ARVs in its programs. MSF provides comprehensive care for people living with HIV/AIDS, including prevention efforts (health education, prevention of mother-to-child transmission of HIV, condom distribution), voluntary counseling and testing, nutritional and psychological support, care and prevention of opportunistic infections and ARV treatment. Between 2002 and 2004, the number of MSF patients on ARVs increased from 1,500 patients in 10 countries to 13,000 patients in 25 countries (Calmy 2004). MSF more than doubled the number of patients under ARV between 2004 and 2005 (MSF 2006).

In 2005, 63% of MSF projects were located in Africa, followed by 23% in Asia. This represented an increase over activities in Asia in 2004 and was the result of natural disasters that affected Central and Southeast Asia in 2005. MSF closed and opened more than 25% of its projects during 2005 in response to evolving developments and crises (MSF 2006). In 2005, 47% of MSF projects took place in unstable settings, such as areas experiencing armed conflicts. Figures 8.2 and 8.3 show the expenditures of MSF by category and continent, respectively. Table 8.3 shows the financial picture for MSF in recent years.

8.3.2 Effectiveness of MSF Operations

MSF has filled a niche with its capacity to respond quickly and flexibly to humanitarian crises, particularly where political considerations or hazardous conditions slow the response of other organizations. In 1999, MSF was awarded the international Nobel Peace Prize, "in recognition of the organization's pioneering humanitarian work on several continents." MSF used the proceeds from the Nobel Peace Prize to establish a Neglected Disease Fund, designed to support pilot projects world-wide that facilitate clinical development, production, procurement and distribution of neglected disease treatments (http://www.doctorswithoutborders.org).

MSF has concluded that the best service for populations in need will come as a result of independence of action rather than participation in an integrated effort. The reasons that MSF gives for its decision to withdraw from collective efforts are: (1) confusion between political and humanitarian agendas, especially in conflict situations, such as Sierra Leone in the 1990s, or more recently Darfur and Lebanon; (2) donors' agendas are not always compatible with humanitarian imperatives; (3)

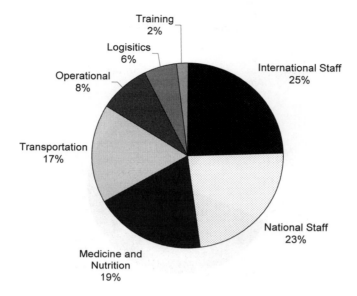

Fig. 8.2 Expenditure of MSF by category. Source: http://www.msf.org/msfinternational/ invoke.cfm? objectid = 992D03D9-5056-AA77-6C9F7BBBE9771A9F&component=toolkit. article&method=full_html

the efforts of donors and multilateral institutions to improve the functioning, coordination, accountability and efficiency of the aid system have resulted in the integration of political, military, civil affairs and humanitarian agendas; (4) the UN decision-making process integrates political and humanitarian agendas, which in practice has led to the subordination of the humanitarian agenda (Stobbaerts 2007). However, as we noted in Chap. 7, duplication and overlap in the activities of the growing number of actors involved in addressing the HIV/ AIDS pandemic can diminish the efficient use of limited resources and act as an impediment to scaling up prevention and treatment.

8.4 US President's Emergency Plan for AIDS Relief (PEPFAR)

The US President's Emergency Plan for AIDS Relief (PEPFAR) is one of the three largest donors of aid for AIDS in the world, the other two being the World Bank and the Global Fund. With the *United States Leadership Against HIV/AIDS, Tuberculosis, and Malaria* Act of 2003 (P.L. 108-25), the Bush administration committed USD 15 billion from 2003 to 2008. The United States Congress placed the following conditions on the funding: (1) 55% of funding would go to treatment

Expenditure by Continent

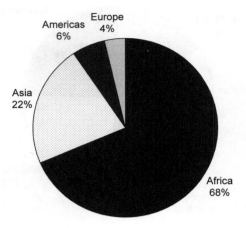

Fig. 8.3 Expenditure of MSF by continent. *Source*: http://www.msf.org /msfinternational/ invoke.cfm?objectid=992D03D9-5056-AA77-6C9F7BBBE9771A9F&component=toolkit. article&method=full_html

Table 8.3 MSF balance sheets 2006 and 2005

	2006 millions €	2005 millions €
Non-current assets	35.5	31.7
Current assets	66.6	91.2
Cash and equivalents	352.1	201.8
Total assets	454.2	324.7
Total retained earnings and equities	388.9	235.8
Non-current liabilities	8.5	7.6
Current liabilities	49.9	43.3
Unspent temporarily restricted funds	6.8	38.0
Total liabilities and retained earnings	65.2	324.7

Source: http://www.msf.org/msfinternational/invoke.cfm?objectid=992D03D9-5056-AA77-6C9F7BB BE9771A9F&component=toolkit.article&method=full_html

of individuals with HIV/AIDS; (2) 15% would go to palliative care for people with AIDS; (3) 20% would be spent on prevention, of which a third would go to abstinence-until-marriage programs; and (4) 10% would help orphans and vulnerable children, of which 50% would fund non-profit organizations, including faith-based organizations. In 2005, PEPFAR increased the percentage of prevention funding that goes to abstinence programs to two-thirds (PEPFAR Fact Sheet 2007; PEPFAR 2005). PEPFAR funding is focused on 15 countries, of which 12 are in Africa, two in the Caribbean and one in Asia (Fillinger 2006). The 15 focus countries receiving PEPFAR funds are Botswana, Côte d'Ivoire, Ethiopia, Guyana, Haiti, Kenya, Mozambique, Namibia, Nigeria, Rwanda, South Africa, Tanzania, Uganda, Vietnam and Zambia. In addition, other countries can receive PEPFAR aid, such as India (http://hivinsite.ucsf.edu/InSite?page=pr-rr-10#S1.7X). In 2007, the Bush administration sought to extend the program a further 5 years and to double the funding to USD 30 billion.

In a study by the Center for Global Development, PEPFAR scored well on making its money move and on collecting data. However, the study also found that PEPFAR could improve its effectiveness by: (1) making the government a true partner in PEPFAR programs; (2) increasing the flexibility of programming and funding; (3) strengthening its capacity-building activities in the host country; (4) adopting 2-year cycles for Country Operational Plans; and (5) publicly disclosing data (Oomman et al., 2007). In a comparative study of US and World Bank funding for HIV/AIDS between 1995 and 1999 (prior to the introduction of PEPFAR), Smith (2007) found that the United States targeted aid for HIV/AIDS to the countries most in need and that used the resources most efficiently, rather than allocating aid for HIV/AIDS in exchange for foreign policy concessions.

PEPFAR has been taken to task for not allocating a larger percentage of funds to prevention. It has been chastised for requiring that generic drugs be approved by the US FDA, Canada, Japan or Western Europe and not funding drugs that have been approved by the WHO. In fiscal year 2006, only 27% of spending on drug procurement went to generic drugs (PEPFAR Fact Sheet 2007). The result of this policy has been that less drug treatments could be purchased than would have been purchased if a greater percentage of generic equivalents had been funded and a large percentage of the PEPFAR budget has been used to purchase drugs from US pharmaceutical companies (Fillinger 2006). In addition, PEPFAR has not enforced appropriate donor guidelines, and it imposed the condition that the majority of the funding for prevention be targeted at abstinence-only programs.

According to PEPFAR guidelines on preventing HIV transmission among injection drug users (IDUs), the most effective strategy for preventing HIV/AIDS is one that decreases drug use and includes information and education, community outreach, risk reduction counseling and substance abuse treatment. Funding may not be used to support needle exchange programs (US Department of State 2006). Needle exchange programs are politically controversial. A 1993 review of needle exchange programs, commissioned by the US Centers for Disease Control and Prevention, reported that ten of fourteen acceptably executed studies found attendance at a needle exchange to be associated with reduced syringe sharing, and four found no such association (Kahn 1993). Four studies that examined the impact of exchange programs on high-risk sexual behaviors were inconclusive (Gibson 1998). In a study that compared HIV prevention strategies in Denmark, Norway and Sweden, researchers concluded that a high level of HIV counseling and testing might be more effective than needle exchange programs alone in preventing HIV transmission among IDUs (Amundsen et al., 2003). However, there is clear evidence that needle exchange programs have reduced HIV transmission rates among IDUs in areas where they have been established. Six US government-funded reports concluded that needle exchange reduces HIV transmission, four of which recommended revoking the federal funding ban on needle exchange programs (Gibson 1998). A 1997 study of 81 cities worldwide found that HIV infection rates increased by 5.9% per year in the 52 cities without needle exchange programs and decreased by 5.8% per year in the 29 cities that did provide needle exchange programs (Hurley et al., 1997). Another study of HIV among IDUs in New York found that HIV prevalence fell from 54 to 13% following the introduction of needle exchange programs (Jarlais et al., 2005). A 2004 WHO report also found that needle exchange programs reduce HIV infection (World Health Organization 2004). In reviewing this evidence, Magee concluded that the refusal to implement such programs for political or moralistic reasons undermines efforts to control the spread of HIV among IDUs (Magee 2007). Indeed, US opposition to needle exchange programs has undermined not just the effectiveness of PEPFAR in HIV prevention and treatment. In 2006, the WHO Asia-Pacific conference withdrew a resolution calling for universal access to HIV/AIDS treatment because the United States insisted on amendments to remove expressions of support for items such as needle exchange programs (Associated Press 2006).

Although PEPFAR guidelines state that men who have sex with men should be a priority for HIV prevention, the Ugandan Information Ministry has protested to UNAIDS about the inclusion of gay people in the planning of HIV prevention initiatives. The Ugandan AIDS commission has defended the lack of any reference to gay or bisexual men in the country's HIV strategy on the grounds that homosexuality is illegal. Organizations that actively promote hatred of gay people and disseminate inaccurate information about the reliability of condoms are barred from receiving PEPFAR funds. However, Pastor Martin Ssempa's Makerere Community Church received USD 40,000 in PEPFAR funding to provide an abstinence education program. The Pastor helped organize a rally demanding government action against gay people, calling homosexual conduct "a criminal act against the laws of nature." The Makerere Community Church also disseminates information stating that condoms do not protect against HIV and has burnt condoms in public. Human Rights Watch has called on the US government to clarify its opposition to attacks on the rights of gay people in Uganda and to articulate that it does not support the use of PEPFAR funds to promote homophobia (Carter 2007).

PEPFAR has been criticized for the preference for abstinence-only programs and for not promoting the use of condoms (The Economist 2007). A recent study indicates that abstinence-only programs are as effective as providing no information at all when it comes to preventing pregnancies, unprotected sex and sexually transmitted diseases. Abstinence-plus interventions, which promote sexual abstinence as the best means of preventing HIV, but also encourage condom use and other safer-sex practices, are more effective than abstinence-only programs (Underhill et al., 2007). PEPFAR's abstinence directive has also resulted in less funding being available for prevention activities that had nothing to do with sex, such as prevention of mother-to-child transmission and strategies to ensure blood transfusion safety (Akukwe 2007).

The US government has been criticized more generally for using its foreign aid policies to advance an ideological agenda for health care in developing countries. Fillinger has noted three areas where this has occurred to the detriment of the efforts to combat HIV/AIDS in developing countries: (1) the Mexico City Policy, which prevents USAID funding for family planning from going to foreign NGOs that use funding from any source to provide counseling and referrals for abortions, advocate making abortion legal or more available in their country or perform abortions in cases not involving a threat to the woman's life, rape or incest; (2) the PEPFAR policy that promotes abstinence only programs, which do not prevent the transmission of HIV within marriages and fail to promote the use of condoms for HIV/AIDS prevention; and (3) the prohibition on requiring prior USAID experience, which allows faith-based organizations to be deemed competitive for US funding based on factors other than experience (Fillinger 2006). The latter was implemented by a USAID policy directive following an Executive Order in 2004. In 2005, USAID issued a policy directive to: (1) permit recipients of funding to not use a multisectoral approach to HIV prevention and to not participate in prevention and treatment programs to which the recipient organization has a moral or religious objection; (2) to prohibit the use of funding to promote the practice or legalization of prostitution and sex trafficking; and (3) to require organizations that receive PEPFAR funding to sign a certification opposing prostitution and sex trafficking (USAID 2005). This policy undermines HIV/AIDS prevention by further stigmatizing sex workers and discouraging programs that address them (Fillinger 2006). Fillinger concluded that these ideological policies undermine best practices in HIV/AIDS programs and disproportionately hurt women, who are already disproportionately affected by HIV/AIDS.

When individual donors come with pre-established priorities, without involving host countries in the setting of priorities, donor coordination is more difficult (Dekay 2004). As we noted in Chap. 7, a lack of donor coordination is an obstacle to expanding treatment and prevention programs. PEPFAR has established priorities that reflect the political interests of the US government and that do not necessarily coincide with the priorities of host governments. This approach undermines coordination and local leadership (Mwale 2004). Moreover, while PEPFAR has a good system for collecting data on the amounts, destination and use of its funds, much of this data (such as how much money is spent on treatment) is not made public and not shared with other stakeholders (or even US government staff that work on PEPFAR, at USAID and the CDC) (Bernstein and Hise 2007). This lack of transparency further complicates donor coordination.

The PEPFAR policy on approved medications has undermined the WHO program on prequalified medications and favored the interests of the US pharmaceutical industry, to the detriment of expanded access to treatment. PEPFAR has made progress expanding the number of patients on ARVs using mainly private health care providers and contractors. However, there is some concern that promoting private care may contribute to the reduction of public health expenditures (Philips 2007). Former Afghan Finance Minister, Ashraf Ghani, has also criticized bilateral donors, particularly the United States. He spent 60% of his time as Finance Minister dealing with a multitude of donors. As a result, he favors multi-lateral coordination of donors. He also noted that one dollar of cash from the World Bank was worth five dollars on the ground, whereas one dollar of US aid was worth only ten cents on the ground, because the other 90 cents got "spread around the beltway" (BBC World 2007). This was likely a reference to a report that USAID was spending 95% of its malaria budget on consultants and 5% on goods like nets, drugs and insecticide (Kyama and McNeil, 2007). The role of the private sector is discussed more broadly in Chap. 7.

8.5 US Centers for Disease Control and Prevention (CDC)

The CDC is part of the US Department of Health and Human Services. In addition to its work in the United States, the CDC is involved in global health activities. The CDC is a recognized source of expertise, particularly in responding to outbreaks of infectious diseases around the world. The CDC is also a valuable source of research and publications on public health issues. Its work outside the United States, with national partners and the WHO, represents a valuable contribution to global health and a recognition of the interconnectedness of global health issues.

The Coordinating Office for Global Health (COGH) coordinates the CDC's global health activities with partners outside the United States and provides leadership to: (1) increase life expectancy and years of quality life, especially among those at highest risk for premature death, particularly vulnerable children and women; and (2) increase the global preparedness to prevent and control naturally-occurring and man-made threats to health (http://www.cdc.gov/about/organization/cogh.htm). The CDC acts as a source of international technical assistance, and is increasing its role in the direct provision of global prevention and prevention research programs. The Division of Global Public Health Capacity Development (formerly called the Division of Epidemiology and Surveillance Capacity Development) works with national and international organizations and foreign governments to improve public health systems through training, consultation, capacity building, and assistance in applied epidemiology, public health surveillance, evaluation, instructional design and other disciplines.

The CDC conducts and publishes research on public health issues, including the Morbidity and Mortality Weekly Report, which provides scientific information recommendations on public health issues (http://www.cdc.gov/mmwr/), the Emerging Infectious Diseases Journal (http://www.cdc.gov/ncidod/EID/index. htm) and the Preventing Chronic Disease Journal (http://www.cdc.gov/pcd/). The CDC has also developed tools to assist in preparing for an influenza pandemic (which we discuss further in Chap. 9).

The CDC responds to health emergencies in the United States and in the rest of the world, responding to outbreaks of infectious diseases by deploying staff, monitoring the spread of disease and training public health staff from other countries. Through the Global Diseases Detection program, CDC staff detects, confirms and stops the spread of infectious diseases in different parts of the world. For example, in 2006 the Global Diseases Detection program investigated more than 60 disease outbreaks in Thailand, Kenya, Guatemala and China. With respect to HIV/AIDS, the CDC provides support to partners in the PEPFAR program, including surveillance, laboratory capacity building, training, monitoring and evaluation and health care for people living with HIV/AIDS. The CDC also works with the WHO, for example in conducting a survey that identified extensively drug-resistant tuberculosis as a global phenomenon (CDC 2006).

With respect to HIV/AIDS, the CDC issues recommendations and guidelines for the United States regarding: community planning; counseling and testing; evaluation; non-occupational post-exposure prophylaxis; occupational exposure and post-exposure prophylaxis; patient care; prevention; surveillance; and treatment. Through its Global AIDS Program, the CDC's physicians, epidemiologists, public health advisors, behavioral scientists and laboratory scientists also work with Ministries of Health and other partners to combat HIV/AIDS in more than 60 developing countries (http://www.cdc.gov/hiv/default.htm).

In the United States, the CDC set a national goal of reducing the number of new HIV infections from an estimated 40,000 to 20,000 per year by the year 2005, focusing particularly on eliminating racial and ethnic disparities in new HIV infections (CDC 2001). Figure 8.4 compares the CDC budget for HIV prevention and

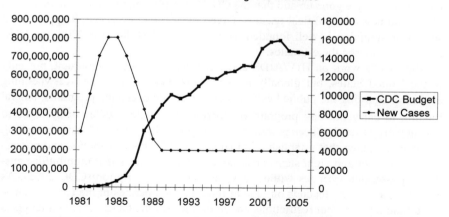

Fig. 8.4 CDC budget for HIV prevention (in constant 1983 dollars) and new infection, United States (1981–2006) *Source*: Holtgrave and Kates (2007)

new infections in the United States between 1981 and 2006. However, for many years, the CDC has used informal methods to estimate that about 40,000 people are newly infected with HIV annually in the United States. A more accurate method is expected to show that the new infections are in fact much higher, possibly by 50%. However, estimating new HIV infections in the United States is also a political issue, since it influences the funding and design of HIV prevention programs. The Bush administration has increased financing for AIDS treatment and prevention programs outside the United States (see the preceding section on PEPFAR), but funding for domestic prevention efforts decreased by 19% in inflation-adjusted terms from 2002 to 2007 (Harris 2007).

The inability of the CDC to provide more accurate estimates of new HIV infections in the United States is puzzling for a number of reasons. First, the number 40,000 is estimated based on just 33 states, with several large states missing from the list. Thus, the number 40,000 is almost surely an underestimate. HIV/AIDS diagnoses were collected from 33 states with name-based reporting systems between 2000 and 2004. Over this 4-year period, 157,252 diagnoses were made in the 33 states. Thus, 33 states alone produced close to 40,000 new cases per year. Second, the national goal in the 2000 Strategic Plan of the CDC was to reduce the number of new HIV infections in the United States from an estimated 40,000 cases to 20,000 cases by 2005, with a particular focus on eliminating racial and ethnic disparities in new HIV infections. The 2000 Strategic Plan also proposed to decrease by at least 50% the number of persons in the United States at high risk for acquiring or transmitting HIV infection by delivering targeted, sustained and evidence-based HIV prevention interventions. The numbers are still above 40,000 per year (CDC HIV Prevention Strategic Plan 2007, Appendix). Third, the resources spent in real terms for prevention has fallen between 2001 and 2005 (see Fig. 8.4).

Some advocacy groups have interpreted the evidence to conclude that the actual numbers have gone up and that the CDC is simply delaying the announcement of the bad news for political reasons. Given the indirect evidence, it appears that such a presumption is well founded. However, as of 31 January 2008, the CDC had not yet revised the estimates.

The CDC's work on HIV/AIDS and infectious diseases is important, not only in the United States, but globally as well. However, in spite the overwhelming evidence regarding the public health benefit of needle exchange programs, federal funding to carry out any program of distributing sterile needles or syringes to injection drug users has been prohibited by Congress since 1988, 47 states have drug paraphernalia laws that establish criminal penalties for the distribution and possession of syringes and eight states and one territory have laws that prohibit dispensing or possessing syringes without a valid medical prescription (CDC 2005). As an organization that depends on federal funding and operates in the United States, these funding and legal restrictions are an obstacle to the CDC achieving its goals with respect to HIV/AIDS prevention in the United States.

8.6 Implications for Other Global Diseases

The ineffectiveness of the WHO in addressing the HIV/AIDS pandemic provides a cautionary tale that requires close evaluation. UNAIDS has moved in to fill the gaps left by the WHO with respect to the HIV/AIDS pandemic, but the creation of such disease-specific agencies is not the best approach to addressing other global diseases that will likely require a rapid global response. Moreover, even the creation of UNAIDS has been insufficient to provide adequate multilateral leadership on HIV/AIDS in the UN system.

MSF has moved in to fill the gaps left by the UN system. However, while MSF has filled an important need, its withdrawal from collective efforts sets an unfortunate precedent in an environment where a multiplicity of players and approaches requires greater harmonization and coordination of efforts in order to ensure the efficient use of resources. Nevertheless, the creation of UNAIDS and the approach of MSF both serve to highlight the need for ongoing reforms to improve the effectiveness of global health institutions and have led to innovative approaches that may serve as models for such reforms.

PEPFAR has injected much-needed funding for HIV/AIDS in several developing countries. However, the policies that have been imposed on funding for treatment have favored the commercial interests of the US pharmaceutical industry, thereby undermining the goal of increasing access to treatment. The policies imposed on funding for prevention have favored the ideological interests of conservative Christian organizations in the United States, thereby undermining the goal of effective, science-based prevention efforts. Ideological or religious doctrines have no place in effectively addressing global diseases. Not only are they often at odds with scientific evidence, but they can hamper efforts to reduce the stigma associated with diseases like HIV/AIDS, at topic we will address in greater detail in the next chapter.

Since the new WHO International Health Regulations only came into force in 2007, their effectiveness in practice has yet to be tested. The obligation of countries to report disease outbreaks to the WHO, together with the economic incentives countries have to report outbreaks and to follow WHO recommendations, reveal a sophisticated approach to regulation design. The focus on reporting outbreaks of fast-moving diseases, rather than slow-moving diseases like HIV/AIDS, endemic diseases like malaria or contagious diseases like tuberculosis, suggests that there is a degree of specialization occurring among organizations that address global health concerns. It also suggests a lack of confidence in the ability of the WHO to move beyond its traditionally narrow focus on the medical aspects of fast-moving, infectious diseases. While the division of responsibilities avoids overlap and duplication of efforts, it will require closer coordination than might be necessary if the WHO were to serve a central leadership role with respect to the manner in which global diseases are addressed. However, despite the global nature of many modern diseases and epidemics, national governments are unlikely to be willing to relinquish control over their ability to protect the health of their citizens. This factor is likely to continue to limit the extent to which the WHO can expand its leadership role in global health issues.

The International Health Regulations avoid overlap with WTO regulation of health-related trade measures, while maintaining a specialized role for the WHO in providing objective risk assessments and making recommendations regarding appropriate responses based on scientific evidence. Disproportionate responses that affect the international movement of people still remain within the discretion of national governments and the WHO does not have the authority to interfere with that discretion. The WTO has not yet negotiated regulations regarding trade-related movement of people, but is likely to be the forum in which such rules will be negotiated on a global basis. It seems both unlikely and unnecessary to extend the mandate of the WHO any further to the regulation of the international movement of goods or intellectual property rights, since the WTO regulates these issues at the international level.

References

Akukwe C (2007) PEPFAR Reauthorization: Issues for Consideration. http://www.worldpress.org/print_article.cfm?article_id=3081&dont=yes. Accessed 12 October 2007

Amundsen EJ, Eskild A, Stigum H, Smith E, Aalen OO (2003) Legal access to needles and syringes/needle exchange programmes versus HIV counselling and testing to prevent transmission of HIV among intravenous drug users: A comparative study of Denmark, Norway and Sweden. European Journal of Public Health 13:252–258

Asia Catalyst (2007) AIDS Blood Scandals: What China Can Learn from the World's Mistakes. http://www.asiacatalyst.org/AIDS_blood_scandals_rpt_0907. pdf. Accessed 14 November 2007

Associated Press (2006) AIDS Treatment Resolution Withdrawn at WHO Meeting Because of U.S. Opposition. http://www.iht.com/articles/ap/2006/09/22/ asia/AS_MED_WHO_Asia_AIDS.php. Accessed 25 September 2006

BBC World (2007) World Debate. 6 October 2007

Bernstein M, Hise SJ (2007) PEPFAR Reauthorization: Improving Transparency in U.S. Funding for HIV/AIDS. Center for Global Development, http://www.cgdev.org/content/publications/detail/14814. Accessed 7 January 2008

Calmy A (2004) MSF and HIV/AIDS: Expanding Treatment, Facing New Challenges. http://www.msf.org/msfinternational/invoke.cfm?component=article&objectid=E5803E3F-48C2-48D0-B63D8771711FB20A&method=full_html. Accessed 5 April 2007

Canadian Commission of Inquiry on the Blood System in Canada (Krever Commission). http://epe.lac-bac.gc.ca/100/200/301/hcan-scan/commission_blood_final_rep-e/vol1-e.pdf. Accessed 15 November 2007

Carter M (2007) PEPFAR Money Being used to 'Promote Homophobia', Charges Human Rights Group. http://www.aidsmap.com/en/news/B990E508-29C7-4F00-A995-9DA9A58385FC.asp, Accessed 22 October 2007

CDC (2001) HIV Prevention Strategic Plan Through 2005. January 2001

CDC (2005) Syringe Exchange Programs. http://www.cdc.gov/idu/facts/aed_idu_syr. htm. Accessed 24 November 2007

CDC (2006) The State of CDC. http://www.cdc.gov/about/stateofcdc/cdrom/SOCDC/SOCDC2006.pdf. Accessed 24 November 2007

CDC HIV Prevention Strategic Plan (2007), http://www.cdc.gov/hiv/resources/reports/psp/pdf/psp.pdf. Accessed 24 November 2007

Day M (2007) Drug industry sponsorship: Who's funding WHO? British Medical Journal 334:338–340

Dekay S (2004) Funding the Response to AIDS: Why are donors not working together? 15th Annual International AIDS Conference, Bangkok, 12 July 2004, http://www.kaisernetwork.org/health_cast/uploaded_files/071204_ias_funding.pdf. Accessed 2 November 2007

Dubuet F, Tronc E (2006) United Nations: Deceptive humanitarian reforms? http://www.msf.org/msfinternational/invoke.cfm?objectid=95542E25-5056-AA77-6C6F0623221C3658&component=toolkit.article&method=full_html. Accessed 4 November 2007

Fidler DP, Heymann DL, Ostroff SM, O'Brien TP (1997) Emerging and reemerging infectious diseases: Challenges for international, national, and state law. International Law 31:773

Fidler DP (1998) The future of the world health organization: What role for international Law? Vanderbilt Journal of Transnational Law 31:1079

Fillinger T (2006) U.S. Policies and their Health Impact on Women in Sup-Saharan Africa. University of Maryland Law Jurnal on Race, Religion, Gender and Class 6:337–352

Gibson DR (1998) HIV Prevention in Injection Drug Users, HIV InSite Knowledge Base Chapter. http://hivinsite.ucsf.edu/InSite?page=kb-07-04-01-01. Accessed 26 November 2007

Harris G (2007) Figures on H.I.V. Rate Expected to Rise. www.nytimes.com, 2 December 2007

Holtgrave DR, Kates J (2007) HIV incidence and CDC's HIV prevention budget: An exploratory correlational analysis. American Journal of Preventive Medicine 32:63–67

Hurley SF et al. (1997) Effectiveness of needle-exchange programmes for prevention of HIV infection. Lancet 349:1797–1800

Jarlais D et al. (2005) Reductions in hepatitis C virus and HIV infections among injecting drug users in New York City, 1990–2001. AIDS 19:3

Kahn JG (1993) Do NEPS affect rates of HIV drug and/or sex risk behaviors? In: Lurie P, Reingold AL et al. The Public Health Impact of Needle Exchange Programs in the United States and Abroad. Centers for Disease Control and Prevention, Atlanta

Kyama R, McNeil DG Jr (2007) Distribution of Nets Splits Malaria Fighters. www. nytimes.com, 9 October 2007

Lewis S (2007) Despite New Figures, Aids Funding Doesn't Meet Needs. http:// allafrica.com/stories/200711231172.html. Accessed 23 November 2007

Magee J (2007) HIV Prevention, Harm Reduction, Injecting Drug Use. http://www. avert.org/injecting.htm. Accessed 14 November 2007

MSF (2006) Overview of MSF Operations – Audited Facts and Figures, http:// www.msf.org/msfinternational/invoke.cfm?objectid=992D03D9-5056-AA77- 6C9F7BBBE 9771A9F&component=toolkit.article&method=full_html. Accessed 24 November 2007

Mwale B (2004) Funding the Response to AIDS: Why are donors not working together? 15th Annual International AIDS Conference, Bangkok, 12 July 2004, http://www. kaisernetwork.org/health_cast/uploaded_files/071204_ias_funding.pdf. Accessed 26 November 2007

Oomman N, Bernstein M, Rosenzweig S (2007) Following the Funding for HIV/AIDS: A Comparative Analysis of the Funding Practices of PEPFAR, the Global Fund and the World Bank MAP in Mozambique, Uganda and Zambia. http://www.cgdev.org/content/ publications/detail/14569/. Accessed 7 November 2007

PEPFAR (2005) FY2006 Country Operation Plan (COP) Guidance for the President's Emergency Plan for AIDS Relief (PEPFAR). http://www.genderhealth.org/pubs/ COP GuidanceFY06.pdf. Accessed 14 November 2007

PEPFAR Fact Sheet (2007) http://www.stopaidsnow.org/documents/PEPFAR_facts. pdf. Accessed 14 November 2007

Philips M (2007) Making AIDS patients pay for their care: Why evidence does not change anything in international donor policies? In: Medicins sans Frontieres, AIDS: Free Access to Treatment, a Public Health Necessity or an Economic Heresy?

Ruger JP (2005) Global Functions at the World Health Organization. British Medical Journal 330:1099–1110

Smith M (2007) To End an Epidemic: A Study of Foreign Aid and HIV/AIDS. International Relations Thesis, New York University

Steenhuysen J (2007) U.S. Regulators Join HIV Transplant Probe. Reuters 16 November 2007

Stein E (2001) International integration and democracy: No love at first sight. American Journal of International Law 95:489

Stobbaerts E (2007) Yet Another Arrogant Move? MSF's Stance on its Relationship with the Rest of the International Aid System. http://www.msf.org/msfinternational/ invoke. cfm?objectid=EE64610A-15C5-F00A-259987366CDE871D &component=toolkit. article&method=full_html. Accessed 14 November 2007

Taylor AL (2004) Governing the Globalization of Public Health. J Law Med Ethics 32:500–508

The Economist (2007) Time to Grow up: "Abstinence only" Education does not Slow the Spread of AIDS. http://www.economist.com/displaystory.cfm?story_id=9831189. Accessed 20 September 2007

Turner J (1997) For WHO or For Whom? World Health Organization's Influence on Health Policy. Lancet 7:1639

UNAIDS (2005a) Intensifying HIV Prevention: UNAIDS Policy Position Paper. http://data.unaids.org/governance/pcb04/pcb_17_05_03_en.pdf. Accessed 25 May 2007

UNAIDS (2005b) Resource Needs for an Expanded Response to AIDS in Low- and Middle-Income Countries. http://www.unaids.org/en/Coordination/FocusAreas/Strategic Information.asp. Accessed 25 June 2007

Underhill K, Operario D, Montgomery P (2007) Systematic Review of Abstinence-Plus HIV Prevention Programs in High-Income Countries. Public Library of Science Medicine 4(9)

USAID (2005) Acquisition and Assistance Policy Directive 05-04, Eligibility Limitation on the Use of Funds and Opposition to Prostitution and Sex Trafficking, http://www.usaid.gov/business/business_opportunities/cib/pdf/aapd05_04.pdf. Accessed 5 August 2007

US Department of State (2006) HIV Prevention among Drug Users Guidance #1: Injection Heroin Use (March 2006). http://www.state.gov/s/gac/partners/guide/prevent/64035.htm. Accessed 25 October 2007

von Tigerstrom B (2005) The revised international health regulations and restraint of national health measures. Health Law Journal 13:35

World Health Organization (2004) Effectiveness of Sterile Needle and Syringe Programming in Reducing HIV/AIDS Among Injecting Drug Users

9 The Way Forward: Prevention, Treatment and Human Rights

"AIDS is no longer just a disease, it is a human rights issue."
Nelson Mandela, at the first 46664 concert held at Greenpoint Stadium, Cape Town (29 November 2003).

There now is a considerable body of evidence to support the view that an effective HIV/AIDS strategy integrates prevention, treatment and human rights. In this chapter, we emphasize the importance of each of these aspects and draw upon the conclusions reached in previous chapters to map out the future of HIV/AIDS. While medicine and science have a crucial role to play in addressing pandemics, whether slow-moving (like HIV/AIDS) or fast-moving (like influenza), the social, legal, political, financial and economic ramifications of pandemics can not be ignored. Well-considered social, legal, political and financial strategies are essential in order to address any pandemic effectively.

9.1 The Importance of HIV/AIDS Prevention

Global access to antiretroviral therapy for people living with HIV/AIDS has been scaled up significantly in recent years, from 8% in 2003 to 28% in 2006 (Global HIV Prevention Working Group 2007). Many developing countries now have universal access to treatment, including low-income countries, such as Rwanda (Perry 2007), and middle-income countries, such as Thailand and Brazil (see Chap. 2). However, prevention needs to be scaled up considerably in order to make universal access to treatment an affordable goal on a global scale. Without adequate prevention, new infections will rise and millions more people will need treatment.

The importance of prevention is illustrated dramatically in Fig. 9.1. Two middle-income countries started out at the same point in 1990 with respect to HIV/AIDS: Thailand and South Africa. However, the course of the epidemic in each has diverged to an extraordinary degree since then.

Low- and middle-income countries are not alone in needing a significant increase in HIV prevention. As Table 9.1 shows, HIV infections have increased in several high-income countries in recent years. In New York City, between 2001 and 2006 the annual number of new HIV infections in men under 30 who have sex with men increased by 32%. The significant factors behind the increase in new infections appear to be higher rates of drug use, optimism that AIDS is treatable and increasing stigma about HIV (Kershaw 2008).

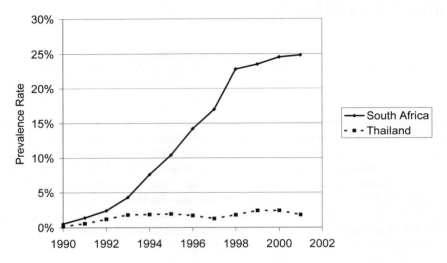

Fig. 9.1 Tale of two countries: South Africa and Thailand. *Source*: UNAIDS

Table 9.1 Rising HIV infection rates in high-income countries

Country	Period	Increase in new HIV infections (%)
Australia	2000–2005	41
Canada	2000–2005	20
United Kingdom	1998–2004	150

Source: Global HIV Prevention Working Group (2007)

In Chap. 2, we discussed how integrated prevention-treatment-human rights strategies aimed at high-risk groups have proved effective in countries like Brazil. In Chap. 7, we explained that limited resources need to focus on high-risk groups and locations to achieve the best possible results. However, as we showed in the example of Ghana, even though almost 80% of people living with HIV/AIDS are sex workers, who are the source of almost 80% of HIV infections, a negligible amount of funding for HIV/AIDS is targeted at this group. The mismatch between the most affected group and the allocation of funding in Ghana highlights the importance of matching funding to prevailing prevalence and transmission patterns in a given country or region. As we saw in Chap. 2, an HIV prevalence rate above 1% is a key threshold for an HIV epidemic to run out of control unless funding for prevention efforts is targeted at high-risk groups, such as commercial sex workers, men who have sex with men, injection drug users and prisoners. However, in Chap. 8 we saw that PEPFAR – the largest bilateral donor of funding for HIV/AIDS programs in developing countries – prohibits the use of funding for programs for commercial sex workers and needle exchange programs.

In Chap. 3, we saw that African-Americans make up 54% of HIV/AIDS patients, even though African-Americans account for less than 15% of the US population. Moreover, black men who have sex with men (MSM) have the highest rates of unrecognized HIV infection, HIV prevalence and incidence rates and AIDS mortality rates among MSM in the United States. In five US cities, 46% of African-American MSM are infected with HIV. HIV and AIDS prevalence rates have affected black MSM disproportionately since the beginning of the epidemic. Black MSM are the only group in the United States with HIV prevalence and incidence rates that are comparable to those in the most affected developing countries. However, the vast majority of HIV prevention intervention for African-Americans does not target homosexual men and for homosexual men does not target black MSM (Millett and Peterson 2007). Thus, the need to focus prevention efforts on the most vulnerable groups remains an issue not just in developing countries.

While prevention strategies need to be tailored to the sources of HIV infections in specific contexts, there are several proven prevention strategies that need to be scaled up. The resources for prevention need to be focused according to the specific nature of the epidemic in different settings, as we showed in Chap. 2. Figure 9.2 shows the source of new HIV infections by region. Table 9.2 summarizes the coverage levels of several essential prevention strategies and Fig. 9.3 shows their deployment by region. It is important to emphasize that prevention and treatment are mutually supportive and need to be addressed simultaneously. Access to treatment supports prevention by reducing risky behaviors, increasing disclosure of HIV status, reducing stigma and reducing infectiousness (Global HIV Prevention Working Group 2007). Prevention supports access to treatment by reducing the number of people that require treatment, thus making universal access to treatment more affordable. HIV treatment and prevention should be integrated, in order to enhance the effectiveness of both.

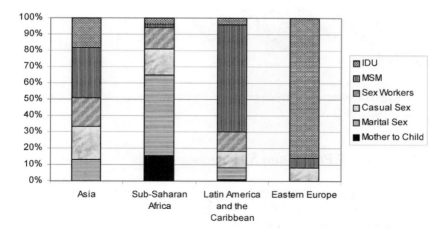

Fig. 9.2 Sources of new HIV infections by region. *Source*: Global HIV Prevention Working Group (2007)

Table 9.2 Estimated coverage levels for essential prevention strategies

Strategy	Coverage
Global condom use in risky sex	9%
Knowledge of HIV status in sub-Saharan Africa	Men 12%/Women 10%
Global treatment for sexually transmitted infections	<20%
Prevention of mother-to-child transmission in developing countries	11%
Global prevention services for men who have sex with men	9%
Global prevention services for injection drug users	8%
Global prevention services for sex workers	<20%
Annual transfusions of unscreened blood in developing countries	6 million units
Unsafe injections in health care settings	40%

Source: Global HIV Prevention Working Group (2007)

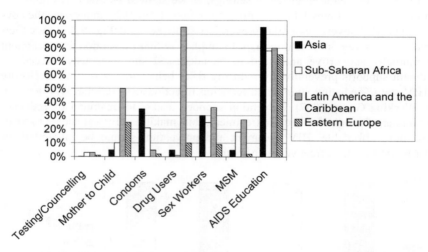

Fig. 9.3 Regional coverage of HIV prevention Services. *Source*: Global HIV Prevention Working Group (2007)

9.1.1 HIV/AIDS Prevention Strategies

HIV prevention strategies fall into four general categories: (1) prevention of sexual transmission; (2) prevention of blood-borne transmission: (3) prevention of mother-to-child transmission; and (4) social strategies.

9.1.1.1 Preventing Sexual Transmission

The strategies for preventing sexual transmission are: (1) behavioral change programs (to increase condom use, to delay the initiation of sexual behavior in young people and to reduce the number of sexual partners); (2) condom promotion; (3) HIV testing (knowledge of HIV status decreases risky behavior); (4) diagnosis and treatment of sexually transmitted infections (which significantly increase the risk of HIV acquisition and transmission, particularly in the case of genital herpes); and (5) adult male circumcision (which reduces the risk of female-to-male transmission by about 60%) (Global HIV Prevention Working Group 2007).

The effectiveness of these strategies varies. The promotion of condoms has been largely successful with respect to commercial sex and casual sex, but condom use remains low within marriage. As we noted in Chap. 4, increasing life expectancy, in areas where it is low due to diseases like malaria, is a cost effective strategy for enhancing behavioral change to lower the risk of HIV infection. A survey by the WHO, on behalf of the Global Fund, reviewed anti-malaria operations in Ethiopia, Ghana, Rwanda and Zambia. In Ethiopia, childhood malaria declined by 60% and the death rate was cut in half within 2 years of the beginning of the mass distribution of mosquito nets. Within a single year, both cases and deaths dropped by two-thirds, in Rwanda, and one-third in Zambia. In Ghana cases fell by an eighth and deaths by a third. In many cases, the distribution of free nets was accompanied by free drugs based on artemisinin, a substance to which the malarial parasite has yet to develop widespread resistance, and spraying DDT inside people's houses. Based on these results, the WHO believes that a 5-year campaign that distributes free nets and malaria drugs would bring malaria under control in most of Africa at a cost of USD 10 billion (Economist 2008). These promising results also bode well for HIV prevention.

Some studies suggest that treating sexually transmitted infections may not reduce HIV transmission significantly (Halperin 2007). However, there is a strong association between the risk of infection with HIV and other sexually transmitted diseases. Moreover, as we noted in Chap. 4, Oster (2005) argues that the explanation for the substantial difference in the transmission rates between the United States and sub-Saharan Africa is due to other untreated sexually transmitted infections, which leave open sores from chlamydia, syphilis and gonorrhea that facilitate HIV transmission. Thus, treating bacterial sexually transmitted infections could prevent as many as 24% of new infections over a decade

There is significant evidence that male circumcision significantly reduces HIV transmission. Box 9.1 discusses the relationship between circumcision and HIV/AIDS.

A similar picture is seen in South and South-East Asia, where overall HIV prevalence is much lower, but the countries with highest HIV prevalence have little male circumcision (Papua New Guinea, Cambodia and Thailand). Conversely, HIV prevalence is extremely low in those countries where most men are circumcised (Pakistan, Bangladesh, Indonesia and Philippines).

Box 9.1 Circumcision and HIV/AIDS

There is ecological evidence that prevalence of circumcision is negatively correlated with prevalence of HIV/AIDS. Specifically, there is a strong inverse correlation between the prevalence of circumcision in countries and the prevalence of HIV in those countries. All the highest HIV prevalence countries are those where circumcision is little practiced. In fact, no country with nearly universal circumcision coverage has ever had an adult HIV prevalence higher than 8%, including countries such as Cameroon, where a 1997 survey found sexual behavior to be higher risk than that in countries with prevalence of around 25%. This fact is illustrated in Fig. 9.4.

Circumsicion versus HIV Prevalence in Sub Saharan Africa

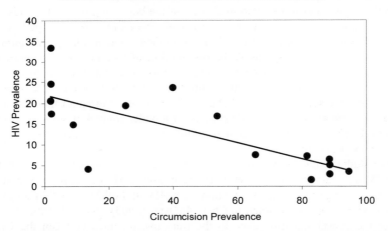

Fig. 9.4 Ecological relationship between circumcision and HIV prevalence. *Source*: Bailey (2007)

A large, randomized controlled trial in 3,274 men between the ages of 18 and 24 years showed that circumcision resulted in a significant 60% reduction in HIV infection (Auvert et al., 2005). These results were confirmed by two other trials.

Vulnerability to HIV varies considerably from one epidemic to the next, as do the issues facing vulnerable groups. For example, in a concentrated epidemic, such as in Asia and Latin America, HIV transmission occurs primarily among vulnerable groups and prevention programs targeted at vulnerable groups would reduce overall infection. However, in a generalized epidemic, such as in several countries in Southern Africa, where HIV transmission occurs primarily outside vulnerable groups, Halperin (2007) argues that transmission would continue unabated despite prevention programs targeted at vulnerable groups. However, as we noted in Chap. 4, research regarding the relationship between trade routes, truckers, sex workers and HIV propagation contradicts this idea. In a generalized epidemic, where HIV is spread along trade routes, prevention programs targeted at truckers and sex workers would be effective in bringing down the growth rate of the spread of the disease.

Having multiple sex partners increases the risk of HIV infection in both concentrated and generalized epidemics, but the impact of this factor on HIV prevalence rates can vary considerably. For example, even though the United States and Uganda have similar rates of multiple sex partners, and the number of sexual partners that men and women had over a 10-year period were much higher in the United States than in Uganda, Uganda's HIV/AIDS prevalence rate was about 18 times higher than that of the United States (Halperin 2007). However, as we noted in Chap. 8, a recent study indicates that abstinence-only programs are as effective as providing no information at all when it comes to preventing pregnancies, unprotected sex and sexually transmitted diseases. Abstinence-plus interventions, which promote sexual abstinence as the best means of preventing HIV, but also encourage condom use and other safer-sex practices, are more effective than abstinence-only programs (Underhill et al., 2007).

9.1.1.2 Preventing Blood-borne Transmission

The proven strategies for preventing blood-borne transmission are: (1) to supply injection drug users with clean injection equipment; (2) methadone or other substitution therapy to reduce drug dependence; (3) blood safety programs, including screening of donated blood; and (4) infection control in health care settings, including injection safety and antiretroviral treatment following exposure to HIV.

As we noted in Chap. 8, the risk of AIDS infection through the use of blood products was recognized as early as 1982, but countries were slow to adopt measures to ensure the safety of the blood supply and the World Health Organization (WHO) passed a resolution on blood products that made no mention of AIDS as late as January 1987. In the 1990s, Chinese health authorities promoted blood-selling by poor farmers to commercial blood collection centers, despite warnings from the WHO, spreading HIV/AIDS through the blood fractionation and re-injection process. In 2007, new HIV infections through hospital blood transfusions continued to be reported in China, and illegal underground blood collection centers have continued to operate. Box 9.2 recounts the story of the Libyan scandal over blood-borne transmission to children.

Box 9.2 The Bulgarian Six

On December 14, 2007, Sixth Sense Productions, Inc., an independent Hollywood producer, announced plans to make a USD 40 million movie about five Bulgarian nurses (Kristiyana Vulcheva, Nasya Nenova, Valya Chervenyashka, Snezhana Dimitrova, Valentina Siropulo) and a Palestinian medical intern (Ashraf Ahmad Djum'a al-Hadjudj) who were jailed in Libya and faced the death penalty for allegedly infecting children with HIV.

This news item is a postscript to a long international drama that began to unfold in 1999 when the medics were arrested on charges of injecting 418 Libyan children with HIV-tainted blood while at a Benghazi hospital. Of them, over 50 had died by the end of 2007.

One important report was submitted by Luc Montagnier and Vittorio Colizzi – two leading experts on HIV/AIDS. Their report concluded that the infection at the hospital resulted from poor hygiene and reuse of syringes. They concluded that the infections began before the arrival of the nurses and doctor in 1998. Through hospital records, and the DNA sequences of the virus, they traced it to patient n.356 who was admitted 28 times between 1994 and 1997 in Ward B, ISO and Ward A. The first cross-contamination occurred during that patient's 1997 admission. Montagnier and Colizzi both testified in person at the trial of record for the defense. On 14 December 2006, *Nature* (446, 836–837) published a report that also concluded that the strain of virus was already present before the arrival of the six accused.

The accused were tried and retried. The Libyans had signed confessions from them – which the accused said were extracted under torture. The final verdict in 2006 sentenced them to death by firing squad. The Libyan President likened the event to the case of Abdel Basset Ali al-Megrahi, who is serving a life sentence in Scotland for the bombing of Pan Am Flight 103 over Lockerbie, Scotland, on 21 December 1988. Thus, it became clear that Libya was trying to extract economic and political favors in exchange for the release of the six.

In the end, Bulgaria, Qatar and a group of European countries funneled USD 460 million into the International Fund Benghazi to finance the treatment of the HIV-infected children and the improvement of the Libyan health care system. France played a pivotal role in the final release of the accused. In exchange for the release, France agreed to sell antitank missiles and nuclear technology to Libya. It was a win-win deal for France: they did multi-million dollar business with Libya and got publicity for helping the release of the accused.

When the nurses returned to Bulgaria, the government endorsed a 10,000 leva reimbursement for each of the nurses. A Bulgarian mobile telephony provider donated an apartment for each nurse.

9.1.1.3 Preventing Mother-to-Child Transmission

The proven strategies for preventing mother-to-child transmission are: (1) general HIV prevention for women of child-bearing age; (2) a brief course of antiretroviral treatment in advance of delivery (which can reduce transmission by 50%, but is only received by an estimated 11% of women in need); (3) prevention of undesired pregnancy in HIV-positive women; (4) breast-feeding alternatives; and (5) cesarean delivery where the mother has a high viral load (Global HIV Prevention Working Group 2007).

In developing countries, a small but growing number of children are dying of HIV/AIDS. As Fig. 9.5 shows, some 4% of children died of HIV/AIDS in 2005.

Causes of Death of Children in Developing Countries

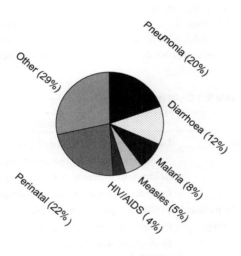

Fig. 9.5 Causes of death among children in developing countries. *Source*: World Health Organization

HIV infected mothers carry additional risks for the baby. In Table 9.3, we indicate some of the major risks. Some risks like stillbirth or high infant mortality have been found only in developing countries but not in developed countries.

For these additional risks, it has been suggested that one way of eliminating mother-to-child transmission is not to have the baby in the first place. This prevents mother-to-child transmission by 100%. Thus, family planning could also help to reduce mother-to-child transmission:

Another often neglected aspect of HIV prevention – one prohibited from funding by the Bush administration's international AIDS program – involves expanding family planning services, including for HIV-positive women who do not want to conceive. Reducing unintended pregnancies could greatly decrease the number of infected infants as well as the number of children who eventually become orphans (Halperin 2007).

If an HIV-positive woman gives birth to a child, there is a risk of transmission of HIV itself, in addition to the other risks listed in Table 9.3. However, the transmission risk of HIV from mother to child is not 100%. It can be minimized through drug treatment of the mother and careful birthing. Figure 9.6 clearly demonstrates this fact, using the data from the United States. The introduction of *zidovudine* (for the mothers before childbirth) has dramatically reduced the risk of HIV infection of the baby.

Since 1998, most countries have applied a regimen of *zidovudine* from 28 weeks, with NVP administered during labor and to the baby, and the addition of a 7 day *zidovudine/lamivudine* postpartum regime. The result has been a dramatic reduction of infected newborns (see Fig. 9.7). Note that the reduction has been evident in Europe and the United States since 1994, when this regime was introduced. In Thailand, the regime was introduced in 1996 and in most parts of Africa 2 years later.

Table 9.3 Risks in pregnancies of HIV-positive women

Pregnancy outcome	Relationship to HIV infection
Spontaneous abortion	Limited data, but evidence of possible increased risk
Stillbirth	Evidence of increased risk in developing countries
Perinatal mortality	Evidence of increased risk in developing countries
Infant mortality	Evidence of increased risk in developing countries
Intrauterine Growth Restriction	Evidence of possible increased risk
Low birth weight (<2,500 g)	Evidence of possible increased risk
Pre-term delivery	Evidence of possible increased risk, especially with more advanced disease
Pre-eclampsia	No data
Gestational diabetes	No data
Chorioamnionitis	Limited data; more recent studies do not suggest an increased risk
Oligohydramnios	Minimal data
Fetal malformation	No evidence of increased risk

Source: French and Brocklehurst (1998)

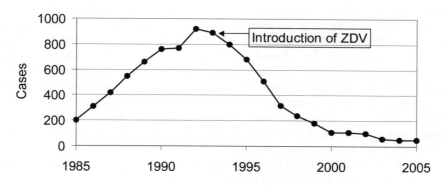

Fig. 9.6 Number of children born with HIV/AIDS in the United States 1985–2005. *Source*: Data collated from CDC database (www.cdc.gov)

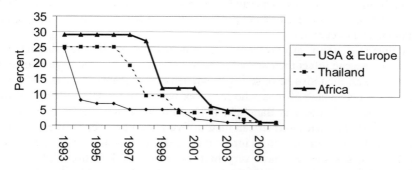

Fig. 9.7 Falling infection rate of newborns 1993–2006. *Source*: Data from Dr. Siripon Kanshana. Ministry of Public Health Thailand

Once a child is born, the question is whether the infected mother should breast-feed the child. On the one hand, UNAIDS estimated that globally there are 300,000 babies infected through breastfeeding. On the other hand, the UNICEF estimates that 1,500,000 children die every year from lack of breastfeeding by the mothers. Thus, it is not clear whether the mothers with HIV should or should not breastfeed the baby.

9.1.1.4 Social Strategies to Reduce Vulnerability to HIV/AIDS

Key factors that increase vulnerability to HIV include: (1) gender inequality (which reduces women's access to information and services, reduces power to negotiate safe sex with partners, increases the risk of sexual violence and may create the need to depend on sex for economic survival); (2) institutionalized discrimination against vulnerable groups (such as criminalizing drug use and needle possession, commercial sex work and sex between men); (3) poverty (which reduces access to information and services and access to prevention tools, such as condoms); (4) HIV stigma (which discourages individuals from seeking testing, disclosing their status, seeking HIV-related services or using alternatives to breast-feeding); and (5) conflict and humanitarian emergencies (which reduce access to services, information and social support by displacing populations and increase the risk of sexual violence) (Global HIV Prevention Working Group 2007).

As we noted in Chap. 4, there is no clear evidence that reducing poverty and income inequality will necessarily reduce HIV/AIDS prevalence. Moreover, poverty reduction is too broad a goal to constitute what might be considered a concrete HIV/AIDS prevention strategy. Thus, if poverty reduces access to information and services and access to prevention tools, such as condoms, a concrete policy response would be to find innovative ways to improve access to information, provide funding to enhance access to services and provide free access to prevention tools, such as condoms and circumcision.

Vulnerable groups are not compartmentalized. People infected through injection drug use can infect their sexual partners. A significant percentage of men who have sex with men also have sex with women (for example, 20% in Asia) and a significant percentage of men who have sex with men are HIV-infected in many parts of the world (28% in Bangkok; 15% in Phnom Penh; 21.5% in urban Senegal; and 46% of African-American men in five US cities). Sex workers can infect their clients, who in turn may infect their spouses or other sexual partners. In many areas, sex workers have very high rates of HIV infection (50% in South Africa; 27% in Guyana; 33% in St. Petersburg, Russia; and 73% in urban Ethiopia) (Global HIV Prevention Working Group 2007). Figure 9.8 shows the linkages between vulnerable groups and the general population in Bangladesh. The linkages between vulnerable groups, and between vulnerable groups and the general population, make effective prevention strategies for vulnerable groups essential.

Social strategies that address the factors that increase vulnerability to HIV include: (1) HIV awareness campaigns, including in the mass media; (2) anti-stigma measures; (3) gender equity initiatives to empower women; (3) involving communities and HIV-positive individuals in HIV/AIDS programs; (4) visible political leadership; (5) engaging a broad range of sectors in HIV awareness and prevention programs; and (6) legal reforms to support HIV prevention strategies, such as laws decriminalizing needle possession and anti-discrimination laws (Global HIV Prevention Working Group 2007). Human rights are the core of most social strategies to

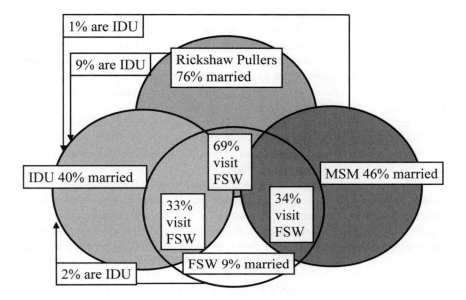

Fig. 9.8 Dynamics of transmission of HIV/AIDS across groups in Bangladesh. *Source*: Evaristo Marowa, UNAIDS Country Coordinator, Bangladesh, Presentation on HIV/AIDS in Bangladesh, 24 April 2005

prevent the spread of HIV/AIDS. We address the various aspects of HIV/AIDS and human rights in greater detail below.

Awareness of HIV status has a significant impact on rates of HIV transmission. When unaware of HIV seropositivity, the transmission rate is estimated at 8.8–10.8 % (as a percentage of PLWH/A), whereas awareness of HIV seropositivity reduces the transmission rate to an estimated 1.7–2.4% (Holtgrave 2005). However, increasing access to HIV testing and counseling also raises human rights issues. In order to balance the need for more testing with the need to respect human rights, it has been recommended that health care providers offer and recommend HIV testing, in conjunction with counseling (the opt-in approach), rather than rely on the client to initiate this process. However, mandatory HIV tests and routine HIV testing unless the client opts out risk violating individuals' rights to informed consent and confidentiality (Jürgens 2007).

9.1.2 Barriers to Increasing HIV Prevention

The major barriers to increasing HIV prevention are: (1) inadequate financing; (2) failure to target limited funding where it will have the greatest impact, due to lack of information on the nature of the epidemic or ideological, non-scientific restrictions on the use of donor funding; (3) limited capacity to administer large increases in funding; (4) failure to integrate HIV prevention in schools, workplaces and other health care programs, such as TB and reproductive health; and (5) stigma and discrimination against HIV-positive people and vulnerable groups, which deter people from seeking testing and prevention services and discourage political leadership (Global HIV Prevention Working Group 2007). We analyze the problems and solutions regarding stigma and discrimination against HIV-positive people and vulnerable groups later in this chapter.

We analyzed the issues of inadequate financing, targeted financing and donor coordination in Chap. 7. As we noted in Chap. 7, a lack of donor coordination is an obstacle to expanding treatment and prevention programs, due to the administrative burden that it imposes on recipients.

As we noted in Chap. 8, the US government's foreign AIDS program, PEPFAR, devotes only 20% of funding to prevention and requires that two-thirds of that amount be spent on abstinence-only programs that do not promote condom use, despite evidence that this approach to prevention is not effective and undermines best practices. PEPFAR guidelines also undermine HIV/AIDS prevention by further stigmatizing sex workers and prohibiting funding of needle exchange programs, despite evidence that such harm reduction programs are effective. The PEPFAR approach assumes that vulnerable groups do not interact with the rest of society. PEPFAR is perhaps the best example of ideological, non-scientific restrictions on the use of donor funding, although it also serves as an example of two of the other significant barriers to HIV prevention, due to its promotion of stigma and discrimination against vulnerable groups and the percentage of funding that it allocates to prevention. However, it is important to emphasize that PEPFAR has done more than any other bilateral funding program to address the need for adequate financing. The key point is that the money that has been made available through PEPFAR could be better spent.

On 26 December 2007, US President Bush signed legislation that lifted a 1999 ban that had made Washington, DC the only US city barred by federal law from using municipal money for needle exchange programs. Officials of the District of Columbia Health Department planned to allocate USD 1 million for such programs in 2008 (Urbina 2007). Extending this change in policy to PEPFAR would enhance the effectiveness of prevention programs in the countries that receive PEPFAR funding.

9.2 The Future of HIV Treatment

In Chap. 3, we provided an overview of the history of drug developments to treat HIV/AIDS and saw the dramatic impact on survival of triple combination therapy. Without this treatment, the chance of surviving 10 years was about 50%. With this treatment, patients have a 50% chance of living another 35 years. In the early 1980s in the United States, the leading causes of death among 25–44 old year men by rank were accidents, cancer and homicide. By 1994, deaths from AIDS had become the leading cause of death in this group. Following the introduction of universal access to triple combination therapy, deaths from AIDS fell to fourth place, behind accidents, cancer and homicide. As a result, whereas 68% of Americans considered HIV/AIDS to be the most urgent health problem facing the United States in 1987, by 2006 only 6% held this view. However, as we saw in the case of Mexico, the introduction of triple combination therapy led to a dramatic rise in the cost of treatment per patient. Thus, with the advent of triple combination therapy, the focus has shifted from the effectiveness of treatments for HIV/AIDS to the cost of making effective treatments accessible. This is why the issue of drug patents became so important, as we saw in Chaps. 5 and 6. This is also why access to health insurance also has become an important issue, which we analyzed in Chap. 3.

There are five classes of anti-HIV drugs, which are known as antiretroviral drugs. (1) Nucleoside/Nucleotide Reverse Transcriptase Inhibitors (NRTIs) were the first type of drug used to treat HIV infection in 1987. NRTIs interfere with reverse transcriptase, an HIV protein that the virus needs to makes copies of itself. (2) Protease Inhibitors, the first of which was approved in 1995, inhibit protease, another protein involved in the HIV replication process. (3) Non-Nucleoside Reverse Transcriptase Inhibitors (NNRTIs), which began to be approved for use in 1997, stop HIV from replicating within cells by inhibiting the reverse transcriptase protein. (4) Fusion or Entry Inhibitors prevent HIV from entering human immune cells and have been available since 2003. (5) Integrase Inhibitors, of which one drug was approved in 2007, inhibit the integrase enzyme, which HIV needs to insert its genetic material into human cells (http://www.avert.org/introtrt.htm).

HIV-positive people are prescribed antiretroviral therapy once the number of CD4 cells falls below a certain threshold or when they develop clinical AIDS symptoms. The CD4 cell count guidelines of the World Health Organization, which depend on the stage of the disease and the particular circumstances of the patient, indicate that antiretroviral treatment should begin when the CD4 cell count falls to the 200–350 mm range (World Health Organization 2003). In 2006, an international panel of experts continued to recommend these guidelines (Hammer et al., 2006). Patients start on what is referred to as "first-line treatment". They then change to "second-line treatment" if the first set of drugs is too toxic for a particular patient to tolerate or if the virus develops resistance to the first set of drugs. The likelihood of drug resistance increases the more doses a patients skips, making daily adherence to treatment extremely important (Hammer et al., 2006).

As of the end of 2006, about 2 million people were receiving of ARV treatment in low- and middle-income countries, which represents 28% of those in need (WHO/UNAIDS Progress Report on Universal Access to Treatment). The "3 by 5" initiative, between December 2003 and December 2005, aimed to have 3 million people on ARV therapy by the end of 2005. During this period, the number of people in low- and middle-income countries receiving ARV treatment increased from 400,000 to 1.3 million (WHO 2006).

9.2.1 Obstacles to Increasing the Number of People Receiving Treatment

One obstacle to increasing the number of people receiving treatment is the capacity constraints of treatment providers, which include limited health infrastructure and human resources, management capacity and the ability to identify new patients through testing and counseling (CHAI 2007). In Chap. 7, we examined multilateral funding programs that address these capacity constraints in developing countries. It is important to note that the estimates of the number of people requiring treatment are just that – estimates. As we have noted, UNAIDS HIV/AIDS estimates were revised in 2007, due to the use of better methodologies. Estimates of the number of people with HIV/AIDS do not necessarily reflect the number of patients that have been identified as requiring treatment.

The reluctance of the United States to allow PEPFAR funding to be spent on WHO-approved drugs has also been criticized as an obstacle to expanding treatment (see Chap. 8 for a discussion of PEPFAR). Indian generic drug manufacturer, Cipla, created a triple-combination drug in a single pill (Triomune) that could be taken twice daily, which it offered to sell for about USD 300 per patient per year in 2001. Cipla's Triomune offer made the 3 by 5 initiative a realizable goal and Cipla has the production capacity to produce four million doses of Triomune per day. The WHO approved Triomune in December 2003 as a first-line treatment for HIV/AIDS (Hamied 2005). The PEPFAR restriction on the use of WHO-approved drugs had the effect of preventing the use of PEPFAR funding to buy Triomune. Moreover, the majority of PEPFAR funds have been used to purchase patented versions of HIV/AIDS drugs, rather than generic versions (see Chap. 8). Figure 9.9 shows how generic competition has lowered the cost of triple combination antiretroviral therapy. Between 2001 and 2007, the price of the generic drugs has brought down the price of the originator substantially – from over USD 10,000 to under USD 350. At the same time, the generic prices have stayed in the 25–30% range of the originator price.

PEPFAR funds can be used to purchase other low-cost generic equivalents of several patented HIV/AIDS drugs, including some produced by Cipla. PEPFAR requires that generic drugs be approved by the US FDA, Canada, Japan or Western Europe to be eligible for funding (see Chap. 8). If US FDA approval is sought for fixed dose combinations of previously approved antiretrovirals for the treatment of HIV, if one or more of the approved drug components are covered by a patent, the FDA cannot approve an application until the patent expires. However, the application can receive tentative approval (which recognizes that at the time the tentative approval action is taken, the application meets the technical and scientific requirements for approval, but final approval is blocked by patent or exclusivity). Products that receive tentative approval are eligible for procurement under the

Price of 3TC/d4T/NVP Generic as a percent of original

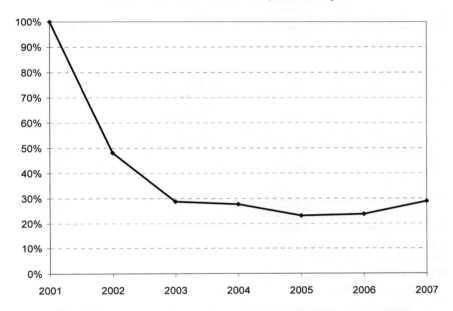

Fig. 9.9 Generic competition has lowered the cost of ARVs. *Source*: MSF

PEPFAR program (US Food and Drug Administration 2006). Table 9.4. lists the generic versions of HIV/AIDS drugs that have been approved by the FDA for purchase with PEPFAR funds, along with the generic companies that own the patents for the specific generic formulations and the country of manufacture.

The fact that the patents for HIV/AIDS drugs are owned by different companies has delayed combining different HIV/AIDS drugs in a single pill in markets protected by patents. One such pill, Atripla, was created through a joint venture between Merck and Bristol-Myers Squibb with Gilead Sciences and combines *efavirenz* (Bristol-Myers Squibb, Merck) with *emtricitabine* and *tenofovir* (Gilead Sciences) (IB Times 2007). Atripla was approved for sale in the United States in 2006, several years after the Indian generic manufacturer, Cipla, had started manufacturing a triple-combination pill and 3 years after Cipla's pill was approved by the WHO. Approval to market Atripla in the European Union was sought in December 2007. Gilead Sciences and Merck have formed a joint venture to market Atripla in developing countries (IB Times 2007). Table 9.5 shows the US patents, patent owners and patent expiry dates for selected HIV/AIDS drugs.

Zidovudine was the first drug to be approved for treatment of HIV infection. As Table 9.5 shows, the patent for *zidovudine* expired in 2005 and the patent for *lamivudine* expires in 2009. However, Glaxo extended the life of these patents to 2016 by combining the two drugs into one pill (called Combivir). While the new

Table 9.4 Generic HIV/AIDS drugs approved by FDA for PEPFAR

Generic drug	Generic manufacturer	Country
Lamivudine/zidovudine (fixed-dose combination)	Aurobindo Pharma	India
Stavudine tablets and oral solution	Aurobindo Pharma	India
Nevirapine tablets and oral solution	Aurobindo Pharma	India
Efavirenz	Aurobindo Pharma	India
Lamivudine tablets and oral solution	Aurobindo Pharma	India
Zidovudine tablets, capsules, and oral solution	Aurobindo Pharma	India
Abacavir tablets	Aurobindo Pharma	India
Lamivudine/nevirapine/zidovudine (fixed-dose combination)	Aurobindo Pharma	India
Didanosine tablets and pediatric powder	Aurobindo Pharma	India
Abacavir copackaged with lamivudine/zidovudine (fixed-dose combination)	Aurobindo Pharma	India
Nevirapine copackaged with lamivudine/zidovudine (fixed-dose combination)	Aspen Pharmacare	South Africa
Didanosine	Barr Laboratories	US
Lamivudine oral solution	Cipla	India
Lamivudine/nevirapine/stavudine (fixed-dose combination for pediatric use)	Cipla	India
Lamivudine/zidovudine (fixed-dose combination)	Cipla	India
Abacavir	Cipla	India
Lamivudine/zidovudine (fixed-dose combination)	Emcure Pharmaceuticals	India
Nevirapine tablets	Hetero Drugs Ltd.	India
Lamivudine/nevirapine/zidovudine (fixed-dose combination)	Pharmacare	South Africa
Nevirapine	Ranbaxy	India
Lamivudine	Ranbaxy	India
Zidovudine	Ranbaxy	India
Nevirapine	Strides Arcolab Ltd.	India
Stavudine	Strides Arcolab Ltd.	India
Nevirapine	Zhejiang Huahai Pharmaceutical	China

Source: http://hivinsite.ucsf.edu/InSite?page=pr-rr-10#S1.7X, July 2007

combination reduces the number of pills that a patient needs to take, it did not involve the invention of any new chemical entities. The patent history of *zidovudine* has been cited as a classic case of "evergreening" – the use of the patent system to extend drug monopolies far beyond the term of the original patent (Hamied 2005). Box 9.3 discussed evergreening.

Table 9.5 US patents, owners and expiry dates for selected HIV/AIDS drugs

Drug	US patent number	Patent owner	Patent expiry date
Zidovudine (AZT)	4724232	Glaxo	September 2005
Didanosine (ddI)	4861759/5616566	US National Institutes of Health, licensed to Bristol-Myers Squibb	October 2006
Stavudine (d4T)	4978655	Yale University, licensed to Bristol-Myers Squibb	June 2008
Lamivudine (3TC)	5047407	IAF Biochem International SA (Canada), licensed to Glaxo	February 2009
Nevirapine	5366972	Boehringer Ingelheim	November 2011
Efavirenz (EFV)	5811423	Merck & Co., Bristol-Myers Squibb	August 2012
Zidovudine + Lamivudine (AZT + 3TC)	5905082	Glaxo	May 2016
Tenofovir (TDF)	5922695	Gilead Sciences	July 2017

Sources: http://drugpatentexpiry.blogspot.com/2006/05/tenofovir-disoproxil-fumarate-patent.html; http://www.answers.com/topic/emtricitabine; Pérez-Casas et al. (2000)

Zidovudine was originally synthesized in 1964, as a potential cancer treatment. Research in 1984 showed that it was effective against HIV/AIDS, which formed the basis for Glaxo's 1984 patent application. Following clinical trials, the US FDA approved *zidovudine* in March 1987 for advanced HIV disease in adults and the patent for *zidovudine* as a treatment for HIV/AIDS was granted in February 1988 (Cochrane 2000). While *zidovudine* alone only extended life by a matter of months, once it was combined with two other classes of HIV/AIDS drugs, it extended life for years. The FDA expanded *zidovudine* approval in 1990 to include less-advanced stages of HIV disease (Coffey and Peiperl, 2006).

Box 9.3 Evergreening patents

Evergreening is a mechanism by which pharmaceutical and other companies can keep extending patents on drugs after the initial patents expire.

The role of patents is to give exclusive rights to manufacture the patented product over a fixed period of time. The intention of providing a monopoly is to provide an incentive to innovate. Granting a patent requires three elements: (1) novelty of the product; (2) non-obviousness of the new product; and (3) demonstrated utility of the product.

To understand evergreening in the United States, we need to examine the Drug Price Competition and Patent Term Restoration Act, informally known as the "Hatch-Waxman Act" [Public Law 98-417]. It is a 1984 United States federal law which established the modern system for generic drug approval. Hatch-Waxman amended the Federal Food, Drug, and Cosmetic Act. Section 505(j) sets forth the process by which would-be marketers of generic drugs can file Abbreviated Abbreviated New Drug Applications (ANDAs) to seek FDA approval of the generic. Section 505(j)(5)(B)(iv), the so-called Paragraph IV, allows 180-day exclusivity to companies that are the "first-to-file" an ANDA against holders of patents for branded counterparts. The Hatch-Waxman Act encouraged the growth of generic industry, whose market share rose from 19% in 1984 to 49% in 2002 (by volume).

For pharmaceutical companies, the Hatch-Waxman Act has created a perverse incentive. It has given them more incentive to try to extend the life of existing drugs by making marginal changes than to try the risky strategy of inventing completely new chemicals. Thus, the two decades following its passage, the Hatch-Waxman Act has resulted in more me-too drugs than drugs with new chemical compounds. The most famous documented case of evergreening occurred in the case of Prilosec – the so-called "Purple Pill" of AstraZeneca (USD 6 billion/year global blockbuster drug), the patent for which expired in 2001 only to be reincarnated as a new patented drug Nexium.

However, on 30 April 2007 the Supreme Court of the United States issued a ruling in KSR International Co v. Teleflex et al., which raises the bar for patent holders to prove that their invention is not obvious, and therefore patentable. This ruling will make many existing patents more vulnerable, make it harder to gain approval for new patents and make evergreening more difficult in the future. If the patent claim extends to what is obvious, it is invalid. For example, a patent's subject matter can be proved obvious if there existed at the time of invention a known problem for which there was an obvious solution encompassed by the patent's claims. The Supreme Court noted that, "granting patent protection to advances that would occur in the ordinary course without real innovation retards progress and may, in the case of patents combining previously known elements, deprive prior inventions of their value or utility." It is worth quoting in full the Court's description of the reason that patents are only granted for non-obvious innovations:

"We build and create by bringing to the tangible and palpable reality around us new works based on instinct, simple logic, ordinary inferences, extraordinary ideas, and sometimes even genius. These advances, once part of our shared knowledge, define a new threshold from which innovation starts once more. And as progress beginning from higher levels of achievement is expected in the normal course, the results of ordinary innovation are not the subject of exclusive rights under the patent laws. Were it otherwise patents might stifle, rather than promote, the progress of useful arts."

WHO guidelines for ARV treatment regimens provide a basis for a range of treatment protocols in individual countries. In individual countries, factors such as prices, drug efficacy and side effects are also taken into account. *Stavudine* (d4T) has been widely used as part of first-line treatment. However, in 2006 the WHO recommended that d4T no longer be used, due to toxicity. Instead, countries should switch to *tenofovir* (TDF) or *zidovudine* (AZT). Of these two, TDF is preferable, because of its efficacy and safety and because it can be taken only once a day.

TDF can be combined with *efavirenz* (EFV), together with *lamiduvine* (3TC) or *emtricitabine* (FTC), in one, triple-combination pill that can be taken once a day. Patients are more likely to adhere to this once-a-day regimen, thereby reducing drug resistance and improving treatment outcomes. However, the higher cost of AZT and TDF, compared to d4T, has delayed the shift to the new regimen in many developing countries (CHAI 2007). In partnership with UNITAID (discussed below), the Clinton Foundation HIV/AIDS Initiative (CHAI) has negotiated price reductions for several HIV/AIDS drugs for use in 27 low- and middle-income countries (see Table 9.6). The Clinton Foundation is discussed in Chap. 7. As of May 2007, 750,000 people were benefiting from medicines purchased under CHAI agreements in 50 countries (CHAI 2007).

Table 9.6 Prices of ARVs per patient per year of May 2007

Product	Strength (mg)	(1)	(2)	(3)	(4)	(5)	(6)
3TC	150	36	55	48	69	96	69
AZT	300	96	147	103	212	216	212
NVP	200	45	72	52	432	130	432
EFV	600	164	243	207	237	300	657
ABC	300	331	773	456	636	816	636
TDF	300	149	211	194	207	287	360
ddI EC	250	156	227	103	248	929	772
ddI EC	400	248	311	132	320	1,096	1,219
LPV/r	200+50	695	536	1,338	500	2,476	1,000
3TC+AZT	150+300	129	180	134	237	301	237
TDF+FTC	300+200	225	689	300	319	328	552
3TC+AZT+NVP	150+300+200	174	217	231	N/A	331	N/A
TDF+FTC+EFV	300+200+600	385	N/A	527	613	N/A	1,033

Source: Clinton Foundation. *Notes*: Each column numbered (1)–(6) refers to price per patient per year in US dollars. (1) Clinton Foundation HIV/AIDS Initiative (CHAI) Ceiling Price. (2) WHO Global Price Reporting Mechanism for the Low Income Countries Average Price. (3) MSF Lowest Price for Generic Drugs for the Low Income Countries. (4) Originator Access Price for the Low Income Countries. (5) WHO Global Price Reporting Mechanism Upper Middle Income Countries Average Price. (6) Originator Lowest Published "Second Tier" Access Program Price (when available)

There are several notable features in Table 9.6. First, the prices are generally higher for middle-income countries than for low-income countries. Thus, the pharmaceutical companies are pursuing a price discrimination strategy across different markets, selling drugs at a price that the markets can bear. Therefore, there is clear room for generic products in these markets, especially for the low-income countries. Compulsory licensing is a distinct possibility (see, however, our discussion in Chap. 6 about the difficulties many developing countries faced importing drugs under compulsory license from Canada). Some companies have used the World Bank's country income index or the Human Development Index as their criteria for setting prices. In Chap. 6, we developed a much more comprehensive index that takes into account not just the level of development of the country but also level of prevalence of HIV/AIDS explicitly. Second, the price of HIV/AIDS drugs in many cases in many developing countries is not necessarily lower than in developed countries. For example, in Guatemala, between 2000 and 2003, prices of most HIV/AIDS drugs were consistently higher than in the United States (Hellerstein 2003).

9.2.2 Second-Line Treatment

According to CHAI, in 2006, 80,000 (4%) of those receiving ARV treatment in low- and middle-income countries were taking second-line treatment. The reason that relatively few are on second-line treatment is that most only began treatment within the last 4 years. As a result, relatively few have experienced treatment failure, which is defined as (1) virologic failure (a viral load of more than 400 copies per milliliter), (2) immunologic failure (a declining CD4 cell count in spite of treatment) or (3) clinical failure (progression to AIDS evidenced by weight loss or the appearance of opportunistic infections). Another reason is that poor diagnostic and laboratory capacity in many countries has made treatment failure difficult to diagnose.

By 2010, CHAI estimates that close to 500,000 people will require second-line treatment in low- and middle-income countries (CHAI 2007). The higher cost of second-line treatment means that access requires further funding. However, patents are not expected to be an obstacle to acquiring affordable second-line treatments in the most affected low-income countries, due to the delay of TRIPS patent rules on pharmaceuticals to 2016, although patent rules may affect affordability in middle-income countries (CHAI 2007). In Chap. 6 we analyzed TRIPS rules on patents for pharmaceuticals in developing countries. However, as we noted in Chap. 5, the problem of regulatory capture in free trade agreements can undermine TRIPS rules so that patents create obstacles to affordable treatment in some low-income countries and political pressure on low- and middle-income countries can discourage the use of TRIPS flexibilities to increase access to treatment.

UNITAID is a global health initiative for HIV/AIDS, tuberculosis and malaria that is funded by several national governments. With respect to HIV/AIDS, UNITAID funding is focused on pediatric and second-line treatment and the prevention of mother-to-child transmission. UNITAID will finance a free supply of second-line HIV/AIDS treatment in 27 countries for 18 months, after which the reduced prices achieved by CHAI will enable other funding sources, such as the Global Fund (discussed in Chap. 7) and PEPFAR (discussed in Chap. 8), to fund the purchase of second-line treatments at lower prices (CHAI 2007).

While high-income countries and middle-income countries with low prevalence rates are in a position to pay for HIV/AIDS treatment, middle-income countries with high prevalence rates and most low-income countries are not. Low-income countries with high prevalence rates in particular will have to depend on external funding sources, such as PEPFAR and the Global Fund, to expand access to treatment and then to maintain treatment. Medical care for people with HIV/AIDS in developing countries costs about USD 1,000 a year, in drugs and support facilities. The Economist estimated that it would cost USD 6–7 billion a year to provide treatment for the 6–7 million people with HIV/AIDS in low-income countries that were in need of treatment in 2006. However, expanding treatment means that fewer people will die. Moreover, millions more will become infected, and even more so if prevention efforts are not improved. Thus, universal treatment in low-income countries could cost USD 40 billion by the end of the next decade. This highlights the need to ensure that external funding is both increased and sustained and the importance of prevention in making universal access to treatment affordable (Economist 2006).

9.2.3 Vaccines for HIV/AIDS

Scientists have been trying to develop an HIV vaccine for more than 20 years, although some have suggested that an effective AIDS vaccine may be a biological impossibility (Epstein 2007). In 2007, about 50 experimental HIV vaccines were being tested in clinical trials.

Most viral vaccines work by generating antibodies that neutralize or inactivate the invading virus. However, unlike other viruses, HIV-1 evades the antibody response, which, together with the large genetic variety found in HIV-1 strains, has made the development of an HIV-1 vaccine difficult. To date, antibody-based HIV-1 vaccines have only succeeded in neutralizing a minority of the copies of the virus that are found in a given patient. HIV-1 antibodies target the mechanism that HIV-1 uses to bind itself to the host immune cells in order to prevent HIV-1 from entering the cell. However, HIV-1 uses shielding mechanisms to prevent the antibodies from recognizing the virus, including a dense coating. Current HIV-1 vaccine research therefore seeks to find vulnerabilities in these shielding mechanisms, but this requires research for multiple genetic subtypes of HIV-1 (Montefiori et al., 2007). For example, one recent study identified a place on the outside of the human immunodeficiency virus that could be vulnerable to antibodies that could block it from infecting human cells, which might be targeted with a vaccine aimed at preventing initial infection (Dunham 2007).

A new class of HIV vaccines was designed to trigger cell-mediated immunity to create an extended immune defense. However, in 2007, Merck reported that its HIV vaccine, V520, had failed. V520 was being tested by Merck and the US National Institutes of Health in a clinical trial involving 3,000 people in high-risk groups in Australia, Brazil, Canada, the Dominican Republic, Haiti, Jamaica, Peru, Puerto Rico and the United States (Associated Press 2007). V520 used the common cold virus (the adenovirus) to transport three synthetic HIV genes into the body's cells (Park 2007). Merck halted the trials after 24 of 741 volunteers who got the V520 vaccine later became infected with HIV, while only 21 of 762 participants that received a placebo also became infected (Associated Press 2007). The V520 vaccine was one of only two AIDS vaccine candidates in advanced human trials, the other being tested by Sanofi-Aventis SA (Dunham 2007).

Other approaches are also being explored. David Ho (the inventor of triple combination therapy) and his team at the Aaron Diamond AIDS Research Center are researching the use of different vectors, or not using vectors at all, to produce stronger immune responses. Scientists at the International AIDS Vaccine Initiative are studying the use of crippled, live strains of HIV and ways to stimulate a special class of antibodies that appear to be able to defuse HIV. The Global HIV Vaccine Enterprise, which is funded by the Gates Foundation (discussed in Chap. 7), Wellcome Trust, the US National Institutes of Health and the European Union, is seeking to accelerate research on HIV vaccines by linking together independent organizations so that researchers can learn from each other, rather than work in isolation (Park 2007).

As we noted in Chap. 5, there are many subtypes of HIV-1 (the most commonly occurring HIV infection in humans). The major HIV-1 subtypes accounting for most infections in Africa are subtype C in southern Africa, subtypes A and D in eastern Africa, and circulating recombinant form 02_AG (CRF02_AG) in west-central Africa (Peeters and Sharp 2000). The most commonly occurring form of HIV-1 in North America and in Europe is subtype B. The first HIV/AIDS vaccine ever to reach Phase III trial was for subtype B. The gp120 vaccine was not effective. However, what vaccine trials have indicated thus far is that, in the case of HIV/AIDS, there is pattern of development of potential vaccines not in the subtypes where the needs are the greatest but in the area where the biggest monetary rewards are expected. The economics of HIV/AIDS vaccines suggest that funding for vaccines for the worst-effected countries are unlikely to come from the private sector (see Box 9.4).

Box 9.4 Why is there no AIDS vaccine?

HIV/AIDS affects hundreds of millions and kills several million people every year. The disease was identified several decades ago. Two Nobel prizes have been awarded in the past two decades for identifying the cause and the transmission mechanism of HIV/AIDS. Yet we still do not have a vaccine for HIV/AIDS. Kremer and Snyder (2004) have developed an argument as to why the private sector is very unlikely to develop a vaccine for AIDS. Here, we illustrate the argument with one example.

Imagine there are 100 people in the world. There are 90 people (type L) who have a small chance of 10% of contracting HIV/AIDS. There are another ten people (type H) who would develop HIV/AIDS with a 100% chance. Let us suppose that the harm from HIV/AIDS is USD 100 for each person. Let us also assume that for each USD 1 decrease in harm, a consumer is willing to pay USD 1 (technically, each consumer is risk neutral). Suppose the drug is perfectly effective, has no side effects and is costless to produce.

How much revenue will a pharmaceutical company generate in each of the following scenarios? (1) It develops a drug D that cures HIV/AIDS (forever). (2) It develops a vaccine V that prevents HIV/AIDS from developing. We show that under the assumption that the pharmaceutical company cannot distinguish between type H and type L, it is more profitable for the drug companies to produce the drug rather than the vaccine.

If the pharmaceutical company develops the drug D, it will be able to sell it to all the people who get HIV/AIDS. By assumption, all the type H people will develop HIV/AIDS. Thus, there will be ten people from type H who will get HIV/AIDS. In addition, nine people of type L will also develop HIV/AIDS. In total, there will be 19 people with HIV/AIDS, including both types. By assumption, each person contracting HIV/AIDS will be willing to pay USD 100 to reduce the effects of HIV/AIDS by 100%. Therefore, the pharmaceutical company will be able to earn USD 1,900 in revenue from the entire population. Given our assumption of zero cost of production, USD 1,900 will also be the profits of the pharmaceutical company.

The vaccine has to be sold before HIV/AIDS strikes. For type L, there is a 10% chance of HIV/AIDS. Thus, they will be willing to pay the average loss of $100 \times (1/10) =$ USD 10 for the vaccine. If the pharmaceutical company cannot distinguish between type L and type H, it can only charge USD 10 to all. In that case, it will generate USD $10 \times 100 =$ USD 1,000 profits by selling the vaccine to all 100 people. The other possibility is the following. The company sets a price of USD 100 for the vaccine. In that case, no person of type L will buy the vaccine ex-ante (as their expected benefit before HIV/AIDS strikes is USD 10 but the cost is USD 100). The only people who will buy the vaccine will be of type H. Since there are ten of type H, the profits will be USD $100 \times 10 =$ USD 1,000. Thus, in either price strategy, the profits of the company will be USD 1,000.

> Therefore, the profits of the company are bigger in the case of the development of drug D instead of the vaccine V. This argument is extremely general as long as the probability of the type L does not get close to the probability of type H getting the disease and the company cannot distinguish between the types.

9.3 Public Health and Human Rights

At the beginning of this book, we highlighted the need to integrate three inter-related issues into any comprehensive AIDS strategy – prevention, treatment and human rights protection. As we showed in Chap. 2, each of these issues must be considered in the context of specific countries or regions, in order to take into account variations in cultural values, affected groups, infection rates, legal systems, economic resources and human resources. In this chapter, we have analyzed prevention and treatment issues in greater detail. The preceding discussion shows that great progress has been made on these two fronts and that greater progress is possible. Our analysis of prevention issues in particular has shown the need to integrate prevention, treatment and human rights strategies. The primary reason that human rights need to be addressed is because discrimination keeps people away from both prevention and treatment programs (Gruskin et al., 2007).

Changing social attitudes in order to overcome stigma and discrimination is not an easy task, particularly given deep-seated fears and prejudices surrounding sex, blood, disease and death and the wide-spread perception that HIV/AIDS is closely tied to deviant or immoral behavior (Jürgens and Cohen, 2007). In this regard, the United Nations International Guidelines on HIV/AIDS and Human Rights recommend that States, in collaboration with and through the community, promote a supportive and enabling environment for women, children and other vulnerable groups by addressing underlying prejudices and inequalities through community dialogue, specially designed social and health services and support to community groups. The Guidelines also recommend that States promote the wide and ongoing distribution of creative education, training and media programs explicitly designed to change attitudes of discrimination and stigmatization associated with HIV/AIDS to understanding and acceptance (United Nations 2007).

Variations in cultural values and legal systems make HIV/AIDS-related human rights particularly difficult to tackle on a global basis. However, HIV/AIDS-related human rights are the area where the least progress has been made and need to become a central focus in the global fight against HIV/AIDS (Jürgens and Cohen 2007). In this section, we focus on three categories of laws: (1) laws that discriminate against vulnerable groups; (2) laws that discriminate against HIV-positive people, such as those that criminalize HIV transmission; and (3) laws that prohibit discrimination against vulnerable groups, including HIV-positive people. We review the United Nations International Guidelines on HIV/AIDS and Human Rights and provide examples in each category.

The law plays different roles with respect to infectious diseases. Some health risks, such as poor access to sterile injection equipment, can be directly attributed to law, and laws have been used to change unhealthy behaviors, such as smoking and drunk driving. Both international and national laws are used in disease control. In addition to the law's role as a source of disease control authority for government, the law has a countervailing role as a source of protection against excessive and unnecessary regulations (Burris 1999).

The United Nations International Guidelines on HIV/AIDS and Human Rights acknowledge the inherent limitations in using law reform to enhance human rights. The effectiveness human rights laws depend on the strength of the legal system in a given society and on the access of its citizens to the system, both of which vary considerably from one country to the next. Moreover, the law cannot serve as the only means of educating, changing attitudes, achieving behavioral change or protecting people's rights. Nevertheless, since laws regulate conduct between the State and the individual and between individuals, they can either support or undermine the observance of human rights, including HIV-related human rights (United Nations 2007). For these reasons, we first consider laws that have a negative impact on HIV-related human rights and then consider laws that support human rights.

9.3.1 Laws that Discriminate Against Vulnerable Groups

While social attitudes may take time to change, an important first step is to reform laws, policies and practices that institutionalize discrimination against the groups of people who are most vulnerable to HIV/AIDS: women and girls; men who have sex with men; commercial sex workers; and injection drug users. The United Nations International Guidelines on HIV/AIDS and Human Rights recommend that States reform criminal laws and correctional systems to ensure that they are consistent with international human rights obligations and are not targeted against vulnerable groups (United Nations 2007). Laws in this category include those that prohibit sexual acts between consenting adults in private, laws prohibiting sex work that involves no victimization and laws prohibiting measures such as needle exchange that can reduce the harm associated with illicit drug use (Elliot 2002).

9.3.1.1 Women and Girls

The United Nations International Guidelines on HIV/AIDS and Human Rights recommend the enactment of anti-discrimination and protective laws to reduce human rights violations against women and children in the context of HIV, to reduce the vulnerability of women and children to HIV infection and to the impact of HIV/AIDS. With respect to women, the Guidelines recommend law reforms to ensure the equality of women regarding property and marital relations and access to employment and economic opportunity, such as equal rights to own and inherit property, to enter into contracts and marriage, to obtain credit and finance, to initiate separation or divorce, to equitably share assets upon divorce or separation and to retain custody of children. In addition, laws should ensure women's reproductive and sexual rights, including the right of independent access to reproductive and sexual health information and services and contraception, the right to demand safer sex practices and the right to legal protection from sexual violence. With respect to children, laws should provide for children's access to HIV-related information, education and means of prevention, govern children's access to voluntary testing with consent, should protect children against mandatory testing, particularly if orphaned by AIDS, and provide for other forms of protection in the context of orphans, including inheritance and/or support. Laws should also protect children against sexual abuse and provide for their rehabilitation if abused and ensure that they are not subject to penalties themselves. Protection under disability laws should also be ensured for children (United Nations 2007).

In sub-Saharan Africa, laws of particular concern include marital rape, property laws, inheritance laws, and child custody laws. In many African countries marital rape does not exist as a legal concept, leaving women with no recourse against sexual abuse by their husbands. When the husband is HIV-positive or engages in unsafe sex or drug use, this increases the risk of infection for women. Child custody laws, customary practice and traditions that favor paternal custody of children make it difficult for women to leave abusive relationships. While statutes allow property ownership regardless of sex, in practice women only have user rights under customary laws, not ownership. Under inheritance laws, property remains in the man's family after he dies. Thus, if a woman wants to leave an abusive husband or her husband dies, she cannot take any property with her, leaving women economically dependant upon their husbands or, as widows, their families. New laws have created inheritance rights for dependants, but are ignored by the man's family and not enforced. As a result, women and children widowed and orphaned by AIDS are left without adequate resources for medical treatment, and women must either rely on their in-laws for support or become commercial sex workers (Kelly 2004). Laws and cultural traditions thus increase women's vulnerability to HIV/AIDS, either within marriage or by forcing them to support themselves and their children as sex workers.

9.3.1.2 Men Who Have Sex with Men

The United Nations International Guidelines on HIV/AIDS and Human Rights recommend the enactment of anti-discrimination and protective laws to reduce human rights violations against men having sex with men, including in the context of HIV, including penalties for vilification of people who engage in same-sex relationships, legal recognition of same-sex marriages or relationships and non-discriminatory property, divorce and inheritance laws for same-sex relationships.

One key purpose of such anti-discrimination laws is to reduce the vulnerability of men who have sex with men to infection by HIV and to the impact of HIV/AIDS. The Guidelines also recommend that the age of consent to sex and marriage be consistent for heterosexual and homosexual relationships and that laws and police practices relating to assaults against men who have sex with men ensure adequate legal protection (United Nations 2007).

In a 2006 internet-based survey of 759 sexually active MSM in New York City, 11% reported being HIV-positive and 74% reported being HIV-negative. The majority were white, college-educated and in their 30s. The race of the respondents was white (77%), latino (13%), black (4%) and other (6%). In the previous 12 months, 45% had more than ten male sex partners, 53% had engaged in unprotected anal sex and 37% had used non-injection drugs. Fifty percent of the HIV-positive men had unprotected anal sex in the previous 12 months and 71% of the HIV-negative men had unprotected anal sex in the previous 12 months (NYC Health 2007).

In a 2006 survey of 614 Black MSM in New York City, 67% were HIV-positive. The median age of the respondents was 42 years, 22% had less than a high school education, 67% were unemployed and 57% had an annual income of less than USD 10,000. Fifty-six percent identified themselves as homosexual, 32% as bisexual, 6% as heterosexual and 6% as other. Sixty-five percent had previously been diagnosed with a sexually transmitted infection and 30% had been raped (80% before they were 18 years old). Eighty-four percent knew that they were HIV-positive. Of the 16% that were unaware that they were HIV-positive, 53% reported having been tested for HIV previously. Of those who had never been tested for HIV, the reasons they gave were: (1) being afraid to learn that they had HIV (48%); (2) being worried that others might treat them differently (26%); (3) the perception of not being at risk because they practiced safe sex (16%); and (4) being afraid that results will be reported to the government (16%). Fifty percent reported unprotected anal sex with a man in the previous 3 months and 31% had exchanged sex for drugs, money or a place to stay in the same period. Among those who had unprotected anal sex with a man in their last sexual encounter, 84% of the HIV-positive men had an HIV-positive sex partner and 89% of the HIV-negative men had an HIV-negative sex partner (NYC Health 2007).

9.3.1.3 Sex Workers

According to the UNAIDS Guidance Note on HIV and Sex Work, despite high HIV prevalence among sex workers, only one in three receive adequate HIV prevention services and even fewer receive adequate treatment and health care (UNAIDS 2007). The UNAIDS Guidance Note focuses on the reduction of HIV vulnerability among sex workers, who are defined as adults over the age of 18 years in order to take into account that sexual exploitation of children under 18 years of age is prohibited under international law. The key factors that lead people into sex work include poverty, gender inequality, indebtedness, migration, criminal coercion, humanitarian emergencies, drug use and dysfunctional families. Laws, policies and practices that drive sex work underground make HIV/AIDS prevention and treatment for sex workers and their clients more difficult. Discrimination against sex workers among the police, health care services and other social services impede access to prevention and treatment. The UNAIDS Guidance Note organizes its recommendations into three categories: (1) reducing vulnerabilities and addressing structural issues; (2) reducing risk of HIV infection; and (3) building supportive environments and expanding choices.

The strategies in the first category are to: (1) address poverty and gender inequality by providing alternatives to sex work through micro-finance programs and reforms to property rights; (2) address the demand for paid sex by seeking to changes men's behavior; (3) expand access to education for girls and women; (4) provide alternative job opportunities through employment growth and vocational training; and (5) provide employment and education opportunities and access to social services for refugees, internally displaced persons and economic migrants.

The strategies in the second category are to: (1) involve sex workers in HIV prevention and treatment programs; (2) make male and female condoms available for free or at low cost; (3) increase access to antiretroviral treatment; (4) address the specific needs of sex workers in sexual and reproductive health programs, taking into account the different needs of female, male and transgender sex workers; (5) make HIV prevention information and condoms readily available to clients; (6) seek to eliminate violence against sex workers by clients, managers, police and other government officials; (7) seek to change attitudes towards sex workers to reduce stigma and discrimination; (8) promote initiatives to enable sex workers to negotiate safe sex practices; and (9) promote access to drug addiction treatment programs and harm reduction programs, such as needle exchange.

The strategies in the third category are to: (1) address sex work stigma and discrimination to reduce economic, cultural and social marginalization in families and communities; (2) improve access to health care, education and training, micro-finance and credit, social services, housing support and legal services; and (3) promote community organizations that work with sex workers.

The UNAIDS Guidance Note on HIV and Sex Work has been criticized for emphasizing alternative livelihoods without offering concrete examples, rather than emphasizing the right to engage in sex work and workplace safety and national laws that undermine sex workers' rights, particularly criminal prohibition of sex work and related activities. The Guidance Note's strategy of reducing demand for sex work has been criticized as implicitly supporting the criminalization or repression of sex work, which can increase the risk of HIV infection by driving sex work underground, limit sex workers' choices regarding working conditions and clients and increase stigmatization. The Guidance Note was further criticized for not advocating enhanced human rights protection for those engaged in sex work – as women, men, transgender persons and workers. The process used for preparing the document was criticized for not meaningfully engaging sex workers. UNAIDS' response to criticism of this document – to withdraw it as a public document and restrict it to internal use – was also criticized (Canadian HIV/AIDS Legal Network 2007b)

The United Nations International Guidelines on HIV/AIDS and Human Rights recommend that criminal law prohibiting sexual acts (including adultery, sodomy, fornication and commercial sexual encounters) between consenting adults in private should not be allowed to impede provision of HIV prevention and care services and should be repealed. With regard to adult sex work that involves no victimization, the International Guidelines on HIV/AIDS and Human Rights recommend de-criminalizing and legally regulating occupational health and safety conditions to protect sex workers and their clients, including support for safe sex during sex work. More generally, criminal law should not impede provision of HIV prevention and care services to sex workers and their clients and should ensure that children and adult sex workers who have been coerced into sex work are not prosecuted for such participation but rather are removed from sex work and provided with medical and psycho-social support services, including those related to HIV (United Nations 2007).

9.3.1.4 Injection Drug Users

In Eastern Europe and Central Asia, UNAIDS (2006) estimates that the use of contaminated injection equipment accounts for more than 80% of HIV/AID cases and accounts for about 30% of new infections outside sub-Saharan Africa. The United Nations International Guidelines on HIV/AIDS and Human Rights recommend that criminal law not be an impediment to measures taken by States to reduce the risk of HIV transmission among injecting drug users and to provide them with HIV-related care and treatment. They further recommend that criminal law be reviewed to consider: (1) the authorization or legalization and promotion of needle and syringe exchange programs; and (2) the repeal of laws criminalizing the possession, distribution and dispensing of needles and syringes (United Nations 2007).

In Saint Petersburg, Russia, a 2002 study found that 48% of injection drug users had shared needles in the 30 days prior to their first use of a needle exchange program. In early 2004, there were four syringe exchange facilities in Saint Petersburg – one mobile service (a bus) and three fixed facilities. However, the most important source of sterile syringes for injection drug users was drug stores. Human Rights Watch found that state-supported impediments to access to both needle exchange points and drug stores were important barriers to HIV prevention, including: (1) police patrols of drug stores, which deterred injection drug users from purchasing syringes; (2) police patrols of needle exchange bus stops; and (3) arrests, fines or bribes for possession of syringes, even though carrying syringes is not illegal in the Russian Federation. However, while police interference with the syringe exchange bus was a problem in the late 1990s, it lessened in the early 2000s. Humanitarian Action, an NGO that delivers syringe exchange services in

Saint Petersburg, visited with police chiefs to talk about the importance of syringe exchange for HIV prevention and organized a training session in 2003 for police officers that included the participation of former drug users and people living with HIV/AIDS. However, due to past incidents, the fear of apprehension by the police kept some drug users from using fixed as well as mobile syringe exchange facilities (Human Rights Watch 2004). Table 9.7 shows the dramatic increase in HIV prevalence among injection drug users in Saint Petersburg from 1998 to 2001.

Table 9.7 HIV prevalence among drug users in Saint Petersburg, Russia

Year	Prevalence rate (%)
1998	4
1999	12
2000	19
2001	36

Source: Dr. Tatjana Smolskaya, Pasteur Institute of Saint Petersburg

A 2005 survey of 500 injection drug users (IDUs) in New York City found that 65% had obtained a syringe from an exchange program in the previous year, 49% at a pharmacy, 10% from a medical provider, 53% from a friend or sexual partner and 25% from a drug dealer. The self-reported HIV prevalence rate in the group was 21%. IDUs who obtained syringes from sterile sources (exchange, pharmacy or provider) were less likely to share syringes than those who obtained them from non-sterile sources (friends, relatives or the street). Those who obtained syringes from exchange programs were significantly less likely to share syringes. Nevertheless, 19% of IDUs had shared a syringe at least once in the previous 12 months and 53% had engaged in unprotected sex. IDUs that had shared a syringe were 2.5 times more likely to engage in unprotected sex (NYC Health 2007).

9.3.2 Laws that Discriminate Against HIV-Positive People

Another category of laws discriminates directly against people with HIV/AIDS, such as laws that criminalize HIV transmission and travel restrictions based on HIV status.

9.3.2.1 Criminalization of HIV Transmission

There is a concern that the criminalization of HIV transmission will discourage people from seeking testing (Tarantola and Gruskin 2007). There is evidence that knowledge of HIV status results in behavioral changes that reduce transmission. In addition, where knowledge of HIV status leads to antiretroviral treatment, treatment also reduces transmission by reducing the amount of virus in the body. Thus, the criminalization of HIV transmission may have the effect of increasing, rather than reducing, HIV transmission. One possible response is mandatory HIV testing in health care settings (that is, testing without the informed consent of the patient). However, this policy, too, may be self-defeating if it discourages people from seeking health care. Moreover, mandatory HIV testing runs counter to the United Nations International Guidelines on HIV/AIDS and Human Rights recommendation that public health legislation ensure that HIV testing of individuals should only be performed with their specific informed consent (United Nations 2007).

Several studies have concluded that the criminalization of HIV transmission is unlikely to serve the goals of public health policy or the goals of criminal law, and thus may do more harm than good. In a UNAIDS policy paper, Elliot (2002) recommended that governments and the judiciary take into account the following principles in determining policy regarding the use of criminal sanctions under public health law: (1) use the best available scientific evidence regarding the modes and risk of HIV transmission to rationally determine when and if conduct should attract criminal liability; (2) the primary objective should be to prevent HIV transmission; (3) legal and policy responses to HIV/AIDS should pursue public health and conform to international human rights norms, particularly non-discrimination and due process; and (4) policy makers should assess the impact of law or policy on human rights and prefer the least-intrusive measures possible to achieve a demonstrably justified objective of preventing disease transmission.

With respect to the four functions of criminal law (harm prevention through imprisonment; prevention of future harm through rehabilitation; punishment/retribution; and deterrence), Elliot (2002) concluded that criminal law is an ineffective response to the epidemic: (1) imprisoning an HIV-positive individual does not prevent transmission through conjugal visits or high-risk behavior with other prisoners; (2) criminal penalties are unlikely to change sexual activity and drug use, due to the complexity of these human behaviors; (3) punishment/retribution do not achieve the goal of HIV prevention and risk reinforcing prejudice and discrimination against already stigmatized HIV-positive people; and (4) criminal sanctions are unlikely to act as a deterrent, given that drug use and sexual activity persist even with the risk of criminal prosecution and are more likely to be driven underground when prosecuted, hindering HIV prevention. Moreover, overly broad use of criminal laws risks spreading misinformation regarding how HIV is transmitted.

In an empirical study conducted in the United States, Burris et al. (2007) found that laws prohibiting unsafe sex or requiring disclosure of infection do not influence people's normative beliefs about risky sex and did not significantly influence sexual behavior. The study concluded that criminal law is not a clearly useful intervention for promoting disclosure by HIV-positive people to their sex partners. Moreover, given concerns about possible negative effects of criminal law, such as stigmatization or reluctance to cooperate with health authorities, criminal law should be used with caution as a behavioral change mechanism for HIV-positive people.

There have been numerous cases in which criminal laws have been applied to HIV transmission in common law countries. In some cases, courts have applied existing criminal laws to cases involving HIV, where the laws themselves do not refer specifically to HIV. In this context, law reforms could come from the legislature, through amendments that clarify the application of relevant criminal laws to cases involving HIV, or through the evolution of precedents in the courts. The United Nations International Guidelines on HIV/AIDS and Human Rights recommend the reform of criminal laws and correctional systems to ensure that they are consistent with international human rights obligations and are not misused in the context of HIV/AIDS (United Nations 2007). They also recommend the sensitization of the judiciary, in ways consistent with judicial independence, on the legal, ethical and human rights issues relative to HIV, including through judicial education and the development of judicial materials (United Nations 2007). Criminal laws should not include specific offences against the intentional transmission of HIV but rather should apply general criminal offences to these exceptional cases. Such application should ensure that the elements of foreseeability, intent, causality and consent are clearly and legally established to support a guilty verdict and/or harsher penalties (United Nations 2007).

In the United States, a series of cases involving spitting have gone in different directions. In Ohio v. Bird (1998), an HIV-positive man was convicted of felonious assault, which requires the knowing attempt to harm by use of a weapon capable of inflicting death, after spitting in a police officer's face, even though all medical and scientific evidence demonstrated that saliva does not transmit HIV. In State v. Jones (2000), another case of an HIV-positive individual accused of spitting on an officer, the New Mexico court of appeals ruled that criminal liability for battery could not be based upon the victims' subjective and unsubstantiated fears that they could develop a disease, and reversed the lower court on this issue. In Weeks v. State (1992), the Texas Court of Appeal sustained the attempted murder conviction of an HIV-positive inmate who spat in a guard's face. The spitting cases show how the application of criminal laws to HIV-positive individuals – when based on HIV status, stigma and discrimination rather than on medical or scientific evidence – can undermine genuine efforts to reduce HIV transmission by spreading misinformation and increasing stigma and discrimination.

In cases involving behavior that does carry a risk of HIV transmission, such as unprotected sexual intercourse or sharing drug injection equipment, the central issue is consent. In R v. Cuerrier (1998) the Supreme Court of Canada established that there is a duty to disclose one's HIV status before engaging in any activity that poses a "significant risk" of HIV transmission. Failure to do so legally invalidates a sexual partner's consent to sexual intercourse. The lack of consent to have intercourse with a partner that is HIV-positive converts the sexual intercourse into a criminal assault. In that case, the complainants did not become infected with HIV as a result of the unprotected sex. However, if the complainants believe that their partner is HIV-free and the accused puts the complainants at significant risk to their health, failure to disclose HIV status vitiates consent to sexual intercourse.

This decision suggests that there might not be a duty to disclose HIV status prior to engaging in activities that do not pose a significant risk of transmission, such as kissing and oral sex, or where an HIV-positive individual uses a condom. In R v. Edwards, a lower court judge ruled that there is no duty to disclose HIV status prior to engaging in unprotected oral sex because it is a low risk activity (Canadian AIDS Society 2004).

In R v. Williams (2003), the defendant began a sexual relationship with the complainant in June 1991, in which they had unprotected sex on numerous occasions. On 15 November 1991, the defendant learned that he was HIV-positive, but did not reveal his status to the complainant and continued to have unprotected sex with her. The Supreme Court of Canada ruled that the defendant was not guilty of aggravated assault under section 268(1) of the Canadian Criminal Code, which requires that the assault "wounds, maims, disfigures or endangers the life of the complainant". What distinguishes aggravated assault from mere assault is not the act itself, but rather the consequences of the act. Because it was likely that the defendant had infected the complainant before he learned of his HIV status, it could not be proved beyond a reasonable doubt that he had endangered the life of the complainant. However, the defendant was guilty of attempted aggravated assault for continuing to have unprotected sex with the complainant after having learned of his HIV status. The court ruled that there is sufficient criminal intent for a conviction on a sexual assault charge if a person acts "recklessly". In Canadian law, a person acts "recklessly" if they know that their conduct risks committing a crime but they commit the act nevertheless. In this case, the Supreme Court ruled that criminal recklessness is established once an individual becomes aware of a risk that he or she has contracted HIV, but continues to have unprotected sex without disclosure of HIV status, thereby creating a risk of further HIV transmission. In this case there was no evidence before the court regarding the defendant's awareness of the risk that he might be HIV-positive, prior to 15 November 1991, other than the fact that he had been asked to take an HIV test. This aspect of the ruling raised the issue of whether there is a duty to disclose the mere awareness of a risk that one might be HIV-positive before having unprotected sex. The court also suggested that an HIV-positive person might be held criminally liable for failure to disclose HIV status before having unprotected sex with another HIV-positive individual, where this results in the transmission of a different strain of HIV or a drug-resistant strain of HIV.

The Supreme Court of Canada cases have been criticized, on the one hand, for discouraging people from seeking testing in order to avoid the possibility of a criminal conviction based on knowledge of HIV status and, on the other hand, for risking undesirable invasions of privacy if courts are required to determine whether an individual was aware that their past activities put them at risk of HIV infection (Canadian HIV/AIDS Legal Network 2003). However, in R v. Williams, the fact that the defendant had been asked to take an HIV test, because he was on a list of former partners provided by an individual who had tested HIV-positive, was not sufficient to establish that he was aware that his past activities had put him at risk of HIV infection. Nevertheless, the decision has been criticized for extending the criminal law beyond cases where individuals know that they are HIV-positive, without defining the nature of the awareness that might be required. More generally, the use of criminal law to prevent HIV transmission has been criticized for stigmatizing all HIV-positive people because of the conduct of a few individuals, for discouraging those most at risk from seeking testing and for being unlikely to stop people from having risky sex or sharing needles and syringes. Moreover, all of the HIV-related criminal prosecutions in Canada have occurred in the context of heterosexual intercourse, rather than homosexual intercourse or injection drug use, creating a perception of discriminatory application (or non-application) of the laws (Betteridge 2007).

In the United Kingdom, there were eleven prosecutions for reckless transmission of HIV/AIDS between 2003 and 2007, in which eight accused pleaded guilty, two were convicted and one was acquitted (Klein 2007). A New Zealand court has ruled that people living with HIV/AIDS are not required to disclose their HIV status if they use condoms during vaginal sex (Klein 2007).

In particular, the use of criminal laws to prevent HIV transmission also has been criticized for not taking into account that HIV-positive individuals living in abusive relationships may fear the consequences of disclosing their status to partners and may not be able to use a condom or insist that their partner use a condom (Canadian AIDS Society 2004). In a literature review of HIV/AIDS and gender-based violence, the Harvard School of Public Health Program on International Health and Human Rights (2006) found that gender-based violence (which is not limited to violence against women) can interfere with safe sex practices and access to treatment. Not only is gender-based violence a risk factor for acquiring HIV/AIDS, but HIV/AIDS is also a risk factor for gender-based violence.

In summary, the use of criminal laws to prevent HIV transmission may undermine overall public health initiatives by: (1) reinforcing HIV/AIDS-related stigma; (2) spreading misinformation about HIV/AIDS; (3) creating a disincentive for HIV testing; (4) hindering access to counseling and support services; (5) creating a false expectation that criminal laws eliminate the danger of unprotected sex for people who believe that they are HIV-negative; (6) creating the risk of selective prosecution of marginalized groups; (7) criminalizing behavior that results from gender inequality, in the case of HIV-positive people living in abusive or economically dependent circumstances; and (8) invading privacy through the disclosure of medical records and HIV status in public court proceedings (Elliot 2002). However, the use of criminal laws may be warranted in some circumstances, where HIV status is an aggravating or otherwise relevant factor in cases involving physical assault that would constitute criminal behavior even in the absence of HIV, such as rape or the use of needles as weapons (Elliot 2002).

Finally, a distinction should be made between criminal laws and public health laws that are quasi-criminal in nature, particularly those regarding quarantine. While quarantine laws, such as isolation, detention or quarantine, may be suitable for casually communicable and curable diseases, such laws run the same risk of misuse as do criminal laws (Elliot 2002). In this regard, the United Nations International Guidelines on HIV/AIDS and Human Rights recommend that public health law provisions applicable to casually transmitted diseases not be applied inappropriately to HIV/AIDS and that they be consistent with international human rights obligations (United Nations 2007).

9.3.2.2 Migration Laws that Discriminate Against HIV-Positive People

Some countries have restricted the entry of people living with HIV/AIDS, for short-term or long-term stays, through mandatory testing or a requirement to declare one's HIV status. As we saw in Chap. 8, the WHO International Health Regulations also contain provisions regarding health measures applied to travelers. These provisions encourage States to base their determinations upon scientific principles, available scientific evidence of a risk to human health and any available specific guidance or advice from the WHO. They also require States to treat travelers with respect for their dignity, human rights and fundamental freedoms and minimize any discomfort or distress associated with such measures.

Governments cite two main reasons for imposing travel restrictions on people living with HIV/AIDS – public health protection and reducing demand on health care and social services (UNAIDS/IOM 2004). In the United Kingdom, another source of demands for HIV screening of migrants has been a concern over "health tourism" – HIV infected migrants from developing countries that go to Europe to receive health care. However, research shows that access to treatment is rarely the reason for migration to Europe, since most migrants only learn of their HIV status after having arrived in the host country, and there is no uniform policy in European Union countries regarding screening of migrants for HIV (Carballo 2007).

HIV/AIDS is not considered to be a condition that poses a threat to public health in relation to travel because HIV/AIDS is already present in virtually every country in the world and HIV is not transmitted through casual contact. Unlike highly contagious diseases with short incubation periods, such as SARS, cholera and plague, HIV transmission can be prevented through safe sex and safe drug injection, which can be used by both the infected and the non-infected to prevent transmission. There is no evidence to support the assumption that both the infected and the non-infected will engage in unsafe practices. As a result, the presence of HIV-positive individuals, by itself, does not pose a risk to public health. In addition, travel restrictions are not effective in preventing the entry of HIV-positive individuals, since HIV tests do not detect the virus in newly infected people and nationals that are returning from travel abroad (who may have been infected while outside the country) are not subject to HIV/AIDS-related travel restrictions and are not prevented from entering their own country. Moreover, travel restrictions can undermine HIV/AIDS-related public health initiatives by increasing stigma and discrimination and mislead the public into thinking that HIV/AIDS can be prevented through border measures, rather than through proven prevention strategies (UNAIDS/IOM 2004).

UNAIDS and the International Organization for Migration (IOM) recommend that exclusion on the basis of possible costs to health care and social services only occur on an individual basis, where the following considerations are shown: (1) the person requires the health care and social services and is likely to use them in the near future; (2) the person has no other means of meeting those costs (for example, through private or employment-based insurance or personal resources); and (3) these costs will not be exceeded by the benefits of the person's skills, talents, contribution to the labor force, payment of taxes, contribution to cultural diversity and capacity for revenue or job creation (UNAIDS/IOM 2004). They also recommend that countries treat similar conditions alike, rather than singling out HIV/AIDS. One study showed that the 10-year economic impact of admitting immigrants with asymptomatic HIV infection would be similar to admitting immigrants with asymptomatic coronary heart disease (Zowall et al., 1994).

The Canadian Immigration and Refugee Protection Act provides that foreign nationals can be deemed "medically inadmissible" based on a medical condition, and therefore denied a visa or entry at the border, if: (1) they are likely to be a danger to public health or public safety; or (2) they might reasonably be expected to cause excessive demand on health or social services. Since 1991, Canadian government policy has been that people living with HIV/AIDS do not represent a danger to public health or public safety by virtue of their HIV status. The issue of excessive demand on health or social services is mainly a consideration in cases of immigration or stays that exceed 6 months, is determined on a case-by-case basis and does not apply to refugees or close family members of Canadian citizens or permanent residents (spouses and children). Demand on health or social services is considered excessive if: (1) the anticipated costs would likely exceed the costs of health or social services for the average Canadian resident; or (2) the demand would add to existing waiting lists for those services and would increase the rate or mortality and morbidity in Canada by denying or delaying access to those services by Canadian citizens or permanent residents. The social or economic contributions the individual is expected to make to Canada are not taken into account. People entering Canada for less than 6 months are not required to disclose their HIV status or to be tested for HIV (Canadian HIV/AIDS Legal Network 2007a).

The United States has had a travel and immigration restriction in place for people living with HIV/AIDS since 1987 (Human Rights Watch 2006). Under the US Immigration and Nationality Act, applicants for a visa or for admission to the United States are inadmissible if they have "a communicable disease of public health significance", which includes HIV infection, although waivers are available on a case-by-case basis. For example, the US Attorney General named the 2006 High Level Meeting on AIDS a "designated event" for which an HIV waiver would be available. Visitors entering the United States on the Visa Waiver Program (which waives the requirement to apply for a visa prior to traveling to the United

States, for certain countries) must fill out an I-94W form, which asks, "Have you ever been afflicted with a communicable disease of public health significance." If the visitor answers yes to the question or the US border authorities suspect a visitor to be HIV-positive the person may be: (1) placed into secondary inspection; (2) questioned by an official of the US Department of Homeland Security; (3) placed into deferred inspection; (4) asked to withdraw the application for admission into the United States; (5) placed into the expedited removal process; or (6) placed into an US Department of Homeland Security Detention Center and detained until the case is heard by an immigration judge (GMHC 2006).

HIV-positive non-immigrants seeking to enter the US on a temporary basis for business, pleasure, or education are eligible for a waiver under which they can be allowed to enter the United States. In practice, a waiver is granted in most cases if: (1) they are not symptomatic; (2) it is a short visit; (3) they have insurance or other assets sufficient to pay medical expenses; and (4) they don't appear to be a public health risk. Permanent residency and immigration applicants can also apply for a waiver, but they are usually rejected. To receive a waiver as an immigrant, the person must be the spouse, unmarried son or adopted child of a United States citizen or permanent resident or have a United States citizen or lawful permanent resident as their son or daughter. In addition, an HIV-positive immigration applicant must prove that: (1) he will not be a danger to public health; (2) the possibility of spreading the disease is minimal; and (3) there will be no cost incurred by any level of government without its prior consent (Tarwater 2001).

The political history of the US HIV travel restrictions is an interesting story. In June 1987 the US Public Health Service added AIDS to the list of excludable conditions, noting that the exclusion was not based on any new scientific knowledge and that AIDS is not spread by casual contact, which is the usual public concept of contagious. In July 1987, Republican Senator Jesse Helms also added HIV infection to the exclusion list, through the US Congress, together with a prohibition on funding from the US Centers for Disease Control for AIDS programs that "promote, encourage or condone homosexual activities" (Koch 1987; AIDS Treatment News 1991). Senator Helms accompanied the introduction of his amendments with the following statement: "We have got to call a spade a spade, and a perverted human being a perverted human being" (Koch 1987). In July 1995, Senator Jesse Helms advocated spending less money on HIV/AIDS, because it resulted from "deliberate, disgusting, revolting conduct" and was "a disease transmitted by people deliberately engaging in unnatural acts" (Associated Press 1995). Ten years later, he had this to say: "It had been my feeling that AIDS was a disease largely spread by reckless and voluntary sexual and drug-abusing behavior, and that it would probably be confined to those in high-risk populations. I was wrong" (Hulse 2005).

In 1990, the US Centers for Disease Control (CDC) recommended that all diseases except active tuberculosis be removed from the list of excludable conditions. HIV was left on the list because it had been put on the list by Congress. In November

1990, the Immigration Reform Act of 1990 directed the CDC to establish a new list of excludable conditions, based solely on current epidemiological principles and medical standards. In January 1991, the CDC again proposed that only active tuberculosis remain on the list of excludable conditions. Religious leaders campaigned to maintain the ban and the US House of Representatives opposed removing the HIV ban (AIDS Treatment News 1991). In August 2007, Democratic Representatives Barbara Lee and Hilda Solis introduced the "HIV Nondiscrimination in Travel and Immigration Act". The proposed legislation would restore the authority of the Secretary of Health and Human Services to determine whether HIV status is a communicable disease of public health significance. The decision to maintain or remove the ban would then be based on public health analysis instead of a formal ban made by Congress (Latino Commission on AIDS 2007). In November 2007, the US Department of Homeland Security proposed a new rule that would allow short-term visas to be granted to HIV-positive people by US consulates in their home countries. However, applicants would have to agree to conditions, including ceding the right to apply for longer stays or permanent residency in the United States. Democratic members of the US House of Representatives objected that the changes would only shift decision-making authority to local consular officers, who may lack the appropriate medical expertise. Moreover, there would be no appeal process (Werner 2007).

The United States and Canada are similar societies, both culturally and economically, but have adopted very different approaches to HIV/AIDS travel restrictions. The HIV prevalence rate in the United States is higher than in Canada. This suggests that the US travel restriction has not been effective in preventing HIV transmission in the United States, and that the lack of such a restriction in Canada has not had the effect of increasing HIV prevalence.

Health care costs, measured as a percentage of GDP, are also higher in the United States than in Canada. While this difference is attributable to many factors, making it difficult to determine the impact of the different travel restriction policies on health care costs without further study, it is an indication that the Canadian approach has not led to a significant increase in health care costs compared to the American approach. In 2003, Americans spent USD 5,711 per capita on health care, compared with USD 2,998 in Canada. Americans spent 15.2% of GDP on health care compared with 9.9% of GDP in Canada. Interestingly, this gap was not always there. In 1970, both countries spent exactly 7.0% of their respective GDP on health care (OECD 2006).

Another factor that suggests that US travel restrictions are unlikely to prove successful is illegal immigration. There are several million illegal entries into the United States each year. They are obviously not screened. Thus, from a practical point of view, travel and immigration restrictions for HIV-positive individuals are unlikely to be effective in preventing the entry of many HIV-positive individuals and may provide additional incentives for some individuals to migrate illegally.

9.3.3 Laws that Prohibit Discrimination Against Vulnerable Groups

The United Nations International Guidelines on HIV/AIDS and Human Rights recommend that States enact or strengthen anti-discrimination laws that protect vulnerable groups, people living with HIV/AIDS and people with disabilities from discrimination in both the public and private sectors, and provide for speedy and effective administrative and civil remedies (United Nations 2007). Human rights laws in many jurisdictions prohibit discrimination against vulnerable groups or against people with HIV/AIDS, as well as providing other rights that are relevant to HIV/AIDS, such as the right to life and the right to health.

Human rights laws fall into two categories. The first category applies to governments, prohibiting governments from passing discriminatory laws or requiring governments to uphold certain human rights. The second category of human rights law prohibits discrimination on the part of private actors, for example with respect to employment practices or rental of housing. While it is not possible to eliminate individual or societal prejudices with legislation, human rights laws provide victims of discrimination with legal recourse against acts of discrimination and create economic disincentives through fines or other legal remedies, thereby contributing to social change.

Canada provides one example of the sources and functioning of human rights laws. Section 15 of the Canadian Charter of Rights and Freedoms, which is part of the Constitution of Canada, guarantees equality rights in the following terms:

> Every individual is equal before and under the law and has the right to the equal protection and equal benefit of the law without discrimination and, in particular, without discrimination based on race, national or ethnic origin, colour, religion, sex, age or mental or physical disability.

Canadian courts have interpreted the term "disability" to include HIV/AIDS, which means that people living with HIV/AIDS have constitutional protection against discrimination by the State. Section 15 is not limited to the grounds that are listed, but also covers analogous grounds, such as sexual orientation. Any law that is inconsistent with constitutional provisions may be struck down or interpreted by courts to make it consistent with the constitution. The Charter applies to all levels and branches of government, all government acts, government corporations and private persons or bodies that exercise authority granted by a statute or that implement government policies or programs.

However, the Charter does not otherwise apply to acts by private citizens. Instead, discrimination by an employer, a landlord or a private business is addressed under other federal and provincial human rights laws, such as the Canadian Human Rights Act, which apply to both the public and private sectors. By virtue of a 1996 policy of the Canadian Human Rights Commission and decisions of Canadian courts and tribunals, the prohibition against disability-based discrimination in the

Canadian Human Rights Act and its provincial counterparts cover discrimination based on HIV/AIDS status (Elliott and Gold 2005).

The remainder of this section provides an overview of court cases in a variety of countries that have applied constitutional law, international law and other legislation to uphold the rights of people living with HIV/AIDS with respect to employment and access to HIV-related medical care and treatment.

9.3.3.1 Cases Involving HIV-Related Discrimination in Employment

In March 2007, Mexico's National Supreme Court of Justice ruled that a provision in article 226 of the Social Security Institute Law for the Armed Forces (ISSFAM) that required HIV-positive individuals to be discharged from the military was unconstitutional, because it was not based on an individual assessment of the person's ability to work, violated constitutional protections of non-discrimination and equality and was inconsistent with Mexico's international obligations regarding people living with HIV/AIDS. The Court ordered that three soldiers be reinstated until medical certificates were issued to determine whether they were fit for duty, which would include an obligation to reinstate their social security benefits (Pearshouse 2007; Medina and Reyes 2007; SCJN 2007a, b). In September 2007, Mexico's National Supreme Court of Justice ruled for a fifth time that this provision was unconstitutional, thereby creating jurisprudence that is binding on all federal judges in Mexico (Avilés Allende 2007). Table 9.8 summarizes several other cases involving HIV-related discrimination in employment from various jurisdictions around the world.

9.3.3.2 Cases Involving Access to HIV-Related Treatment

With respect to HIV/AIDS, laws in South Africa and Latin America that provide a right to health care have been used to induce governments to provide access to antiretroviral treatment (Gruskin et al., 2007). The South African constitution provides a right to health care that is binding on the government. The Treatment Action Campaign used this provision to challenge the government's program that limited the use of *nevirapine* to prevent mother-to-child HIV transmission to 18 test sites. The court ruled that the government's restriction on the use of *nevirapine* was unreasonable and that the policy should be reformed to meet the government's constitutional obligation (Singh et al., 2007; Elliot et al., 2006).

In Argentina, five court cases between 1996 and 2003 repeatedly ordered the Argentine Ministry of Health to supply antiretroviral treatment to people living with HIV/AIDS, in accordance with the right to health set out in international treaties, which had been incorporated into domestic law. The failure of the Ministry of Health to act in a timely fashion, which led to interruptions in the supply of antiretroviral drugs, ultimately led to a court order that would fine the Ministry of Health USD 1,000 per day (funds which would then be used to implement the national AIDS plan) until it complied with the courts' previous orders, and the threat

Table 9.8 HIV-related discrimination in employment

Case	Relevant legislation	Issues	Outcome
Canada v. Thwaites, Federal Court (1994)	Canadian Human Rights Act	Discharge from Armed Forces based on HIV status	CAD 160,000 paid for unlawful discrimination
XX v. Gun Club Corp., Colombian Constitutional Court (1996)	Constitution of Colombia	Dismissal from job based on HIV status; violation of privacy by doctor	Doctor reported to Medical Ethics Tribunal for violating patient's privacy; Compensation paid for unlawful discrimination; Entitlement to social security restored
MX v. ZY, Bombay High Court of Judicature (1997)	Constitution of India	Employment at public corporation denied based on HIV status	Discriminatory workplace policy unconstitutional; Worker ordered reinstated; Lost wages paid from date of illegal dismissal
JRB et al. v. Ministry of Defense, Supreme Court of Justice of Venezuela	Constitution of Venezuela; International treaties	Mandatory medical leave from Armed Forces based on HIV status; violation of privacy by superior officers	HIV found incompatible with military service; Armed Forces ordered to respect privacy and to provide medical treatment
Haindongo Nghidi-pohamba Nanditume v. Minister of Defence, Labour Court of Namibia (2000)	Labour Act	Denial of entry into Namibian Defence Force based on HIV status	Namibian Defence Force found guilty of unfair discrimination; Ordered to admit plaintiff, unless his CD4 count was below 200 and viral load above 100,000; Ordered medical exam to include also CD4 and viral load, not just HIV
Hoffmann v. South African Airways, Constitutional Court of South Africa (2000)	South African Constitution	Government airline's prohibition on employing HIV-positive people as cabin crew	Unfair discrimination; Airline ordered to hire plaintiff and pay legal costs
XX v. Ministry of National Defense, Colombian Constitutional Court (2003)	Constitution of Colombia; Universal Declaration of Human Rights	Expulsion of student from military school based on HIV status	Unconstitutional discrimination; School ordered to provide medical treatment, including ARVs, and appropriate activity to minimize risk to cadet's health
Diau v. Botswana Building Society	Employment Act; Constitution of Botswana	Employment terminated for refusal to take HIV test	Infringement of right not to be subject to inhuman and degrading treatment and right to liberty; Employer ordered to reinstate employee and pay compensation for lost wages

Source: Elliot et al. (2006) Courting Rights: Case Studies in Litigating the Human Rights of People Living with HIV, UNAIDS/Canadian HIV/AIDS Legal Network, http://www.aidslaw.ca/ publications/ interfaces/downloadFile.php?ref=1013

Table 9.9 Cases involving access to HIV-related treatment

Case	Relevant legislation	Issues	Outcome
Alonso Muñoz Ceballos v. Instituto de Seguros Sociales, Constitutional Court of Colombia (2002)	Constitution of Colombia	Eligibility to receive public health care for HIV	Discontinuing access to treatment violated right to health and freedom from discrimination; Public social security obliged to cover patient's health care
Luis Guillermo Murillo Rodríguez et al. v. Caja Costarricense de Seguro Social, Supreme Court of Justice of Costa Rica (1997)	Constitution of Costa Rica; International Human Rights Conventions	Refusal to provide ARVs	Refusal violated right to life and health; Social Security system ordered to provide ARVs and pay court costs and damages; If cost of ARVs relevant, so are costs of withholding treatment
D v. United Kingdom, European Court of Human Rights (1997)	European Convention on Human Rights	Deportation of person with advanced AIDS, receiving treatment and palliative care	Deportation would amount to inhuman treatment, due to risk of dying in most distressing circumstances
N (FC) v. Secretary of State for the Home Department, House of on Human Rights Lords (2005)	European Convention	Deportation of person living with HIV, receiving ARV treatment	Deportation not inhuman treatment, because N was healthy
Cruz del Valle Bermudez el al. v. Ministry of Health and Social Action, Supreme Court of Venezuela (1999)	Constitution of Venezuela	HIV+ persons not covered by social security system through employment	Court ordered Ministry to provide coverage for ARVs and HIV-related treatment to all Venezuelans, even if not eligible for social security
Jorge Odir Miranda Cortez et al. v. El Salvador, Inter-American Commission on Human Rights (2001)	American Convention on Human Rights	Access to ARVs pending delayed decision of Supreme Court	El Salvador ordered to provide ARVs and other HIV-related treatment pending decision of Supreme Court of El Salvador; Case rendered moot when Supreme Court ordered Salvadoran Social Security Institute to provide access to HIV treatment
Van Biljon and Others v. Minister of Correctional Services and Others, High Court, South Africa (1997)	South African Constitution	Access to ARVs for HIV+ prisoners	Government ordered to provide free ARVs to HIV + prisoners, even though not available outside prisons

Source: Elliot et al. (2006) Courting Rights: Case Studies in Litigating the Human Rights of People Living with HIV, UNAIDS/Canadian HIV/AIDS Legal Network, http://www.aidslaw.ca/publications/interfaces/downloadFile.php?ref=1013

of criminal charges for contempt of court (Elliot et al., 2006). An Argentine court also relied on the right to health set out in international treaties to order the government to produce and administer a vaccine within a set period of time, in order to protect people living in a region affected by Argentine haemorrhagic fever (Singh et al., 2007). The constitutional court of Ecuador relied on the right to health set out in international treaties to rule that the Ministry of Health had failed to meet its obligations when it suspended its HIV treatment program (Singh et al., 2007; Elliot et al., 2006). In Costa Rica, the Supreme Court ruled in 1997 that the Costa Rican Social Security Fund could not argue that financial constraints justified failure to comply with its very reason for its existence, which is to provide coverage for necessary medical care. Shortly after this ruling, the Supreme Court ordered the Social Security Fund to develop a plan to provide coverage to all persons living with HIV/AIDS that were in need of antiretroviral treatment. A few weeks later, Costa Rica became the first Central American country to include coverage for antiretroviral drugs in its national health insurance plan (Elliot et al., 2006).

In India, the courts have interpreted the right to life in the Indian constitution to include a right to health, and have obliged the Indian government to dedicate resources to uphold the right to health in a variety of cases (Singh et al., 2007).

Table 9.9 summarizes several other cases from various jurisdictions around the world where litigation has increased access to HIV-related medical treatment. These cases suggest that human rights laws can be instrumental in promoting health care reforms through litigation, provided that judicial authorities are independent and competent and governments respect the rule of law (Singh et al., 2007).

9.3.3.3 Institutional Policies and Practices

In addition to laws that institutionalize or prohibit discrimination, institutional policies and practices can represent an important force with respect to stigma, discrimination and access to health care. The United Nations International Guidelines on HIV/AIDS and Human Rights recommend that States ensure that government and the private sector develop codes of conduct regarding HIV/AIDS issues that translate human rights principles into codes of professional responsibility and practice, with accompanying mechanisms to implement and enforce those codes. In many jurisdictions, the courts have the power to order changes in policies and practices of both governmental and non-governmental institutions. However, litigation is an expensive and time-consuming process that creates additional stress for the people living with HIV/AIDS who choose to litigate. Thus, it is important to promote the voluntary adoption of appropriate policies and practices.

One example in this category is the policies and practices of health care institutions. For example, in the mid 1980s, in British Columbia, Canada, all hospitals refused to treat AIDS patients, with the exception of St. Paul's Hospital, which adopted appropriate policies based on the commitment of the founding Sisters of

Providence to care for all who were in need, regardless of financial or social standing (Gratham 2007). In 2006, the City of Philadelphia agreed to resolve a complaint regarding the refusal of emergency medical services personnel to touch or lift a patient because of his HIV status, by paying monetary compensation and agreeing to implement a mandatory paramedic/EMT training program on HIV and infectious diseases (John Gill Smith and United States v. City of Philadelphia 2006). Ironically, "Philadelphia" was the name and setting of the first high-profile Hollywood film to take AIDS seriously, in 1993.

Another example in this category is the policies and practices of employers. As we showed in Chap. 3, HIV/AIDS affects the productivity of workers substantially, making it cost effective for companies to have prevention programs and to provide treatment for employees, from a purely financial point of view. Business leaders have an economic incentive to invest resources in fighting the epidemic. Moreover, as we saw in Chap. 7, firms can have a tremendous impact in promoting prevention among employees and their families and providing access to treatment. However, it is important to have an overarching framework that ensures the adoption of best practices by individual firms and to minimize overlap between the private sector and the other players that are involved in addressing the pandemic. In this regard, the Global Business Coalition on HIV/AIDS has provided leadership, particularly in its efforts to identify ways to improve the global business community's response to HIV/AIDS, including through leadership to dispel myths and stigma, break down workplace barriers and influence community change. Given the economic and legal incentives, an effective HIV/AIDS response must be a core component of an overall business strategy.

9.3.4 Risk Management: The Tradeoff Between Human Rights and HIV Prevention

We can think of HIV/AIDS as a disaster from the point of view of a country as a whole. Unlike other disasters (such as an outbreak of an influenza pandemic), this disaster unfolds over many years. However, the standard operating procedure for disaster management also applies to managing HIV/AIDS risk. For managing any kind of risk, we need to measure the severity and the frequency of occurrence of that risk. Once we measure the risk, we need to find ways of managing the risk in a dynamic way. That means putting a risk management plan in place, monitoring the plan and modifying the plan as events unfold.

Most often, at the national level, HIV/AIDS is seen as a public health problem and is managed as such. Thus, various measures are taken to reduce the incidence of HIV/AIDS by taking steps against the main channels through which the disease strikes: (1) actions to reduce the contamination of the blood supply; (2) special steps to promote health care for key groups, such as sex workers; (3) needle exchange programs; (4) promoting safe sex through the use of condoms; and (5) minimizing HIV transmission from infected mothers to newborns.

Another approach to risk management is risk avoidance. At the country level, risk avoidance could imply two extreme actions: quarantining people who are already infected and preventing infected people from coming into the country. Neither of these policies is feasible for most countries, as they directly go against human rights. Thus, extreme forms of risk management and the respect for human rights pose a tradeoff for a country.

Cuba provides a striking example of how containment of HIV/AIDS can be conducted at a national level. Cuba started promoting public health messages against HIV/AIDS in 1983, 3 years before the first HIV case was reported in the country. Between 1986 and 1989, Cuba undertook a massive testing exercise, which tested more than 80% of the adult population. Those who were seropositive were quarantined indefinitely in sanitariums. Over the years, Cuba has relaxed the rule. Today, anybody found seropositive is required to attend an 8 week course. After that, they are free to leave. Nearly half the people choose to stay in the sanitariums, where they get free food and a place to stay, along with retraining if they choose to help with the logistics of the sanitariums.

Such a curtailment of freedom of movement without committing a crime is unprecedented anywhere in the world. It has been criticized by many. It did produce a result that is also unprecedented. Cuba has an HIV incidence rate of 0.05%. In the neighboring island of Haiti, the rate is 120 times as high, at 6.1%.

It should be noted that quarantine of individuals who have committed no crime is not unheard of. There was the case of Mary Mallon in the United States in 1908 – better known as the "Typhoid Mary" – who carried typhoid without every showing any symptoms. She was quarantined against her will for a number of years. Similarly, during the outbreak of influenza in the United States in 1918, many families were quarantined on public health grounds. Individuals with SARS were also quarantined in Toronto.

9.4 The Future of HIV/AIDS

The future of HIV/AIDS presents a mixed picture. While HIV/AIDS incidence has begun to level off in some high-prevalence countries, new infections have increased in many developed countries. While several science-based prevention strategies need to be scaled up significantly, the increase in mother-to-child prevention has dramatically reduced infections among newborns and male circumcision is a promising new prevention strategy. While millions still lack access to treatment, there has been a large increase in funding, drug prices have dropped dramatically, several key drug patents will expire in the near future and efforts to develop new treatments continue. While stigma and discrimination remain obstacles to effective prevention and treatment, human rights laws have proved to be an effective vehicle for addressing discrimination and increasing access to treatment around the world. Thus, while HIV/AIDS continues to pose a significant threat to public health, there are many signs that progress in fighting this pandemic can and will continue, as knowledge gradually replaces ignorance.

References

AIDS Treatment News (1991) Travel/Immigration Ban: Background, Documentation. http://www.aids.org/atn/a-128-03.html. Accessed 5 December 2007

Associated Press (1995) Senator Jesse Helms: Cut AIDS Funding. http://ww2.aegis.org/news/ap/1995/AP950702.html. Accessed 1 December 2007

Associated Press (2007) Experimental AIDS vaccine falls short. 21 September 2007

Auvert B, Taljaard D, Lagarde E, Sobngwi-Tambekou J, Sitta R, Puren A (2005) Randomized, controlled intervention trial of male circumcision for reduction of HIV infection risk: The ANRS 1265 trial. PLoS Medicine 2:298

Avilés Allende C (2007) Amplía Corte protección a militares con VIH. El Universal, 24 September 2007. http://www.el-universal.com.mx/notas/450935.html. Accessed 10 December 2007

Bailey RC (2007) Male Circumcision: The Road from Evidence to Practice. Division of Epidemiology, School of Public Health, University of Illinois at Chicago

Betteridge G (2007) Criminal law and HIV transmission or exposure: New cases and developments. HIV/AIDS Policy and Law Review 12:40–44

Burris, S (1999) Law as a structural factor in the spread of communicable disease. Houston Law Review 36:1755

Burris S, Beletsky L, Burleson JA, Case P, Lazzarini Z (2007) Do Criminal Laws Influence HIV Risk Behavior? An Empirical Trial. http://ssrn.com/abstract=977274. Accessed 5 November 2007

Canadian AIDS Society (2004) HIV Disclosure & the Criminal Law in Canada. http://www.aidslaw.ca/publications/interfaces/downloadFile.php?ref=24. Accessed 15 November 2007

Canadian HIV/AIDS Legal Network (2003) Supreme Court of Canada Decision in R v. Williams. http://www.aidslaw.ca/publications/interfaces/downloadFile.php?ref=22. Accessed 25 November 2007

Canadian HIV/AIDS Legal Network (2007a) Canada's Immigration Policy as it Affects People Living with HIV/AIDS, February 2007. http://www.aidslaw.ca/publications/interfaces/downloadFile.php?ref=1254. Accessed 5 November 2007

Canadian HIV/AIDS Legal Network (2007b) A Human Rights-based Commentary on UNAIDS Guidance Note: HIV and Sex Work. http://www.hivlawandpolicy.org/resources/A%20Human%20Rights-based%20Commentary%20on%20UNAIDS%20Guidance%20 20on%20Sex%20Work%20&%20HIV-sept%2007.pdf. Accessed 5 November 2007

Carballo M (2007) Communicable Diseases: Challenges for Health in the Age of Migration. http://www.eu2007.min-saude.pt/NR/rdonlyres/84DA4983-F26D-4C53-899A-A9138 2C1FE1C/10624/Chpt4EU.PDF. Accessed 7 November 2007

CHAI (2007) Q & A on Second-Line HIV/AIDS Treatment. http://www.cptech.org/ip/health/aids/2g/clinton-qa05082007.pdf. Accessed 5 November 2007

Cochrane J (2000) Zidovudine's patent history. Lancet 356:1611–1612

Coffey S, Peiperl L (2006) Zidovudine. http://hivinsite.ucsf.edu/InSite?page=ar-01-01. Accessed 5 November 2007

Dunham W (2007) AIDS virus weakness detected. Reuters, 14 February 2007

Economist (2006) Look to the future: The war against AIDS. The Economist, 19 August 2006

Economist (2008) Net benefits: Giving bed nets and drugs away free may be the way to deal with malaria. The Economist, 31 January 2008

Elliot R (2002) Criminal Law, Public Health and HIV Transmission: A Policy Options Paper. http://data.unaids.org/publications/IRC-pub02/JC733-CriminalLaw_en.pdf. Accessed 15 November 2007

Elliott R, Gold J (2005) Protection against discrimination based on HIV/AIDS status in Canada: The legal framework. HIV/AIDS Policy and Law Review 10:1

Epstein H (2007) The Invisible Cure: Africa, the West, and the Fight Against AIDS. London, Farrar, Straus and Giroux

French R, Brocklehurst P (1998) The effect of pregnancy on survival in women infected with HIV: A systematic review of the literature and meta-analysis. British Journal of Obstetrics and Gynaecology VI: 105(IP: 8):827–835

Global HIV Prevention Working Group (2007) Bringing HIV Prevention to Scale: An Urgent Global Priority. http://www.icaso.org/resources/bringing_ HIV_prev_to_scale_2007. pdf. Accessed 5 November 2007

GMHC (2006) To All HIV Positive Visitors Coming to the United States to Attend the 2006 High Level Meeting on AIDS. http://www.ua2010.org/index.php/en/content/download/2400/24423/file/2006%20High%20Level%20Meeting%20on%20AIDS%20HIV%20Waiver.pdf. Accessed 25 November 2007

Gratham N (2007) A Salute to the Sisters. Promise Fall/Winter 2007, St. Paul's Foundation

Gruskin S, Mills E, Tarantola D (2007) History, principles and practice of health and human rights. Lancet 370:449–455

Halperin D (2007) Evidence-Based Behavior Change HIV Prevention Approaches for Sub-Saharan Africa. Harvard Center for Population and Development Studies. http://www.harvardaidsprp.org/research/daniel-halperin-hupa-011707.pdf. Accessed 5 December 2007

Hamied YK (2005) Trading in Death. Health Administrator XIX:1

Hammer et al. (2006) Treatment for Adult HIV Infection: 2006 Recommendations of the International AIDS Society–USA Panel. JAMA 296:827–843

Harvard School of Public Health Program on International Health and Human Rights (2006) HIV/AIDS and Gender-Based Violence (GBV), Literature Review. http://www.hsph.harvard.edu/pihhr/files/Final_Literature_Review.pdf. Accessed 5 November 2007

Hulse C (2005) In Memoir, Jesse Helms Says He Was No Racist. http://www.nytimes.com/2005/08/31/politics/31helms.html?_r=1&oref=slogin. Accessed 25 November 2007

Human Rights Watch (2004) Lessons Not Learned: Human Rights Abuses and HIV/AIDS in the Russian Federation. http://hrw.org/reports/2004/russia0404/. Accessed 15 November 2007

Human Rights Watch (2006) Family, Unvalued: Discrimination, Denial, and the Fate of Binational Same-Sex Couples under U.S. Law. http://hrw.org/reports/2006/us0506/. Accessed 8 November 2007

Hulse C (2005) In Memoir, Jesse Helms Says He Was No Racist. http://www.nytimes.com/2005/08/31/politics/31helms.html?_r=1&oref=slogin. Accessed 25 November 2007

Human Rights Watch (2004) Lessons Not Learned: Human Rights Abuses and HIV/AIDS in the Russian Federation. http://hrw.org/reports/2004/russia0404/. Accessed 15 November 2007

Human Rights Watch (2006) Family, Unvalued: Discrimination, Denial, and the Fate of Binational Same-Sex Couples under U.S. Law. http://hrw.org/reports/2006/us0506/. Accessed 8 November 2007

IB Times (2007) Gilead, Bristol-Myers to Market HIV Drug. http://www.ibtimes.com/articles/20071211/gilead-bristol-myers-to-market-hiv-drug.htm. Accessed 5 November 2007

John Gill Smith and United States v. City of Philadelphia (2006) Settlement Order. http://www.hivlawandpolicy.org/resources/settlement%20order-EMTS-Phila%20Nov%202006.pdf. Accessed 25 November 2007

Jürgens R (2007) Increasing access to HIV testing and counseling while respecting human rights. New York, Public Health Program of the Open Society Institute

Jürgens R, Cohen J (2007) Human Rights and HIV/AIDS: Now More Than Ever, 10 Reasons Why Human Rights Should Occupy the Center of the Global AIDS Struggle. Open Society Institute. http://www.soros.org/initiatives/health/focus/law/articles_publications/publications/human_20071017/nowmore_20070901.pdf. Accessed 12 November 2007

Kelly C (2004) Conspiring to kill: gender-biased legislation, culture, and aids in sub-Saharan Africa. Journal of Law and Family Studies 6:439

Kershaw S (2008) New HIV Cases Drop but Rise in Young Gay Men. www.nytimes.com. Accessed 2 January 2008

Klein A (2007) Criminal law and HIV/AIDS. HIV/AIDS Policy and Law Review 12: 51–53

Koch E (1987) Senator Helms's Callousness Toward AIDS Victims. http://query.nytimes.com/gst/fullpage.html?res=9B0DE3DA1530F934A35752C1A961948260. Accessed 25 November 2007

Latino Commission on AIDS (2007) The Latino Commission on AIDS Supports the HIV Nondiscrimination in Travel and Immigration Act. http://www.latinoaids.org/mediaadvisory/travel.htm. Accessed 11 November 2007

Medina A, Reyes MA (2007) Discriminación por vivir con VIH: Fuerzas Armadas, a punto del revés, Letra S 128. http://www.jornada.unam.mx/2007/03/01/ls-fuerzasarmadas.html. Accessed 2 December 2007

Millett G, Peterson J (2007) The known hidden HIV/AIDS epidemic among Black men who have sex with men in the United States. American Journal of Preventive Medicine 32:31–33

Montefiori D et al. (2007) Antibody-based HIV-1 vaccine: Recent developments and future directions. PLoS Medicine 4:12

NYC Health (2007) HIV Epidemiology and Field Services Research Unit Report, October 2007. http://www.nyc.gov/html/doh/downloads/pdf/dires/dires-2007-research-report.pdf. Accessed 12 December 2007

OECD (2006) OECD Health Data 2006. http://www.oecd.org/health/healthdata. Accessed 5 January 2008

Ohio v. Bird (1998) Ohio State Court Appellate Amicus Brief. http://www. hivlawandpolicy.org/resources/Larry%20Bird%20Amicus%20Appellate%20Brief.pdf. Accessed 20 December 2007

Oster E (2005) Sexually transmitted infections, sexual behavior, and the HIV/AIDS epidemic. The Quarterly Journal of Economics120(2):467–514

Park A (2007) Assessing a Failed AIDS Vaccine. http://www.time.com/time/health/ article/0,8599,1681526,00.html?xid=feed-cnn-topics. Accessed 12 December 2007

Pearshouse R (2007) Mexico: Supreme court rules discharge of HIV-positive troops unconstitutional. HIV/AIDS Policy and Law Review 12:47–48

Peeters M, Sharp PM (2000) Genetic diversity of HIV-1: The moving target. AIDS 14:S129–S130

Pérez-Casas C et al. (2000) HIV/AIDS Pricing Report. Médicins sans Frontières. http://www.bioltrop.fr/09-diagautre/durban-hiv.htm. Accessed 7 December 2007

Perry A (2007) Seeds of Change in Rwanda. Time/CNN, 26 September 2007. http:// www.ambassadorprograms.org/upcomingprograms/extensions/2008/time-rwanda.pdf. Accessed 2 December 2007

R v. Cuerrier (1998) 2 SCR 371, Supreme Court of Canada. http://scc.lexum.umontreal. ca/ en/1998/1998rcs2-371/1998rcs2-371.html. Accessed 12 December 2007

R v. Williams (2003) 2 SCR 134, Supreme Court of Canada. http://scc.lexum.umontreal. ca/ en/2003/2003scc41/2003scc41.html. Accessed 22 December 2007

SCJN (2007a) Sesión Pública Núm. 27, Amparo en revisión 510/2004. http:// www.scjn.gob.mx/NR/rdonlyres/F8F3CE48-E2D1-4A3A-BEEE-594EA57353B0/0/276 MARDE2007.pdf. Accessed 2 December 2007

SCJN (2007b) Sesión Pública Núm. 26, Amparo en revisión 510/2004. http://www.scjn. gob.mx/NR/rdonlyres/98EF667E-CF50-4ABB-AB9F-107ADF012927/0/265DEMARZODE 2007.pdf. Accessed 2 December 2007

Singh JA, Govender M, Mills E (2007) Do human rights matter to health? Lancet 370:521–527

State v. Jones (2000) New Mexico Court of Appeals, 129 NM 165. http://www. hivlawandpolicy.org/resources/State%20v%20Jones%20-%20NM%20spitting%20case-2000.pdf. Accessed 4 December 2007

Tarantola D, Gruskin S (2007) New guidance on recommended HIV testing and couselling. Lancet 370:202–203

Tarwater J (2001) The tuberculosis & HIV debate in immigration law: Critical flaws in United States academic anti-exclusion arguments. Georgetown Immigration Law Journal 15:357

US Food and Drug Administration (2006) Guidance for Industry Fixed Dose Combinations, Co-Packaged Drug Products, and Single-Entity Versions of Previously Approved Antiretrovirals for the Treatment of HIV. http://www.fda.gov/cder/guidance/6360fnl.htm. Accessed 8 December 2007

Weeks v. State (1992) Texas Court of Appeal, 834 SW 2d 559. http://www. hivlawandpolicy.org/resources/partial%20case%20&resource%20list-Lambda.pdf. Accessed 4 December 2007

Werner E (2007) Lawmakers, Gay-Rights Groups Protesting New HIV/AIDS Travel Rule in US. http://news.lp.findlaw.com/ap/o/55/12-11-2007/f0a90026bc21dacb.html. Accessed 2 December 2007

WHO (2006) Progress on Global Access to HIV Antiretroviral Therapy: A Report on "3 by 5" and Beyond. www.who.int/hiv/fullreport_en_highres.pdf. Accessed 9 December 2007

UNAIDS/IOM (2004) Statement on HIV/AIDS-Related Travel Restrictions. http://www.aegis.com/files/unaids/UNAIDS_IOM_on%20travel%20restrictions.pdf. Accessed 2 December 2007

UNAIDS (2006) Report on the Global AIDS Epidemic. http://www.unaids.org/en/HIV_data/2006GlobalReport/default.asp. Accessed 22 November 2007

UNAIDS (2007) UNAIDS Guidance Note HIV and Sex Work. http://www.aids.md/files/library/2007/1144/unaids-guidance-note-hiv-sex-work-apr-2007.pdf. Accessed 2 December 2007

Underhill K, Operario D, Montgomery P (2007) Systematic Review of Abstinence-Plus HIV Prevention Programs in High-Income Countries. PLoS Medicine 4:9

United Nations (2007) International Guidelines on HIV/AIDS and Human Rights: 2006 Consolidated Version. http://data.unaids.org/Publications/IRC-pub07/jc1252-internguidelines_en.pdf. Accessed 5 December 2007

Urbina I (2007) New Law Allows Needle Exchanges in Washington. http://www.nytimes.com. Accessed 27 December 2007

World Health Organization (2003) Scaling Up Antiretroviral Therapy in Resouurce-Limited Setting: Treatment Guidelines for a Public Health Approach. http://www.who.int/hiv/pub/prev_care/en/arvrevision2003en.pdf. Accessed 20 November 2007

Zowall et al. (1994) Modeling Health Care Costs Attributable to HIV Infection and Coronary Heart Disease in Immigrants to Canada. In: Kaplan, Brandeau (eds) Modeling the AIDS Epidemic – Planning, Policy and Predictions. Raven Press, New York

Index

About the Authors

Dr. Bradly J. Condon is a professor of international trade law and international business at the Instituto Tecnológico Autónomo de México (ITAM) and is a senior fellow, Tim Fischer Centre for Global Trade and Finance, School of Law, Bond University, Australia. He is a member of the Mexican National Research System. He has served as the director of the Centre for North American Business Studies at Simon Fraser University, Canada, expert witness before the Canadian Parliament, advisor for the Commonwealth Law Association, guest of the United States Congress on international trade issues and visiting professor in the Mexican delegation to the World Trade Organization. He is listed in Who's Who in the World. He has also authored eight books and over 50 research papers.

Dr. Tapen Sinha is the ING Comercial America chair professor in the Department of Actuarial Studies at the Instituto Tecnológico Autónomo de Mexico (ITAM) where he is also the director of the International Center for Pension Research. He has a concurrent appointment as professor at the University of Nottingham, UK. He is a research associate at the Centre for Risk and Insurance (CRIS), at the School of Business of the University of Nottingham. He is a member of the Mexican National Research System and the Mexican Academy of Sciences. He is a senior consultant with Cranes Software Inc. He has also published over 120 research papers and authored/edited nine books.